The Other Route into College:
Alternative Admission

the OTHER ROUTE INTO COLLEGE

>>>>>>>>>>>>> *Alternative Admission*

STACY NEEDLE, M.S. ED.

WITH A FOREWORD BY JOAN ISAAC MOHR

**ASSISTANT VICE PRESIDENT FOR ENROLLMENT MANAGEMENT AND
DEAN OF ADMISSIONS, HOFSTRA UNIVERSITY**

RANDOM HOUSE NEW YORK

104106

Random House publications are available at special discounts for corporate use, in bulk purchases of one hundred copies or more for promotions or premiums. Special editions, including personalized covers and corporate imprints, can be created in large quantities for special needs. For more information, write to the Director of Special Markets, Random House, Inc., 201 East 50th Street, New York, NY 10022.

Library of Congress Catalog Card Number: 90-23298

ISBN 0-679-73140-7

Manufactured in the United States of America
9 8 7 6 5 4   3 2
First Edition

Design by Susan Hood

ACKNOWLEDGMENTS

While writing *The Other Route into College: Alternative Admission* has been a great pleasure for me, I have never lost sight of the fact that the contributions of others have enriched it and certainly, in a large way, made it possible.

My agent, Carole Abel, deserves special recognition. She supported this book from the very moment I approached her with the idea.

Charlotte Mayerson, my editor at Random House, is a true professional, whose intelligence, support, and thoroughness improved the book immeasurably.

My sincere thanks to the hundreds of college administrators who provided information for this book.

I am fortunate to have had the very special help of an experienced writer, Joseph Bilby. His contributions were crucial and I am deeply grateful.

This book could not have been produced without the assistance of Elizabeth Cooner. I genuinely appreciate her efforts.

I wish to acknowledge, with deep gratitude, Joan Isaac Mohr, Vice President for Enrollment and Dean of Admissions at Hofstra University, for writing the Foreword.

Deborah Izzo is to be thanked for spending countless hours typing the manuscripts.

A major contribution was made by Michael Fine, who gave generously of his time.

Martha O'Connell, Nancy Rothschild, and Joan Rudinski have indirectly contributed to this book. Through the years, they have served as an inspiration to me, both personally and professionally. Working with them was a special joy.

My last word of appreciation is to Steve, whose optimism and encouragement kept me going even when my own faltered. Thank you, Steve Needle, for believing in my dream.

FOREWORD

Dear Student, Parent, Counselor, or Individual interested in the college admission process:

If you've studied the college admission process, you've quickly discovered that each college seems unique in its requirements, deadlines, programs, and fees, among other things. To add to the confusion, the very mention of "admission standards" conjures up all sorts of half-truths and anxieties about SAT scores, rank in class, grade point average, and prior academic records. The confusion further deepens when you learn that colleges may use other admission criteria, such as financial need, legacies, extracurricular activities, special talents, recommendations, and the dreaded essay. For a student or parent, it seems like an unmanageable task.

Is there one college that is right for a particular student? No. There are numerous schools that would be a good match for the student. I often talk with high school juniors and their parents who will face this formidable task within a year. I assure them that applying to college is really a process, not a crisis. If you do the research, and put time and effort into the decisions you need to make, you will make good choices. Ultimately, you'll reach a decision about which college to attend. The task at hand is to identify some of the colleges that have caught your interest—and make a final decision based on the information you have gathered over a period of time.

But first, a gentle word of caution. Few students—no matter how strong their academic or extracurricular record—are likely to be admitted to all the schools to which they have applied. A great deal depends on the academic profile of the institution. Students may be above, equal to, or below the "typical" applicant pool of the colleges that interest them.

To accommodate the various types of applications, many colleges and universities have developed several admissions policies. These "alternative admission programs" are designed on behalf of students who do not meet regular admission standards, but have the potential to perform better in college than their high school record and test scores may indicate. If you are accepted through an alternative program or policy, you may be certain that the college believes that you have what it takes to succeed in an undergraduate program. Remember: Colleges are not in the business of admitting students whom they expect to fail. They *are* in the business of helping students to do well and of providing the support needed to encourage strengths and overcome weaknesses.

This book covers alternative programs that augment the regular admission process at close to 240 colleges and universities in 47 states. It does not, however, cover programs specifically for students with learning disabilities.

Many students need an alternative program when applying to college. They need the extra support or program that will assist them in succeeding at a particular college or university. This assistance may take many forms. For example, a student may simply be limited in the number of courses that she or he may register for in the first year. Assistance may involve a tutoring program, special summer study just before the freshman year, or a complete separate class program during the student's first year or two of college. The offerings are as varied as the number of institutions in this volume.

There are many paths leading to a college education. Choose the one that best fits your needs and goals, has the type of program and environment that meets your needs, and, above all, is a school in which you are comfortable.

No two of us are alike. When reading admission applications, we see that there are no two students with the same credentials, background, or needs. Yet a college may be the home of a very diverse student body exposing individuals to a broad array of ideas, topics, and intellectual tools.

Best wishes as you use this resource to help in your decision process.

Joan Isaac Mohr
Assistant Vice President for Enrollment
Management and Dean of Admissions
Hofstra University

CONTENTS

ALL ABOUT
ALTERNATIVE ADMISSION

Michael graduated from a New Jersey college with a 3.0 grade point average (GPA). President of several student organizations and active in many others, a member of student government and resident adviser, Michael received the college's Outstanding Student award in recognition of his overall achievement and contributions to the community.

Lainie's admission as a freshman at a major New England university fulfilled a longtime dream. Her ambition and determination led to academic success and personal fulfillment in her college career.

Robert, who received superior grades in his high school science and mathematics courses, was accepted by an upstate New York technical college and finished his sophomore year with a 3.4 GPA.

On the surface these appear to be typical stories of today's success-oriented college generation. *They are not.* Motivation came late to Michael, Lainie, and Robert. All three had high school records and/or Scholastic Aptitude Test (SAT) scores that seemed to destine them to academic oblivion. But they got a second chance—a chance provided by alternative admissions to the colleges they attended.

Michael, who graduated from high school with a 1.94 GPA and combined SAT scores of 840, says that "almost any college would have rejected me." A special college program gave him his "opportunity to excel." Lainie, an indifferent student in high school, maintains that, if it were not for the alternative freshman year program she enrolled in, she would never have been able to attend the institution of her choice and might have ended up, like a number of her friends, attending no college at all. Robert's excellence in high school mathematics was not matched by his written and oral communication skills, and he needed assistance in filling out his college applications. Successful completion of an intensive ten-week summer program demonstrated his potential for college-level work, however, and enabled him to attend a competitive school that otherwise would not have accepted him.

WHAT IS ALTERNATIVE ADMISSION?

Alternative admission policies and programs provide enrollment opportunities for high school or college transfer applicants who do not meet the regular admissions requirements of many colleges and universities. Although most prospective college students are unaware of alternative admission programs, they are offered by hundreds of schools across the United States.

There are no national alternative admission standards, however, and each policy or program is unique to the individual institution. In general, the ideal alternative admission candidate is a student who has the ability to complete his or her studies for a college degree, but whose high school record and/or Scholastic Aptitude Test/American College Test (SAT/ACT) scores do not reflect that ability.

Alternative admission benefits a wide spectrum of potential college students. Although some alternative admission opportunities are directed at specific target groups, including minorities or older students, most are open to anyone with the motivation and desire to succeed in college. It is important for a college applicant to evaluate carefully various offerings and determine which ones meet his or her particular needs. This book provides the information needed to make such an evaluation.

WHY SHOULD YOU CONSIDER ALTERNATIVE ADMISSION?

- It can mean the difference between acceptance and nonacceptance to college!
- It can mean acceptance to the college of your choice even if you do not meet the regular admissions standards!
- It can mean attendance at a more competitive college than you otherwise would have been accepted by!
- It can provide you with the opportunity to transfer to the college of your choice!
- It can provide the chance to establish a sound academic record before transferring to a more competitive college!
- It can provide you with the opportunity to transfer to a college which will provide the support services you need to succeed!
- It can provide students already enrolled in two-year colleges an opportunity to enter a four-year degree program!

- It can provide the skills and confidence needed to let you ultimately succeed in your college career—and beyond!

WHAT IS AN ALTERNATIVE ADMISSION POLICY OR PROGRAM?

Although all alternative admission policies and programs strive to offer opportunities to those students who do not meet ordinary admissions criteria, they vary in the means used to achieve that goal. There are two basic offerings: alternative policies and structured alternative programs.

A school with an alternative admission policy may require separate freshman orientation and also require its alternative students to complete certain courses. It may also offer some support services, but not a special alternative faculty or curriculum. Policy schools generally do not charge alternative students additional fees.

Colleges with structured alternative admission programs generally require alternative students to complete a certain curriculum over a specified period of time (usually a summer, or one or two semesters) and offer extensive support services. Programs may be offered in the summer preceding freshman year or during the regular academic year, and must be successfully completed in order for the student to matriculate. Program faculty are sometimes specially trained to deal with the needs of alternative students. Participation may involve additional cost to the student, although financial aid is often available.

Since the vast majority of schools listed in this guide offer formal programs, that term will be used henceforth to define alternative admissions. Most programs share some or all of the following characteristics:

COURSES

Mainstream: Students who "mainstream" are not enrolled in special classes, but usually take a reduced credit load within the college's normal curriculum, attending classes with the rest of the student body.

Separate Classes: Many programs require that alternative students take classes together, rather than with the rest of the student body, during the duration of the program. These classes are often taught by special faculty.

Remedial Classes: These classes, often not credit-bearing, prepare academically deficient students before they are admitted to regular classes. Remedial classes are most often offered in basic subjects, like mathematics or English.

All About Alternative Admission

Required Courses: Alternative students are sometimes required to take special courses, including freshman-orientation seminars, study skills courses, and so forth.

SPECIAL ASSISTANCE

Special Faculty: These faculty members instruct only alternative students. In some cases these teachers are trained to meet the special needs of alternative students.

Tutors: Such instructors, sometimes professional ones or sometimes students' peers, instruct and assist students in one-on-one or small-group situations as a supplement to classroom instruction.

Support Services: These special counselors are trained to deal with the needs of alternative admission students and are often available for help with academic and personal problems. There may be study technique workshops, which focus on improving a student's study habits; academic skills centers, which help a student in specific academic areas; and testing facilities.

Special New-Student Orientation: Colleges usually conduct special orientation programs to acquaint the new alternative student with the range of courses and support services available, as well as program requirements.

WHO IS A GOOD CANDIDATE FOR ALTERNATIVE ADMISSION?

- The high school student who has average grades with above-average SAT or ACT scores. This student has good academic potential, but is not working to capacity for any number of reasons, possibly including lack of motivation.
- The high school student who has above-average grades with low SAT or ACT scores. This student, who does well in the classroom, may lack the necessary background in test-taking, reading comprehension, or basic verbal or mathematical skills.
- The high school student who has both low grades and low standardized tests but is motivated highly enough to convince the program that he or she will succeed.
- The high school student who had previously done good work but whose performance has been affected by family problems, a lack of educational continuity due to frequent moving, or other problems.
- The high school student who may fit into several of the above categories.

- The college student who has established a satisfactory academic record at a junior or community college offering extensive student support services and wishes to transfer and obtain his or her bachelor's degree at a four-year college offering similar services.
- The college student who wishes to transfer from a two-year or four-year college that does not offer the necessary support services (i.e., testing, small class size, and personal contact with faculty) the student needs in order to excel in school.

WHAT COLLEGES LOOK FOR

In considering freshman alternative admission candidates, colleges may consider some or all of the following criteria. In addition, the alternative candidate's level of motivation and maturity, as well as significant academic improvement in the last year of high school, are particularly important:

- SAT or ACT scores
- High school grade point average
- High school class rank
- Type of high school attended
- Difficulty of high school courses
- Extracurricular activities
- Community service and volunteer work
- Interview with admissions counselor
- Essay/personal statement
- Letters of recommendation
- Minority status
- Age of applicant
- State residence

Considerations for Transfer Students: All or some of the criteria listed below are considered by admissions personnel when considering alternative admission applicants transferring from another college or university. As with applicants for the freshman class, demonstrations of maturity, motivation, and academic improvement are particularly important for alternative transfer candidates.

- Grade point average at previous institution
- Difficulty of coursework
- Type of college attended

- Number of credits completed (often must be less than 30 credits)
- Community service or volunteer work
- Interview with admissions counselor
- Essay/personal statement
- Letters of recommendation
- Minority status
- Age of applicant
- State residence

MATCHING THE COLLEGE TO THE STUDENT

After deciding that you would like to try the alternative admission route to college, consider what kind of school you are looking for. We have listed first the general considerations *any* student considering a school would keep in mind. The second category includes specific issues for alternative admission:

GENERAL CONSIDERATIONS

- What is the school's geographic location?
- What is the campus setting—urban, suburban, or rural?
- What is the size and composition of the school's student population?
- Is the school coeducational or single sex?
- Is the school public, or does it have a private or religious affiliation?
- What is the tuition?
- What is the cost of room and board and the meal plan?
- What are the most common undergraduate academic majors?
- What types of social life and extracurricular activities are available?
- What is the composition and size of the student body?

ALTERNATIVE ADMISSIONS CONSIDERATIONS

- Is alternative admission a policy or a structured program? If a program, how structured is it?
- Do alternative students attend mainstream classes or classes composed entirely of alternative students?
- Is there a limited course load for alternative students?
- What is the student-faculty ratio?

- What academic and personal support services are available?
- Do alternative students have access to special faculty members trained to deal with their special problems?
- Is tutoring available? Is it required or voluntary?

THE COLLEGE VISIT

THE ADMISSIONS INTERVIEW

When you have narrowed your choices to the schools that appear to meet your needs best, you should arrange visits to the campuses. The admissions interview gives the interviewer a chance to assess you personally as a potential alternative admission student; it is the centerpiece of the campus visit.

The interviewer will carefully examine your motivation and assess your level of maturity. Because of the importance of these characteristics in alternative admission, the interview is often more important than it would be to the applicant for regular admission. Review probable questions beforehand so that you enter the interview feeling relaxed. The following list of potential questions will help you prepare:

- Why are you interested in this college?
- Why do you think alternative admission is appropriate for you?
- What are your academic and social goals?
- How do you feel your academic performance in high school reflects your potential?
- What do you expect from an alternative admission program?
- What is your best method of preparing for exams?
- How would you prepare to do a term paper?
- What do you expect from the college in the way of support?
- What are the traits that make you stand out and show why you should be accepted over hundreds of other applicants?
- Why do you feel a college degree is important?
- What is your philosophy toward education?

The interview is also *your* chance to learn about alternative admission in more detail. There are some key questions you can ask the interviewer to help you decide if a school's alternative admission policy or program is right for you. Asking perceptive questions will give you the information you need, and will also indicate to the interviewer that you are a mature person. The following sample questions will give you an idea of what to ask. Others will occur to you as you read the individual college entries. Don't ask so many questions, however, that you take too much of the interviewer's time:

- What are the requirements for alternative admission?
- How many alternative admission students are accepted each year?
- If alternative admission is a separate program, do alternative admission students take the same courses as other students?
- Do the courses taken by alternative students earn credits toward a degree?
- What is the average class size for alternative students?
- Are tutorial services available? Are available tutors faculty members, students, or both? Is there an additional fee for tutoring?
- What will happen if I do not do well the first semester?
- What percentage of alternative students eventually complete their degrees?
- Does completion of the alternative admission program mean automatic admission into a regular program?
- Is there a college skills center? If so, is it available on a walk-in basis?
- Do the professors hold regular office hours for consultation?
- Will I have a faculty adviser?
- Is a summer program required prior to fall enrollment?
- Am I expected to choose a major while I am still in the program?
- Is skills-building part of the program?

THE CAMPUS TOUR

Another feature of the college visit is the campus tour. The tour should include the school's academic buildings, study skills center, and counseling center. Ask your student guide enough questions so that you get a student's perspective on alternative admissions and the school. The decision you make is important. You want to be sure that you and the college are well matched.

HOW TO READ THE GUIDE

This section contains profiles of 239 colleges and universities offering alternative admission. Each entry presents pertinent information about the school in a standard format. The categories include institutional summary, alternative admission summary, academic coursework and related features, required courses, profile of alternative admission students, other features and accommodations, and deadlines. Should one of these categories not apply to a given institution, it doesn't appear in the profile. The following list details the type of information to be found in each section:

Institutional Summary: This section provides general information about an individual college or university. It includes, where applicable, the following details about each school:
- Name
- Address
- Admissions phone number
- Tuition, room, and meal plan costs during the 1989–90 academic year
- Number of full-time and part-time undergraduates
- Student/faculty ratio
- Percentage of students enrolled in largest academic program
- Date founded
- Public or private
- Religious affiliation
- Coed or single sex
- Location
- Campus size
- Campus setting

Alternative Admission Summary: This section outlines alternative admission requirements, policies, and programs. Although some schools only have policies, you will find that most offerings are structured, with a specified coursework schedule for a specified length of time. Included in this section, where applicable, are the following:
- Contact person and his or her phone number
- Title of program
- Duration of program
- Additional cost of program
- Percentage of students who complete the program within the allotted time span
- Degree received at completion of program

Academic Coursework and Related Features: This section describes general alternative admission academic information, including the following:
- Availability of support services, including all or some of the following: special freshman orientation, college survival-skills classes, academic counseling, drug/alcohol coun-

seling, peer counseling, psychological counseling, career counseling, women's center, academic skills center, study technique workshops, health center, aptitude testing, extended time for tests
- Tutoring: required or optional, by whom administered, in what academic areas and frequency
- Academic advisers: availability and percentage who serve alternative students exclusively
- Placement testing
- Number of full-time faculty at the institution
- Number of faculty assigned to alternative admission; whether they are specially trained to deal with the problems of alternative students
- Percentage of classes open to alternative admission students
- Limits on class size
- Evening courses
- Credit load

Required Courses: This section includes specific coursework requirements, including:
- Courses mandated by alternative admission, including remedial, required, and those only required of students who demonstrate deficiencies
- Definition of which courses may be credit-bearing, mainstreamed, and calculated in student's GPA
- GPA needed to stay in the program or at the college

Profile of Alternative Admissions Students: This section provides available statistical information on the school's alternative admission population. It may include the following:
- Number of students enrolled in alternative admission
- Percentage of students accepted who actually enrolled
- Percentage of new students and/or transfer students
- Percentage of students who transfer after freshman and sophomore years
- Percentage of minority students
- Percentage of female students
- Percentage of state residents
- Percentage of international students
- Percentage of adult students (25 years old or older)
- Percentage of intercollegiate athletes
- Percentage of learning-disabled students
- Percentage in top 50 percent of their high school class
- Percentage that completed degrees within 4 or 5 years

All About Alternative Admission

Other Features and Accommodations: This section details the following:
- On-campus housing and meal plans available to alternative admission students
- Availability of financial aid

Deadlines: Along with pertinent deadlines, this section may include a brief evaluation of the type of student most fitted for a given institution's alternative admission policy or program. The relevant deadlines and related information include:
- Alternative admission applications
- Information on whether a school will accept students on a space-available basis after application deadlines
- Financial aid
- Notification of acceptance
- Confirmation of acceptance by applicant

GLOSSARY

ACT (American College Test): Similar to the SAT, although scored differently, the ACT is also used as an aptitude indicator in various areas of the country.

Academic probation: A student is placed on academic probation for failing to achieve academic standards. Probationary status may place restrictions on the number of courses a student may take and may involve counseling as well. Academic improvement, generally signified by obtaining a certain GPA, is usually necessary to terminate probation.

Academic skills center: A center on campus that offers assistance in bolstering and improving academic skills.

Academic suspension: Should a student's record not improve under the stimulus and guidance of probation, he or she may be suspended and not allowed to take further courses. Suspension may be for a semester or permanent. In some cases, suspended students may have to reapply formally for readmission.

Alternative admission policies/programs: Admissions procedure and schedule of coursework designed to enable those who would not otherwise meet the standards of a given college or university to attend that institution.

Aptitude testing: Testing to indicate an individual's areas of ability and talents.

Associate's degree: This degree (AA) is normally awarded by a community or junior college after 2 years of full-time study, sometimes in a technical or paraprofessional field. A student with an associate's degree who wishes to complete a bachelor's degree usually transfers to another institution to complete further requirements.

Bachelor's degree: A bachelor's degree is normally awarded after 4 years of full-time study. (Some programs require 5 years.) The degree is usually awarded as a Bachelor of

Science (BS) or Bachelor of Arts (BA), most often in specific subject areas such as history, English, marketing, or chemistry.

Class rank: Where a student stands academically in relation to his or her classmates. Class rank is expressed in a numerical figure; for example, a rank of 50/100 would put a student in the top half of the class. Sometimes this number is expressed in deciles (tenths) or quintiles (fifths).

College survival skills: Social and academic skills needed for a successful college career, including test-taking and dealing with such problems as getting along with a roommate and homesickness.

Freshman: A first-year student at a college or university.

Freshman orientation: An introduction to the college and its programs. Orientation may also include registration procedures.

GED (Graduate Equivalency Diploma): This diploma is awarded after a candidate who has not completed high school classes passes a test that measures the skills necessary to graduate. It is accepted in lieu of a regular high school diploma.

Major: A major (short for major field) is an intensive course of study taken in addition to required courses. A student could major in English, accounting, chemistry, or elementary education. The bachelor's degree usually is awarded in a major field. Most courses in a major are offered to a student in the final 2 or 3 years of a 4-year program.

Matriculated student: A student who has been formally accepted into a program at a degree-granting institution.

Nonmatriculated student: A student who is attending an institution and taking courses, but has not been formally admitted into a degree-granting program.

Open-admissions policy: Anyone who applies to an institution with open admissions is accepted. This type of policy is usually confined to community colleges.

Placement testing: Tests administered prior to registration in order to determine the level of courses a student will be permitted to take. These tests are generally given in English, mathematics, reading, and foreign languages.

Quarter: One fourth of an academic year. Under the quarter system, individual courses do not bear as much academic credit as those in the more traditional, 2-semester-a-year system. A student usually goes to school for 3 quarters (fall, winter, and spring).

Reply date: The date, after formal admissions, by which the college wishes a student to inform it if he or she will be attending.

Rolling admissions: As an application arrives at a college, it is processed and acceptance decisions are made on an ongoing basis rather than at a specific time of the year.

SAT (Scholastic Aptitude Test): Administered by the College Board and required by most colleges as one indication of an applicant's aptitude to perform college-level work. The test is designed to measure verbal and mathematical abilities. The minimum score for each section is 200, the maximum, 800.

Glossary

Semester: One half of the academic year. In traditional schools, courses last for half an academic year, and academic credit is awarded at the end of each semester.

Student-faculty ratio: The number of students divided by the number of faculty. A college with 1,000 students and 300 faculty members would have a student-faculty ratio of 10:3. The lower the ratio, generally speaking, the smaller the class size.

Study technique workshops: These workshops provide intensive instruction on note-taking and improvement of study skills.

Transfer student: A student who, after completing courses at one college or university, transfers and continues his or her education at another. Courses taken at one school are often, although not always, accepted by another.

TSWE (Test of Standard Written English): This is a section of the SAT (see above) designed to measure a student's ability in such areas as sentence structure and choice of words.

Waiting list: An applicant placed on an admissions waiting list may be accepted if an already accepted applicant does not matriculate at the institution.

COLLEGE PROFILES

ADELPHI UNIVERSITY

>>>>>>>>>>>>>>>>>>>>>>>>>>>

Garden City, NY 11530
(516) 663-1100

$8,600 Tuition and Fees
$4,550 Average Double Room and Meal Plan

3,497 full-time undergraduates, 1,625 part-time
   undergraduates
16:1 student/faculty ratio

>>

Founded in 1896, Adelphi University is a private institution, coed. Located on 75 acres in a town 20 miles from
New York City. Bachelor's degrees are offered.

ALTERNATIVE ADMISSIONS:

Contact: Dr. John Donohue, Coordinator of Student
Services (516) 663-1080

Adelphi University has a structured program, General
Studies, initiated in 1985 for alternative admissions students. The formal program of studies begins in the fall
and lasts for 1 year. Sixty-six percent of the students
complete the program in that time.

ADMISSION POLICIES:

- New students are eligible for alternative admissions

- Requirements for admission as a freshman:
   350 — minimum verbal SAT
   350 — minimum math SAT
   2.0 — minimum GPA
Other considerations: ACT scores (in place of SAT),
high school rank, essay/personal statement

ACADEMIC COURSEWORK AND RELATED FEATURES:

- Support services: freshman orientation, college survival skills, academic advising, drug/alcohol counseling, psychological counseling, academic skills center,
study technique workshops, career advising, peer
counseling, health center, aptitude testing
- Separate new-student orientation
- Students are required to work with tutors 1 hour per
week
- Group and one-on-one tutoring by professional tutors in math and writing
- Counseling is required
- Students are assigned an academic adviser. All advisers serve alternative admissions students exclusively
- Placement testing is required in math, reading, and
writing
- A total of 320 full-time faculty at the institution
- Eleven faculty members assigned to the program
- Students take all of their classes with alternative
admissions students only

- Alternative admissions classes average 20 students
- Students are limited to a credit load of 13 credits per semester through spring semester of freshman year

REQUIRED COURSES:
Critical Reading and Writing (credit-bearing)
The Modern Condition (credit-bearing)
Origins of the Modern Condition (credit-bearing)
Society and the Individual (credit-bearing)
Expository Writing (credit-bearing)

- Required courses are calculated in GPA

PROFILE OF ALTERNATIVE ADMISSIONS STUDENTS:
- 155 alternative admissions students enrolled
- 38% of accepted students enrolled
- 100% enter as new students
- 31% minority, 70% female
- 80% state residents, no international students
- None 25 years or older
- No learning disabled
- 5% in top 50% of high school class
- 66% graduate within 5 years

OTHER FEATURES/ACCOMMODATIONS:
- On-campus housing is available for alternative admissions students
- A meal plan is available
- Financial aid is available

DEADLINES:
- Rolling admission
- May 1 for financial aid
- May 1 for reply date

ALASKA PACIFIC UNIVERSITY
>>>>>>>>>>>>>>>>>>>>>>>>>>>

Anchorage, AK 99508
(907) 564-8248

$5,800 Tuition and Fees
$3,770 Average Double Room and Meal Plan

400 full-time undergraduates, 1,400 part-time undergraduates
12:1 student/faculty ratio
35% of undergraduates study business

>>
Founded in 1957, Alaska Pacific University is a private institution, coed, affiliated with the United Methodist church. Located on 200 acres in a small city. Associate's and bachelor's degrees are offered.

ALTERNATIVE ADMISSIONS:
Contact: Alice Bosshard, Director of Academic Support Center (907) 561-1266

Alaska Pacific University has a policy, Provisional Admittance, initiated in 1987 for alternative admissions students.

ADMISSION POLICIES:
- New and transfer students are eligible for alternative admissions

- Requirements for admission as a freshman:
  560 — minimum combined verbal and math SAT
  11 — minimum ACT
  2.5 — minimum GPA

- Requirements for admission as a transfer student:
  1.75 — minimum GPA
Other considerations: number of credits completed (less than 16 credits)

ACADEMIC COURSEWORK AND RELATED FEATURES:
- Support services: freshman orientation, college survival skills, academic advising, drug/alcohol counseling, study technique workshops, career advising, aptitude testing
- Students are not required to work with tutors
- Counseling is not required
- Students are assigned an academic adviser. All advisers serve alternative admissions students exclusively. Students meet with advisers 3 times per semester
- Placement testing is required in math, reading, and writing
- Students take classes with alternative admissions students
- Alternative admissions classes average 15 students
- Students are limited to a credit load of 15 credits per semester until they attain a 2.0 GPA

REQUIRED COURSES:
Success skills (credit-bearing)—alternative admissions students only
- Required courses are calculated in GPA

PROFILE OF ALTERNATIVE ADMISSIONS STUDENTS:
- 63 alternative admissions students enrolled
- 85% of the accepted students enrolled

Stacy Needle

- 30% minority, 60% female
- 75% state residents
- 30% 25 years or older
- 40% intercollegiate athletes, Division NAIA sports available:
  basketball, wrestling (men)
  volleyball, basketball (women)
- No learning disabled
- 50% in top 50% of high school class

OTHER FEATURES/ACCOMMODATIONS:
- On-campus housing is available, but is not guaranteed for alternative admissions students
- A meal plan is available
- Financial aid is available

DEADLINES:
- Rolling admission
- August 1 for financial aid

ALBRIGHT COLLEGE
>>>>>>>>>>>>>>>>>>>>>>>>>>>

Reading, PA 19612-5234
(215) 921-7512

$10,715 Tuition and Fees
$ 1,775 Average Double Room
$ 1,475 Average Meal Plan

1,326 full-time undergraduates, 629 part-time
  undergraduates
13:1 student/faculty ratio
40% of undergraduates study math/sciences

>>

Founded in 1856, Albright College is a private institution, coed, affiliated with the United Methodist church. Located on 90 acres in a small city 60 miles from Philadelphia. Bachelor's degrees are offered.

ALTERNATIVE ADMISSIONS:
Additional cost: $2,100 basic program fee
Contact: Dale Reinhart, Dean of Admissions and Enrollment (215) 921-7512

Albright College has a structured summer program, Summer Freshmen Program, initiated in 1979 for alternative admissions students. The program begins in June and lasts for 8 weeks. One hundred percent of the students complete the program in that time.

ADMISSION POLICIES:
- New students are eligible for alternative admissions, with a limit of 20 students. There is no wait list
- Requirements for admission as a freshman:
  485 — average verbal SAT
  460 — average math SAT
     or
   19 — average ACT

  2.7 — average GPA
Other considerations: high school rank, essay/personal statement, letters of recommendation

ACADEMIC COURSEWORK AND RELATED FEATURES:
- Support services: freshman orientation, college survival skills, academic advising, psychological counseling, academic skills center, study technique workshops, career advising, peer counseling, health center
- Separate new-student orientation
- Students are not required to work with tutors
- One-on-one tutoring by peer tutors as well as professional tutors in all academic areas
- Counseling is not required
- Students are assigned an academic adviser. None of the advisers serve alternative admissions students exclusively. Students meet with advisers 8 times
- Placement testing is not required
- Students take all of their classes with alternative admissions students
- Alternative admissions classes average 20 students

REQUIRED COURSES:
English (credit-bearing)—alternative admissions students only
Social science (credit-bearing)—alternative admissions students only
History (credit-bearing)—alternative admissions students only

- Required courses are calculated in GPA
- Minimum of 2.0 GPA required to stay in program; if below 2.0 GPA, a student may not enroll for the fall semester

PROFILE OF ALTERNATIVE ADMISSIONS STUDENTS:
- 16 alternative admissions students enrolled
- 80% of the accepted students enrolled
- 100% enter as new students
- 4% transfer to another college after sophomore year
- 5% minority, 30% female
- 30% state residents, no international students

The Other Route into College

- None 25 years or older
- No intercollegiate athletes
- 10% learning disabled
- 90% in top 50% of high school class
- 65% graduate within 4 years

OTHER FEATURES/ACCOMMODATIONS:

- On-campus housing is available and is guaranteed for alternative admissions students
- A meal plan is available
- Financial aid is available

DEADLINES:

- Rolling admission
- April 1 for financial aid
- May 1 for reply date

The program is best suited for a bright, capable, under-achiever who needs to be motivated.

ALCORN STATE UNIVERSITY

>>>>>>>>>>>>>>>>>>>>>>>>>>>>

Lorman, MS 39096
(601) 877-6147

$3,600 In-State Tuition and Fees
$4,782 Out-of-State Tuition and Fees
$ 455 Average Double Room
$ 455 Average Meal Plan

2,411 full-time undergraduates, 256 part-time
   undergraduates
20:1 student/faculty ratio
30% of undergraduates study math/sciences

>>

Founded in 1871, Alcorn State University is a public institution, coed. Located on 1,700 acres in a rural community 44 miles from Vicksburg. Associate's and bachelor's degrees are offered.

ALTERNATIVE ADMISSIONS:

Contact: Albert Johnson, Director of Admissions (601) 877-6147

Alcorn State University has a structured summer program for alternative admissions students. The program lasts for 5 weeks. Ninety-five percent of the students complete the program in that time.

ADMISSION POLICIES:

- New students are eligible for alternative admissions
- Admission considerations: SAT or ACT scores

ACADEMIC COURSEWORK AND RELATED FEATURES:

- Placement testing is required
- Alternative admissions students do not take separate classes

DEADLINES:

- Rolling admission
- April 15 for financial aid
- May 30 for reply date

ALVERNIA COLLEGE

>>>>>>>>>>>>>>>>>>>>>>>>>>>>

Reading, PA 19607
(215) 775-0525

$5,606 Tuition and Fees
$3,200 Average Double Room and Meal Plan

631 full-time undergraduates, 460 part-time
   undergraduates
14:1 student/faculty ratio
55% of undergraduates study business

>>

Founded in 1958, Alvernia College is a private institution, coed, affiliated with the Roman Catholic church. Located on 80 acres in a small city. Associate's and bachelor's degrees are offered.

ALTERNATIVE ADMISSIONS:

Contact: Dr. Mary Ann Konsin, Vice President of Academic Affairs (215) 777-5411

Alvernia College has a structured program, Educational Development Growth Environment (E.D.G.E.), initiated in 1987 for alternative admissions students. The formal program of studies begins in the fall and lasts for 1 year.

Stacy Needle

ADMISSION POLICIES:

- New students are eligible for alternative admissions, with a limit of 50 students. There is no wait list

- Requirements for admission as a freshman:
  370 — average verbal SAT
  360 — average math SAT
  32 — average TSWE
  2.0 — average GPA
Other considerations: high school rank, difficulty of high school courses taken, letters of recommendation

ACADEMIC COURSEWORK AND RELATED FEATURES:

- Support services: freshman orientation, college survival skills, academic advising, drug/alcohol counseling, psychological counseling, academic skills center, study technique workshops, career advising, peer counseling, health center
- Students are required to work with tutors
- Group and one-on-one tutoring by professional tutors in English and math
- Counseling is not required
- Students are assigned an academic adviser. None of the advisers serve alternative admissions students exclusively. Students meet with advisers 17 times per semester
- Placement testing is required in English and math
- A total of 50 full-time faculty at the institution
- Special faculty assigned to the program
- Students take all of their classes with alternative admissions students
- Students are limited to a credit load of 14 credits per semester through spring semester of freshman year

REQUIRED COURSES:

English (credit-bearing)—alternative admissions students only
Math (credit-bearing)—alternative admissions students only
Humanities I and II (credit-bearing)—alternative admissions students only
Psychology (credit-bearing)—alternative admissions students only
Physical education (credit-bearing)—alternative admissions students only
Study skills (credit-bearing)—alternative admissions students only

- Required courses are calculated in GPA

PROFILE OF ALTERNATIVE ADMISSIONS STUDENTS:

- 30 alternative admissions students enrolled
- 80% of accepted students enrolled
- 100% enter as new students
- 5% minority, 50% female
- 65% state residents, no international students
- None 25 years or older
- 25% intercollegiate athletes, Division NAIA sports available:
  baseball, basketball, tennis, golf, cross-country (men)
  basketball, softball, field hockey, tennis, cross-country, volleyball, golf (women)
- No learning disabled
- 30% in top 50% of high school class

OTHER FEATURES/ACCOMMODATIONS:

- On-campus housing is available, but is not guaranteed for alternative admissions students
- A meal plan is available
- Financial aid is available

DEADLINES:

- Rolling admission—1 week after acceptance is sent, notification of admission
- April 1 for financial aid

ANDREWS UNIVERSITY

>>>>>>>>>>>>>>>>>>>>>>>>>>>>

Berrien Springs, MI 49104
(616) 471-3353

$7,761 Tuition and Fees
$1,506 Average Double Room
$1,500 Average Meal Plan

1,595 full-time undergraduates, 414 part-time undergraduates
12:1 student/faculty ratio
48% of undergraduates study arts/humanities

>>

Founded in 1874, Andrews University is a private institution, coed, affiliated with the Seventh-day Adventist church. Located on 1,600 acres in a rural community 15 miles from Benton Harbor. Associate's and bachelor's degrees are offered.

ALTERNATIVE ADMISSIONS:

Contact: Dr. Cyril Connelley, Director of Admissions
(616) 471-3353

The Other Route into College

Andrews University has a policy for alternative admissions students.

ADMISSION POLICIES:

- New and transfer students are eligible for alternative admissions

- Requirements for admission as a freshman:
    12 — average ACT
    1.97 — average GPA
Other considerations: letters of recommendation

- Requirements for admission as a transfer student:
    1.17 — minimum GPA
Other considerations: number of credits completed, letters of recommendation

ACADEMIC COURSEWORK AND RELATED FEATURES:

- Support services: freshman orientation, college survival skills, academic advising, drug/alcohol counseling, psychological counseling, academic skills center, study technique workshops, career advising, health center
- Students are not required to work with tutors
- Counseling is not required
- Students are assigned an academic adviser. None of the advisers serve alternative admissions students exclusively. Students meet with advisers at least 1 time per semester
- Placement testing is not required
- Alternative admissions students do not take separate classes
- Students are not limited to credit load

REQUIRED COURSES:

College Success Strategies (credit-bearing)
Basic Writing Skills (credit-bearing)
Reading Techniques (credit-bearing)
Mathematics Skills Lab (credit-bearing)
Mathematics Skills—Algebra (credit-bearing)

- Required courses are calculated in GPA

PROFILE OF ALTERNATIVE ADMISSIONS STUDENTS:

- 293 alternative admissions students enrolled
- 59% of the accepted students enrolled
- 82% enter as new students, 18% as transfer students
- 56% minority, 35% female
- 26% state residents, 29% international students
- 55% 25 years or older
- No intercollegiate athletes

OTHER FEATURES/ACCOMMODATIONS:

- On-campus housing is available, but is not guaranteed for alternative admissions students

- A meal plan is available
- Financial aid is available

DEADLINES:

- Rolling admission
- June 1 for financial aid

ANGELO STATE UNIVERSITY
>>>>>>>>>>>>>>>>>>>>>>>>>>>>

San Angelo, TX 76909
(915) 942-2041

$ 822 In-State Tuition and Fees
$3,270 Out-of-State Tuition and Fees
$ 900 Average Double Room
$ 550 Average Meal Plan

4,364 full-time undergraduates, 1,528 part-time
    undergraduates
26:1 student/faculty ratio
44% of undergraduates study business

>>

Founded in 1928, Angelo State University is a public institution, coed. Located on 268 acres in a small city. Associate's and bachelor's degrees are offered.

ALTERNATIVE ADMISSIONS:

Additional cost: $206 basic program fee
Contact: William Bowen, Director of Admissions (915) 942-2041

Angelo State University has a structured summer program, Summer Provisional, for alternative admissions students. The program begins in June and lasts for 2 terms. Forty percent of the students complete the program in that time.

ADMISSION POLICIES:

- New students are eligible for alternative admissions

- Admission considerations: SAT or ACT scores, high school GPA, high school rank

ACADEMIC COURSEWORK AND RELATED FEATURES:

- Support services: freshman orientation, academic advising, psychological counseling, study technique workshops, career advising, health center

Stacy Needle

- Students are not required to work with tutors
- Counseling is not required
- Students are assigned an academic adviser. None of the advisers serve alternative admissions students exclusively
- Placement testing is required in English and math
- Alternative admissions students do not take separate classes

REQUIRED COURSES:
- Remedial courses required:
  Writing Fundamentals and/or Reading Fundamentals (credit-bearing)
  Math Fundamentals I and/or Math Fundamentals II (credit-bearing)
- Remedial courses are calculated in GPA
- Minimum of 2.0 GPA required to stay in program; if below 2.0 GPA, a student may not enroll for the fall semester

PROFILE OF ALTERNATIVE ADMISSIONS STUDENTS:
- 67 alternative admissions students enrolled
- 40% of accepted students enrolled
- 100% enter as new students
- No international students
- No intercollegiate athletes

OTHER FEATURES/ACCOMMODATIONS:
- On-campus housing is available, but is not guaranteed for alternative admissions students
- A meal plan is available

DEADLINES:
- Rolling admission

The program is best suited for a student who has the maturity to be able to withstand a very demanding program.

ANNA MARIA COLLEGE

>>>>>>>>>>>>>>>>>>>>>>>>>>

Paxton, MA 01612
(508) 757-4586

$8,100 Tuition and Fees
$4,020 Average Double Room and Meal Plan

423 full-time undergraduates, 127 part-time undergraduates
16:1 student/faculty ratio
67% of undergraduates study arts/humanities

>>

Founded in 1946, Anna Maria College is a private institution, coed, affiliated with the Roman Catholic church. Located on 180 acres in a rural community 8 miles from Worcester. Associate's and bachelor's degrees are offered.

ALTERNATIVE ADMISSIONS:

Contact: Christopher Lydon, Director of Admissions (508) 757-4586

Anna Maria College has a policy for alternative admissions students.

ADMISSION POLICIES:
- New and transfer students are eligible for alternative admissions

- Requirements for admission as a freshman:
  370 — average verbal SAT
  385 — average math SAT
  2.4 — average GPA
Other considerations: TSWE scores, high school rank, difficulty of high school courses taken, interview with admissions counselor, essay/personal statement, letters of recommendation

- Requirements for admission as a transfer student:
  2.2 — average GPA
Other considerations: difficulty of coursework, interview with admissions counselor, essay/personal statement, letters of recommendation

ACADEMIC COURSEWORK AND RELATED FEATURES:
- Support services: freshman orientation, college survival skills, academic advising, academic skills center, study technique workshops, career advising, health center, aptitude testing
- Students are not required to work with tutors
- Counseling is not required
- Students are assigned an academic adviser
- Placement testing is required
- Alternative admissions students do not take separate classes
- Students are not limited to credit load

PROFILE OF ALTERNATIVE ADMISSIONS STUDENTS:
- 25 alternative admissions students enrolled
- 55% of the accepted students enrolled
- 85% enter as new students, 15% as transfer students

- 70% female
- 5% international students
- 10% 25 years or older

OTHER FEATURES/ACCOMMODATIONS:
- On-campus housing is available and is guaranteed for alternative admissions students
- A meal plan is available
- Financial aid is available

DEADLINES:
- Rolling admission
- June 1 for financial aid

ANTIOCH COLLEGE
>>>>>>>>>>>>>>>>>>>>>>>>>>>

Yellow Springs, OH 45387
(513) 767-6400

$11,200 Tuition and Fees
$ 3,330 Average Double Room and Meal Plan

564 full-time undergraduates, 27 part-time
   undergraduates
11:1 student/faculty ratio

>>

Founded in 1852, Antioch College is a private institution, coed. Located on 100 acres in a rural community. Bachelor's degrees are offered.

ALTERNATIVE ADMISSIONS:

Contact: Jimmy Williams, Director of Admissions (513) 767-6400

Antioch College has a policy for alternative admissions students.

ADMISSION POLICIES:
- New and transfer students are eligible for alternative admissions
- Admission considerations—new student: high school GPA, high school rank, type of high school attended, essay/personal statement, letters of recommendation, age of applicant
- Admission considerations—transfer student: GPA at previous institution, difficulty of coursework, type of college attended, essay/personal statement, letters of recommendation

Stacy Needle

8

ACADEMIC COURSEWORK AND RELATED FEATURES:
- Support services: freshman orientation, academic advising, drug/alcohol counseling, women's center, psychological counseling, academic skills center, career advising, peer counseling, health center, aptitude testing
- Students are not required to work with tutors
- Group and one-on-one tutoring by peer tutors as well as professional tutors in writing, science, math, computers, and foreign languages
- Counseling is not required
- Students are assigned an academic adviser
- Placement testing is required in math and writing
- Alternative admissions students do not take separate classes
- Students are not limited to credit load

OTHER FEATURES/ACCOMMODATIONS:
- On-campus housing is available and is guaranteed for alternative admissions students
- A meal plan is available
- Financial aid is available

DEADLINES:
- Rolling admission

AQUINAS COLLEGE
>>>>>>>>>>>>>>>>>>>>>>>>>>>

Grand Rapids, MI 49506
(616) 732-4460

$7,494 Tuition and Fees
$3,484 Average Double Room and Meal Plan

1,200 full-time undergraduates, 900 part-time
   undergraduates
16:1 student/faculty ratio

>>

Founded in 1931, Aquinas College is a private institution, coed, affiliated with the Roman Catholic church. Located on 101 acres in a large city 150 miles from Detroit. Associate's and bachelor's degrees are offered.

ALTERNATIVE ADMISSIONS:

Contact: Paula Meehan, Dean of Admissions (616) 732-4460

Aquinas College has a policy for alternative admissions students.

ADMISSION POLICIES:

- New students are eligible for alternative admissions

- Admission considerations: ACT scores, high school GPA

ACADEMIC COURSEWORK AND RELATED FEATURES:

- Support services: freshman orientation, college survival skills, academic advising, drug/alcohol counseling, women's center, psychological counseling, academic skills center, study technique workshops, career advising, health center
- Students are not required to work with tutors
- Group and one-on-one tutoring by peer tutors as well as professional tutors
- Counseling is not required
- Students are assigned an academic adviser
- Placement testing is required in math, English, and reading
- Alternative admissions students do not take separate classes
- Students are not limited to credit load

OTHER FEATURES/ACCOMMODATIONS:

- On-campus housing is available, but is not guaranteed for alternative admissions students
- A meal plan is available

DEADLINES:

- Rolling admission
- March 1 for financial aid

ATLANTIC UNION COLLEGE

>>>>>>>>>>>>>>>>>>>>>>>>>>

South Lancaster, MA 01561
(508) 368-2235

$8,275 Tuition and Fees
$1,500 Average Double Room
$1,350 Average Meal Plan

795 full-time undergraduates, 169 part-time
  undergraduates
12:1 student/faculty ratio
30% of undergraduates study education

>>

Founded in 1882, Atlantic Union College is a private institution, coed, affiliated with the Seventh-day Adventist church. Located on 314 acres in a rural community 20 miles from Worcester. Associate's and bachelor's degrees are offered.

ALTERNATIVE ADMISSIONS:

Contact: James Norcliffe, Director of Admissions (508) 368-2235

Atlantic Union College has a policy for alternative admissions students.

ADMISSION POLICIES:

- New and transfer students are eligible for alternative admissions

- Admission considerations—new student: SAT or ACT scores, high school GPA, essay/personal statement, letters of recommendation

- Admission considerations—transfer student: GPA at previous institution, essay/personal statement, letters of recommendation

ACADEMIC COURSEWORK AND RELATED FEATURES:

- Support services: freshman orientation, academic advising, psychological counseling, academic skills center, study technique workshops, career advising, aptitude testing
- Students are required to work with tutors
- One-on-one tutoring by peer tutors in all academic areas
- Academic counseling is required
- Students are assigned an academic adviser. None of the advisers serve alternative admissions students exclusively
- Placement testing is required in English and math
- Students take classes with alternative admissions students only
- Alternative admissions classes average 15 students
- Students are limited to a credit load of 12 credits per semester until they attain a 2.0 GPA

REQUIRED COURSES:

- Remedial courses required:
  Preface to Rhetoric Writing (credit-bearing)—alternative admissions students only
  Reading (credit-bearing)—alternative admissions students only
  Math (credit-bearing)—alternative admissions students only

- Remedial courses are calculated in GPA

OTHER FEATURES/ACCOMMODATIONS:
- On-campus housing is available and is guaranteed for alternative admissions students
- A meal plan is available

DEADLINES:
- Rolling admission
- August 15 for financial aid
- August 25 for reply date

AUBURN UNIVERSITY AT MONTGOMERY

>>>>>>>>>>>>>>>>>>>>>>>>>>>

Montgomery, AL 36193
(205) 884-4080

$1,205 In-State Tuition and Fees
$3,645 Out-of-State Tuition and Fees
$1,260 Average Double Room

3,831 full-time undergraduates, 721 part-time
   undergraduates
22:1 student/faculty ratio

>>

Founded in 1969, Auburn University at Montgomery is a public institution, coed. Located on 500 acres in a large city. Bachelor's degrees are offered.

ALTERNATIVE ADMISSIONS:

Contact: Nancy Wong, Admissions Counselor (205) 884-4080

Auburn University at Montgomery has a structured program, Special Student Admissions, initiated in 1969 for alternative admissions students. The formal program of studies begins in the fall and lasts for approximately 2–3 quarters; however, students can also enter the program in the spring and continue for approximately 2–3 quarters.

ADMISSION POLICIES:
- New and transfer students are eligible for alternative admissions
- Admission based on individual criteria

ACADEMIC COURSEWORK AND RELATED FEATURES:
- Support services: freshman orientation, college survival skills, academic advising, drug/alcohol counseling, psychological counseling, academic skills center, study technique workshops, career advising, health center
- Separate new-student orientation
- Students are not required to work with tutors
- Placement testing is required in math and English
- Alternative admissions students do not take separate classes
- Students are limited to a credit load of 10 credits per quarter through completion of program

REQUIRED COURSES:
- Courses required of students who demonstrate deficiency:
  Developmental English (credit-bearing)
  Developmental Math (credit-bearing)
  Developmental Study Skills (credit-bearing)

- Remedial courses are not calculated in GPA
- Minimum of 2.0 GPA required to stay in program; if below 2.0 GPA, a student is not permitted to continue at the college

PROFILE OF ALTERNATIVE ADMISSIONS STUDENTS:
- 450 alternative admissions students enrolled
- 75% of accepted students enrolled

OTHER FEATURES/ACCOMMODATIONS:
- On-campus housing is available, but is not guaranteed for alternative admissions students
- A meal plan is not available
- Financial aid is available

DEADLINES:
- Rolling admission

AUGUSTA COLLEGE

>>>>>>>>>>>>>>>>>>>>>>>>>>>>

Augusta, GA 30910
(404) 737-1405

$1,368 In-State Tuition and Fees
$3,750 Out-of-State Tuition and Fees
$1,440 Average Double Room
$3,240 Average Meal Plan

Stacy Needle

2,363 full-time undergraduates, 1,677 part-time
  undergraduates
32:1 student/faculty ratio
33% of undergraduates study business

\>\>

Founded in 1925, Augusta College is a public institution, coed. Located on 72 acres in a city 148 miles from
Atlanta. Associate's and bachelor's degrees are offered.

ALTERNATIVE ADMISSIONS:

Contact: Dr. William Dodd, Director of Developmental
Studies (404) 737-1685

Augusta College has a structured program, Developmental Studies, for alternative admissions students.

ADMISSION POLICIES:

• New and transfer students are eligible for alternative
  admissions

• Requirements for admission as a freshman:
  450 — average verbal SAT
  430 — average math SAT
Other considerations: high school GPA, interview with
admissions counselor

• Admission considerations—transfer student: GPA at
  previous institution, number of credits completed
  (less than 29 credits)

ACADEMIC COURSEWORK AND RELATED FEATURES:

• Support services: freshman orientation, college survival skills, academic advising, drug/alcohol counsel-
  ing, psychological counseling, academic skills center,
  study technique workshops, career advising, aptitude
  testing, extended time for tests
• Separate new-student orientation
• Students are not required to work with tutors
• Group and one-on-one tutoring by peer tutors as well
  as professional tutors
• Counseling is not required
• Students are assigned an academic adviser. Students
  meet with advisers at least 1 time per semester
• Placement testing is required
• A total of 154 full-time faculty at the institution
• Nine faculty members assigned to the program, who
  are trained to work with alternative admissions stu-
  dents
• Students take classes with alternative admissions
  students only
• Courses are also offered in the evening
• Students are not limited to credit load

REQUIRED COURSES:

• Courses required of students who demonstrate defi-
  ciency:
  Developmental Math (credit-bearing)
  Developmental English (credit-bearing)
  Developmental Reading (credit-bearing)

• Remedial courses are not calculated in GPA

PROFILE OF ALTERNATIVE ADMISSIONS STUDENTS:

• 22% minority

OTHER FEATURES/ACCOMMODATIONS:

• On-campus housing is available, but is not guaranteed
  for alternative admissions students
• A meal plan is available
• Financial aid is available

DEADLINES:

• Rolling admission

AURORA UNIVERSITY
\>

Aurora, IL 60506
(312) 896-1975

_____

$7,570 Tuition and Fees
$1,620 Average Double Room
$1,725 Average Meal Plan

773 full-time undergraduates, 771 part-time
  undergraduates
14:1 student/faculty ratio
30% of undergraduates study math/sciences

\>\>

Founded in 1893, Aurora University is a private institution, coed. Located on 26 acres in a small city 40 miles
from Chicago. Bachelor's degrees are offered.

ALTERNATIVE ADMISSIONS:

Contact: John Milroy, Director of Admissions (312)
896-1975

Aurora University has a policy for alternative admissions students.

The Other Route into College

ADMISSION POLICIES:

- New and transfer students are eligible for alternative admissions, with a limit of 15–20 students. There is a wait list

- Requirements for admission as a freshman:
  13 — minimum ACT
  1.9 — minimum GPA

Other considerations: SAT scores (in place of ACT), high school rank, type of high school attended, difficulty of high school courses taken, interview with admissions counselor, essay/personal statement, letters of recommendation

- Requirements for admission as a transfer student:
  2.0 — minimum GPA

Other considerations: interview with admissions counselor, essay/personal statement, letters of recommendation

ACADEMIC COURSEWORK AND RELATED FEATURES:

- Support services: freshman orientation, college survival skills, academic advising, drug/alcohol counseling, academic skills center, study technique workshops, career advising, health center, aptitude testing
- Students are not required to work with tutors
- One-on-one tutoring by peer tutors
- Counseling is not required
- Students are assigned an academic adviser. Students meet with advisers at least 1 time per trimester
- Placement testing is required in math
- Students take an average of 40% of the classes with alternative admissions students
- Alternative admissions classes average 10 students
- Students are not limited to credit load

REQUIRED COURSES:

- Remedial courses required:
  Approaches to Learning (credit-bearing)—alternative admissions students only
- Courses required of students who demonstrate deficiency:
  Pre-Algebra
  Principles of Composition

PROFILE OF ALTERNATIVE ADMISSIONS STUDENTS:

- 15 alternative admissions students enrolled
- 30% of the accepted students enrolled
- 50% minority, 40% female
- 100% state residents, no international students
- None 25 years or older
- 50% intercollegiate athletes, Division III sports available:

soccer, tennis, football, basketball, baseball, golf, cross-country (men)
volleyball softball, basketball, tennis, cross-country (women)
- 60% in top 50% of high school class

OTHER FEATURES/ACCOMMODATIONS:

- On-campus housing is available, but is not guaranteed for alternative admissions students
- A meal plan is available
- Financial aid is available

DEADLINES:

- Rolling admission

AVILA COLLEGE

>>>>>>>>>>>>>>>>>>>>>>>>>>>

Kansas City, MO 64145
(816) 942-8400

———

$6,030 Tuition and Fees
$2,750 Average Double Room and Meal Plan

491 full-time undergraduates, 629 part-time undergraduates
11:1 student/faculty ratio

>>

Founded in 1916, Avila College is a private institution, coed, affiliated with the Roman Catholic church. Located on 48 acres in a large city. Bachelor's degrees are offered.

ALTERNATIVE ADMISSIONS:

Contact: James Millard, Director of Admissions (816) 942-8400

Avila College has a structured program, Restricted Provisional Acceptance, for alternative admissions students. The formal program of studies begins in the fall and lasts for 1 semester; however, students can also enter the program in the spring and continue for 1 semester.

ADMISSION POLICIES:

- New and transfer students are eligible for alternative admissions

Stacy Needle

- Admission considerations—new student: SAT or ACT scores, high school GPA, high school rank
- Admission considerations—transfer student: GPA at previous institution, number of credits completed

ACADEMIC COURSEWORK AND RELATED FEATURES:

- Support services: freshman orientation, college survival skills, academic advising, drug/alcohol counseling, psychological counseling, academic skills center, career advising, peer counseling, health center, aptitude testing
- Students are not required to work with tutors
- Placement testing is required in math
- Students take 1 class with alternative admissions students only
- Alternative admissions classes average 5–10 students
- Courses are also offered in the evening
- Students are limited to a credit load of 12 credits per semester through first semester of program

REQUIRED COURSES:
Strategies for Academic Success

- Required courses are not calculated in GPA
- Minimum of 2.0 GPA required to stay in program; if below 2.0 GPA, a student is academically dismissed

OTHER FEATURES/ACCOMMODATIONS:
- On-campus housing is available, but is not guaranteed for alternative admissions students
- A meal plan is available
- Financial aid is available

DEADLINES:
- Rolling admission
- April for financial aid

BALL STATE UNIVERSITY

>>>>>>>>>>>>>>>>>>>>>>>>>

Muncie, IN 47306-0855
(317) 285-8300

$1,992 In-State Tuition and Fees
$5,990 Out-of-State Tuition and Fees
$2,600 Average Double Room and Meal Plan

15,214 full-time undergraduates, 2,942 part-time undergraduates
17:1 student/faculty ratio
45% of undergraduates study sciences and humanities

>>

Founded in 1918, Ball State University is a public institution, coed. Located on 955 acres in a small city 50 miles from Indianapolis. Associate's and bachelor's degrees are offered.

ALTERNATIVE ADMISSIONS:
Additional cost: $980 basic program fee
Contact: Dr. Charles Martin, Assistant Dean of University College (317) 285-3682

Ball State University has a structured summer program, Project Start, initiated in 1985 for alternative admissions students. The program begins in June and lasts for 5 weeks. Ninety-six of the students complete the program in that time.

ADMISSION POLICIES:
- New students are eligible for alternative admissions, with a limit of 100 students. There is no wait list

- Requirements for admission as a freshman:
  354 — average verbal SAT
  376 — average math SAT
   35 — average TSWE
Other considerations: ACT scores (in place of SAT), high school GPA, high school rank, state residence

ACADEMIC COURSEWORK AND RELATED FEATURES:
- Support services: freshman orientation, college survival skills, academic advising, drug/alcohol counseling, women's center, psychological counseling, academic skills center, study technique workshops, career advising, peer counseling, health center, aptitude testing
- Separate new-student orientation
- Students are not required to work with tutors
- Group and one-on-one tutoring by peer tutors as well as professional tutors in all academic areas
- Academic counseling is required
- Students are assigned an academic adviser. None of the advisers serve alternative admissions students exclusively. Students meet with advisers at least 2 times per semester
- Placement testing is required in math
- Alternative admissions students do not take separate classes

REQUIRED COURSES:

- Minimum of 2.0 GPA required to stay in program; if below, 2.0 GPA, a student may not enroll for the fall semester.

PROFILE OF ALTERNATIVE ADMISSIONS STUDENTS:

- 95 alternative admissions students enrolled
- 76% of the accepted students enrolled
- 100% enter as new students
- 20% minority, 55% female
- 100% state residents, no international students
- None 25 years or older
- 4% intercollegiate athletes
- No learning disabled
- None in top 50% of high school class

OTHER FEATURES/ACCOMMODATIONS:

- On-campus housing is available and is guaranteed for alternative admissions students
- A meal plan is available. It is required of alternative admissions students
- Financial aid is available

DEADLINES:

- Rolling admission
- March 1 for financial aid
- April 1 for reply date

The program is best suited for a motivated late bloomer with academic potential that has yet to be realized, encouraged, or utilized.

BARTLESVILLE WESLEYAN COLLEGE

>>>>>>>>>>>>>>>>>>>>>>>>>

Bartlesville, OK 74006
(918) 333-6151

$4,670 Tuition and Fees
$1,300 Average Double Room
$1,400 Average Meal Plan

334 full-time undergraduates, 131 part-time undergraduates
12:1 student/faculty ratio
29% of undergraduates study business

>>

Founded in 1909, Bartlesville Wesleyan College is a private institution, coed, affiliated with the Wesleyan church. Located on 115 acres in a small city 40 miles from Tulsa. Associate's and bachelor's degrees are offered.

ALTERNATIVE ADMISSIONS:

Contact: Keat Wade, Director of Personal Development Learning Center (918) 333-6151

Bartlesville Wesleyan College has a structured program, Conditional Acceptance, initiated in 1986 for alternative admissions students. The formal program of studies begins in the fall and lasts for 1–4 semesters; however, students can also enter the program in the spring and continue for 1–4 semesters.

ADMISSION POLICIES:

- New students are eligible for alternative admissions
- Admission considerations: SAT or ACT scores, high school GPA, high school rank

ACADEMIC COURSEWORK AND RELATED FEATURES:

- Support services: freshman orientation, college survival skills, academic advising, drug/alcohol counseling, psychological counseling, academic skills center, study technique workshops, career advising, peer counseling, aptitude testing, extended time for tests
- Students are not required to work with tutors
- Group and one-on-one tutoring by peer tutors as well as professional tutors in all academic areas
- Counseling is not required
- Students are assigned an academic adviser. All advisers serve alternative admissions students exclusively. Students meet with advisers 3 times per semester
- Placement testing is required in English, math, and reading
- Alternative admissions students do not take separate classes
- Students are limited to a credit load of 13 credits per semester until they attain a 2.0 GPA

REQUIRED COURSES:

- Courses required of students who demonstrate deficiency:
  Developmental English
  Developmental Math
  Analytical Thinking or Developmental Reading
- Minimum of 1.5 GPA required to stay in program; if below 1.5 GPA, a student is academically suspended

PROFILE OF ALTERNATIVE ADMISSIONS STUDENTS:

- 17 alternative admissions students enrolled
- 90% of the accepted students enrolled

Stacy Needle

- 20% graduate within 4 years
- 33% graduate within 5 years

OTHER FEATURES/ACCOMMODATIONS:
- On-campus housing is available and is guaranteed for alternative admissions students
- A meal plan is available
- Financial aid is available

DEADLINES:
- Rolling admission

BELMONT ABBEY COLLEGE

>>>>>>>>>>>>>>>>>>>>>>>>>>>

Belmont, NC 28012
(704) 825-6665

———

$6,764 Tuition and Fees
$3,262 Average Double Room and Meal Plan

909 full-time undergraduates, 120 part-time
   undergraduates
17:1 student/faculty ratio
22% of undergraduates study business

>>

Founded in 1876, Belmont Abbey College is a private institution, coed, affiliated with the Roman Catholic church. Located on 650 acres in a town 12 miles from Charlotte. Bachelor's degrees are offered.

ALTERNATIVE ADMISSIONS:
Contact: Denis Stokes, Director of Admissions (704) 825-6665

Belmont Abbey College has a policy for alternative admissions students.

ADMISSION POLICIES:
- New and transfer students are eligible for alternative admissions

- Requirements for admission as a freshman:
   360 — average verbal SAT
   390 — average math SAT
   2.2 — average GPA

Other considerations: difficulty of high school courses taken, essay/personal statement, letters of recommendation

- Admission considerations—transfer student: GPA at previous institution, difficulty of coursework, number of credits completed, essay/personal statement

ACADEMIC COURSEWORK AND RELATED FEATURES:
- Support services: freshman orientation, college survival skills, academic advising, drug/alcohol counseling, psychological counseling, academic skills center, study technique workshops, career advising, peer counseling, health center, aptitude testing
- Students are not required to work with tutors
- Counseling is not required
- Students are assigned an academic adviser. None of the advisers serve alternative admissions students exclusively
- Placement testing is required in math, English, and foreign language
- Alternative admissions students do not take separate classes
- Students are not limited to credit load

OTHER FEATURES/ACCOMMODATIONS:
- On-campus housing is available and is guaranteed for alternative admissions students
- On-campus housing is required of alternative admissions students
- A meal plan is available. It is required of alternative admissions students
- Financial aid is available

DEADLINES:
- Rolling admission
- March 1 for financial aid

BELMONT COLLEGE

>>>>>>>>>>>>>>>>>>>>>>>>>>>

Nashville, TN 37212
(615) 385-6785

———

$4,650 Tuition and Fees
$1,370 Average Double Room
$1,500 Average Meal Plan

1,977 full-time undergraduates, 711 part-time
   undergraduates
16:1 student/faculty ratio
46% of undergraduates study business

>>

Founded in 1951, Belmont College is a private institution, coed, affiliated with the Southern Baptist church. Located on 40 acres in a large city. Associate's and bachelor's degrees are offered.

ALTERNATIVE ADMISSIONS:

Contact: Dr. Norma Stevens, Director of Opportunity Admissions (615) 373-7001

Belmont College has a structured program, Opportunity Admissions, initiated in 1986 for alternative admissions students. The formal program of studies begins in the fall and lasts for 1 semester. Ninety-seven percent of the students complete the program in that time.

ADMISSION POLICIES:

- New students are eligible for alternative admissions, with a limit of 20 students. There is a wait list

- Requirements for admission as a freshman:
    13 — minimum ACT
    2.0 — minimum GPA
Other considerations: high school rank

ACADEMIC COURSEWORK AND RELATED FEATURES:

- Support services: freshman orientation, college survival skills, academic advising, drug/alcohol counseling, psychological counseling, academic skills center, study technique workshops, career advising, peer counseling, health center, aptitude testing
- Students are not required to work with tutors
- Group and one-on-one tutoring by peer tutors as well as professional tutors
- Counseling is not required
- Students are assigned an academic adviser. None of the advisers serve alternative admissions students exclusively. Students meet with advisers 4 times per semester
- Placement testing is not required
- A total of 158 full-time faculty at the institution
- Four faculty members assigned to the program, who are trained to work with alternative admissions students
- Students take an average of 75% of their classes with alternative admissions students
- Alternative admissions classes average 12 students
- Students are limited to a credit load of 13 credits per semester through spring semester of freshman year

REQUIRED COURSES:

- Remedial courses required:
    English (noncredit)—alternative admissions students only
    Math (noncredit)—alternative admissions students only

Stacy Needle

Science with Lab (noncredit)—alternative admissions students only

- Other required courses:
    Study Skills Lab (noncredit)—alternative admissions students only

PROFILE OF ALTERNATIVE ADMISSIONS STUDENTS:

- 26 alternative admissions students enrolled
- 49% of the accepted students enrolled
- 100% enter as new students
- 31% minority, 53% female
- 82% state residents, 4% international students
- 12% 25 years or older
- No intercollegiate athletes
- 17% learning disabled
- 22% in top 50% of high school class
- 10% graduate within 4 years
- 25% graduate within 5 years

OTHER FEATURES/ACCOMMODATIONS:

- On-campus housing is available and is guaranteed for alternative admissions students
- On-campus housing is required of alternative admissions students
- A meal plan is available. It is required of alternative admissions students
- Financial aid is not available

DEADLINES:

- Rolling admission
- March 15 for financial aid

BEMIDJI STATE UNIVERSITY

>>>>>>>>>>>>>>>>>>>>>>>>>>>

Bemidji, MN 56601-2699
(218) 755-2040

$1,715 In-State Tuition and Fees
$2,798 Out-of-State Tuition and Fees
$2,255 Average Double Room and Meal Plan

3,885 full-time undergraduates, 755 part-time undergraduates
19:1 student/faculty ratio

>>

Founded in 1919, Bemidji State University is a public institution, coed. Located on 89 acres in a small city 200 miles from Minneapolis. Associate's and bachelor's degrees are offered.

ALTERNATIVE ADMISSIONS:

Contact: Louise Churack, Director of Educational Development Center (218) 755-2614

Bemidji State University has a structured summer program, Summer Prep Program, initiated in 1989 for alternative admissions students. The program lasts for 5 weeks. Eighty-one percent of the students complete the program in that time.

ADMISSION POLICIES:

• New students are eligible for alternative admissions, with a limit of 30 students. There is a wait list

• Requirements for admission as a freshman:
   340 — minimum verbal SAT
   340 — minimum math SAT
        or
    12 — minimum ACT

Other considerations: high school GPA, high school rank, type of high school attended, difficulty of high school courses taken, age of applicant, state residence

ACADEMIC COURSEWORK AND RELATED FEATURES:

• Support services: freshman orientation, college survival skills, academic advising, academic skills center, study technique workshops, career advising, health center, aptitude testing, extended time for tests
• Separate new-student orientation
• Students are not required to work with tutors
• Counseling is not required
• Students are assigned an academic adviser. None of the advisers serve alternative admissions students exclusively. Students meet with advisers 3 times per quarter
• Placement testing is required in English, reading, and math
• A total of 220 full-time faculty at the institution
• Three faculty members assigned to the program, who are trained to work with alternative admissions students
• Students take all of their classes with alternative admissions students only
• Alternative admissions students average 20–25 students

REQUIRED COURSES:

Orientation/College Success (credit-bearing)—alternative admissions students only
• Courses required of students who demonstrate deficiency:

Basic Grammar and Writing (credit-bearing)—alternative admissions students only
Basic Algebra (credit-bearing)—alternative admissions students only
• Remedial courses are calculated in GPA
• Required courses are calculated in GPA

OTHER FEATURES/ACCOMMODATIONS:

• On-campus housing is available and is guaranteed for alternative admissions students
• A meal plan is available

DEADLINES:

• Rolling admission

BETHANY COLLEGE

>>>>>>>>>>>>>>>>>>>>>>>>>>>>

Lindsborg, KS 67456-1897
(913) 227-3311

$5,992 Tuition and Fees
$1,257 Average Double Room
$1,655 Average Meal Plan

684 full-time undergraduates, 38 part-time
   undergraduates
13:1 student/faculty ratio

>>

Founded in 1881, Bethany College is a private institution, coed, affiliated with the Lutheran church. Located on 40 acres in a rural community 15 miles from Salina. Bachelor's degrees are offered.

ALTERNATIVE ADMISSIONS:

Contact: Dr. Sally Mowery, Director of Academic Support Center (913) 227-3311, Ext. 200

Bethany College has a structured program, Academic Support Program, initiated in 1974 for alternative admissions students. The formal program of studies begins in the fall and lasts for 1 semester. One hundred percent of the students complete the program in that time.

ADMISSION POLICIES:

• New and transfer students are eligible for alternative admissions

The Other Route into College

- Admission considerations—new student: SAT or ACT scores, high school GPA, high school rank
- Admission considerations—transfer student: GPA at previous institution, number of credits completed, interview with admissions counselor

ACADEMIC COURSEWORK AND RELATED FEATURES:

- Support services: freshman orientation, academic advising, drug/alcohol counseling, psychological counseling, academic skills center, study technique workshops, career advising, peer counseling, health center, aptitude testing
- Students are not required to work with tutors
- Counseling is not required
- Students are assigned an academic adviser. None of the advisers serve alternative admissions students exclusively. Students meet with advisers 2 times per semester
- Placement testing is not required
- A total of 57 full-time faculty at the institution
- One faculty member assigned to the program, who is trained to work with alternative admissions students
- Alternative admissions students do not take separate classes
- Students are not limited to credit load

REQUIRED COURSES:

- Minimum of 1.7 GPA required to stay in program; if below 1.7 GPA, a student is academically dismissed and may not enroll for 1 or more semesters

OTHER FEATURES/ACCOMMODATIONS:

- On-campus housing is available, but is not guaranteed for alternative admissions students
- A meal plan is available
- Financial aid is available

DEADLINES:

- Rolling admission
- March 15 for financial aid
- April 1 for reply date

BETHEL COLLEGE

>>>>>>>>>>>>>>>>>>>>>>>>>>>

St. Paul, MN 55112
(612) 638-6242

$8,500 Tuition and Fees
$1,760 Average Double Room
$1,420 Average Meal Plan

1,683 full-time undergraduates, 117 part-time
   undergraduates
15:1 student/faculty ratio

>>

Founded in 1871, Bethel College is a private institution, coed, affiliated with the Baptist General Conference. Located on 231 acres in a large city. Associate's and bachelor's degrees are offered.

ALTERNATIVE ADMISSIONS:

Contact: Douglas Briggs, Director of Admissions (612) 638-6242

Bethel College has a structured program, Fresh Start, initiated in 1987 for alternative admissions students. The formal program of studies begins in the fall and lasts for 1 semester. One hundred percent of the students complete the program in that time.

ADMISSION POLICIES:

- New students are eligible for alternative admissions, with a limit of 10 students. There is no wait list

- Requirements for admission as a freshman:
   377 — average verbal SAT
   412 — average math SAT
         or
    15 — average ACT
Other considerations: high school GPA, high school rank, interview with admissions counselor, letters of recommendation

ACADEMIC COURSEWORK AND RELATED FEATURES:

- Support services: freshman orientation, college survival skills, academic advising, drug/alcohol counseling, psychological counseling, academic skills center, study techniques workshops, career advising, peer counseling, health center, aptitude testing, extended time for tests
- Students are not required to work with tutors
- One-on-one tutoring by peer tutors in all academic areas

Stacy Needle

- Counseling is not required
- Students are assigned an academic adviser. All advisers serve alternative admissions students exclusively. Students meet with advisers 3 hours per week
- A total of 102 full-time faculty at the institution
- One faculty member assigned to the program, who is trained to work with alternative admissions students
- Students take an average of 10% of their classes with alternative admissions students only
- Alternative admissions classes average 10 students
- Students are limited to a credit load of 12 credits per semester through fall semester of freshman year

REQUIRED COURSES:

Freshman Seminar (credit-bearing)—alternative admissions students only
Study Skills Seminar (credit-bearing)

- Minimum of 3.0 GPA required to stay in program; if below 3.0 GPA, a student is either placed on academic probation or dismissed

PROFILE OF ALTERNATIVE ADMISSIONS STUDENTS:

- 10 alternative admissions students enrolled
- 100% of accepted students enrolled
- 100% enter as new students
- 10% minority, 30% female
- No international students
- None 25 years or older
- 20% intercollegiate athletes, Division III sports available:
  baseball, basketball, cross-country, football, golf, hockey, soccer, tennis, track and field (men)
  basketball, cross-country, tennis, track and field, volleyball (women)
- No learning disabled
- 10% in top 50% of high school class

OTHER FEATURES/ACCOMMODATIONS:

- On-campus housing is available and is guaranteed for alternative admissions students
- A meal plan is available
- Financial aid is available

DEADLINES:

- Rolling admission
- April 1 for financial aid
- April 25 for reply date

BOSTON UNIVERSITY

>>>>>>>>>>>>>>>>>>>>>>>>>>>

Boston, MA 02215
(617) 353-2300

_____

$11,950 Tuition and Fees
$ 4,900 Average Double Room and Meal Plan

13,626 full-time undergraduates, 823 part-time undergraduates

>>

Founded in 1839, Boston University is a private institution, coed. Located on 86 acres in a large city. Associate's and bachelor's degrees are offered.

ALTERNATIVE ADMISSIONS:

Contact: Brendan Gilbane, Dean of College of Basic Studies (617) 353-2850

Boston University has a structured program, College of Basic Studies, initiated in 1952 for alternative admissions students. The formal program of studies begins in the fall and lasts for 2 years. Forty-five percent of the students complete the program in that time. Students receive an associate's degree upon completion of their studies.

ADMISSION POLICIES:

- New students are eligible for alternative admissions with a limit of 940 students

- Requirements for admission as a freshman:
  1000 — average combined verbal and math SAT
  2.8 — average GPA

ACADEMIC COURSEWORK AND RELATED FEATURES:

- Students are not required to work with tutors
- Placement testing is not required
- Students take all of their classes with alternative admissions students only
- Alternative admissions classes average 30 students

REQUIRED COURSES:

Humanities (credit-bearing)
Social Science (credit-bearing)
Rhetoric (credit-bearing)
Psychology (credit-bearing)
Science (credit-bearing)

PROFILE OF ALTERNATIVE ADMISSIONS STUDENTS:

- 42% graduate within 4 years
- 50% graduate within 5 years

The Other Route into College

OTHER FEATURES/ACCOMMODATIONS:

- On-campus housing is available and is guaranteed for alternative admissions students
- A meal plan is available
- Financial aid is available

DEADLINES:

- January 15 for admission
- May 1 for reply date

The above information was compiled from Boston University's *Undergraduate Programs Bulletin.*

CALIFORNIA STATE UNIVERSITY AT CHICO

>>>>>>>>>>>>>>>>>>>>>>>>>>

Chico, CA 95929
(916) 895-6321

$ 842 In-State Tuition and Fees
$6,512 Out-of-State Tuition and Fees
$3,400 Average Double Room and Meal Plan

12,255 full-time undergraduates, 1,815 part-time undergraduates
15:1 student/faculty ratio
31% of undergraduates study arts/humanities

>>

Founded in 1887, California State University at Chico is a public institution, coed. Located on 130 acres in a rural community, 90 miles from Sacramento. Bachelor's degrees are offered.

ALTERNATIVE ADMISSIONS:

Contact: Dr. Kenneth Edson, Director of Admissions
(916) 895-6321

California State University at Chico has a policy, Alternative Admission in Creative Arts, initiated in 1976 for alternative admissions students.

ADMISSION POLICIES:

- New and transfer students are eligible for alternative admissions

- Requirements for admission as a freshman:
  350 — minimum verbal SAT
  350 — minimum math SAT
     or
   15 — minimum ACT

  2.0 — minimum GPA
  Other considerations: interview with faculty, essay/personal statement, letters of recommendation, audition or portfolio

- Requirements for admission as a transfer student:
  2.0 — minimum GPA
  Other considerations: difficulty of coursework, type of college attended, number of credits completed, extracurricular activities, interview with faculty, essay/personal statement, letters of recommendation, portfolio or audition

ACADEMIC COURSEWORK AND RELATED FEATURES:

- Support services: freshman orientation, college survival skills, academic advising, drug/alcohol counseling, women's center, psychological counseling, academic skills center, study technique workshops, career advising, health center
- Students are not required to work with tutors
- Group and one-on-one tutoring by peer tutors as well as professional tutors in all academic areas
- Counseling is not required
- Students are assigned an academic adviser. None of the advisers serve alternative admissions students exclusively. Students meet with advisers 1–2 times per semester
- Placement testing is not required
- Alternative admissions students do not take separate classes
- Students are not limited to credit load

REQUIRED COURSES:

- Minimum of 2.0 GPA required to stay at college; if below 2.0 GPA, a student is placed on academic probation

PROFILE OF ALTERNATIVE ADMISSIONS STUDENTS:

- 5 alternative admissions students enrolled
- 100% of accepted students enrolled

OTHER FEATURES/ACCOMMODATIONS:

- On-campus housing is available, but is not guaranteed for alternative admissions students
- A meal plan is available
- Financial aid is available

Stacy Needle

DEADLINES:
- Rolling admission
- March 1 for financial aid

CALIFORNIA STATE UNIVERSITY AT HAYWARD

>>>>>>>>>>>>>>>>>>>>>>>>>>>

Hayward, CA 94542
(415) 881-3817

$ 822 In-State Tuition and Fees
$6,534 Out-of-State Tuition and Fees
$2,140 Average Double Room

6,350 full-time undergraduates, 2,902 part-time
    undergraduates
19:1 student/faculty ratio

>>

Founded in 1957, California State University at Hayward is a public institution, coed. Located on 365 acres in a large city 15 miles from Oakland. Bachelor's degrees are offered.

ALTERNATIVE ADMISSIONS:

Contact: Glenn Perry, Director of Administrative and Admissions Services (415) 881-4091

California State University at Hayward has a policy for alternative admissions students.

ADMISSION POLICIES:
- New and transfer students are eligible for alternative admissions
- Admission considerations—new student: SAT or ACT scores, high school GPA
- Admission considerations—transfer student: GPA at previous institution

ACADEMIC COURSEWORK AND RELATED FEATURES:
- Support services: freshman orientation, college survival skills, academic advising, academic skills center, study technique workshops, career advising, peer counseling, health center, aptitude testing

- Students are not required to work with tutors
- One-on-one tutoring by peer tutors as well as professional tutors
- Counseling is not required
- Students are not assigned an academic adviser
- Placement testing is required in English and math
- Alternative admissions students do not take separate classes
- Students are not limited to credit load

OTHER FEATURES/ACCOMMODATIONS:
- On-campus housing is available, but is not guaranteed for alternative admissions students
- A meal plan is available
- Financial aid is available

DEADLINES:
- Rolling admission

CALUMET COLLEGE OF SAINT JOSEPH

>>>>>>>>>>>>>>>>>>>>>>>>>>>

Whiting, IN 46394
(219) 473-4215

$3,285 Tuition and Fees

410 full-time undergraduates, 649 part-time
    undergraduates
15:1 student/faculty ratio
54% of undergraduates study business

>>

Founded in 1951, Calumet College of Saint Joseph is a private institution, coed, affiliated with the Roman Catholic church. Located on 256 acres in a small city 20 miles from Chicago. Associate's and bachelor's degrees are offered.

ALTERNATIVE ADMISSIONS:

Contact: Sharon Sweeney, Director of Admissions (219) 473-4215

Calumet College of Saint Joseph has a policy for alternative admissions students.

ADMISSION POLICIES:

- New and transfer students are eligible for alternative admissions

- Requirements for admission as a freshman:
  280 — minimum verbal SAT
  300 — minimum math SAT
  28 — minimum TSWE
      or

  13 — minimum ACT

  1.7 — minimum GPA
Other considerations: high school rank, essay/personal statement

- Requirements for admission as a transfer student:
  1.5 — minimum GPA
Other considerations: number of credits completed, essay/personal statement

ACADEMIC COURSEWORK AND RELATED FEATURES:

- Support services: freshman orientation, academic advising
- Students are not required to work with tutors
- Academic counseling is required
- Students are not assigned an academic adviser
- Placement testing is not required
- Alternative admissions students do not take separate classes
- Students are limited to a credit load of 9 credits per semester through fall semester of college

REQUIRED COURSES:

- Courses required of students who demonstrate deficiency:
  Developmental English (credit-bearing)

- Remedial courses are calculated in GPA

PROFILE OF ALTERNATIVE ADMISSIONS STUDENTS:

- 27 alternative admissions students enrolled
- 20% of the accepted students enrolled
- 50% enter as new students, 50% as transfer students
- 27% of the students transfer to another college after freshman year, 13% transfer after sophomore year
- 70% minority, 68% female
- 75% state residents, no international students
- 65% 25 years or older
- No intercollegiate athletes
- 5% learning disabled
- None in top 50% of high school class
- 15% graduate within 4 years
- 20% graduate within 5 years

OTHER FEATURES/ACCOMMODATIONS:

- On-campus housing is not available for alternative admissions students
- A meal plan is not available
- Financial aid is available

DEADLINES:

- Rolling admission

CAMERON UNIVERSITY

>>>>>>>>>>>>>>>>>>>>>>>>>>>>

Lawton, OK 73505
(405) 581-2230

$1,209 In-State Tuition and Fees
$2,382 Out-of-State Tuition and Fees
$1,720 Average Double Room and Meal Plan

3,012 full-time undergraduates, 2,430 part-time undergraduates
18:1 student/faculty ratio

>>

Founded in 1908, Cameron University is a public institution, coed. Located on 160 acres in a small city. Associate's and bachelor's degrees are offered.

ALTERNATIVE ADMISSIONS:

Contact: Louise Brown, Director of Admissions (405) 581-2230

Cameron University has a policy for alternative admissions students.

ADMISSION POLICIES:

- New and transfer students are eligible for alternative admissions

- Admission considerations—new student: ACT scores, high school GPA, high school rank

- Admission considerations—transfer student: GPA at previous institution, number of credits completed (less than 24 credits)

Stacy Needle

ACADEMIC COURSEWORK AND RELATED FEATURES:

- Support services: freshman orientation, college survival skills, academic advising, drug/alcohol counseling, study technique workshops, career advising, peer counseling, aptitude testing, extended time for tests
- Students are not required to work with tutors
- Group and one-on-one tutoring by peer tutors as well as professional tutors in accounting, computer science, English, fine arts, reading, and science
- Counseling is not required
- Students are assigned an academic adviser
- Placement testing is required in English and math
- Alternative admissions students do not take separate classes
- Students are not limited to credit load

REQUIRED COURSES:

- Courses required of students who demonstrate deficiency:
  Fundamentals of English (noncredit)
  Developmental Writing (noncredit)
  Fundamentals of Math (noncredit)
  Beginning Algebra (noncredit)
  Intermediate Algebra (noncredit)

PROFILE OF ALTERNATIVE ADMISSIONS STUDENTS:

- 11 alternative admissions students enrolled

OTHER FEATURES/ACCOMMODATIONS:

- On-campus housing is available, but is not guaranteed for alternative admissions students
- A meal plan is available
- Financial aid is available

DEADLINES:

- Rolling admission—1 month after application is sent, notification of admission
- June for financial aid

CASTLETON STATE COLLEGE

>>>>>>>>>>>>>>>>>>>>>>>>>>>>

Castleton, VT 05735
(802) 468-5611, Ext. 213

$2,328 In-State Tuition and Fees
$5,376 Out-of-State Tuition and Fees
$3,990 Average Double Room and Meal Plan

1,450 full-time undergraduates, 500 part-time undergraduates
15:1 student/faculty ratio
27% of undergraduates study business

>>

Founded in 1787, Castleton State College is a public institution, coed. Located on 135 acres in a rural community 9 miles from Rutland. Associate's and bachelor's degrees are offered.

ALTERNATIVE ADMISSIONS:

Contact: Gary Fallis, Director of Admissions (802) 468-5611, Ext. 213

Castleton State College has a policy for alternative admissions students.

ADMISSION POLICIES:

- New students are eligible for alternative admissions

- Requirements for admission as a freshman:
  369 — average verbal SAT
  427 — average math SAT
  2.2 — average GPA
Other considerations: essay/personal statement

ACADEMIC COURSEWORK AND RELATED FEATURES:

- Support services: freshman orientation, college survival skills, academic advising, drug/alcohol counseling, psychological counseling, academic skills center, study technique workshops, career advising, peer counseling, health center, extended time for tests
- Students are not required to work with tutors
- One-on-one tutoring by peer tutors in all academic areas
- Counseling is not required
- Students are assigned an academic adviser. None of the advisers serve alternative admissions students exclusively
- Placement testing is required in writing, reading, and math

The Other Route into College

- Alternative admissions students do not take separate classes
- Students are limited to a credit load of 13 credits per semester until all academic skill deficiencies are successfully met

PROFILE OF ALTERNATIVE ADMISSIONS STUDENTS:
- 6% state residents
- 3% in top 50% of high school class

OTHER FEATURES/ACCOMMODATIONS:
- On-campus housing is available, but is not guaranteed for alternative admissions students
- A meal plan is available
- Financial aid is available

DEADLINES:
- Rolling admission
- March 15 for financial aid
- May 1 for reply date

CEDARVILLE COLLEGE

>>>>>>>>>>>>>>>>>>>>>>>>>>>

Cedarville, OH 45314
(513) 766-2211

$4,912 Tuition and Fees
$1,455 Average Double Room
$1,635 Average Meal Plan

1,814 full-time undergraduates, 65 part-time undergraduates
18:1 student/faculty ratio
24% of undergraduates study business

>>

Founded in 1887, Cedarville College is a private institution, coed, affiliated with the Baptist church. Located on 100 acres in a rural community 8 miles from Xenia. Associate's and bachelor's degrees are offered.

ALTERNATIVE ADMISSIONS:
Contact: Pat Bates, Dean of Women (513) 766-2211

Cedarville College has a structured program, Academic Development Program, initiated in 1984 for alternative admissions students. The formal program of studies begins in the fall and lasts for 1 quarter. Ninety-nine percent of the students complete the program in that time.

ADMISSION POLICIES:
- New students are eligible for alternative admissions with a limit of 50–55 students. There is a wait list
- Requirements for admission as a freshman:
  480 — average verbal SAT
  515 — average math SAT
     or
   12 — minimum ACT

  1.5 — minimum GPA

Other considerations: high school rank, type of high school attended, essay/personal statement, letters of recommendation

ACADEMIC COURSEWORK AND RELATED FEATURES:
- Support services: freshman orientation, college survival skills, academic advising, psychological counseling, career advising, health center
- Students are not required to work with tutors
- Counseling is not required
- Students are assigned an academic adviser. All advisers serve alternative admissions students exclusively. Students meet with advisers 5 times per quarter
- Placement testing is required in English and math
- Alternative admissions students do not take separate classes
- Students are limited to a credit load of 15 credits per semester until a satisfactory GPA is attained

REQUIRED COURSES:
- Courses required of students who demonstrate deficiency:
  Basic English (credit-bearing)
  Basic Math (credit-bearing)
- Remedial courses are not calculated in GPA

OTHER FEATURES/ACCOMMODATIONS:
- On-campus housing is available, but is not guaranteed for alternative admissions students
- A meal plan is available

DEADLINES:
- Rolling admission

Stacy Needle

CENTRAL CONNECTICUT STATE UNIVERSITY

>>>>>>>>>>>>>>>>>>>>>>>>>>>

New Britain, CT 06050
(203) 827-7543

$1,625 In-State Tuition and Fees
$4,034 Out-of-State Tuition and Fees
$1,804 Average Double Room
$1,540 Average Meal Plan

6,763 full-time undergraduates, 4,487 part-time
  undergraduates
17:1 student/faculty ratio
35% of undergraduates study business

>>

Founded in 1849, Central Connecticut State University is a public institution, coed. Located on 140 acres in a small city 10 miles from Hartford. Bachelor's degrees are offered.

ALTERNATIVE ADMISSIONS:

Contact: Charles Jones, Jr., Director of Educational Support Services (203) 827-7119

Central Connecticut State University has a structured summer program, Educational Opportunity Program, initiated in 1969 for alternative admissions students. The program begins in July and lasts for 5 weeks. Ninety-five percent of the students complete the program in that time.

ADMISSION POLICIES:

- New students are eligible for alternative admissions, with a limit of 44 students. There is no wait list

- Requirements for admission as a freshman:
  300 — average verbal SAT
  300 — average math SAT
  2.5 — average GPA
Other considerations: interview with admissions counselor, essay/personal statement, financial need, state residence

ACADEMIC COURSEWORK AND RELATED FEATURES:

- Support services: freshman orientation, college survival skills, academic advising, drug/alcohol counseling, women's center, psychological counseling, academic skills center, study technique workshops, career advising, health center, aptitude testing
- Separate new-student orientation
- Students are required to work with tutors at least 3 hours per week
- Group and one-on-one tutoring by peer tutors in accounting, math, and English
- Counseling is not required
- Students are assigned an academic adviser
- Placement testing is required in English and math
- A total of 384 full-time faculty at the institution
- Six faculty members assigned to the program, who are trained to work with alternative admissions students

REQUIRED COURSES:

Reading Efficiency—alternative admissions students only
Fundamentals of Mathematics—alternative admissions students only
- Courses required of students who demonstrate deficiency:
  Remediation in Mathematics
  Remediation in English

- Required courses are calculated in GPA

PROFILE OF ALTERNATIVE ADMISSIONS STUDENTS:

- 42 alternative admissions students enrolled
- 100% of accepted students enrolled
- 83% minority, 59% female
- 88% state residents, no international students
- None 25 years or older
- 2% intercollegiate athletes
- No learning disabled
- 47% in top 50% of high school class
- 35% graduate within 5 years

OTHER FEATURES/ACCOMMODATIONS:

- On-campus housing is available and is guaranteed for alternative admissions students
- On-campus housing is required of alternative admissions students
- A meal plan is available. It is required of alternative admissions students
- Financial aid is available

DEADLINES:

- March 15 for admission; after March 15, applications are reviewed on a space-available basis
- March 15 for financial aid
- March–June for notification of admission

The Other Route into College

CENTRAL MICHIGAN UNIVERSITY

>>>>>>>>>>>>>>>>>>>>>>>>>>>>

Mount Pleasant, MI 48859
(517) 774-3076

———

$1,945 In-State Tuition and Fees
$4,635 Out-of-State Tuition and Fees
$3,160 Average Double Room and Meal Plan

14,333 full-time undergraduates, 1,020 part-time
   undergraduates
20:1 student/faculty ratio
25% of undergraduates study education

>>

Founded in 1892, Central Michigan University is a public institution, coed. Located on 900 acres in a small city 60 miles from Lansing. Bachelor's degrees are offered.

ALTERNATIVE ADMISSIONS:

Contact: Joyce Carter, Director of Academic Assistance Program (517) 774-3465

Central Michigan University has a structured summer program, Summer Academic Advancement Program, initiated in 1980 for alternative admissions students. The program begins in June and lasts for 6 weeks. One hundred percent of the students complete the program in that time.

ADMISSION POLICIES:

- New students are eligible for alternative admissions, with a limit of 20 students. There is a wait list

- Requirements for admission as a freshman:
   22 — minimum ACT
   2.0 — minimum GPA
Other considerations: high school rank, type of high school attended, difficulty of high school courses taken

ACADEMIC COURSEWORK AND RELATED FEATURES:

- Support services: freshman orientation, college survival skills, academic advising, drug/alcohol counseling, psychological counseling, academic skills center, study technique workshops, career advising, peer counseling, health center, aptitude testing
- Separate new-student orientation
- Students are not required to work with tutors
- Counseling is not required

- Students are assigned an academic adviser. None of the advisers serve alternative admissions students exclusively. Students meet with advisers 2 times per semester
- Placement testing is not required
- A total of 699 full-time faculty at the institution
- Two faculty members assigned to the program, who are trained to work with alternative admissions students
- Students take an average of 50% of their classes with alternative admissions students only
- Alternative admissions classes average 20 students
- Students are not limited to credit load

REQUIRED COURSES:

- Minimum of 2.0 GPA required to stay in program; if below 2.0 GPA, a student may not enroll for the fall semester

PROFILE OF ALTERNATIVE ADMISSIONS STUDENTS:

- 19 alternative admissions students enrolled
- 100% of the accepted students enrolled
- 100% enter as new students
- 5% of the students transfer to another college after sophomore year
- 16% female
- 95% state residents
- 60% in top 50% of high school class
- 80% graduate within 4 years

OTHER FEATURES/ACCOMMODATIONS:

- On-campus housing is available and is guaranteed for alternative admissions students
- A meal plan is available

DEADLINES:

- Rolling admission
- April for reply date

The program is best suited for a bright, energetic individual who needs to learn educational motivation.

Stacy Needle

CENTRAL STATE UNIVERSITY

>>>>>>>>>>>>>>>>>>>>>>>>>

Edmond, OK 73034
(405) 341-2980, Ext. 2338

$1,000 In-State Tuition and Fees
$2,232–$2,790 Out-of-State Tuition and Fees
$1,992 Average Double Room and Meal Plan

6,317 full-time undergraduates, 4,623 part-time
  undergraduates
24:1 student/faculty ratio
25% of undergraduates study education

>>

Founded in 1890, Central State University is a public institution, coed. Located on 200 acres in a town 10 miles from Oklahoma City. Bachelor's degrees are offered.

ALTERNATIVE ADMISSIONS:

Contact: Darrell Gilliland, Director of Admissions (405) 341-2980, Ext. 2338

Central State University has a policy for alternative admissions students.

ADMISSION POLICIES:

- New and transfer students are eligible for alternative admissions

- Admission considerations—new student: SAT or ACT scores, high school GPA, high school rank, type of high school attended

- Requirements for admission as a transfer student: 1.4 — minimum GPA
Other considerations: type of college attended, number of credits completed (less than 24 credits), essay/personal statement

ACADEMIC COURSEWORK AND RELATED FEATURES:

- Support services: freshman orientation, academic advising, drug/alcohol counseling, psychological counseling, career advising, health center, aptitude testing
- Students are not required to work with tutors
- Counseling is not required
- Students are assigned an academic adviser. None of the advisers serve alternative admissions students exclusively. Students meet with advisers at least 1 time per semester

- Placement testing is not required
- Alternative admissions students do not take separate classes

REQUIRED COURSES:

- Courses required of students who demonstrate deficiency:
  Principles of Science (credit-bearing)
  English Fundamentals (credit-bearing)
  Elementary Algebra (credit-bearing)
  Intermediate Algebra (credit-bearing)
  United States History (credit-bearing)
  Developmental Reading (credit-bearing)

- Remedial courses are not calculated in GPA

PROFILE OF ALTERNATIVE ADMISSIONS STUDENTS:

- 99% of the accepted students enrolled
- 23% minority, 51% female
- 100% state residents, no international students
- None 25 years or older
- 1% intercollegiate athletes
- 1% learning disabled

OTHER FEATURES/ACCOMMODATIONS:

- On-campus housing is available, but is not guaranteed for alternative admissions students
- A meal plan is available
- Financial aid is available

DEADLINES:

- August 1 for admission
- July 1 for financial aid

The program is best suited for a student who (1) has a demonstrated talent or ability in an area such as art, drama, or music, or (2) is educationally or economically disadvantaged, yet shows promise of being able to succeed, or (3) has national test scores that indicate a potential not shown on high school transcripts, or (4) shows identification of characteristics that would allude to an individual's potential and belie his/her past academic performance.

CENTRAL WASHINGTON UNIVERSITY

>>>>>>>>>>>>>>>>>>>>>>>>>>>>

Ellensburg, WA 98926
(509) 963-1211

$1,518 In-State Tuition and Fees
$5,325 Out-of-State Tuition and Fees
$2,993 Average Double Room and Meal Plan

5,898 full-time undergraduates, 877 part-time
   undergraduates
23:1 student/faculty ratio

>>

Founded in 1891, Central Washington University is a
public institution, coed. Located on 350 acres in a small
city 100 miles from Seattle. Bachelor's degrees are
offered.

ALTERNATIVE ADMISSIONS:

Contact: E. Rose Clayton, Director of Special Services/
Access Program (509) 963-2131

Central Washington University has a structured program, Access Program, initiated in 1979 for alternative
admissions students. The formal program of studies
begins in the fall and lasts approximately 1 year; however, students can also enter the program in the winter
and continue for approximately 1 year.

ADMISSION POLICIES:

- New and transfer students are eligible for alternative
  admissions, with a limit of 60 students. There is no
  wait list

- Requirements for admission as a freshman:
  2.15 — average GPA
Other considerations: SAT or ACT scores, interview
with admissions counselor, essay/personal statement

- Admission considerations—transfer student: GPA
  at previous institution, difficulty of coursework,
  number of credits completed (less than 40 credits),
  interview with director of Access Program, essay/
  personal statement
- Admission into the Access Program is limited to individuals who are members of groups traditionally
  underrepresented in the college population (e.g., disabled persons or minorities), or who are beyond the
  usual college age at the time of application (e.g.,

veterans, displaced homemakers, and reentry students). Individuals who have experienced an inter-
ruption in the educational process (i.e., have not been
enrolled in a formal educational program for 1 or
more years) will be given preference.

ACADEMIC COURSEWORK AND RELATED FEATURES:

- Support services: freshman orientation, college survival skills, academic advising, drug/alcohol counseling, women's center, psychological counseling,
  academic skills center, study technique workshops,
  career advising, peer counseling, health center, aptitude testing, extended time for tests (if learning disabled)
- Separate new-student orientation
- Group and one-on-one tutoring by peer tutors
- Counseling is not required
- Students are assigned an academic adviser. None of
  the advisers serve alternative admissions students
  exclusively. Students meet with advisers 10–13
  times per quarter
- Alternative admissions students do not take separate
  classes
- Students are not limited to credit load

REQUIRED COURSES:

Exploratory Studies (credit-bearing)
- Courses required of students who demonstrate defi-
  ciency:
  Improvement of Basic Reading Skills (credit-bearing)
  Basic English (credit-bearing)
  Basic English and Spelling (credit-bearing)
  Basic Mathematics (credit-bearing)

- Remedial courses are not calculated in GPA
- Required courses are calculated in GPA

PROFILE OF ALTERNATIVE ADMISSIONS STUDENTS:

- 49 alternative admissions students enrolled
- 95% enter as new students, 5% as transfer students
- 25% minority, 25% female
- 100% state residents, no international students
- 10% 25 years or older
- No intercollegiate athletes
- 10% learning disabled
- 25% graduate within 5 years

OTHER FEATURES/ACCOMMODATIONS:

- On-campus housing is available, but is not guaranteed
  for alternative admissions students
- A meal plan is available
- Financial aid is available

Stacy Needle

CLEMSON UNIVERSITY

>>>>>>>>>>>>>>>>>>>>>>>>>

Clemson, SC 29634-4024
(803) 656-2287

$2,374 In-State Tuition and Fees
$6,116 Out-of-State Tuition and Fees
$1,400 Average Double Room
$1,404 Average Meal Plan

11,147 full-time undergraduates, 627 part-time
  undergraduates
19:1 student/faculty ratio
28% of undergraduates study business

>>

Founded in 1889, Clemson University is a public institution, coed. Located on 600 acres in a town 17 miles from Anderson. Bachelor's degrees are offered.

ALTERNATIVE ADMISSIONS:

Additional cost: $1,005 basic program fee
Contact: Dr. George Carter, Jr., Director of Undergraduate Academic Services (803) 656-0199

Clemson University has a structured summer program, Science and Technology Entrance Program (STEP), initiated in 1988 for alternative admissions students. The program begins in June and lasts for 7 weeks. Ninety percent of the students complete the program in that time.

ADMISSION POLICIES:

• New students are eligible for alternative admissions

• Requirements for admission as a freshman:
  831 — average combined verbal and math SAT
  2.5 — average GPA
Other considerations: high school rank, type of high school attended, interview with admissions counselor, state residence

ACADEMIC COURSEWORK AND RELATED FEATURES:

• Support services: freshman orientation, college survival skills, academic advising, drug/alcohol counseling, women's center, psychological counseling, study technique workshops, career advising, peer counseling, health center, aptitude testing
• Separate new-student orientation
• Students are not required to work with tutors
• One-on-one tutoring by peer tutors
• Counseling is not required

• Students are assigned an academic adviser. Twenty-five percent of the advisers serve alternative admissions students exclusively. Students meet with advisers 8 times per semester
• Placement testing is not required
• A total of 1,114 full-time faculty at the institution
• Eight faculty members assigned to the program, who are trained to work with alternative admissions students
• Students take all of their classes with alternative admissions students
• Alternative admissions classes average 15 students
• Students are limited to a credit load of 13 credits per semester through spring semester of freshman year

REQUIRED COURSES:

Reading Improvement (credit-bearing)—alternative admissions students only
Efficient Reading (credit-bearing)—alternative admissions students only
Study Techniques (credit-bearing)—alternative admissions students only

• Required courses are calculated in GPA

PROFILE OF ALTERNATIVE ADMISSIONS STUDENTS:

• 36 alternative admissions students enrolled
• 80% of accepted students enrolled
• 100% enter as new students
• 10% minority, 14% female
• 86% state residents, no international students
• None 25 years or older
• No intercollegiate athletes
• No learning disabled
• 30% in top 50% of high school class

OTHER FEATURES/ACCOMMODATIONS:

• On-campus housing is available, but is not guaranteed for alternative admissions students
• A meal plan is available
• Financial aid is available

DEADLINES:

• Rolling admission
• February for financial aid
• April for reply date

The program is best suited for a person interested in the academic fields of agriculture, textile management, forestry, or industrial technology education.

COKER COLLEGE

>>>>>>>>>>>>>>>>>>>>>>>>>>

Hartsville, SC 29550
(803) 332-1381

$6,964 Tuition and Fees
$1,260 Average Double Room
$1,968 Average Meal Plan

540 full-time undergraduates, 119 part-time
  undergraduates
10:1 student/faculty ratio

>>

Founded in 1908, Coker College is a private institution,
coed. Located on 15 acres in a town 30 miles from
Florence. Bachelor's degrees are offered.

ALTERNATIVE ADMISSIONS:

Contact: Mary Catherine Stuckey, Director of Admissions (803) 332-1381

Coker College has a structured program, Provisional
Acceptance, initiated in 1987 for alternative admissions
students. The formal program of studies begins in the
fall and lasts for 1 semester. One hundred percent of
the students complete the program in that time.

ADMISSION POLICIES:

• New and transfer students are eligible for alternative
  admissions

• Requirements for admission as a freshman:
  648 — average combined verbal and math SAT
  2.5 — average GPA
Other considerations: high school rank, type of high
school attended, difficulty of high school courses taken,
extracurricular activities, community service/volunteer
work, essay/personal statement, letters of recommendation

• Requirements for admission as a transfer student:
  2.5 — average GPA
Other considerations: difficulty of coursework, type of
college attended, number of credits completed, extracurricular activities, community service/volunteer
work, essay/personal statement, letters of recommendation

ACADEMIC COURSEWORK AND RELATED FEATURES:

• Students are not required to work with tutors
• Counseling is required

• Students are assigned an academic adviser. All advisers serve alternative admissions students exclusively
• Placement testing is required in English and math
• Alternative admissions students do not take separate
  classes
• Students are limited to a credit load of 13 credits per
  semester through fall semester of program

REQUIRED COURSES:
Freshman Course (credit-bearing)

• Required courses are calculated in GPA
• Minimum of 1.5 GPA required to stay in program; if
  below 1.5 GPA, a student may not return to the
  college

PROFILE OF ALTERNATIVE ADMISSIONS STUDENTS:

• 20% minority, 60% female
• 30% intercollegiate athletes, Division NAIA sports
  available:
  soccer, basketball, tennis, golf (men)
  soccer, basketball, tennis, softball, volleyball
  (women)

OTHER FEATURES/ACCOMMODATIONS:

• On-campus housing is available, but is not guaranteed
  for alternative admissions students
• A meal plan is available
• Financial aid is available

DEADLINES:

• Rolling admission

COLGATE UNIVERSITY

>>>>>>>>>>>>>>>>>>>>>>>>>>

Hamilton, NY 13346
(315) 824-1000, Ext. 401

$13,710 Tuition and Fees
$ 2,230 Average Double Room
$ 2,310 Average Meal Plan

2,709 full-time undergraduates, 8 part-time
  undergraduates
12:1 student/faculty ratio

Stacy Needle

Founded in 1819, Colgate University is a private institution, coed. Located on 1,100 acres in a rural community 45 miles from Syracuse. Bachelor's degrees are offered.

ALTERNATIVE ADMISSIONS:

Contact: Charles Rice, Assistant Dean of Undergraduate Studies (315) 824-1000, Ext. 375

Colgate University has a structured summer program, Office of Undergraduate Studies Program, initiated in 1968 for alternative admissions students. The program begins in late June and lasts for 6 weeks. Ninety-nine percent of the students complete the program in that time.

ADMISSION POLICIES:

- New students are eligible for alternative admissions

- Admission considerations: SAT or ACT scores, essay/personal statement, letters of recommendation

- Program is specifically for economically and educationally disadvantaged students

ACADEMIC COURSEWORK AND RELATED FEATURES:

- Support services: freshman orientation, college survival skills, academic advising, drug/alcohol counseling, women's center, psychological counseling, academic skills center, career advising, peer counseling, health center
- Separate new-student orientation
- Students are not required to work with tutors
- One-on-one tutoring by peer tutors as well as professional tutors in all academic areas
- Counseling is available
- Students are assigned an academic adviser
- Placement testing is required
- Alternative admissions students do not take separate classes

REQUIRED COURSES:

Writing Segment
Humanities or Social Science course
Science/Math elective
Physical Science class

- Minimum of 1.35 GPA required to stay in program; if below 1.35 GPA, students cannot remain at the college

PROFILE OF ALTERNATIVE ADMISSIONS STUDENTS:

- 42 alternative admissions students enrolled
- 100% enter as new students

- 2% of the students transfer to another college after freshman year, 3% transfer after sophomore year
- 98% minority, 48% female
- 50% state residents, no international students
- None 25 years or older
- 10% intercollegiate athletes
- No learning disabled
- 100% in top 50% of high school class
- 86% graduate within 4 years

OTHER FEATURES/ACCOMMODATIONS:

- On-campus housing is available for alternative admissions students
- A meal plan is available
- Financial aid is available

DEADLINES:

- January 15 for admission
- February 1 for financial aid
- March 26 for notification of admission
- May 1 for reply date

COLLEGE OF NEW ROCHELLE
>>>>>>>>>>>>>>>>>>>>>>>>>>>>

New Rochelle, NY 10805
(914) 654-5452

$8,500 Tuition and Fees
$2,120 Average Double Room
$1,800 Average Meal Plan

561 full-time undergraduates, 176 part-time undergraduates
11:1 student/faculty ratio
55% of undergraduates study arts/humanities

>>

Founded in 1904, the College of New Rochelle is a private institution, women only. Located on 16 acres in a small city 15 miles from New York City. Bachelor's degrees are offered.

ALTERNATIVE ADMISSIONS:

Contact: Dr. Ann Raia, Associate Dean of the School of Arts and Sciences (914) 654-5398

The College of New Rochelle has a structured program, Special Advisement Program, initiated in 1985 for alternative admissions students. The formal program of studies begins in the fall and lasts for 1 year. Ninety-nine percent of the students complete the program in that time.

ADMISSION POLICIES:
- New students are eligible for alternative admissions

- Requirements for admission as a freshman:
  - 300 — minimum verbal SAT
  - 300 — minimum math SAT

Other considerations: high school GPA, high school rank, type of high school attended

ACADEMIC COURSEWORK AND RELATED FEATURES:
- Support services: freshman orientation, college survival skills, academic advising, women's center, academic skills center, study technique workshops, career advising, peer counseling, health center
- Counseling is required
- Students are assigned an academic adviser. None of the advisers serve alternative admissions students exclusively. Students meet with advisers 2 times per semester
- Placement testing is required in math and writing
- A total of 54 full-time faculty at the institution
- Five faculty members assigned to the program, who are trained to work with alternative admissions students
- Alternative admissions students do not take separate classes
- Students are limited to a credit load of 12 credits per semester through spring semester of freshman year

REQUIRED COURSES:
Techniques of Inquiry (credit-bearing)
- Courses required of students who demonstrate deficiency:
  - Writers Workshop
  - Seminar on Research Essay
  - Developmental Mathematics
  - Applied Mathematics

- Remedial courses are calculated in GPA
- Required courses are calculated in GPA

PROFILE OF ALTERNATIVE ADMISSIONS STUDENTS:
- 28 alternative admissions students enrolled
- 35% of the accepted students enrolled
- 100% enter as new students
- 15% minority, 100% female
- 75% state residents, no international students
- None 25 years or older
- 15% intercollegiate athletes, Division III sports available:

basketball, volleyball, swimming, softball, tennis (women)
- No learning disabled
- 60% in top 50% of high school class

OTHER FEATURES/ACCOMMODATIONS:
- On-campus housing is available, but is not guaranteed for alternative admissions students
- A meal plan is available
- Financial aid is available

DEADLINES:
- Rolling admission
- June 15 for financial aid

COLLEGE OF SAINT ELIZABETH

>>>>>>>>>>>>>>>>>>>>>>>>>>>>>

Convent Station, NJ 07961
(201) 292-6351

$7,500 Tuition and Fees
$3,700 Average Double Room and Meal Plan

446 full-time undergraduates, 594 part-time undergraduates
10:1 student/faculty ratio
44% of undergraduates study business

>>

Founded in 1899, the College of Saint Elizabeth is a private institution, women only, affiliated with the Roman Catholic church. Located on 200 acres in a town 40 miles from New York City. Bachelor's degrees are offered.

ALTERNATIVE ADMISSIONS:

Contact: Mary Beth Carey, Director of Admissions
(201) 292-6351

The College of Saint Elizabeth has a structured program, Special Admittance Program, for alternative admissions students. The formal program of studies begins in the fall and lasts for 1 semester; however, students can also enter program in the spring and continue for 1 semester.

Stacy Needle

ADMISSION POLICIES:

- New students are eligible for alternative admissions

- Requirements for admission as a freshman:
  300 — minimum verbal SAT
  300 — minimum math SAT
  2.0 — minimum GPA
  Other considerations: TSWE scores, essay/personal statement, letters of recommendation

ACADEMIC COURSEWORK AND RELATED FEATURES:

- Support services: freshman orientation, college survival skills, academic advising, drug/alcohol counseling, women's center, psychological counseling, academic skills center, study technique workshops, career advising, peer counseling, health center, aptitude testing
- Students are not required to work with tutors
- One-on-one tutoring by peer turors
- Counseling is not required
- Students are assigned an academic adviser. None of the advisers serve alternative admissions students exclusively
- Placement testing is required in English, math, and reading
- Alternative admissions students do not take separate classes
- Students are limited to a credit load of 12 credits per semester through first semester of program

REQUIRED COURSES:

- Courses required of students who demonstrate deficiency:
  Basic Skills Math (noncredit)
  Basic Skills English (noncredit)
  Basic Skills Reading (noncredit)

- Minimum of 2.0 GPA required to stay in program; if below 2.0 GPA, a student is academically dismissed.

PROFILE OF ALTERNATIVE ADMISSIONS STUDENTS:

- 19 alternative admissions students enrolled
- 19% of the accepted students enrolled

OTHER FEATURES/ACCOMMODATIONS:

- On-campus housing is available and is guaranteed for alternative admissions students
- A meal plan is available
- Financial aid is available

DEADLINES:

- Rolling admission
- March 15 for financial aid
- May 1 for reply date

COLLEGE OF ST. JOSEPH

>>>>>>>>>>>>>>>>>>>>>>>>>>

Rutland, VT 05701
(802) 773-5900, Ext. 205

$5,900 Tuition and Fees
$3,550 Average Double Room and Meal Plan

200 full-time undergraduates, 260 part-time undergraduates

>>

Founded in 1954, the College of St. Joseph is a private institution, coed. Located on 100 acres in a town 160 miles from Boston, Massachusetts. Associate's and bachelor's degrees are offered.

ALTERNATIVE ADMISSIONS:

Contact: Robert A. McDermott, Dean of Admissions
(802) 773-5900, Ext. 205

The College of St. Joseph has a structured program for alternative admissions students. The formal program of studies begins in the fall and lasts for 1 year. Seventy-five percent of the students complete the program in that time.

ADMISSION POLICIES:

- New students are eligible for alternative admissions, with a limit of 15 students

- Admission considerations: interview with admissions counselor, letters of recommendation

ACADEMIC COURSEWORK AND RELATED FEATURES:

- Students are required to work with tutors
- Counseling is available
- Students take classes with alternative admissions students only
- Alternative admissions classes average 15 students

REQUIRED COURSES:

- Remedial courses required:
  Developmental Math
  Developmental English
  Developmental Reading
  Study Skills

- Minimum of 1.5 GPA required to stay in program; if below 1.5 GPA, a student is placed on academic probation

The Other Route into College

PROFILE OF ALTERNATIVE ADMISSIONS STUDENTS:
- 50% of the accepted students enrolled
- 75% graduate within 4 years

PROFILE OF ALTERNATIVE ADMISSIONS STUDENTS:
- 100% of the accepted students enrolled
- 80% graduate within 4 years

OTHER FEATURES/ACCOMMODATIONS:
- On-campus housing is available
- A meal plan is available

DEADLINES:
- Rolling admission

COLLEGE OF SAINT ROSE

>>>>>>>>>>>>>>>>>>>>>>>>

Albany, NY 12203
(518) 454-5150

$7,184 Tuition and Fees
$3,542–$4,850 Average Double Room and Meal Plan

1,350 full-time undergraduates, 921 part-time
undergraduates

>>

Founded in 1920, the College of Saint Rose is a private institution, coed. Located on 22 acres in a city. Bachelor's degrees are offered.

ALTERNATIVE ADMISSIONS:

Contact: Mary O'Donnell, Director of Admissions (518) 454-5150

The College of Saint Rose has a structured summer program, Access, for alternative admissions students. The program lasts for 6 weeks. One hundred percent of the students complete the program in that time.

ADMISSION POLICIES:

- New students are eligible for alternative admissions, with a limit of 20 students
- Admission considerations: interview with admissions counselor, letters of recommendation

ACADEMIC COURSEWORK AND RELATED FEATURES:

- Students are required to work with tutors
- Counseling is available
- Alternative admissions students do not take separate classes

REQUIRED COURSES:

- Minimum of 2.0 GPA required to stay in program; if below 2.0 GPA, a student may not enroll for the fall semester

COLLEGE OF ST. SCHOLASTICA

>>>>>>>>>>>>>>>>>>>>>>>>>

Duluth, MN 55811
(218) 723-6046

$7,932 Tuition and Fees
$2,796 Average Double Room and Meal Plan

1,600 full-time undergraduates, 148 part-time
undergraduates
13:1 student/faculty ratio
60% of undergraduates study math/sciences

>>

Founded in 1912, the College of St. Scholastica is a private institution, coed, affiliated with the Benedictine Catholic church. Located on 160 acres in a small city 150 miles from Minneapolis. Bachelor's degrees are offered.

ALTERNATIVE ADMISSIONS:

Contact: Jay Newcomb, Director of Academic Support Services (218) 723-6552

The College of St. Scholastica has a structured program, Special Status Admission, initiated in 1969 for alternative admissions students. The formal program of studies begins in the fall and lasts for 3 quarters; however, students can also enter the program in the winter or spring and continue for 3 quarters. Eighty-five percent of the students complete the program in that time.

ADMISSION POLICIES:

- New and transfer students are eligible for alternative admissions, with a limit of 30 students. There is a wait list

Stacy Needle

- Requirements for admission as a freshman:
  500 — average verbal SAT
  550 — average math SAT
  or
  22 — average ACT

  3.0 — average GPA
  Other considerations: high school rank

- Requirements for admission as a transfer student:
  2.0 — minimum GPA

ACADEMIC COURSEWORK AND RELATED FEATURES:

- Support services: freshman orientation, college survival skills, academic advising, drug/alcohol counseling, women's center, psychological counseling, academic skills center, study technique workshops, career advising, peer counseling, health center, aptitude testing, extended time for tests
- Separate new-student orientation
- Students are not required to work with tutors
- Group and one-on-one tutoring by peer tutors as well as professional tutors in all academic areas
- Peer and academic counseling is required
- Students are assigned an academic adviser. None of the advisers serve alternative admissions students exclusively. Students meet with advisers 10 times per quarter
- Placement testing is required in English, math, and sciences
- A total of 90 full-time faculty at the institution
- Special faculty assigned to the program, who are trained to work with alternative admissions students
- Students take an average of 15% of their classes with alternative admissions students only
- Alternative admissions classes average 15 students
- Courses are also offered in the evening
- Students are limited to a credit load of 12 credits per semester until they attain a 2.0 GPA

REQUIRED COURSES:

Introduction to College Study (credit-bearing)—alternative admissions students only

- Required courses are calculated in GPA

PROFILE OF ALTERNATIVE ADMISSIONS STUDENTS:

- 30 alternative admissions students enrolled
- 100% of the accepted students enrolled
- 85% enter as new students, 15% as transfer students
- 15% of the students transfer to another college after freshman year, 5% transfer after sophomore year
- 2% minority, 60% female
- 90% state residents, 1% international students
- 30% 25 years or older

- 25% intercollegiate athletes, Division III sports available:
  soccer, cross-country, hockey, basketball, baseball (men)
  volleyball, cross-country, basketball, softball (women)
- 3% learning disabled
- 85% in top 50% of high school class
- 85% graduate within 5 years

OTHER FEATURES/ACCOMMODATIONS:

- On-campus housing is available, but is not guaranteed for alternative admissions students
- A meal plan is available
- Financial aid is available

DEADLINES:

- Rolling admission—2 weeks after application is sent, notification of admission
- May 1 for financial aid

The program is best suited for a person interested in a challenging curriculum in a small atmosphere.

COLUMBIA UNION COLLEGE

>>>>>>>>>>>>>>>>>>>>>>>>>>

Takoma Park, MD 20912
(800) 492-1715 (in Maryland)
(800) 835-4212 (outside Maryland)

$12,000 Tuition and Fees, Average Double Room, and Meal Plan

551 full-time undergraduates, 685 part-time undergraduates

>>

Founded in 1904, Columbia Union College is a private institution, coed, affiliated with the Seventh-day Adventist church. Located on 19 acres in a town 10 miles from Washington, D.C. Associate's and bachelor's degrees are offered.

ALTERNATIVE ADMISSIONS:

Contact: Sheila Burnette, Assistant Director of Admissions (800) 492-1715 or (800) 835-4212

Columbia Union College has a structured summer program, Summer Start, for alternative admissions students. The program lasts for 6 weeks. Ninety percent of the students complete the program in that time.

ADMISSION POLICIES:

- New students are eligible for alternative admissions, with a limit of 50 students

- Requirements for admission as a freshman:
  210 — minimum verbal SAT
  240 — minimum math SAT
  1.75 — minimum GPA

ACADEMIC COURSEWORK AND RELATED FEATURES:

- Students are not required to work with tutors
- Counseling is available
- Alternative admissions students do not take separate classes

REQUIRED COURSES:

- Remedial courses required:
  Study Skills
  Learning Assistance Lab
  Remedial Math
  Remedial English

PROFILE OF ALTERNATIVE ADMISSIONS STUDENTS:

- 90% of the accepted students enrolled

OTHER FEATURES/ACCOMMODATIONS:

- On-campus housing is available for alternative admissions students
- A meal plan is available

CONCORDIA COLLEGE

>>>>>>>>>>>>>>>>>>>>>>>>>

St. Paul, MN 55104
(612) 647-8231

$6,690 Tuition and Fees
$2,550 Average Double Room and Meal Plan

1,039 full-time undergraduates, 94 part-time
  undergraduates
13:1 student/faculty ratio
41% of undergraduates study business

Stacy Needle

>>

Founded in 1893, Concordia College is a private institution, coed, affiliated with the Missouri Synod of the Lutheran Church. Located on 26 acres in a large city. Associate's and bachelor's degrees are offered.

ALTERNATIVE ADMISSIONS:

Contact: Joan Hagman, Director of Study Skills (612) 647-8272

Concordia College has a structured program, Academic Development Program, initiated in 1979 for alternative admissions students. The formal program of studies begins in the fall and lasts for approximately 1 year.

ADMISSION POLICIES:

- New and transfer students are eligible for alternative admissions, with a limit of 30 students. There is a wait list

- Requirements for admission as a freshman:
  13 — average ACT
Other considerations: high school GPA, high school rank, letters of recommendation

- Requirements for admission as a transfer student:
  1.75 — minimum GPA
Other considerations: number of credits completed (less than 15 credits)

ACADEMIC COURSEWORK AND RELATED FEATURES:

- Support services: freshman orientation, college survival skills, academic advising, psychological counseling, academic skills center, career advising, peer counseling, health center, aptitude testing, extended time for tests
- Students are required to work with tutors 3 hours per week
- Group and one-on-one tutoring by peer tutors in all academic areas
- Counseling is not required
- Students are assigned an academic adviser. None of the advisers serve alternative admissions students exclusively. Students meet with advisers two times per semester
- Placement testing is required in reading
- A total of 61 full-time faculty at the institution
- One faculty member assigned to the program, who is trained to work with alternative admissions students
- Students take an average of 25% of their classes with alternative admissions students only
- Alternative admissions classes average 15 students
- Students are limited to a credit load of 14 credits per semester through fall semester of program

REQUIRED COURSES:

- Remedial courses required:
  Fundamentals of Writing (credit-bearing)
  Principles of Algebra (credit-bearing)
- Courses required of students who demonstrate deficiency:
  Efficient Reading (credit-bearing)—alternative admissions students only
- Remedial courses are calculated in GPA

PROFILE OF ALTERNATIVE ADMISSIONS STUDENTS:

- 34 alternative admissions students enrolled
- 75% of accepted students enrolled
- 15% of the students transfer to another college after freshman year, 15% transfer after sophomore year
- 18% minority, 55% female
- 91% state residents, no international students
- None 25 years or older
- 40% intercollegiate athletes, Division NAA sports available:
  football, basketball, soccer, golf, baseball, tennis (men)
  volleyball, basketball, softball, tennis, golf (women)
- 6% learning disabled
- None in top 50% of high school class

OTHER FEATURES/ACCOMMODATIONS:

- On-campus housing is available, but is not guaranteed for alternative admissions students
- A meal plan is available
- Financial aid is available

DEADLINES:

- Rolling admission
- June 1 for financial aid

CONVERSE COLLEGE

>>>>>>>>>>>>>>>>>>>>>>>>>>>

Spartanburg, SC 29301
(803) 596-9040

$8,350 Tuition and Fees
$3,000 Average Double Room and Meal Plan

846 full-time undergraduates, 73 part-time undergraduates
11:1 student/faculty ratio

>>
Founded in 1889, Converse College is a private institution, women only. Located on 71 acres in a small city. Bachelor's degrees are offered.

ALTERNATIVE ADMISSIONS:

Additional cost: $125 basic program fee
Contact: Dr. Thomas McDaniels, Dean of College of Arts and Sciences (803) 596-9015

Converse College has a structured program, Special III, for alternative admissions students. The formal program of studies begins in the fall and lasts for 1 semester. Ninety-eight percent of the students complete the program in that time.

ADMISSION POLICIES:

- New students are eligible for alternative admissions, with a limit of 20 students. There is a wait list

- Requirements for admission as a freshman:
  410 — average verbal SAT
  370 — average math SAT
  2.6 — average GPA
  Other considerations: high school rank, type of high school attended, difficulty of high school courses taken

ACADEMIC COURSEWORK AND RELATED FEATURES:

- Support services: freshman orientation, academic advising, drug/alcohol counseling, psychological counseling, academic skills center, study technique workshops, career advising, health center, aptitude testing
- Students are not required to work with tutors
- One-on-one tutoring by peer tutors
- Counseling is not required
- Students are assigned an academic adviser. Two percent of the advisers serve alternative admissions students exclusively. Students meet with advisers 6–10 times per semester
- Placement testing is not required
- Alternative admissions students do not take separate classes
- Students are limited to a credit load of 9 credits per semester through winter semester of freshman year

REQUIRED COURSES:

Reading and Study Skills (noncredit)

PROFILE OF ALTERNATIVE ADMISSIONS STUDENTS:

- 20 alternative admissions students enrolled
- 60% of accepted students enrolled
- 100% enter as new students

The Other Route into College

- 2% of the students transfer to another college after freshman year, 5% transfer after sophomore year
- 2% minority, 100% female
- No international students
- None 25 years or older
- 3% intercollegiate athletes
- 90% in top 50% of high school class
- 50% graduate within 4 years

OTHER FEATURES/ACCOMMODATIONS:
- On-campus housing is available and is guaranteed for alternative admissions students
- On-campus housing is required of alternative admissions students
- A meal plan is available. It is required of alternative admissions students
- Financial aid is available

DEADLINES:
- Rolling admission
- February 15 for financial aid
- March 30 for reply date

The program is best suited for a student with a good academic record but slightly lower standardized test scores.

COVENANT COLLEGE

>>>>>>>>>>>>>>>>>>>>>>>>>

Lookout Mountain, GA 30750
(404) 820-1560

$6,600 Tuition and Fees
$1,450 Average Double Room
$ 800 Average Meal Plan

547 full-time undergraduates, 32 part-time undergraduates
12:1 student/faculty ratio
24% of undergraduates study arts/humanities

>>

Founded in 1955, Covenant College is a private institution, coed, affiliated with the Presbyterian Church in America. Located on 300 acres in a rural community 5 miles from Chattanooga, Tennessee. Associate's and bachelor's degrees are offered.

ALTERNATIVE ADMISSIONS:

Contact: Nick Arnett, Director of Admissions (404) 820-1560

Covenant College has a policy for alternative admissions students.

ADMISSION POLICIES:
- New and transfer students are eligible for alternative admissions, with a limit of 15 students. There is a wait list

- Requirements for admission as a freshman:
  365 — average verbal SAT
  410 — average math SAT
  or
  15 — average ACT

  2.3 — average GPA
Other considerations: interview with admissions counselor, essay/personal statement, letters of recommendation

- Requirements for admission as a transfer student:
  2.0 — minimum GPA
Other considerations: difficulty of coursework, type of college attended, number of credits completed (less than 30 credits), interview with admissions counselor, essay/personal statement, letters of recommendation

ACADEMIC COURSEWORK AND RELATED FEATURES:
- Support services: freshman orientation, college survival skills, academic advising, drug/alcohol counseling, psychological counseling, academic skills center, study technique workshops, career advising, peer counseling, health center, aptitude testing, extended time for tests
- Separate new-student orientation
- Students are required to work with tutors 5 hours per week
- Group and one-on-one tutoring by peer as well as professional tutors in English and math
- Academic and personal counseling is required
- Students are assigned an academic adviser. None of the advisers serve alternative admissions students exclusively. Students meet with advisers 3 times per semester
- Placement testing is required in English
- Students take classes with alternative admissions students
- Alternative admissions classes average 10 students
- Students are limited to a credit load of 14 credits per semester

Stacy Needle

REQUIRED COURSES:
- Courses required of students who demonstrate deficiency:
  Remedial English (noncredit)—alternative admissions students only

PROFILE OF ALTERNATIVE ADMISSIONS STUDENTS:
- 15 alternative admissions students enrolled
- 5% of accepted students enrolled
- 10% transfer to another college after freshman year, 10% transfer after sophomore year
- 20% minority, 50% female
- 10% state residents, no international students
- None 25 years or older
- 8% intercollegiate athletes
- 10% learning disabled
- 50% in top 50% of high school class
- 35% graduate within 4 years
- 50% graduate within 5 years

OTHER FEATURES/ACCOMMODATIONS:
- On-campus housing is available and is guaranteed for alternative admissions students
- A meal plan is available. It is required of alternative admissions students
- Financial aid is available

DEADLINES:
- Rolling admission
- February for financial aid
- May 1 for reply date

The program is best suited for a hardworking student from a strong Christian background.

DAKOTA STATE UNIVERSITY
>>>>>>>>>>>>>>>>>>>>>>>>>

Madison, SD 57042
(605) 256-5139

$1,690 In-State Tuition and Fees
$1,690 Out-of-State Tuition and Fees
$ 950 Average Double Room
$ 950 Average Meal Plan

829 full-time undergraduates, 282 part-time undergraduates
15:1 student/faculty ratio
41% of undergraduates study business

>>

Founded in 1881, Dakota State University is a public institution, coed. Located on 10 acres in a rural community, 45 miles from Sioux Falls. Associate's and bachelor's degrees are offered.

ALTERNATIVE ADMISSIONS:
Contact: Mark Weiss, Director of Admissions (605) 256-5139

Dakota State University has a structured program, Conditional/At Risk, initiated in 1989 for alternative admissions students. The formal program of studies begins in the fall; however, students can also enter the program in the spring.

ADMISSION POLICIES:
- New and transfer students are eligible for alternative admissions

- Requirements for admission as a freshman:
    14 — average ACT
    1.9 — average GPA
  Other considerations: high school rank

- Requirements for admission as a transfer student:
    2.0 — minimum GPA
  Other considerations: type of college attended, number of credits completed (less than 32 credits)

ACADEMIC COURSEWORK AND RELATED FEATURES:
- Support services: freshman orientation, academic advising, drug/alcohol counseling, psychological counseling, academic skills center, career advising, peer counseling
- Separate new-student orientation
- Students are not required to work with tutors
- One-on-one tutoring by peer tutors as well as professional tutors in math, science, and computers
- Counseling is not required
- Students are assigned an academic adviser
- Placement testing is required in reading, writing, and math
- A total of 60 full-time faculty at the institution
- Eight faculty members assigned to the program
- Alternative admissions students do not take separate classes
- Students are limited to a credit load of 14 credits per semester through second semester of program

The Other Route into College

REQUIRED COURSES:

- Remedial courses required:
  Reading Development (credit-bearing)
  Writing Development (credit-bearing)
  Math (credit-bearing)
- Remedial courses are not calculated in GPA
- Minimum of 2.0 GPA required to stay in program; if below 2.0 GPA, a student is academically suspended

PROFILE OF ALTERNATIVE ADMISSIONS STUDENTS:

- 26 alternative admissions students enrolled
- 61% of accepted students enrolled
- 60% female
- 100% state residents

OTHER FEATURES/ACCOMMODATIONS:

- On-campus housing is available, but is not guaranteed for alternative admissions students
- A meal plan is available
- Financial aid is available

DEADLINES:

- Rolling admission
- January 1 for financial aid

DAVIS & ELKINS COLLEGE

>>>>>>>>>>>>>>>>>>>>>>>>>>

Elkins, WV 26241
(304) 636-1900

$10,350 Tuition and Fees, Average Double Room, and Meal Plan

617 full-time undergraduates, 201 part-time undergraduates
15:1 student/faculty ratio
30% of undergraduates study business

>>

Founded in 1904, Davis & Elkins College is a private institution, coed, affiliated with the Presbyterian church. Located on 170 acres in a small city 150 miles from Charleston, South Carolina. Associate's and bachelor's degrees are offered.

Stacy Needle

ALTERNATIVE ADMISSIONS:

Contact: Dr. M. Godden, Director of Summer Programs
(304) 636-1900

Davis & Elkins College has a structured program, initiated in 1973 for alternative admissions students. The formal program of studies begins in the fall and lasts for 1 semester. Ninety percent of the students complete the program in that time.

ADMISSION POLICIES:

- New and transfer students are eligible for alternative admissions

- Requirements for admission as a freshman:
  820 — average combined verbal and math SAT
  21 — average ACT
  2.4 — average GPA
  Other considerations: letters of recommendation

- Requirements for admission as a transfer student:
  2.0 — minimum GPA
  Other considerations: letters of recommendation

ACADEMIC COURSEWORK AND RELATED FEATURES:

- Support services: freshman orientation, college survival skills, academic advising, drug/alcohol counseling, women's center, psychological counseling, academic skills center, study technique workshops, career advising, peer counseling, health center, aptitude testing, extended time for tests
- Separate new-student orientation
- Students are not required to work with tutors
- Counseling is required
- Students are assigned an academic adviser. None of the advisers serve alternative admissions students exclusively. Students meet with advisers 2 times per semester
- Placement testing is required
- A total of 44 full-time faculty at the institution
- Special faculty assigned to the program, who are trained to work with alternative admissions students
- Students are limited to a credit load of 12 credits per semester through fall semester of program

REQUIRED COURSES:

- Remedial courses required:
  Writing (noncredit)
  Reading (noncredit)
  Math (noncredit)

PROFILE OF ALTERNATIVE ADMISSIONS STUDENTS:

- 80 alternative admissions students enrolled

OTHER FEATURES/ACCOMMODATIONS:
- On-campus housing is available and is guaranteed for alternative admissions students
- On-campus housing is required of alternative admissions students
- A meal plan is available. It is required of alternative admissions students
- Financial aid is available

DEADLINES:
- Rolling admission
- March 1 for financial aid
- May 1 for reply date

DEFIANCE COLLEGE
>>>>>>>>>>>>>>>>>>>>>>>>>>>

Defiance, OH 43512
(419) 784-4010, Ext. 354

$7,184 Tuition and Fees
$3,040 Average Double Room and Meal Plan

735 full-time undergraduates, 298 part-time
  undergraduates
14:1 student/faculty ratio
26% of undergraduates study business

>>

Founded in 1850, the Defiance College is a private institution, coed, affiliated with United Church of Christ. Located on 150 acres in a small city 55 miles from Toledo. Associate's and bachelor's degrees are offered.

ALTERNATIVE ADMISSIONS:

Contact: Russell Levthold, Senior Lecturer of Developmental Education (419) 784-4010

The Defiance College has a structured program, Conditional Admission, initiated in 1987 for alternative admissions students. The formal program of studies begins in the fall and lasts for 1 semester; however, students can also enter the program in the spring and continue for 1 semester. Ninety percent of the students complete the program in that time.

ADMISSION POLICIES:
- New students are eligible for alternative admissions
- Requirements for admission as a freshman:
  350 — minimum verbal SAT
  350 — minimum math SAT
    or
  12 — minimum ACT

  1.8 — minimum GPA
Other considerations: high school rank

ACADEMIC COURSEWORK AND RELATED FEATURES:
- Support services: freshman orientation, academic advising, drug/alcohol counseling, psychological counseling, academic skills center, study technique workshops, career advising, health center
- Separate new-student orientation
- Students are required to work with tutors 5 hours per week
- Group and one-on-one tutoring by peer tutors in all academic areas
- Counseling is not required
- Students are assigned an academic adviser
- Placement testing is required
- A total of 55 full-time faculty at the institution
- Five faculty members assigned to the program, who are trained to work with alternative admissions students
- Alternative admissions students do not take separate classes
- Students are not limited to credit load

REQUIRED COURSES:
Freshman Seminar (credit-bearing)
- Required courses are calculated in GPA

PROFILE OF ALTERNATIVE ADMISSIONS STUDENTS:
- 63 alternative admissions students enrolled
- 80% of the accepted students enrolled

OTHER FEATURES/ACCOMMODATIONS:
- On-campus housing is available and is guaranteed for alternative admissions students
- A meal plan is available
- Financial aid is available

DEADLINES:
- Rolling admission
- March 1 for financial aid
- May 1 for reply date

DELAWARE VALLEY COLLEGE

>>>>>>>>>>>>>>>>>>>>>>>>>>

Doylestown, PA 18901
(215) 345-1500

$8,200 Tuition and Fees
$1,600 Average Double Room
$1,840 Average Meal Plan

1,150 full-time undergraduates, 20 part-time
   undergraduates
14:1 student/faculty ratio
63% of undergraduates study math/sciences

>>

Founded in 1896, Delaware Valley College is a private
institution, coed. Located on 800 acres in a rural community 20 miles from Philadelphia. Associate's and
bachelor's degrees are offered.

ALTERNATIVE ADMISSIONS:

Contact: Joseph Folcocy, Director of Counseling (215)
345-1500, Ext. 2278

Delaware Valley College has a structured program,
Special Students, initiated in 1978 for alternative admissions students. The formal program of studies begins
in the fall; however, students can also enter the program in the spring.

ADMISSION POLICIES:

- New and transfer students are eligible for alternative
  admissions

- Requirements for admission as a freshman:
  350 — minimum verbal SAT
  350 — minimum math SAT
       or
   14 — minimum ACT

  2.0 — minimum GPA
Other considerations: high school rank, interview with
admissions counselor, essay/personal statement, letters of recommendation

- Requirements for admission as a transfer student:
  2.0 — minimum GPA
Other considerations: interview with admissions counselor, essay/personal statement, letters of recommendation

ACADEMIC COURSEWORK AND RELATED FEATURES:

- Support services: freshman orientation, college survival skills, academic advising, drug/alcohol counseling, psychological counseling, academic skills center,
  study technique workshops, career advising, peer
  counseling, health center, aptitude testing, extended
  time for tests
- Separate new-student orientation
- Students are not required to work with tutors
- Group and one-on-one tutoring by peers as well as
  professional tutors in English, math, and sciences
- Counseling is required
- Students are assigned an academic adviser. Students
  meet with advisers 10 times per semester
- Placement testing is required in English and math

REQUIRED COURSES:

- Courses required of students who demonstrate defi-
  ciency:
  Preparatory English (credit-bearing)
  Preparatory Math (credit-bearing)
  Reading (credit-bearing)

- Remedial courses are not calculated in GPA

PROFILE OF ALTERNATIVE ADMISSIONS STUDENTS:

- 70 alternative admissions students enrolled
- 12% of the accepted students enrolled
- 98% enter as new students, 2% as transfer students
- 5% of the students transfer to another college after
  freshman year, 2% transfer after sophomore year
- 25% minority, 15% female
- 65% state residents, 5% international students
- 2% 25 years or older
- 45% intercollegiate athletes, Division III sports available:
  football, basketball, baseball, wrestling, cross-coun-
     try, track, soccer, lacrosse (men)
  basketball, softball, volleyball, field hockey, soccer,
     track, cross-country (women)
- 3% learning disabled
- 31% in top 50% of high school class

OTHER FEATURES/ACCOMMODATIONS:

- On-campus housing is available, but is not guaranteed
  for alternative admissions students
- A meal plan is available
- Financial aid is available

DEADLINES:

- Rolling admission—30 days after application is sent,
  notification of admission
- April 1 for financial aid

Stacy Needle

42

DELTA STATE UNIVERSITY

>>>>>>>>>>>>>>>>>>>>>>>>>>>>

Cleveland, MS 38733
(601) 846-4655

$1,604 In-State Tuition and Fees
$2,786 Out-of-State Tuition and Fees
$ 325 Average Double Room
$ 404 Average Meal Plan

1,164 full-time undergraduates, 172 part-time
   undergraduates
16:1 student/faculty ratio

>>

Founded in 1924, Delta State University is a public institution, coed. Located on 524 acres in a small city 116 miles from Memphis, Tennessee. Bachelor's degrees are offered.

ALTERNATIVE ADMISSIONS:

Contact: Besty Elliott, Director of Admissions (601) 846-4655

Delta State University has a policy, Over 21, initiated in 1986 for alternative admissions students. The formal program of studies begins in the fall and lasts for 1 semester; however, students can also enter the program in the spring and continue for 1 semester.

ADMISSION POLICIES:

• New and transfer students are eligible for alternative admissions

• Admission based on individual criteria

ACADEMIC COURSEWORK AND RELATED FEATURES:

• Placement testing is not required
• Alternative admissions students do not take separate classes
• Students are not limited to credit load

OTHER FEATURES/ACCOMMODATIONS:

• On-campus housing is available, but is not guaranteed for alternative admissions students
• A meal plan is available

DOMINICAN COLLEGE OF BLAUVELT

>>>>>>>>>>>>>>>>>>>>>>>>>>>

Orangeburg, NY 10962
(914) 359-7800

$5,500 Tuition and Fees
$4,500 Average Double Room and Meal Plan

675 full-time undergraduates, 685 part-time
   undergraduates
12:1 student/faculty ratio
30% of undergraduates study business

>>

Founded in 1952, Dominican College of Blauvelt is a private institution, coed, affiliated with the Roman Catholic church. Located on 17 acres in a town 17 miles from New York City. Associate's and bachelor's degrees are offered.

ALTERNATIVE ADMISSIONS:

Contact: Harry White, Director of Admissions (914) 359-7800

Dominican College of Blauvelt has a structured program, Conditional Admissions, initiated in 1984 for alternative admissions students. The formal program of studies begins in the fall and lasts for 4 years; however, students can also enter the program in the spring and continue for 4 years. Forty percent of the students complete the program in that time. Students receive a bachelor's degree upon completion of their studies.

ADMISSION POLICIES:

• New students are eligible for alternative admissions

• Requirements for admission as a freshman:
   430 — average verbal SAT
   420 — average math SAT
Other considerations: high school GPA, high school rank, type of high school attended, difficulty of high school courses taken, extracurricular activities, community service/volunteer work, interview with admissions counselor, alumni affiliation/recommendation, minority status

ACADEMIC COURSEWORK AND RELATED FEATURES:

• Support services: freshman orientation, college survival skills, academic advising, academic skills center, study technique workshops, career advising, peer counseling, aptitude testing

The Other Route into College

- Students are not required to work with tutors
- One-on-one tutoring by peers as well as professional tutors in English, math, and reading
- Counseling is not required
- Students are assigned an academic adviser
- Placement testing is required in English, math, and reading
- A total of 80 full-time faculty at the institution
- Special faculty assigned to the program, who are trained to work with alternative admissions students
- Students take an average of 60% of their classes with alternative admissions students
- Alternative admissions classes average 18 students
- Courses are also offered in the evening
- Students are limited to a credit load of 12 credits per semester until they attain a 2.0 GPA

REQUIRED COURSES:
- Courses required of students who demonstrate deficiency:
  Remedial English (credit-bearing)—alternative admissions students only
  Remedial Math (credit-bearing)—alternative admissions students only
  Remedial Reading (credit-bearing)—alternative admissions students only
- Remedial courses are calculated in GPA
- Minimum of 1.7 GPA required to stay in program; if below 1.7 GPA, the student meets with the Committee on Academic Standards

PROFILE OF ALTERNATIVE ADMISSIONS STUDENTS:
- 28 alternative admissions students enrolled
- 26% of the accepted students enrolled
- 100% enter as new students
- 20% of the students transfer to another college after freshman year, 24% transfer after sophomore year
- 10% minority, 60% female
- 65% state residents
- 35% intercollegiate athletes, Division NAIA sports available:
  baseball, soccer, basketball (men)
  basketball, softball, volleyball (women)
- 40% graduate within 4 years

OTHER FEATURES/ACCOMMODATIONS:
- On-campus housing is available, but is not guaranteed for alternative admissions students
- A meal plan is available

DEADLINES:
- Rolling admission

D'YOUVILLE COLLEGE
>>>>>>>>>>>>>>>>>>>>>>>>>>>>

Buffalo, NY 14201
(716) 881-7600

$7,120 Tuition and Fees
$3,350 Average Double Room and Meal Plan

1,027 full-time undergraduates, 273 part-time undergraduates
13:1 student/faculty ratio
30% of undergraduates study math/sciences

>>

Founded in 1908, D'Youville College is a private institution, coed. Located on 1 acre in a large city. Bachelor's degrees are offered.

ALTERNATIVE ADMISSIONS:
Contact: Frank Vastola, Director of Admissions (716) 881-7600

D'Youville College has a policy for alternative admissions students.

ADMISSION POLICIES:
- New or transfer students are eligible for alternative admissions

- Requirements for admission as a freshman:
  350 — average verbal SAT
  300 — average math SAT
       or
   15 — minimum ACT
Other considerations: high school GPA, high school rank

- Requirements for admission as a transfer student:
  1.3 — minimum GPA

ACADEMIC COURSEWORK AND RELATED FEATURES:
- Support services: freshman orientation, academic advising, drug/alcohol counseling, psychological counseling, academic skills center, study technique workshops, career advising, peer counseling, health center, aptitude testing, extended time for tests
- Students are not required to work with tutors
- Group and one-on-one tutoring by peer tutors as well as professional tutors in reading, writing, math, and science
- Counseling is not required

Stacy Needle

- Students are assigned an academic adviser. None of the advisers serve alternative admissions students exclusively. Students meet with advisers 2 times per semester
- Placement testing is required
- Alternative admissions students do not take separate classes
- Students are limited to a credit load of 12 credits per semester through first semester at college

REQUIRED COURSES:
- Remedial courses required:
  Writing Skills (non-credit)
  Reading and Study Skills (non-credit)
  College Math Skills (non-credit)

PROFILE OF ALTERNATIVE ADMISSIONS STUDENTS:
- 28 alternative admissions students enrolled
- 35% of accepted students enrolled
- 80% enter as new students, 20% as transfer students
- 6% of the students transfer to another college after freshman year, 4% transfer after sophomore year
- 40% minority, 79% female
- 90% state residents, no international students
- 12% 25 years or older
- No intercollegiate athletes
- 3% learning disabled
- 10% in top 50% of high school class
- 74% graduate within 4 years

OTHER FEATURES/ACCOMMODATIONS:
- On-campus housing is available and is guaranteed for alternative admissions students
- A meal plan is available
- Financial aid is available

DEADLINES:
- Rolling admission
- April 15 for financial aid

EAST CENTRAL UNIVERSITY
>>>>>>>>>>>>>>>>>>>>>>>>>>>>

Ada, OK 74820
(405) 332-8000

$ 824 In-State Tuition and Fees
$2,352–$2,940 Out-of-State Tuition and Fees
$ 600 Average Double Room
$1,324 Average Meal Plan

3,139 full-time undergraduates, 476 part-time undergraduates
23:1 student/faculty ratio
25% of undergraduates study education

>>

Founded in 1909, East Central University is a public institution, coed. Located on 132 acres in a small city 90 miles from Oklahoma City. Bachelor's degrees are offered.

ALTERNATIVE ADMISSIONS:

Contact: Pamla Armstrong, Director of Admissions (405) 332-8000

East Central University has a policy for alternative admissions students.

ADMISSION POLICIES:
- New students are eligible for alternative admissions
- Requirements for admission as a freshman:
  15 — minimum ACT
  2.6 — minimum GPA
Other considerations: high school rank, type of high school attended

ACADEMIC COURSEWORK AND RELATED FEATURES:
- Support services: freshman orientation, college survival skills, academic advising, academic skills center, study technique workshops, career advising, peer counseling, health center, aptitude testing, writing center
- Separate new-student orientation
- Students are not required to work with tutors
- Group and one-on-one tutoring by peers tutors in all academic areas
- Counseling is not required
- Students are assigned an academic adviser. None of the advisers serve alternative admissions students exclusively. Students meet with advisers 1 time per semester

The Other Route into College

- Placement testing is not required
- Alternative admissions students do not take separate classes

REQUIRED COURSES:
- Remedial courses required:
  Fundamentals of English (non-credit)
  Beginning Algebra (non-credit)
  Intermediate Algebra (non-credit)

PROFILE OF ALTERNATIVE ADMISSIONS STUDENTS:
- 25 alternative admissions students enrolled
- 5% of the accepted students enrolled
- 10% of the students transfer to another college after freshman year
- 3% minority, 11% female
- 21% state residents, no international students
- 5% 25 years or older
- None in top 50% of high school class

OTHER FEATURES/ACCOMMODATIONS:
- On-campus housing is available, but is not guaranteed for alternative admissions students
- A meal plan is available
- Financial aid is available

DEADLINES:
- July for admission

EAST STROUDSBURG UNIVERSITY OF PENNSYLVANIA

>>>>>>>>>>>>>>>>>>>>>>>>>>

East Stroudsburg, PA 18301
(717) 424-3542

$2,382 In-State Tuition and Fees
$4,000 Out-of-State Tuition and Fees
$1,720 Average Double Room
$ 912 Average Meal Plan

3,710 full-time undergraduates, 600 part-time undergraduates
16:1 student/faculty ratio
27% of undergraduates study social sciences

>>

Founded in 1893, East Stroudsburg University is a public institution, coed. Located on 551 acres in a town 40 miles from Allentown. Associate's and bachelor's degrees are offered

ALTERNATIVE ADMISSIONS:
Contact: Alan Chesterton, Director of Admissions (717) 424-3542

East Stroudsburg University has a structured summer program, June–January Freshman Program, for alternative admissions students. The program begins in late June and lasts for 9 weeks. Ninety-five percent of the students complete the program in that time.

ADMISSION POLICIES:
- New students are eligible for alternative admissions, with a limit of 150–200 students. There is no wait list

- Requirements for admission as a freshman:
  384 — average verbal SAT
  423 — average math SAT
Other considerations: high school rank

ACADEMIC COURSEWORK AND RELATED FEATURES:
- Support services: freshman orientation, college survival skills, academic advising, drug/alcohol counseling, women's center, psychological counseling, academic skills center, study techniques workshop, career advising, peer counseling, health center, aptitude testing, extended time for tests (if learning disabled)
- Separate new-student orientation
- Students are not required to work with tutors
- One-on-one tutoring by peer tutors as well as professional tutors
- Counseling is not required
- Students are assigned an academic adviser. None of the advisers serve alternative admissions students exclusively. Students meet with advisers 1 time per semester
- Placement testing is required in writing
- Alternative admissions students do not take separate classes
- Students are not limited to credit load

PROFILE OF ALTERNATIVE ADMISSIONS STUDENTS:
- 186 alternative admissions students enrolled
- 18% of accepted students enrolled
- 100% enter as new students
- 3% minority, 41% female
- 77% state residents
- None 25 years or older

Stacy Needle

- 45% in top 50% of high school class
- 30% graduate within 4 years
- 32% graduate within 5 years

OTHER FEATURES/ACCOMMODATIONS:
- On-campus housing is available and is guaranteed for alternative admissions students
- A meal plan is available
- Financial aid is available

DEADLINES:
- March 1 for admission
- May 1 for financial aid
- March 1 for notification of admission
- April 1 for reply date

EAST TEXAS STATE UNIVERSITY
>>>>>>>>>>>>>>>>>>>>>>>>>>>

Commerce, TX 75428
(214) 886-5081

———

$834 In-State Tuition and Fees
$3,200 Out-of-State Tuition and Fees
$1,937 Average Double Room and Meal Plan

2,965 full-time undergraduates, 1,118 part-time undergraduates
34:1 student/faculty ratio

>>

Founded in 1889, East Texas State University is a public institution, coed. Located on 1,883 acres in a small city. Bachelor's degrees are offered.

ALTERNATIVE ADMISSIONS:
Contact: Wanda Simpson, Assistant Director of Admissions (214) 886-5081

East Texas State University has a structured summer program for alternative admissions students. The program begins in June and lasts for 11 weeks.

ADMISSION POLICIES:
- New and transfer students are eligible for alternative admissions

- Admission considerations—new student: SAT or ACT scores

- Admission considerations—transfer student: admission based on individual criteria

ACADEMIC COURSEWORK AND RELATED FEATURES:
- Support services: freshman orientation, college survival skills, academic advising, drug/alcohol counseling, psychological counseling, academic skills center, study technique workshops, career advising, peer counseling, health center, aptitude testing, extended time for tests
- Students are not required to work with tutors
- One-on-one tutoring by peer tutors as well as professional tutors in math and English
- Counseling is not required
- Placement testing is required in math
- A total of 231 full-time faculty at the institution
- Special faculty assigned to the program
- Students take classes with alternative admissions students only
- Alternative admissions classes average 20 students

REQUIRED COURSES:
- Remedial courses required:
  Developmental English (credit-bearing)—alternative admissions students only
  Developmental Math (credit-bearing)

- Remedial courses are calculated in GPA

OTHER FEATURES/ACCOMMODATIONS:
- On-campus housing is available, but is not guaranteed for alternative admissions students
- A meal plan is available
- Financial aid is available

EASTERN CONNECTICUT STATE UNIVERSITY
>>>>>>>>>>>>>>>>>>>>>>>>>>>

Willimantic, CT 06226
(203) 456-5286

———

$1,632 In-State Tuition and Fees
$3,511 Out-of-State Tuition and Fees
$1,614 Average Double Room
$1,400 Average Meal Plan

2,670 full-time undergraduates, 1,434 part-time
  undergraduates
16:1 student/faculty ratio
40% of undergraduates study business

>>

Founded in 1889, Eastern Connecticut State University
is a public institution, coed. Located on 100 acres in a
small city 28 miles from Hartford. Associate's and bachelor's degrees are offered.

ALTERNATIVE ADMISSIONS:

Contact: Floyd Baywell, Director of the Learning Center (203) 456-5492

Eastern Connecticut State University has a structured
summer program, Contract Admissions Program
(C.A.P.), initiated in 1969 for alternative admissions
students. The program begins in late June and lasts for
6 weeks. Ninety-five percent of the students complete
the program in that time.

ADMISSION POLICIES:

• New students are eligible for alternative admissions,
  with a limit of 50 students. There is no wait list

• Requirements for admission as a freshman:
  300 — average verbal SAT
  300 — average math SAT
Other considerations: TSWE scores, high school rank,
interview with admissions counselor

ACADEMIC COURSEWORK AND RELATED FEATURES:

• Support services: freshman orientation, college survival skills, academic advising, drug/alcohol counseling, women's center, psychological counseling,
  academic skills center, study technique workshops,
  career advising, peer counseling, health center, aptitude testing
• Separate new-student orientation
• Students are required to work with tutors
• Group and one-on-one tutoring by peers as well as
  professional tutors in all academic areas
• Academic counseling is required
• Students are assigned an academic adviser. All advisers serve alternative admissions students exclusively
• Placement testing is required in reading and writing
• A total of 133 faculty at the institution
• Seven faculty members assigned to the program,
  who are trained to work with alternative admissions
  students
• Students take an average of 20% of their classes with
  alternative admissions students only
• Alternative admissions classes average 15 students

REQUIRED COURSES:

• Remedial courses required:
  Freshman Seminar (credit-bearing)—alternative admissions students only

• Remedial courses are calculated in GPA

PROFILE OF ALTERNATIVE ADMISSIONS STUDENTS:

• 50 alternative admissions students enrolled
• 85% of the accepted students enrolled
• 100% enter as new students
• 70% minority, 50% female
• 100% state residents, no international students
• None 25 years or older
• 10% intercollegiate athletes
• No learning disabled

OTHER FEATURES/ACCOMMODATIONS:

• On-campus housing is available and is guaranteed for
  alternative admissions students
• On-campus housing is reserved for alternative admissions students
• A meal plan is available. It is required of alternative
  admissions students
• Financial aid is available

DEADLINES:

• Rolling admission
• March 15 for financial aid
• May 1 for reply date

EASTERN MICHIGAN UNIVERSITY

>>>>>>>>>>>>>>>>>>>>>>>>>>

Ypsilanti, MI 48197
(313) 487-3060

$1,975 In-State Tuition and Fees
$2,310 Out-of-State Tuition and Fees
$3,192 Average Double Room and Meal Plan

17,506 full-time undergraduates
20:1 student/faculty ratio
73% of undergraduates study arts/humanities

Stacy Needle

>>

Founded in 1849, Eastern Michigan University is a public institution, coed. Located on 460 acres in a small city 30 miles from Detroit. Bachelor's degrees are offered.

ALTERNATIVE ADMISSIONS:

Contact: Joan Schiller, Coordinator of PASS Program (313) 487-3148

Eastern Michigan University has a structured program, Promote Academic Success (PASS), initiated in 1972 for alternative admissions students. The formal program of studies begins in the fall and lasts for 1 year. Ninety percent of the students complete the program in that time.

ADMISSION POLICIES:

- New students are eligible for alternative admissions, with a limit of 200 students. There is no wait list

- Requirements for admission as a freshman:
  812 — minimum combined verbal and math SAT
  or
  18 — minimum ACT

  2.2 — minimum GPA

ACADEMIC COURSEWORK AND RELATED FEATURES:

- Support services: freshman orientation, college survival skills, academic advising, drug/alcohol counseling, psychological counseling, academic skills center, study technique workshops, career advising, peer counseling, health center
- Students are required to work with tutors
- One-on-one tutoring by peers as well as professional tutors in math, history, and government
- Academic counseling is required
- Students are assigned an academic adviser. Students meet with advisers 2–3 times per semester
- Placement testing is not required
- A total of 650 full-time faculty at the institution
- Four faculty members assigned to the program
- Students take classes with alternative admissions students only
- Alternative admissions classes average 20 students
- Students are limited to a credit load of 12 credits per semester through fall semester of freshman year

REQUIRED COURSES:

- Remedial courses required:
  Basic English (credit-bearing)—alternative admissions students only
  Educational Psychology—Study Habits (credit-bearing)—alternative admissions students only

- Minimum of 2.0 GPA required to stay in program; if below 2.0 GPA, a student is placed on academic probation

PROFILE OF ALTERNATIVE ADMISSIONS STUDENTS:

- 185 alternative admissions students enrolled
- 50% of the accepted students enrolled
- 100% enter as new students
- 90% state residents
- None 25 years or older

OTHER FEATURES/ACCOMMODATIONS:

- On-campus housing is available, but is not guaranteed for alternative admissions students
- A meal plan is available
- Financial aid is available

DEADLINES:

- Rolling admission

EASTERN NAZARENE COLLEGE

>>>>>>>>>>>>>>>>>>>>>>>>>>>

Quincy, MA 02170
(617) 773-2373

$6,047 Tuition and Fees
$2,950 Average Double Room and Meal Plan

668 full-time undergraduates, 45 part-time undergraduates

>>

Founded in 1900, Eastern Nazarene College is a private institution, coed, affiliated with the Church of the Nazarene. Located on 15 acres in a town 7 miles from Boston. Associate's and bachelor's degrees are offered.

ALTERNATIVE ADMISSIONS:

Contact: Dr. Donald Yerxa, Director of Admissions (617) 773-2373

Eastern Nazarene College has a structured program, College Achievement Program, for alternative admissions students. The formal program of studies begins in the fall and lasts for 1 year. Eighty percent of the students complete the program in that time.

The Other Route into College

ADMISSION POLICIES:

- New students are eligible for alternative admissions
- Admission based on individual criteria

ACADEMIC COURSEWORK AND RELATED FEATURES:

- Students are not required to work with tutors
- Counseling is available
- Students take classes with alternative admissions students only
- Students are limited to a credit load of 12 credits per semester through fall semester of freshman year, if a 2.0 GPA is attained

REQUIRED COURSES:

- Courses required of students who demonstrate deficiency:
  Math for College
  Reading for College
  Basic Writing

OTHER FEATURES/ACCOMMODATIONS:

- On-campus housing is available
- A meal plan is available

DEADLINES:

- Rolling admission

EASTERN OREGON STATE COLLEGE

>>>>>>>>>>>>>>>>>>>>>>>>>

La Grande, OR 97850
(503) 963-1393

$1,662 In-State Tuition and Fees
$1,662 Out-of-State Tuition and Fees
$2,745 Average Double Room and Meal Plan

1,568 full-time undergraduates, 207 part-time undergraduates
11:1 student/faculty ratio
30% of undergraduates study arts/humanities

>>

Founded in 1929, Eastern Oregon State College is a public institution, coed. Located on 21 acres in a rural community 250 miles from Portland. Associate's and bachelor's degrees are offered.

Stacy Needle

ALTERNATIVE ADMISSIONS:

Contact: Terral Schut, Director of Admissions (503) 963-1393

Eastern Oregon State College has a policy, Special Admissions, initiated in 1972 for alternative admissions students.

ADMISSION POLICIES:

- New and transfer students are eligible for alternative admissions

- Admission considerations—new student: SAT or ACT scores, high school GPA, interview with admissions counselor, essay/personal statement, letters of recommendation

- Requirements for admission as a transfer student: 1.8 — minimum GPA

ACADEMIC COURSEWORK AND RELATED FEATURES:

- Support services: freshman orientation, college survival skills, academic advising, drug/alcohol counseling, academic skills center, study technique workshops, career advising, peer counseling, health center, aptitude testing
- Students are not required to work with tutors
- Group and one-on-one tutoring by peer tutors as well as professional tutors in all academic areas
- Counseling is not required
- Students are assigned an academic adviser. None of the advisers serve alternative admissions students exclusively. Students meet with advisers 2 times per semester
- Placement testing is required in math
- Alternative admissions students do not take separate classes
- Students are not limited to credit load

REQUIRED COURSES:

- Courses required of students who demonstrate deficiency:
  Elementary Algebra
  Survey of Calculus

- Remedial courses are calculated in GPA

PROFILE OF ALTERNATIVE ADMISSIONS STUDENTS:

- 21 alternative admissions students enrolled
- 23% of accepted students enrolled

OTHER FEATURES/ACCOMMODATIONS:

- On-campus housing is available, but is not guaranteed for alternative admissions students

- A meal plan is available
- Financial aid is available

DEADLINES:
- Rolling admission
- February 1 for financial aid

EASTERN WASHINGTON UNIVERSITY

>>>>>>>>>>>>>>>>>>>>>>>>>>

Cheney, WA 99004
(509) 359-2397

$1,272 In-State Tuition and Fees
$4,425 Out-of-State Tuition and Fees
$2,574 Average Double Room and Meal Plan

6,720 full-time undergraduates, 1,478 part-time
  undergraduates
25:1 student/faculty ratio
37% of undergraduates study arts/humanities

>>

Founded in 1882, Eastern Washington University is a public institution, coed. Located on 350 acres in a town 18 miles from Spokane. Bachelor's degrees are offered.

ALTERNATIVE ADMISSIONS:
Contact: Sally Burge, Director of Learning Skills Center
(509) 359-2487

Eastern Washington University has a structured program, Freshman Success, initiated in 1986 for alternative admissions students. The formal program of studies begins in the fall and lasts for 1 year. Eighty-nine percent of the students complete the program in that time.

ADMISSION POLICIES:
- New students are eligible for alternative admissions, with a limit of 30 students. There is no wait list
- Admission considerations: SAT or ACT scores, high school GPA, type of high school attended, difficulty of high school courses taken, essay/personal statement

ACADEMIC COURSEWORK AND RELATED FEATURES:
- Support services: freshman orientation, college survival skills, academic advising, drug/alcohol counseling, women's center, psychological counseling, academic skills center, study technique workshops, career advising, health center, aptitude testing, extended time for tests
- Students are required to work with tutors
- One-on-one tutoring by peer tutors as well as professional tutors
- Counseling is not required
- Students are assigned an academic adviser
- Placement testing is required in math and English
- Alternative admissions students do not take separate classes
- Students are limited to a credit load of 12–15 credits per semester through 2 quarters

REQUIRED COURSES:
Learning Skills
- Courses required of students who demonstrate deficiency:
  Basic Arithmetic (credit-bearing)
  Basic Algebra (credit-bearing)
  Basic Geometry (credit-bearing)
  English Composition (credit-bearing)
- Remedial courses are not calculated in GPA
- Required courses are calculated in GPA

PROFILE OF ALTERNATIVE ADMISSIONS STUDENTS:
- 100% enter as new students
- 75% minority
- 100% state residents
- None 25 years or older
- 2% intercollegiate athletes

OTHER FEATURES/ACCOMMODATIONS:
- On-campus housing is available, but is not guaranteed for alternative admissions students
- A meal plan is available
- Financial aid is available

DEADLINES:
- Rolling admission
- February 15 for financial aid

EDGEWOOD COLLEGE
>>>>>>>>>>>>>>>>>>>>>>>>>>>

Madison, WI 53711
(608) 257-4861

$6,000 Tuition and Fees
$3,000 Average Double Room and Meal Plan

388 full-time undergraduates, 469 part-time
   undergraduates
17:1 student/faculty ratio

>>

Founded in 1927, Edgewood College is a private institution, coed, affiliated with Sinsinawa Dominican church.
Located on 55 acres in a small city. Bachelor's degrees
are offered.

ALTERNATIVE ADMISSIONS:

Contact: Jo Meier Jonquer, Administrative Associate,
(608) 257-4861, Ext. 2214.

Edgewood College has a policy for alternative admissions students.

ADMISSION POLICIES:

• New and transfer students are eligible for alternative
  admissions

• Admission considerations—new student: SAT or
  ACT scores, high school GPA, high school rank,
  essay/personal statement, letters of recommendation

• Admissions considerations—transfer student: GPA
  at previous institution, number of credits completed,
  essay/personal statement, letters of recommendation

ACADEMIC COURSEWORK AND RELATED FEATURES:

• Support services: freshman orientation, college survival skills, academic advising, drug/alcohol counseling, psychological counseling, study technique
  workshops, career advising, peer counseling, aptitude testing
• Students are not required to work with tutors
• Counseling is not required
• Students are assigned an academic adviser. None of
  the advisers serve alternative admissions students
  exclusively
• Placement testing is required

• Alternative admissions students do not take separate
  classes
• Students are not limited to credit load

REQUIRED COURSES:

• Minimum of 2.0 GPA required to stay in program; if
  below 2.0 GPA, a student is placed on academic probation

OTHER FEATURES/ACCOMMODATIONS:

• On-campus housing is available, but is not guaranteed
  for alternative admissions students
• A meal plan is available
• Financial aid is available

DEADLINES:

• Rolling admission
• March 1 for financial aid

ELIZABETHTOWN COLLEGE
>>>>>>>>>>>>>>>>>>>>>>>>>>

Elizabethtown, PA 17022
(717) 367-1151, Ext. 164

$9,700 Tuition and Fees
$1,700 Average Double Room
$1,800 Average Meal Plan

1,451 full-time undergraduates, 322 part-time
   undergraduates
14:1 student/faculty ratio
45% of undergraduates study business

>>

Founded in 1899, Elizabethtown College is a private
institution, coed, affiliated with the Church of the Brethren. Located on 110 acres in a town 10 miles from
Harrisburg. Bachelor's degrees are offered.

ALTERNATIVE ADMISSIONS:

Contact: Dr. Robert Wheelersburg, Assistant Dean of
Faculty (717) 367-1151

Elizabethtown College has a structured program, Development Studies, for alternative admissions students.
The formal program of studies begins in the fall and
lasts for 1 semester. One hundred percent of the students complete the program in that time.

Stacy Needle

ADMISSION POLICIES:

- New students are eligible for alternative admissions, with a limit of 45 students. There is a wait list
- Requirements for admission as a freshman:
  - 350 — minimum verbal SAT
  - 350 — minimum math SAT
  - 35 — minimum TSWE
  - 2.0 — minimum GPA

Other considerations: type of high school attended, difficulty of high school courses taken, interview with admissions counselor, letters of recommendation

ACADEMIC COURSEWORK AND RELATED FEATURES:

- Support services: freshman orientation, academic advising, drug/alcohol counseling, psychological counseling, academic skills center, study technique workshops, career advising, peer counseling, health center, aptitude testing
- Separate new-student orientation
- Students are not required to work with tutors
- One-on-one tutoring by peer tutors
- Counseling is not required
- Students are assigned an academic adviser
- Placement testing is required in reading and math
- A total of 105 full-time faculty at the institution
- Two faculty members assigned to the program
- Students take an average of 20% of their classes with alternative admissions students only
- Alternative admissions classes average 15 students
- Students are not limited to credit load

REQUIRED COURSES:

- Remedial courses required:
  Intermediate Algebra (credit-bearing)
  Basic Writing (credit-bearing)

- Other required courses:
  Introduction to College (credit-bearing)—alternative admissions students only

- Remedial courses are calculated in GPA
- Required courses are calculated in GPA

PROFILE OF ALTERNATIVE ADMISSIONS STUDENTS:

- 60 alternative admissions students enrolled
- 60% of accepted students enrolled
- 100% enter as new students
- None 25 years or older

OTHER FEATURES/ACCOMMODATIONS:

- On-campus housing is available and is guaranteed for alternative admissions students
- On-campus housing is required of alternative admissions students
- A meal plan is available. It is required of alternative admissions students
- Financial aid is available

DEADLINES:

- Rolling admission
- March 1 for financial aid
- May 1 for reply date

ELMHURST COLLEGE
>>>>>>>>>>>>>>>>>>>>>>>>>>>>

Elmhurst, IL 60126
(708) 617-3400

$7,166 Tuition and Fees
$1,520 Average Double Room
$1,540 Average Meal Plan

1,650 full-time undergraduates, 1,500 part-time
  undergraduates
15:1 student/faculty ratio
45% of undergraduates study business

>>

Founded in 1871, Elmhurst College is a private institution, coed, affiliated with the United Church of Christ. Located on 38 acres in a small city 15 miles from Chicago. Bachelor's degrees are offered.

ALTERNATIVE ADMISSIONS:

Contact: Michael E. Dessimoz, Director of Admissions
(708) 617-3400

Elmhurst College has a policy for alternative admissions students.

ADMISSION POLICIES:

- New and transfer students are eligible for alternative admissions

- Requirements for admission as a freshman:
  - 16 — average ACT
  - 2.25 — average GPA

- Requirements for admission as a transfer student:
  - 2.8 — average GPA

ACADEMIC COURSEWORK AND RELATED FEATURES:

- Support services: freshman orientation, college survival skills, academic advising, drug/alcohol counsel-

The Other Route into College

ing, psychological counseling, academic skills center, study technique workshops, career advising, health center, aptitude testing
- Students are not required to work with tutors
- Group and one-on-one tutoring by peer tutors as well as professional tutors in all academic areas
- Counseling is not required
- Students are assigned an academic adviser. Five percent of the advisers serve alternative admissions students exclusively. Students meet with advisers 4–6 times per semester
- Placement testing is required in English
- Students take classes with alternative admissions students only
- Alternative admissions classes average 15 students
- Courses are also offered in the evening
- Students are limited to a credit load of 12 credits per semester through fall semester of college

REQUIRED COURSES:

Introduction to College Study (credit-bearing)—alternative admissions students only

- Required courses are calculated in GPA
- Minimum of 2.0 GPA required to stay at college; if below 2.0 GPA, a student is placed on academic probation

PROFILE OF ALTERNATIVE ADMISSIONS STUDENTS:

- 55% of accepted students enrolled
- 95% enter as new students, 5% transfer students
- 8% minority, 50% female
- 95% state residents, 5% international students
- 5% 25 years or older
- 40% intercollegiate athletes, Division III sports available:
  football, baseball, basketball, wrestling, golf, track and field, cross-country, tennis (men)
  volleyball, tennis, softball, basketball, cross-country, track and field (women)
- 33% in top 50% of high school class
- Approximately 30% graduate within 4 years
- Approximately 40% graduate within 5 years

OTHER FEATURES/ACCOMMODATIONS:

- On-campus housing is available and is guaranteed for alternative admissions students
- A meal plan is available
- Financial aid is available

DEADLINES:

- Rolling admission
- May 1 for financial aid
- August 15 for reply date

Stacy Needle

54

The program is best suited for an adult with evidence of recent success in high school and strong course patterns.

ELMS COLLEGE
>>>>>>>>>>>>>>>>>>>>>>>>>>>>

Chicopee, MA 01013
(413) 592-3189

$8,100 Tuition and Fees
$3,100 Average Double Room and Meal Plan

650 full-time undergraduates, 608 part-time
  undergraduates
13:1 student/faculty ratio
44% of undergraduates study math/science

>>

Founded in 1928, Elms College is a private institution, women only, affiliated with the Roman Catholic church. Located in a small city 2 miles from Springfield. Associate's and bachelor's degrees are offered.

ALTERNATIVE ADMISSIONS:

Contact: Daniel Casey, Academic Dean (413) 594-2761

Elms College has a structured program, Reduced Load Program, for alternative admissions students. The formal program of studies begins in the fall and lasts for 1–2 semesters; however, students can also enter the program in the spring and continue for 1–2 semesters.

ADMISSION POLICIES:

- New and transfer students are eligible for alternative admissions, with a limit of 16–20 students. There is a wait list

- Requirements for admission as a freshman:
  400 — minimum verbal SAT
  400 — minimum math SAT
  2.0 — minimum GPA
Other considerations: high school rank, difficulty of high school courses taken, extracurricular activities, essay/personal statement, letters of recommendation

- Requirements for admission as a transfer student: 2.0 — minimum GPA

Other considerations: interview with admissions counselor, essay/personal statement, 2 letters of recommendation

ACADEMIC COURSEWORK AND RELATED FEATURES:

- Support services: freshman orientation, college survival skills, academic advising, drug/alcohol counseling, women's center, psychological counseling, academic skills center, study technique workshops, career advising, peer counseling, health center
- Separate new-student orientation
- Students are not required to work with tutors
- Group and one-on-one tutoring by peer tutors
- Counseling is not required
- Students are assigned an academic adviser. Students meet with advisers 3–4 times per semester
- Placement testing is required in math, English, and foreign language
- Students taken an average of 20% of their classes with alternative admissions students
- Alternative admissions classes average 15–20 students
- Students are limited to a credit load of 15 credits per semester either through the end of the first semester of the program or the end of the second semester of the program

REQUIRED COURSES:

Study Skills Course (credit-bearing)—alternative admissions students only

- Required courses are calculated in GPA
- Minimum of 2.0 GPA required to stay in program; if below 2.0 GPA, a student is placed on academic probation for 1 semester

PROFILE OF ALTERNATIVE ADMISSIONS STUDENTS:

- 18 alternative admissions students enrolled
- 50% of accepted students enrolled
- 10% of the students transfer to another college after freshman year, 5% transfer after sophomore year
- 6% minority, 100% female
- 3% state residents, 2% international students
- 3% intercollegiate athletes
- 95% graduate within 4 years
- 5% graduate within 5 years

OTHER FEATURES/ACCOMMODATIONS:

- On-campus housing is available and is guaranteed for alternative admissions students
- A meal plan is available
- Financial aid is available

DEADLINES:

- Rolling admission 2–3 weeks after application is sent, notification of admission
- March 1 for financial aid
- May 1 for reply date

EMERSON COLLEGE

>>>>>>>>>>>>>>>>>>>>>>>>>>>>

Boston, MA 02116
(617) 578-8600

$8,000 Tuition and Fees
$4,357 Average Double Room
$2,376 Average Meal Plan

1,939 full-time undergraduates, 315 part-time undergraduates
15:1 student/faculty ratio
100% of undergraduates study arts/humanities

>>

Founded in 1880, Emerson College is a private institution, coed. Located on 2 acres in a large city. Bachelor's degrees are offered.

ALTERNATIVE ADMISSIONS:

Contact: Dr. Harold Lawson, Dean of Division of Continuing Education/Alternative Learning Program (617) 578-8615

Emerson College has a structured program, The Alternative Freshman Year Program, initiated in 1989 for alternative admissions students. The formal program of studies begins in the fall and lasts for 1 year.

ADMISSION POLICIES:

- New students are eligible for alternative admissions, with a limit of 50 students. There is a wait list

- Admission considerations: SAT or ACT scores, high school GPA, high school rank, type of high school attended, essay/personal statement, letters of recommendation

The Other Route into College

ACADEMIC COURSEWORK AND RELATED FEATURES:

- Support services: freshman orientation, college survival skills, academic advising, drug/alcohol counseling, psychological counseling, academic skills center, career advising, peer counseling, health center, aptitude testing, extended time for tests
- Students are required to work with tutors
- Group and one-on-one tutoring by professional tutors
- Academic counseling is required
- Students are assigned an academic adviser. All advisers serve alternative admissions students exclusively
- Placement testing is required in grammar, oral competency, and reading
- A total of 90 full-time faculty at the institution
- Six faculty members assigned to the program, who are trained to work with alternative admissions students
- Students take an average of 75% of their classes with alternative admissions students
- Alternative admissions classes average 16 students
- Students are limited to a credit load of 12 credits per semester through spring semester of freshman year

REQUIRED COURSES:

- Remedial courses required:
  Introduction to Academic Communication Skills (non-credit)—alternative admissions students only
  Advanced Academic Communication Skills (non-credit)—alternative admissions students only

- Other required courses:
  Freshman Composition (credit-bearing)—alternative admissions students only
  Public Speaking (credit-bearing)—alternative admissions students only
  Introduction to Literature (credit-bearing)—alternative admissions students only
  Western Civilization and Culture (credit-bearing)—alternative admissions students only
  Expository Writing (credit-bearing)—alternative admissions students only

- Required courses are calculated in GPA

OTHER FEATURES/ACCOMMODATIONS:

- On-campus housing is available and is guaranteed for alternative admissions students
- On-campus housing is required of alternative admissions students
- A meal plan is available. It is required of alternative admissions students

DEADLINES:

- Rolling admission
- March 1 for financial aid
- May 1 for reply date

The program is best suited for a student committed to a career in communications or performing arts, but with an academic record that does not meet regular admission standards.

EMMANUEL COLLEGE
>>>>>>>>>>>>>>>>>>>>>>>>>>

Boston, MA 02115
(617) 735-9715

$8,635 Tuition and Fees
$4,666 Average Double Room and Meal Plan

577 full-time undergraduates, 237 part-time
  undergraduates

>>

Founded in 1919, Emmanuel College is a private institution, women only, affiliated with the Roman Catholic church. Located in a large city. Bachelor's degrees are offered.

ALTERNATIVE ADMISSIONS:

Contact: Maureen Ferrari, Director of Admissions
(617) 735-9715

Emmanuel College has a policy for alternative admissions students.

ADMISSION POLICIES:

- New students are eligible for alternative admissions

- Requirements for admission as a freshman:
  1.8 — minimum GPA

ACADEMIC COURSEWORK AND RELATED FEATURES:

- Students are required to work with tutors
- Counseling is available
- Alternative admissions students do not take separate classes
- Students are limited to a credit load of 12 credits per semester through fall semester of freshman year

Stacy Needle

REQUIRED COURSES:
- Remedial courses required:
  Writing Skills
  Math Review

- Minimum of 2.0 GPA required to stay at college; if below 2.0 GPA, a student is placed on academic probation

PROFILE OF ALTERNATIVE ADMISSION STUDENTS:
- 8% of the accepted students enrolled
- 90% graduate within 4 years
- 10% graduate within 5 years

OTHER FEATURES/ACCOMMODATIONS:
- On-campus housing is available
- A meal plan is available

DEADLINES:
- Rolling admission

FAIRLEIGH DICKINSON UNIVERSITY, FLORHAM–MADISON CAMPUS

>>>>>>>>>>>>>>>>>>>>>>>>>>>

Madison, NJ 07940
(201) 377-4700

$7,440 Tuition and Fees
$4,500 Average Double Room and Meal Plan

1,434 full-time undergraduates, 1,040 part-time undergraduates

>>

Founded in 1942, Fairleigh Dickinson University, Florham–Madison Campus is a private institution, coed. Located on 175 acres in a town. Associate's and bachelor's degrees are offered.

ALTERNATIVE ADMISSIONS:

Contact: Kathryn Douglas, Director of Freshmen Intensive Studies (201) 593-8500

Fairleigh Dickinson University, Florham–Madison Campus has a structured program, Freshmen Intensive Studies, initiated in 1984 for alternative admissions students. The formal program of studies begins in the fall and lasts for 1 year. Eighty percent of the students complete the program in that time.

ADMISSION POLICIES:
- New students are eligible for alternative admissions, with a limit of 35 students. There is a wait list

- Admission considerations: SAT or ACT scores, high school GPA, high school rank, interview with admissions counselor

ACADEMIC COURSEWORK AND RELATED FEATURES:
- Support services: freshman orientation, college survival skills, academic advising, drug/alcohol counseling, psychological counseling, academic skills center, study technique workshops, career advising, health center, aptitude testing, extended time for tests (if learning disabled)
- Students are required to work with tutors 1 hour per week
- Group and one-on-one tutoring by professional tutors
- Counseling is not required
- Students are assigned an academic adviser. All advisers serve alternative admissions students exclusively. Students meet with advisers 15 times per semester
- Placement testing is required in math and English
- Three faculty members assigned to the program, who are trained to work with alternative admissions students
- Alternative admissions students do not take separate classes
- Students are limited to a credit load of 12 credits per semester through spring semester of freshman year

REQUIRED COURSES:
General Psychology (credit-bearing)
Math (credit-bearing)
English (credit-bearing)

- Required courses are calculated in GPA

PROFILE OF ALTERNATIVE ADMISSIONS STUDENTS:
- 35 alternative admissions students enrolled
- 55% of the accepted students enrolled
- 100% enter as new students
- 10% minority, 50% female
- 70% state residents, no international students
- None 25 years or older

The Other Route into College

- 35% intercollegiate athletes, Division III sports available:
baseball, basketball, lacrosse, football, golf, soccer, tennis (men)
basketball, field hockey, golf, softball, tennis, volleyball (women)
- No learning disabled
- 65% graduate within 4 years

OTHER FEATURES/ACCOMMODATIONS:
- On-campus housing is available, but is not guaranteed for alternative admissions students
- A meal plan is available
- Financial aid is available

DEADLINES:
- Rolling admission
- March 15 for financial aid
- May 1 for reply date

FLORIDA INTERNATIONAL UNIVERSITY

>>>>>>>>>>>>>>>>>>>>>>>>>>

Miami, FL 33199
(305) 348-2363

$1,140 In-State Tuition and Fees
$3,900 Out-of-State Tuition and Fees
$1,850 Average Double Room
$1,556 Average Meal Plan

7,201 full-time undergraduates, 7,613 part-time undergraduates
13:1 student/faculty ratio
30% of undergraduates study business

>>

Founded in 1965, Florida International University is a public institution, coed. Located on 537 acres in a large city. Bachelor's degrees are offered.

ALTERNATIVE ADMISSIONS:
Contact: Carmen Brown, Director of Admissions (305) 348-2363

Florida International University has a policy for alternative admissions students.

ADMISSION POLICIES:
- New students are eligible for alternative admissions
- Requirements for admission as a freshman:
  940 — average combined verbal and math SAT
  21 — average ACT
  2.7 — average GPA
Other considerations: essay/personal statement

ACADEMIC COURSEWORK AND RELATED FEATURES:
- Support services: freshman orientation, college survival skills, academic advising, drug/alcohol counseling, women's center, psychological counseling, academic skills center, study technique workshops, career advising, peer counseling, health center, aptitude testing, extended time for tests
- Students are not required to work with tutors
- Group and one-on-one tutoring by peer tutors in all academic areas
- Counseling is not required
- Students are assigned an academic adviser. None of the advisers serve alternative admissions students exclusively. Students meet with advisers 1–2 times per semester
- Placement testing is required in essay writing, math, trigonometry, and foreign language
- Alternative admissions students do not take separate classes
- Students are not limited to credit load

OTHER FEATURES/ACCOMMODATIONS:
- On-campus housing is available, but is not guaranteed for alternative admissions students
- A meal plan is available
- Financial aid is available

DEADLINES:
- Rolling admission
- April 15 for financial aid

Stacy Needle

FORT LEWIS COLLEGE

>>>>>>>>>>>>>>>>>>>>>>>>>>

Durango, CO 81301
(303) 247-7184

$1,348 In-State Tuition and Fees
$4,692 Out-of-State Tuition and Fees
$ 950 Average Double Room
$1,534 Average Meal Plan

3,700 full-time undergraduates, 200 part-time
   undergraduates
22:1 student/faculty ratio
39% of undergraduates study arts/humanities

>>

Founded in 1911, Fort Lewis College is a public institution, coed. Located on 600 acres in a town 220 miles from Albuquerque, New Mexico. Associate's and bachelor's degrees are offered.

ALTERNATIVE ADMISSIONS:

Contact: Sheri Rochford, Director of Admissions (303) 247-7184

Fort Lewis College has a policy for alternative admissions students.

ADMISSION POLICIES:

- New and transfer students are eligible for alternative admissions
- Admission considerations—new student: SAT or ACT scores, high school GPA, high school rank
- Requirements for admission as a transfer student: 2.0 — minimum GPA

Other considerations: number of credits completed

ACADEMIC COURSEWORK AND RELATED FEATURES:

- Support services: freshman orientation, academic advising, drug/alcohol counseling, psychological counseling, academic skills center, study technique workshops, health center, extended time for tests
- Students are not required to work with tutors
- One-on-one tutoring by peer tutors in all academic areas
- Counseling is not required
- Students are assigned an academic adviser. None of the advisers serve alternative admissions students exclusively. Students meet with advisers at least 1 time per semester
- Placement testing is required in math and English

- Alternative admissions students do not take separate classes
- Students are not limited to credit load

REQUIRED COURSES:

- Minimum of 2.0 GPA required to stay at college; if below 2.0 GPA, a student is subject to academic probation or suspension

OTHER FEATURES/ACCOMMODATIONS:

- On-campus housing is available, but is not guaranteed for alternative admissions students
- A meal plan is available
- Financial aid is available

DEADLINES:

- Rolling admission
- April 15 for financial aid

GANNON UNIVERSITY

>>>>>>>>>>>>>>>>>>>>>>>>>>

Erie, PA 16541
(814) 871-7407

$7,000 Tuition and Fees
$1,750 Average Double Room
$1,750 Average Meal Plan

2,355 full-time undergraduates, 860 part-time
   undergraduates
15:1 student/faculty ratio
20% of undergraduates study business

>>

Founded in 1925, Gannon University is a private institution, coed, affiliated with the Roman Catholic church. Located in a small city 100 miles from Cleveland, Ohio. Associate's and bachelor's degrees are offered.

ALTERNATIVE ADMISSIONS:

Contact: Ellen Schumann, Director of General Studies (814) 871-7330

Gannon University has a structured program, General Studies, initiated in 1989 for alternative admissions students. The formal program of studies begins in the fall and lasts for 1–3 semesters.

The Other Route into College

ADMISSION POLICIES:

- New students are eligible for alternative admissions, with a limit of 36 students. There is a wait list

- Requirements for admission as a freshman:
  400 — average verbal SAT
  367 — average math SAT
  2.1 — average GPA
Other considerations: high school rank, type of high school attended, difficulty of high school courses taken

ACADEMIC COURSEWORK AND RELATED FEATURES:

- Support services: freshman orientation, college survival skills, academic advising, psychological counseling, academic skills center, study technique workshops, career advising, peer counseling, health center
- Students are not required to work with tutors
- Group and one-on-one tutoring by peer tutors as well as professional tutors in all academic areas
- Counseling is not required
- Students are assigned an academic adviser. All advisers serve alternative admissions students exclusively. Students meet with advisers at least 4 times per semester
- Placement testing is required in English, math, and reading
- Students take an average of 20% of their classes with alternative admissions students only
- Alternative admissions classes average 16 students
- Students are limited to a credit load of 16 credits per semester

REQUIRED COURSES:

Self-Development (credit-bearing)—alternative admissions students only

- Courses required of students who demonstrate deficiency:
  Introduction to Composition (credit-bearing)
  Algebra Refresher (credit-bearing)

- Remedial courses are calculated in GPA
- Minimum of 2.0 GPA required to stay in program; if below 2.0 GPA, after the third semester, a student is asked to leave the program

PROFILE OF ALTERNATIVE ADMISSIONS STUDENTS:

- 100% enter as new students
- 8% minority, 22% female
- 72% state residents, no international students
- None 25 years or older
- No intercollegiate athletes
- 5% learning disabled
- None in top 50% of high school class

OTHER FEATURES/ACCOMMODATIONS:

- On-campus housing is available and is guaranteed for alternative admissions students
- A meal plan is available
- Financial aid is available

DEADLINES:

- Rolling admission—3 weeks after application is sent, notification of admission
- February 28 for financial aid
- May 1 for reply date

GENEVA COLLEGE
>>>>>>>>>>>>>>>>>>>>>>>>>>>>>>

Beaver Falls, PA 15010
(412) 847-6500

$6,670 Tuition and Fees
$3,250 Average Double Room and Meal Plan

1,061 full-time undergraduates, 203 part-time
  undergraduates
20:1 student/faculty ratio
28% of undergraduates study business

>>

Founded in 1848, Geneva College is a private institution, coed, affiliated with the Reformed Presbyterian Church of North America. Located on 50 acres in a small city 35 miles from Pittsburgh. Associate's and bachelor's degrees are offered.

ALTERNATIVE ADMISSIONS:

Contact: Robin Ware, Director of Admissions (412) 847-6500

Geneva College has a structured program, Program for Adults Continuing Education (PACE), for alternative admissions students. The formal program of studies begins in the fall and lasts for 1 year; however, students can also enter the program in the spring and continue for 1 year.

ADMISSION POLICIES:

- New and transfer students are eligible for alternative admissions

- Admission based on individual criteria

Stacy Needle

ACADEMIC COURSEWORK AND RELATED FEATURES:

- Support services: freshman orientation, college survival skills, academic advising, drug/alcohol counseling, psychological counseling, study technique workshops, career advising, health center, aptitude testing, extended time for tests
- Students are not required to work with tutors
- Group and one-on-one tutoring by peer tutors
- Counseling is not required
- Students are not assigned an academic adviser
- Placement testing is required in English, math, and speech
- Alternative admissions students do not take separate classes
- Students are not limited to credit load

PROFILE OF ALTERNATIVE ADMISSIONS STUDENTS:

- 20 alternative admissions students enrolled

OTHER FEATURES/ACCOMMODATIONS:

- On-campus housing is available and is guaranteed for alternative admissions students
- On-campus housing is required of alternative admissions students
- A meal plan is available. It is required of alternative admissions students
- Financial aid is not available

DEADLINES:

- Rolling admission

GEORGE FOX COLLEGE

▶▶▶▶▶▶▶▶▶▶▶▶▶▶▶▶▶▶▶▶▶▶▶▶▶▶

Newberg, OR 97132
(503) 538-8383, Ext. 234

$7,585 Tuition and Fees
$1,560 Average Double Room
$1,560 Average Meal Plan

901 full-time undergraduates, 23 part-time undergraduates
16:1 student/faculty ratio
35% of undergraduates study arts/humanities

▶▶

Founded in 1891, George Fox College is a private institution, coed, affiliated with the Northwest Yearly Meeting of Friends Church (Quaker). Located on 60 acres in a town 23 miles from Portland. Bachelor's degrees are offered.

ALTERNATIVE ADMISSIONS:

Contact: Bonnie Jerke, Director of Academic Success Program (503) 538-8383

George Fox College has a structured program, Academic Success Program, initiated in 1985 for alternative admissions students. The formal program of studies begins in the fall and lasts for 1 semester. Eighty-six percent of the students complete the program in that time.

ADMISSION POLICIES:

- New students are eligible for alternative admissions, with a limit of 25 students. There is a wait list

- Requirements for admission as a freshman:
  260 — minimum verbal SAT
  260 — minimum math SAT
  2.01 — minimum GPA
Other considerations: interview with admissions counselor, essay/personal statement, letters of recommendation

ACADEMIC COURSEWORK AND RELATED FEATURES:

- Support services: freshman orientation, college survival skills, academic advising, drug/alcohol counseling, psychological counseling, academic skills center, study technique workshops, career advising, peer counseling, health center, aptitude testing, extended time for tests
- Separate new-student orientation
- Group and one-on-one tutoring by peer tutors
- Counseling is not required
- Students are assigned an academic adviser. All advisers serve alternative admissions students exclusively. Students meet with advisers 15 times per semester
- Placement testing is not required
- A total of 57 full-time faculty at the institution
- Three faculty members assigned to the program, who are trained to work with alternative admissions students
- Students take an average of 14% of their classes with alternative admissions students only
- Alternative admissions classes average 12 students
- Students are limited to a credit load of 14 credits per semester through fall semester of freshman year

The Other Route into College

REQUIRED COURSES:

Effective College Learner (credit-bearing)—alternative admissions students only

• Required courses are calculated in GPA

PROFILE OF ALTERNATIVE ADMISSIONS STUDENTS:

• 25 alternative admissions students enrolled
• 63% of accepted students enrolled
• 100% enter as new students
• 16% minority, 44% female
• 52% state residents, no international students
• None 25 years or older
• 24% intercollegiate athletes, Division NAIA sports available:
  soccer, cross-country, basketball, baseball, track (men)
  volleyball, cross-country, basketball, softball, track (women)
• 24% learning disabled
• 8% in top 50% of high school class
• 34% graduate within 4 years
• 36% graduate within 5 years

OTHER FEATURES/ACCOMMODATIONS:

• On-campus housing is available and is guaranteed for alternative admissions students
• On-campus housing is required of alternative admissions students
• A meal plan is available. It is required of alternative admissions students
• Financial aid is available

DEADLINES:

• Rolling admission
• March 1 for financial aid

GEORGIA COLLEGE

>>>>>>>>>>>>>>>>>>>>>>>>>>>>

Milledgeville, GA 30161
(912) 453-5234

$1,098 In-State Tuition and Fees
$2,882 Out-of-State Tuition and Fees
$ 612 Average Double Room
$ 740 Average Meal Plan

Stacy Needle

2,198 full-time undergraduates, 378 part-time undergraduates
10:1 student/faculty ratio
35% of undergraduates study education

>>

Founded in 1889, Georgia College is a public institution, coed. Located on 46 acres in a small city 33 miles from Macon. Bachelor's degrees are offered

ALTERNATIVE ADMISSIONS:

Contact: Dr. John Britt, Chairperson of Developmental Studies (912) 453-5016

Georgia College has a structured program, Developmental Studies, for alternative admissions students. The formal program of studies begins in the fall and lasts for a maximum of 3 quarters; however, students can also enter the program in the spring and continue for a maximum of 3 quarters

ADMISSION POLICIES:

• New and transfer students are eligible for alternative admissions

• Requirements for admission as a freshman:
  250 — minimum verbal SAT
  280 — minimum math SAT
  1.8 — minimum GPA
Other considerations: ACT scores (in place of SAT)

• Requirements for admission as a transfer student:
  1.5 — minimum GPA
Other considerations: type of college attended, number of credits completed (less than 20 credits)

ACADEMIC COURSEWORK AND RELATED FEATURES:

• Support services: freshman orientation, college survival skills, academic advising, drug/alcohol counseling, women's center, academic skills center, career advising, peer counseling, health center, aptitude testing, extended time for tests
• Separate new-student orientation
• Students are not required to work with tutors
• Group and one-on-one tutoring by peer tutors as well as professional tutors in math, English, and reading
• Counseling is not required
• Students are assigned an academic adviser. Ninety percent of the advisers serve alternative admissions students exclusively. Students meet with advisers at least 1 time per semester
• Placement testing is required
• A total of 100 full-time faculty at the institution

- Six faculty members assigned to the program, who are trained to work with alternative admissions students
- Students take all of their classes with alternative admissions students
- Alternative admissions classes average 20–25 students
- Students are not limited to credit load

REQUIRED COURSES:

- Courses required of students who demonstrate deficiency:
  Developmental Studies Math (noncredit)—alternative admissions students only
  Developmental Studies Reading (noncredit)—alternative admissions students only
  Developmental Studies English (noncredit)—alternative admissions students only

PROFILE OF ALTERNATIVE ADMISSIONS STUDENTS:

- 350 alternative admissions students enrolled
- 70% of accepted students enrolled
- 4% of the students transfer to another college after freshman year, 5% transfer after sophomore year
- 17% minority, 60% female
- 84% state residents, 4% international students
- 35% 25 years or older
- 75% in top 50% of high school class

OTHER FEATURES/ACCOMMODATIONS:

- On-campus housing is available, but is not guaranteed for alternative admissions students
- A meal plan is available
- Financial aid is available

DEADLINES:

- September 1 for admission
- February 1 for financial aid
- September 1 for reply date

GEORGIA STATE UNIVERSITY

>>>>>>>>>>>>>>>>>>>>>>>>>>>>

Atlanta, GA 30303-3085
(404) 651-2365

$2,880–$3,600 In-State Tuition and Fees
$ 840–$1,050 Out-of-State Tuition and Fees

3,850 full-time undergraduates, 11,560 part-time undergraduates
22:1 student/faculty ratio
38% of undergraduates study business

>>

Founded in 1913, Georgia State University is a public institution, coed. Located on 17 acres in a large city. Bachelor's degrees are offered.

ALTERNATIVE ADMISSIONS:

Contact: Dr. Joan Elifson, Director of Developmental Studies (404) 651-3360

Georgia State University has a structured program, Developmental Studies, initiated in 1975 for alternative admissions students. The formal program of studies begins in the fall and lasts for a maximum of 4 quarters; however, students can also enter the program in the spring and continue for a maximum of 4 quarters.

ADMISSION POLICIES:

- New students are eligible for alternative admissions

- Requirements for admission as a freshman:
  280 — minimum verbal SAT
  250 — minimum math SAT
  1.8 — minimum GPA
Other considerations: difficulty of high school courses taken, state residence

ACADEMIC COURSEWORK AND RELATED FEATURES:

- Support services: freshman orientation, college survival skills, academic advising, drug/alcohol counseling, women's center, psychological counseling, academic skills center, study technique workshops, career advising, health center, aptitude testing
- Separate new-student orientation
- Students are not required to work with tutors
- Academic counseling is required
- Students are not assigned an academic adviser
- Placement testing is required in English, reading, and math

The Other Route into College

- A total of 877 full-time faculty at the institution
- Twenty-two faculty members assigned to the program, who are trained to work with alternative admissions students
- Students take all of their classes with alternative admissions students only
- Courses are also offered in the evening
- Students are not limited to credit load

REQUIRED COURSES:

- Courses required of students who demonstrate deficiency:
  Developmental English (noncredit)—alternative admissions students only
  Developmental Math (noncredit)—alternative admissions students only
  Developmental Reading (noncredit)—alternative admissions students only

PROFILE OF ALTERNATIVE ADMISSIONS STUDENTS:

- 816 alternative admissions students enrolled
- 100% of accepted students enrolled
- 100% enter as new students
- 40% minority, 61% female
- 97% state residents
- 9% 25 years or older
- 1% learning disabled

OTHER FEATURES/ACCOMMODATIONS:

- On-campus housing is not available for alternative admissions students
- A meal plan is not available
- Financial aid is available

DEADLINES:

- Rolling admission

GOLDEY-BEACOM COLLEGE

>>>>>>>>>>>>>>>>>>>>>>>>>>

Wilmington, DE 19808
(302) 998-8814

$4,500 Tuition and Fees
$2,300 Average Double Room and Meal Plan

Stacy Needle

1,100 full-time undergraduates, 1,100 part-time undergraduates
30:1 student/faculty ratio
100% of undergraduates study business

>>

Founded in 1886, Goldey-Beacom College is a private institution, coed. Located on 30 acres in a small city. Associate's and bachelor's degrees are offered.

ALTERNATIVE ADMISSIONS:

Contact: S. Hale Humphery, Director of Admissions
(302) 998-8814

Goldey-Beacom College has a structured program, Probational Acceptance, initiated in 1976 for alternative admissions students. The formal program of studies begins in the fall and lasts for approximately 1 semester.

ADMISSION POLICIES:

- New and transfer students are eligible for alternative admissions

- Requirements for admission as a freshman:
  320 — average verbal SAT
  350 — average math SAT
  2.0 — average GPA

- Requirements for admission as a transfer student:
  2.0 — average GPA

ACADEMIC COURSEWORK AND RELATED FEATURES:

- Support services: freshman orientation, college survival skills, academic advising, drug/alcohol counseling, psychological counseling, academic skills center, study technique workshops, career advising, peer counseling, health center, aptitude testing, extended time for tests
- Students are not required to work with tutors
- One-on-one tutoring by peer tutors as well as professional tutors in all academic areas
- Counseling is not required
- Students are assigned an academic adviser
- Placement testing is required
- Students take all of their classes with alternative admissions students only
- Alternative admissions classes average 20–30 students
- Students are limited to a credit load of 12 credits per semester until they attain a 2.0 GPA

REQUIRED COURSES:

- Remedial courses required:
  Reading and Study Skills (credit-bearing)—alternative admissions students only

Basic English Principles (credit-bearing)—alternative admissions students only

Basic Arithmetic (credit-bearing)—alternative admissions students only

- Remedial courses are calculated in GPA

PROFILE OF ALTERNATIVE ADMISSIONS STUDENTS:

- 10 alternative admissions students enrolled
- 20% of accepted students enrolled
- 93% enter as new students, 7% as transfer students
- 46% minority, 67% female
- 27% state residents, 7% international students
- None 25 years or older
- No intercollegiate athletes
- 20% in top 50% of high school class

OTHER FEATUERS/ACCOMMODATIONS:

- On-campus housing is available, but is not guaranteed for alternative admissions students
- A meal plan is available
- Financial aid is not available

DEADLINES:

- Rolling admission—1 month after application is sent, notification of admission
- March 31 for financial aid
- May 1 for reply date

GRAND VALLEY STATE UNIVERSITY

>>>>>>>>>>>>>>>>>>>>>>>>>>

Allendale, MI 49401
(616) 895-2025

$1,245 In-State Tuition and Fees
$2,271 Out-of-State Tuition and Fees
$3,340 Average Double Room and Meal Plan

6,368 full-time undergraduates, 2,463 part-time undergraduates
23:1 student/faculty ratio

>>

Founded in 1960, Grand Valley State University is a public institution, coed. Located on 800 acres in a rural community 12 miles from Grand Rapids. Bachelor's degrees are offered.

ALTERNATIVE ADMISSIONS:

Contact: Jo Ann Foerster, Director of Admissions (616) 895-2025

Grand Valley State University has a policy, Non-Degree Status, for alternative admissions students.

ADMISSION POLICIES:

- New and transfer students are eligible for alternative admissions
- Admission considerations—new student: high school GPA
- Students who are 21 years of age or have been graduated from high school at least 3 years are eligible for Non-Degree Status
- Admission considerations—transfer student: GPA at previous institution, number of credits completed
- Transfer students are eligible for Non-Degree Status if they are not on academic probation at their home institution

ACADEMIC COURSEWORK AND RELATED FEATURES:

- Support services: drug/alcohol counseling, psychological counseling, academic skills center, study technique workshops, career advising, extended time for tests
- Students are not required to work with tutors
- Group and one-on-one tutoring by peer tutors as well as professional tutors in all academic areas
- Counseling is not required
- Students are not assigned an academic adviser
- Placement testing is not required
- Alternative admissions students do not take separate classes
- Students are not limited to credit load

OTHER FEATURES/ACCOMMODATIONS:

- On-campus housing is available, but is not guaranteed for alternative admissions students
- A meal plan is available

DEADLINES:

- Rolling admission

The Other Route into College

GREEN MOUNTAIN COLLEGE

>>>>>>>>>>>>>>>>>>>>>>>>>>>

Poultney, VT 05764
(802) 287-9313

$11,310 Tuition and Fees, Average Double Room,
and Average Meal Plan

600 full-time undergraduates, 30 part-time
undergraduates
14:1 student/faculty ratio
51% of undergraduates study business

>>

Founded in 1834, Green Mountain College is a private
institution, coed. Located on 155 acres in a town 20
miles from Rutland. Bachelor's degrees are offered.

ALTERNATIVE ADMISSIONS:

Contact: Jeanette Marcy, Instructor of Developmental
Studies (802) 287-9313

Green Mountain College has a structured program, The
Skills Advancement Program, initiated in 1984 for alternative admissions students. The formal program of
studies begins in the fall and lasts 1–3 semesters.

ADMISSION POLICIES:

- New and transfer students are eligible for alternative
  admissions

- Requirements for admission as a freshman:
  320 — minimum verbal SAT
  320 — minimum math SAT
      or
  15 — minimum ACT

  1.75 — minimum GPA
Other considerations: high school rank, type of high
school attended, difficulty of high school courses taken,
essay/personal statement, letters of recommendation

- Requirements for admission as a transfer student:
  2.0 — minimum GPA
Other considerations: difficulty of coursework, type of
college attended, essay/personal statement, letters of
recommendation

ACADEMIC COURSEWORK AND RELATED FEATURES:

- Support services: freshman orientation, college survival skills, academic advising, drug/alcohol counseling, women's center, psychological counseling,
  academic skills center, study technique workshops,
  career advising, peer counseling, health center, aptitude testing
- Students are not required to work with tutors
- Group and one-on-one tutoring by peer tutors as well
  as professional tutors in all academic areas
- Counseling is not required
- Students are assigned an academic adviser
- Placement testing is required in math and verbal
  skills
- A total of 45 full-time faculty at the institution
- Four faculty members assigned to the program, who
  are trained to work with alternative admissions stu-
  dents
- Alternative admissions students do not take separate
  classes

REQUIRED COURSES:

- Remedial courses required:
  Foundations of English (noncredit)
  Foundations of Math (noncredit)

PROFILE OF ALTERNATIVE ADMISSIONS STUDENTS:

- 60 alternative admissions students enrolled
- 45% of accepted students enrolled
- 2% minority, 45% female
- 5% state residents, no international students
- 1% 25 years or older
- 60% in top 50% of high school class

OTHER FEATURES/ACCOMMODATIONS:

- On-campus housing is available and is guaranteed for
  alternative admissions students
- On-campus housing is required of alternative admissions students
- A meal plan is available. It is required of alternative
  admissions students
- Financial aid is available

DEADLINES:

- Rolling admission—3–4 weeks after application is
  sent, notification of admission
- February 15 for financial aid
- May 1 for reply date

The program is best suited for a student who has the
ability to succeed in college, yet needs to strengthen
his/her skills and motivation level.

Stacy Needle

GWYNEDD-MERCY COLLEGE

>>>>>>>>>>>>>>>>>>>>>>>>>>

Gwynedd Valley, PA 19437
(215) 641-5510

$6,650 Tuition and Fees
$3,500 Average Double Room and Meal Plan

711 full-time undergraduates, 1,223 part-time
   undergraduates
11:1 student/faculty ratio
57% of undergraduates study health sciences

>>

Founded in 1948, Gwynedd-Mercy College is a private
institution, coed, affiliated with the Roman Catholic
church. Located on 170 acres in a town 20 miles from
Philadelphia. Associate's and bachelor's degrees are
offered.

ALTERNATIVE ADMISSIONS:

Contact: Sister Maureen McCann, Assistant Chairperson of Allied Health Division (215) 646-7300, Ext. 476

Gwynedd-Mercy College has a structured summer program, Health Careers Opportunity Program (H.C.O.P.),
initiated in 1988, for alternative admissions students.
The program begins in July and lasts for 5 weeks. One
hundred percent of the students complete the program
in that time.

ADMISSION POLICIES:

- New students are eligible for alternative admissions,
  with a limit of 15 students. There is a wait list

- Requirements for admission as a freshman:
  365 — average verbal SAT
  378 — average math SAT
Other considerations: ACT scores (in place of SAT),
high school rank, letters of recommendation, financial
need, minority status

ACADEMIC COURSEWORK AND RELATED FEATURES:

- Support services: freshman orientation, college survival skills, academic advising, psychological counseling, career advising, peer counseling, health center
- Students are required to work with tutors 4 hours
  per week
- Group tutoring in math, reading, and writing
- Counseling is not required

- Students are assigned an academic adviser. All advis-
  ers serve alternative admissions students exclu-
  sively. Students meet with advisers 1 time per
  semester
- Placement testing is not required
- A total of 91 full-time faculty at the institution
- Five faculty members assigned to the program
- Students take classes with alternative admissions
  students
- Alternative admissions classes average 20 students
- Students are limited to a credit load of 12 credits per
  semester through spring semester of freshman year

REQUIRED COURSES:

- Remedial courses required:
  Basic Skills Math (noncredit)—alternative admis-
    sions students only
  Basic Skills Reading (noncredit)—alternative admis-
    sions students only
  Basic Skills Writing (noncredit)—alternative admis-
    sions students only

PROFILE OF ALTERNATIVE ADMISSIONS STUDENTS:

- 20 alternative admissions students enrolled
- 3% of accepted students enrolled
- 100% enter as new students
- 100% minority, 83% female
- 100% state residents, no international students
- None 25 years or older
- No intercollegiate athletes
- No learning disabled
- 35% in top 50% of high school class

OTHER FEATURES/ACCOMMODATIONS:

- On-campus housing is available and is guaranteed for
  alternative admissions students
- A meal plan is available
- Financial aid is available

DEADLINES:

- Rolling admission
- March 1 for financial aid
- July 1 for reply date

The Other Route into College

GWYNEDD-MERCY COLLEGE

>>>>>>>>>>>>>>>>>>>>>>>>>>>>

Gwynedd Valley, PA 19437
(215) 641-5510

$6,650 Tuition and Fees
$3,500 Average Double Room and Meal Plan

711 full-time undergraduates, 1,223 part-time
 undergraduates
11:1 student/faculty ratio
57% of undergraduates study health sciences

>>

Founded in 1948, Gwynedd-Mercy College is a private
institution, coed, affiliated with the Roman Catholic
church. Located on 170 acres in a town 20 miles from
Philadelphia. Associate's and bachelor's degrees are
offered.

ALTERNATIVE ADMISSIONS:

Contact: Marjorie DeSimone, Dean of Admissions (215)
641-5510

Gwynedd-Mercy College has a structured program,
Entry Program, initiated in 1988 for alternative admissions students. The formal program of studies begins
in the fall and lasts for 1 year.

ADMISSION POLICIES:

- New students are eligible for alternative admissions,
  with a limit of 20 students. There is a wait list

- Requirements for admission as a freshman:
  365 — average verbal SAT
  378 — average math SAT
Other considerations: ACT scores (in place of SAT),
high school rank, letters of recommendation

ACADEMIC COURSEWORK AND RELATED FEATURES:

- Support services: freshman orientation, college survival skills, academic advising, psychological counseling, career advising, peer counseling, health center
- Students are required to work with tutors 4 hours
  per week
- Group tutoring in math, reading, and writing
- Counseling is not required
- Students are assigned an academic adviser. All advisers serve alternative admissions students exclusively. Students meet with advisers 1 time per
  semester

- Placement testing is not required
- A total of 91 full-time faculty at the institution
- Two faculty members assigned to the program
- Students take classes with alternative admissions
  students
- Alternative admissions classes average 20 students
- Students are limited to a credit load of 12 credits per
  semester through spring semester of freshman year

REQUIRED COURSES:

- Remedial courses required:
  Basic Skills Math (noncredit)—alternative admissions students only
  Basic Skills Reading (noncredit)—alternative admissions students only
  Basic Skills Writing (noncredit)—alternative admissions students only

PROFILE OF ALTERNATIVE ADMISSIONS STUDENTS:

- 20 alternative admissions students enrolled
- 3% of accepted students enrolled
- 100% enter as new students
- 20% minority, 85% female
- 96% state residents, no international students
- 1% 25 years or older
- No intercollegiate athletes
- No learning disabled
- 35% in top 50% of high school class

OTHER FEATURES/ACCOMMODATIONS:

- On-campus housing is available and is guaranteed for
  alternative admissions students
- A meal plan is available
- Financial aid is available

DEADLINES:

- Rolling admission
- March 1 for financial aid
- August 1 for reply date

Stacy Needle

HARDING UNIVERSITY

>>>>>>>>>>>>>>>>>>>>>>>>>>

Searcy, AR 72143
(800) 632-4751 (in Arkansas)
(800) 643-3792 (outside Arkansas)

$4,000 Tuition and Fees
$1,000 Average Double Room
$2,000 Average Meal Plan

2,900 full-time undergraduates, 300 part-time
   undergraduates
17:1 student/faculty ratio
27% of undergraduates study business

>>

Founded in 1924, Harding University is a private institution, coed. Located on 200 acres in a town 45 miles
from Little Rock. Bachelor's degrees are offered.

ALTERNATIVE ADMISSIONS:

Contact: Linda Thompson, Director of Program for Academic Success (501) 279-4416

Harding University has a structured summer program,
Program for Academic Success, initiated in 1986 for
alternative admissions students. The program begins in
June and lasts for 6 weeks. Fifty percent of the students
complete the program in that time.

ADMISSION POLICIES:

• New students are eligible for alternative admissions,
  with a limit of 30 students. There is a wait list

• Requirements for admission as a freshman:
     14 — minimum ACT
Other considerations: SAT scores (in place of ACT),
high school GPA, letters of recommendation

ACADEMIC COURSEWORK AND RELATED FEATURES:

• Support services: freshman orientation, college survival skills, academic advising, drug/alcohol counseling, psychological counseling, academic skills center,
  study technique workshops, career advising, health
  center, aptitude testing
• Separate new-student orientation
• Group and one-on-one tutoring by peer tutors in all
  academic areas
• Academic and career counseling is required
• Students are assigned an academic adviser. All advisers serve alternative admissions students exclusively
• Placement testing is required in reading, algebra,
  arithmetic, and sentence structure

• A total of 180 full-time faculty at the institution
• Five faculty members assigned to the program, who
  are trained to work with alternative admissions students
• Students take classes with alternative admissions
  students only
• Alternative admissions classes average 20 students

REQUIRED COURSES:

• Remedial courses required:
  Effective College Reading and Lab (credit-bearing)—
     alternative admissions students only
  Critical Reading/Reasoning and Lab (credit-bearing)
     —alternative admissions students only
  Basic English (credit-bearing)—alternative admis-
     sions students only
  Beginning Algebra (credit-bearing)—alternative ad-
     missions students only
  Grammar and Composition (credit-bearing)
  Intermediate Algebra (credit-bearing)

• Other required courses:
  Study Skills/Personal Development (credit-bearing)
     —alternative admissions students only

• Remedial courses are calculated in GPA
• Required courses are calculated in GPA

PROFILE OF ALTERNATIVE ADMISSIONS STUDENTS:

• 50 alternative admissions students enrolled
• 100% enter as new students
• 70% female
• 30% state residents

OTHER FEATURES/ACCOMMODATIONS:

• On-campus housing is available and is guaranteed for
  alternative admissions students
• On-campus housing is required of alternative admissions students
• A meal plan is available. It is required of alternative
  admissions students
• Financial aid is available

DEADLINES:

• Rolling admission
• April 1 for financial aid
• June 30 for reply date

The program is best suited for a student who needs to
build his/her skills in reading, writing, math, and study
skills.

HOFSTRA UNIVERSITY

>>>>>>>>>>>>>>>>>>>>>>>>>>

Hempstead, NY 11550
(516) 560-6700

$8,430 Tuition and Fees
$2,440 Average Double Room
$2,040 Average Meal Plan

7,100 full-time undergraduates, 2,000 part-time
  undergraduates
17:1 student/faculty ratio
45% of undergraduates study business

>>

Founded in 1935, Hofstra University is a private institution, coed. Located on 240 acres in a town 25 miles from
New York City. Bachelor's degrees are offered.

ALTERNATIVE ADMISSIONS:

Contact: Dr. Ignacio Gotz, Director of Division of Special Studies (516) 560-5840

Hofstra University has a structured program, Division
of Special Studies, initiated in 1973 for alternative admissions students. The formal program of studies begins in the fall and lasts for 1 year; however, students
can also enter the program in the spring and continue
for 1 year. Ninety-five percent of the students complete
the program in that time.

ADMISSION POLICIES:

- New students are eligible for alternative admissions,
  with a limit of 100 students. There is a wait list.

- Requirements for admission as a freshman:
  800 — minimum combined verbal and math SAT
        or
  19 — minimum ACT
Other considerations: high school GPA, high school
rank, type of high school attended, difficulty of high
school courses taken, interview with admissions counselor

ACADEMIC COURSEWORK AND RELATED FEATURES:

- Support services: freshman orientation, college survival skills, academic advising, drug/alcohol counseling, psychological counseling, academic skills center,
  study technique workshops, career advising, peer
  counseling, health center, extended time for tests (if
  learning disabled)
- Separate new-student orientation

- Students are not required to work with tutors
- Counseling is not required
- Students are assigned an academic adviser. All advis-
  ers serve alternative admissions students exclusively
- Placement testing is not required
- Students take all of their classes with alternative
  admissions students only
- Alternative admissions classes average 24 students
- Students are not limited to credit load

REQUIRED COURSES:

- Minimum of 2.0 GPA required to stay in program; if
  below 2.0 GPA, a student may be academically dismissed

PROFILE OF ALTERNATIVE ADMISSIONS STUDENTS:

- 100 alternative admissions students enrolled
- 50% of accepted students enrolled
- 100% enter as new students
- Approximately 5% of the students transfer to another college after freshman year
- 5% minority, 52% female
- 60% state residents, 1% international students
- None 25 years or older
- 5% intercollegiate athletes
- 10% learning disabled
- 65% graduate within 4 years

OTHER FEATURES/ACCOMMODATIONS:

- On-campus housing is available and is guaranteed for
  alternative admissions students
- A meal plan is available
- Financial aid is available

DEADLINES:

- Rolling admission
- May 1 for reply date

The program is best suited for an underachiever in high
school who had poor grades in ninth and tenth grades,
but an improving academic record in eleventh and
twelfth grades.

Stacy Needle

70

HOUGHTON COLLEGE

>>>>>>>>>>>>>>>>>>>>>>>>>>>>

Houghton, NY 14744
(716) 567-2211

$7,468 Tuition and Fees
$1,360 Average Double Room
$1,540 Average Meal Plan

1,107 full-time undergraduates, 57 part-time
  undergraduates
14:1 student/faculty ratio
26% of undergraduates study education

>>

Founded in 1883, Houghton College is a private institution, coed, affiliated with the Wesleyan church. Located
on 1,300 acres in a rural community, 55 miles from
Buffalo. Associate's and bachelor's degrees are offered.

ALTERNATIVE ADMISSIONS:

Contact: Richard Wing, Coordinator of Achievement
Program (716) 567-2211

Houghton College has a structured program, Achievement, initiated in 1982 for alternative admissions students. The formal program of studies begins in the fall
and lasts approximately 1 year.

ADMISSION POLICIES:

- New students are eligible for alternative admissions,
  with a limit of 35 students. There is a wait list

- Requirements for admission as a freshman:
  392 — average verbal SAT
  423 — average math SAT
   38 — average TSWE
       or
   16 — average ACT
Other considerations: high school GPA, high school
rank, type of high school attended, difficulty of high
school courses taken, letters of recommendation

ACADEMIC COURSEWORK AND RELATED FEATURES:

- Support services: freshman orientation, college
  survival skills, academic advising, psychological
  counseling, academic skills center, study technique
  workshops, career advising, peer counseling, health
  center, aptitude testing
- Students are required to work with tutors 4–5 hours
  per week
- Group and one-on-one tutoring by peer tutors in psychology, math, history, and writing

- Counseling is not required
- Students are assigned an academic adviser. None of
  the advisers serve alternative admissions students
  exclusively. Students meet with advisers 5 times per
  semester
- Placement testing is not required
- Students take an average of 35% of their classes with
  alternative admissions students only
- Alternative admissions classes average 18 students
- Students are limited to a credit load of 13 credits per
  semester through spring semester of freshman year

REQUIRED COURSES:

English Composition (credit-bearing)—alternative admissions students only
Study Skills (credit-bearing)—alternative admissions
students only

- Required courses are calculated in GPA
- Minimum of 1.5 GPA required to stay in program; if
  below 1.5 GPA, a student is placed on academic probation

PROFILE OF ALTERNATIVE ADMISSIONS STUDENTS:

- 34 alternative admissions students enrolled
- 52% of accepted students enrolled
- 100% enter as new students
- 5% of the students transfer to another college after
  freshman year, 11% transfer after sophomore year
- 11% minority, 55% female
- 70% state residents, no international students
- None 25 years or older
- 14% intercollegiate athletes, Division NAIA sports
  available:
  basketball, track and field, cross-country, soccer
    (men)
  basketball, field hockey, cross-country, track and
    field, soccer, volleyball (women)
- 1% learning disabled
- 87% in top 50% of high school class
- 49% graduate within 4 years

OTHER FEATURES/ACCOMMODATIONS:

- On-campus housing is available and is guaranteed for
  alternative admissions students
- A meal plan is available
- Financial aid is available

DEADLINES:

- Rolling admission
- March 15 for financial aid

The program is best suited for an Evangelical Christian
who is motivated to correct his/her academic deficiencies.

The Other Route into College

HUNTINGTON COLLEGE

>>>>>>>>>>>>>>>>>>>>>>>>>>>>

Huntington, IN 46750
(219) 356-6000

$6,800 Tuition and Fees
$1,620 Average Double Room
$1,100 Average Meal Plan

469 full-time undergraduates, 65 part-time
  undergraduates
13:1 student/faculty ratio
51% of undergraduates study arts/humanities

>>

Founded in 1897, Huntington College is a private insti-
tution, coed, affiliated with the Church of the United
Brethren in Christ. Located on 100 acres in a small city.
Associate's and bachelor's degrees are offered.

ALTERNATIVE ADMISSIONS:

Contact: Jerry Davis, Associate Dean of Students and
Director of Student Counseling Services (219) 356-
6000, Ext. 1027

Huntington College has a structured program, Limited
Load, initiated in 1986 for alternative admissions students. The formal program of studies begins in the fall
and lasts for 10 weeks. Ninety-eight percent of the
students complete the program in that time.

ADMISSION POLICIES:

- New and transfer students are eligible for alternative
  admissions

- Requirements for admission as a freshman:
  330 — average verbal SAT
  370 — average math SAT
   30 — average TSWE
      or
   14 — average ACT

  2.1 — average GPA
  Other considerations: high school rank, difficulty of high
  school courses taken

- Admission considerations—transfer student: GPA at
  previous institution, difficulty of coursework, type of
  college attended, number of credits completed

ACADEMIC COURSEWORK AND RELATED FEATURES:

- Support services: freshman orientation, college survival skills, academic advising, drug/alcohol counseling, psychological counseling, study technique
  workshops, career advising, peer counseling, health
  center, aptitude testing
- Students are not required to work with tutors
- Group and one-on-one tutoring by peer tutors as well
  as professional tutors in most academic areas
- Counseling is required
- Students are assigned an academic adviser. None of
  the advisers serve alternative admissions students
  exclusively. Students meet with advisers 2 times per
  semester
- Placement testing is not required
- Students take classes with alternative admissions
  students only
- Alternative admissions classes average 20 students
- Students are limited to a credit load of 13 credits per
  semester through 10 weeks

REQUIRED COURSES:

- Remedial courses required:
  College Success Seminar (credit-bearing)—alterna-
    tive admissions students only
- Other required courses:
  College Life (credit-bearing)

- Remedial course are calculated in GPA
- Required courses are calculated in GPA

PROFILE OF ALTERNATIVE ADMISSIONS STUDENTS:

- 20 alternative admissions students enrolled
- 60% of accepted students enrolled
- 5% of the students transfer to another college after
  freshman year, 3% transfer after sophomore year
- 2% minority, 40% female
- 85% state residents, 3% international students
- 6% 25 years or older
- 10% intercollegiate athletes
- 1% learning disabled
- 5% in top 50% of high school class

OTHER FEATURES/ACCOMMODATIONS:

- On-campus housing is available, but is not guaranteed
  for alternative admissions students
- A meal plan is available
- Financial aid is available

DEADLINES:

- December 31 for admission; after December 31, applications are reviewed on a space-available basis
- February 15 for financial aid

Stacy Needle

HUSSON COLLEGE

>>>>>>>>>>>>>>>>>>>>>>>>>

Bangor, ME 04401
(207) 947-1121, Ext. 218

$6,700 Tuition and Fees
$3,400 Average Double Room and Meal Plan
572 full-time undergraduates, 1,062 part-time
undergraduates

>>

Founded in 1898, Husson College is a private institution, coed. Located on 215 acres in a town. Associate's and bachelor's degrees are offered.

ALTERNATIVE ADMISSIONS:

Contact: Carlena Bean, Assistant Director of Admissions (207) 947-1121, Ext. 218

Husson College has a structured program, Academic Development, for alternative admissions students.

ADMISSION POLICIES:

• New students are eligible for alternative admissions

• Admission based on individual criteria

ACADEMIC COURSEWORK AND RELATED FEATURES:

• Students are required to work with tutors
• Counseling is available
• Students take classes with alternative admissions students only
• Alternative admissions classes average 10–15 students
• Students are limited to a credit load of 12 credits per semester

REQUIRED COURSES:

• Courses required of students who demonstrate deficiency:
Remedial Math
Remedial English

• Minimum of 1.5 GPA required to stay in program; if below 1.5 GPA, a student is placed on academic probation

OTHER FEATURES/ACCOMMODATIONS:

• On-campus housing is available
• A meal plan is available

DEADLINES:

• Rolling admission

IDAHO STATE UNIVERSITY

>>>>>>>>>>>>>>>>>>>>>>>>>

Pocatello, ID 83209
(208) 236-2475

$1,086 In-State Tuition and Fees
$2,986 Out-of-State Tuition and Fees
$2,378 Average Double Room and Meal Plan

4,645 full-time undergraduates, 1,856 part-time
undergraduates
15:1 student/faculty ratio
24% of undergraduates study math/sciences

>>

Founded in 1901, Idaho State University is a public institution, coed. Located on 735 acres in a town. Associate's and bachelor's degrees are offered.

ALTERNATIVE ADMISSIONS:

Contact: Mike Echamis, Director of Admissions (208) 236-2475

Idaho State University has a policy for alternative admissions students.

ADMISSION POLICIES:

• New and transfer students are eligible for alternative admissions

• Requirements for admission as a freshman:
600 — minimum combined verbal and math SAT
or
12 — minimum ACT
Other considerations: high school GPA, difficulty of high school courses taken

• Requirements for admission as a transfer student:
1.65 — average GPA

ACADEMIC COURSEWORK AND RELATED FEATURES:

• Support services: freshman orientation, college survival skills, academic advising, drug/alcohol counseling, psychological counseling, academic skills center, study technique workshops, career advising, peer counseling, health center, aptitude testing
• Students are not required to work with tutors
• Group and one-on-one tutoring by peer tutors in English, math, and sciences
• Counseling is not required
• Students are assigned an academic adviser. Students meet with advisers 3–4 times per semester

The Other Route into College

- Placement testing is required in English composition and math
- Alternative admissions students do not take separate classes

REQUIRED COURSES:
- Courses required of students who demonstrate deficiency:
  Developmental Algebra (noncredit)
  Developmental Math (noncredit)
  Basic Writing (noncredit)
  Reading and Study Skills (credit-bearing)

PROFILE OF ALTERNATIVE ADMISSIONS STUDENTS:
- 27 alternative admissions students enrolled
- 95% of accepted students enrolled
- 5% minority, 50% female
- 50% state residents, 1% international students
- 60% 25 years or older

OTHER FEATURES/ACCOMMODATIONS:
- On-campus housing is available, but is not guaranteed for alternative admissions students
- A meal plan is available
- Financial aid is available

DEADLINES:
- Rolling admission
- March 15 for financial aid

IMMACULATA COLLEGE

>>>>>>>>>>>>>>>>>>>>>>>>>

Immaculata, PA 19345
(215) 296-9067

$7,100 Tuition and Fees
$4,100 Average Double Room and Meal Plan

800 full-time undergraduates, 900 part-time undergraduates

>>
Founded in 1920, Immaculata College is a private institution, women only, affiliated with the Roman Catholic church. Located on 400 acres in a town 20 miles from Philadelphia. Associate's and bachelor's degrees are offered.

ALTERNATIVE ADMISSIONS:
Contact: Sr. Maria Claudia, Director of Admissions (215) 296-9067

Immaculata College has a policy for alternative admissions students.

ADMISSION POLICIES:
- New students are eligible for alternative admissions, with a limit of 20 students
- Requirements for admission as a freshman:
  350 — minimum verbal SAT
  350 — minimum math SAT
  1.8 — minimum GPA
Other considerations: interview with admissions counselor

ACADEMIC COURSEWORK AND RELATED FEATURES:
- Students are required to work with tutors
- Counseling is available
- Alternative admissions students do not take separate classes
- Students are limited to a credit load of 12 credits per semester through spring semester of freshman year

REQUIRED COURSES:
- Minimum of 2.0 GPA required to stay at college; if below 2.0 GPA, a student is placed on academic probation

PROFILE OF ALTERNATIVE ADMISSIONS STUDENTS:
- 75% of the accepted students enrolled
- 50% graduate within 4 years

OTHER FEATURES/ACCOMMODATIONS:
- On-campus housing is available
- A meal plan is available

DEADLINES:
- Rolling admission

Stacy Needle

INDIANA INSTITUTE OF TECHNOLOGY

▶▶▶▶▶▶▶▶▶▶▶▶▶▶▶▶▶▶▶▶▶▶▶▶▶▶

Fort Wayne, IN 46803
(219) 422-5561, Ext. 205

$5,400 Tuition and Fees
$1,040 Average Double Room
$1,600 Average Meal Plan

460 full-time undergraduates, 230 part-time
  undergraduates
20:1 student/faculty ratio
50% of undergraduates study business

▶▶

Founded in 1930, Indiana Institute of Technology is a
private institution, coed. Located on 25 acres in a small
city 165 miles from Indianapolis. Associate's and bachelor's degrees are offered.

ALTERNATIVE ADMISSIONS:

Contact: Dr. Stephen Rowe, Academic Dean (219) 422-
5561, Ext. 207

Indiana Institute of Technology has a structured program, Freshman College, initiated in 1989 for alternative admissions students. The formal program of
studies begins in the fall and lasts for 1 year; however,
students can also enter the program in the spring and
continue for 1 year.

ADMISSION POLICIES:

- New and transfer students are eligible for alternative
  admissions

- Requirements for admission as a freshman:
  360 — average verbal SAT
  500 — average math SAT
    or
   15 — average ACT

  1.9 — average GPA
Other considerations: high school rank

- Requirements for admission as a transfer student:
  2.0 — minimum GPA
Other considerations: type of college attended

ACADEMIC COURSEWORK AND RELATED FEATURES:

- Support services: freshman orientation, college survival skills, academic advising, drug/alcohol counsel-

ing, psychological counseling, academic skills center,
study technique workshops, career advising, peer
counseling, extended time for tests
- Separate new-student orientation
- Students are required to work with tutors 4–8 hours
  per week
- Group and one-on-one tutoring by peer tutors as well
  as professional tutors in all academic areas
- Academic counseling is required
- Students are assigned an academic adviser. All advisers serve alternative admissions students exclusively. Students meet with advisers 15 times per
  semester
- Placement testing is required in math and English
- A total of 20 full-time faculty at the institution
- Two faculty members assigned to the program
- Alternative admissions students do not take separate
  classes
- Students are limited to a credit load of 12 credits per
  semester until ability to survive academically is evi-
  dent by GPA

REQUIRED COURSES:

- Remedial courses required:
  Developmental Reading (credit-bearing)
  Basic Grammar (credit-bearing)
  Elementary Algebra (credit-bearing)
  Basic Algebra (credit-bearing)
- Other required courses:
  Trigonometry (credit-bearing)

- Remedial courses are calculated in GPA
- Required courses are calculated in GPA
- Minimum of 2.0 GPA required to stay at college; if
  below 2.0 GPA, a student is placed on academic probation

PROFILE OF ALTERNATIVE ADMISSIONS STUDENTS:

- 25% minority, 20% female
- 30% state residents, no international students
- None 25 years or older
- 10% intercollegiate athletes
- 5% learning disabled
- 5% in top 50% of high school class

OTHER FEATURES/ACCOMMODATIONS:

- On-campus housing is available, but is not guaranteed
  for alternative admissions students
- A meal plan is available
- Financial aid is available

DEADLINES:

- Rolling admission
- March 1 for financial aid

The Other Route into College

INDIANA STATE UNIVERSITY

>>>>>>>>>>>>>>>>>>>>>>>>>>

Terre Haute, IN 47809
(812) 237-2121

———

$1,992 In-State Tuition and Fees
$4,720 Out-of-State Tuition and Fees
$2,752 Average Double Room and Meal Plan

8,337 full-time undergraduates, 1,769 part-time
    undergraduates
19:1 student/faculty ratio

>>

Founded in 1865, Indiana State University is a public
institution, coed. Located on 90 acres in a town 75 miles
from Indianapolis. Associate's and bachelor's degrees
are offered.

ALTERNATIVE ADMISSIONS:

Contact: Charles Hedrick, Director of Enrichment and
Learning Skills (812) 237-4135

Indiana State University has a structured program,
Conditional Admission, for alternative admissions students. The formal program of studies begins in the fall
and lasts for 1 semester; however, students can also
enter the program in the spring and continue for 1
semester.

ADMISSION POLICIES:

• New students are eligible for alternative admissions

• Admission considerations: SAT or ACT scores, high
  school GPA, high school rank

ACADEMIC COURSEWORK AND RELATED FEATURES:

• Support services: freshman orientation, college sur-
  vival skills, academic advising, drug/alcohol counsel-
  ing, women's center, psychological counseling,
  academic skills center, career advising, health center
• Students are required to work with tutors
• Students are assigned an academic adviser
• Placement testing is required
• Alternative admissions students do not take separate
  classes
• Students are not limited to credit load

OTHER FEATURES/ACCOMMODATIONS:

• On-campus housing is available, but is not guaranteed
  for alternative admissions students

• A meal plan is available
• Financial aid is available

DEADLINES:

• Rolling admission
• January 1 for financial aid

INDIANA UNIVERSITY OF PENNSYLVANIA

>>>>>>>>>>>>>>>>>>>>>>>>>>

Indiana, PA 15705
(412) 357-2230

———

$2,026 In-State Tuition and Fees
$3,552 Out-of-State Tuition and Fees
$1,244 Average Double Room
$1,106 Average Meal Plan

11,030 full-time undergraduates, 1,161 part-time
    undergraduates
19:1 student/faculty ratio

>>

Founded in 1875, Indiana University of Pennsylvania is
a public institution, coed. Located on 162 acres in a
town 65 miles from Pittsburgh. Associate's and bachelor's degrees are offered.

ALTERNATIVE ADMISSIONS:

Contact: Carolyn Wilkie, Director of Learning Center
(412) 357-2729

Indiana University of Pennsylvania has a structured
summer program, Learning Center, initiated in 1972 for
alternative admissions students. The program lasts for
5 weeks. Eighty-five percent of the students complete
the program in that time.

ADMISSION POLICIES:

• New students are eligible for alternative admissions

• Admission considerations: SAT or ACT scores, high
  school rank, minority status, age of applicant

ACADEMIC COURSEWORK AND RELATED FEATURES:

• Support services: freshman orientation, college survival skills, academic advising, drug/alcohol counsel-

Stacy Needle

ing, psychological counseling, academic skills center, study technique workshops, career advising, health center, extended time for tests
- Separate new-student orientation
- Students are not required to work with tutors
- Group and one-on-one tutoring by peer tutors
- Developmental counseling is required
- Students are assigned an academic adviser. All advisers serve alternative admissions students exclusively. Students meet with advisers 18 times per semester
- Placement testing is required in algebra, reading, writing, and foreign language
- Sixteen faculty members assigned to the program, who are trained to work with alternative admissions students
- Students take classes with alternative admissions students only
- Alternative admissions classes average 20–25 students

REQUIRED COURSES:

Educational Planning and Development (credit-bearing)—alternative admissions students only
Strategies for Academic Success (credit-bearing)
Career Exploration (credit-bearing)
- Courses required of students who demonstrate deficiency:
  Reading Skills for College Study (credit-bearing)—alternative admissions students only
  Introduction to College Math I (credit-bearing)—alternative admissions students only
  Introduction to College Math II (credit-bearing)
- Remedial courses are not calculated in GPA
- Required courses are calculated in GPA
- Minimum of 1.8 GPA required to stay in program; if below 1.8 GPA, a student may not enroll for the fall semester

PROFILE OF ALTERNATIVE ADMISSIONS STUDENTS:

- 287 alternative admissions students enrolled
- 100% enter as new students
- 62% minority, 63% female
- 90% state residents, no international students
- 1% 25 years or older
- 2%–3% learning disabled
- 53% in top 50% of high school class

OTHER FEATURES/ACCOMMODATIONS:

- On-campus housing is available, but is not guaranteed for alternative admissions students
- A meal plan is available
- Financial aid is available

DEADLINES:

- December 31 for admission; after December 31, applications are reviewed on a space-available basis
- May 1 for financial aid
- January 31 for notification of admission
- April 15 for reply date

INDIANA UNIVERSITY-PURDUE UNIVERSITY AT INDIANAPOLIS

>>>>>>>>>>>>>>>>>>>>>>>>>>>>

Indianapolis, IN 46202
(317) 274-4591

———

$1,560–$1,950 In-State Tuition and Fees
$4,608–$5,760 Out-of-State Tuition and Fees
$1,187 Average Double Room
$1,094 Average Meal Plan

7,347 full-time undergraduates, 10,986 part-time undergraduates
25:1 student/faculty ratio

>>

Founded in 1969, Indiana University–Purdue University at Indianapolis is a public institution, coed. Located on 300 acres in a large city. Associate's and bachelor's degrees are offered.

ALTERNATIVE ADMISSIONS:

Contact: Nancy Obergfel, Director of University Access Center (317) 274-2237

Indiana University–Purdue University at Indianapolis has a structured program, Guided Study Program, initiated in 1969 for alternative admissions students. The formal program of studies begins in the fall and lasts for a minimum of 1 semester; however, students can also enter the program in the spring and continue for a minimum of 1 semester.

ADMISSION POLICIES:

- New and transfer students are eligible for alternative admissions

The Other Route into College

- Admission considerations—new student: SAT or ACT scores, high school rank
- Admission considerations—transfer student: GPA at previous institution, number of credits completed

ACADEMIC COURSEWORK AND RELATED FEATURES:
- Placement testing is required in math, English, and reading
- A total of 1,120 full-time faculty at the institution
- Three faculty members assigned to the program, who are trained to work with alternative admissions students

REQUIRED COURSES:
- Courses required of students who demonstrate deficiency:
  Study Skills (credit-bearing)
  General Math (credit-bearing)
  Introduction to Algebra (credit-bearing)
  Access to Writing (credit-bearing)
  Basic College Writing (credit-bearing)
  Advanced College Writing (credit-bearing)

- Remedial courses are calculated in GPA
- Minimum of 2.0 GPA required to stay in program; if below 2.0 GPA, a student is given 2 semesters to attain a 2.0 GPA

OTHER FEATURES/ACCOMMODATIONS:
- On-campus housing is available for alternative admissions students
- A meal plan is available

DEADLINES:
- Rolling admission

INDIANA UNIVERSITY SOUTHEAST

>>>>>>>>>>>>>>>>>>>>>>>>>>>>>

New Albany, IN 47150
(812) 945-2731

$1,344–$1,680 In-State Tuition and Fees
$3,336–$4,170 Out-of-State Tuition and Fees

2,404 full-time undergraduates, 3,048 part-time undergraduates
18:1 student/faculty ratio

>>

Founded in 1941, Indiana University Southeast is a public institution, coed. Located on 180 acres in a town 5 miles from Louisville, Kentucky. Associate's and bachelor's degrees are offered.

ALTERNATIVE ADMISSIONS:
Contact: Stanley Wheeler, Director of Admissions
(812) 945-2731

Indiana University Southeast has a policy, Probation, for alternative admissions students.

ADMISSION POLICIES:
- New and transfer students are eligible for alternative admissions

- Requirements for admission as a freshman:
  400 — minimum verbal SAT
  400 — minimum math SAT
      or
   19 — minimum ACT
Other considerations: high school rank, difficulty of high school courses taken

- Admission considerations—transfer student: GPA at previous institution, type of college attended

ACADEMIC COURSEWORK AND RELATED FEATURES:
- Support services: freshman orientation, academic advising, psychological counseling, study technique workshops, career advising
- Students are not required to work with tutors
- Group and one-on-one tutoring by peer tutors as well as professional tutors
- Students are assigned an academic adviser. Students meet with advisers 1 time per semester
- Placement testing is required

Stacy Needle

78

- Alternative admissions students do not take separate classes
- Students are not limited to credit load

REQUIRED COURSES:
- Remedial courses required:
  Math (credit-bearing)
  English (credit-bearing)
- Remedial courses are not calculated in GPA

PROFILE OF ALTERNATIVE ADMISSIONS STUDENTS:
- 15% of accepted students enrolled

OTHER FEATURES/ACCOMMODATIONS:
- On-campus housing is not available
- A meal plan is not available
- Financial aid is available

DEADLINES:
- Rolling admission
- March 1 for financial aid

IONA COLLEGE
>>>>>>>>>>>>>>>>>>>>>>>>>>

New Rochelle, NY 10801
(914) 969-3500

___

$5,920 Tuition and Fees
$4,100 Average Double Room and Meal Plan

595 full-time undergraduates, 560 part-time
  undergraduates
20:1 student/faculty ratio
55% of undergraduates study business

>>

Founded in 1960, Iona College is a private institution, coed. Located on 21 acres in a large city 15 miles from New York City. Associate's and bachelor's degrees are offered.

ALTERNATIVE ADMISSIONS:

Contact: Barbara Christie, Associate Dean of Admissions at Seton School (914) 633-2503

Iona College has a structured program, SCOPE (located at Seton School, a 2-year college in Yonkers, New York), initiated in 1986 for alternative admissions students. The formal program of studies begins in the fall and lasts for 2 years; however, students can also enter the program in the spring and continue for 2 years. Seventy-five percent of the students complete the program in that time. Students receive an associate's degree upon completion of their studies.

ADMISSION POLICIES:
- New and transfer students are eligible for alternative admissions
- Admission considerations—new student: high school GPA, high school rank, interview with admissions counselor
- Requirements for admission as a transfer student:
  2.0 — minimum GPA
Other considerations: number of credits completed (less than 30 credits), interview with admissions counselor

ACADEMIC COURSEWORK AND RELATED FEATURES:
- Support services: freshman orientation, college survival skills, academic advising, drug/alcohol counseling, psychological counseling, academic skills center, study technique workshops, career advising, peer counseling, health center
- Separate new-student orientation
- Students are not required to work with tutors
- Group and one-on-one tutoring by peer tutors as well as professional tutors in all academic areas
- Counseling is not required
- Students are assigned an academic adviser
- Placement testing is required in math, reading, and writing
- A total of 26 full-time faculty at the institution
- Special faculty assigned to the program, who are trained to work with alternative admissions students
- Alternative admissions students do not take separate classes
- Students are not limited to credit load

REQUIRED COURSES:
- Minimum of 1.8 GPA required to stay in program; if below 1.8 GPA, a student may be academically dismissed

PROFILE OF ALTERNATIVE ADMISSIONS STUDENTS:
- 199 alternative admissions students enrolled
- 100% of accepted students enrolled
- 97% enter as new students, 3% as transfer students
- 70% transfer to another college after sophomore year

- 52% minority, 55% female
- 93% state residents, 10% international students

OTHER FEATURES/ACCOMMODATIONS:
- On-campus housing is available, but is not guaranteed for alternative admissions students
- A meal plan is available
- Financial aid is available

DEADLINES:
- Rolling admission
- April 15 for financial aid
- May 1 for reply date

The program is best suited for a student who has followed an academic program in high school.

JOHN BROWN UNIVERSITY
>>>>>>>>>>>>>>>>>>>>>>>>>>>

Siloam Springs, AR 72761
(501) 524-3131

$4,500 Tuition and Fees
$1,010 Average Double Room
$1,670 Average Meal Plan

780 full-time undergraduates, 94 part-time
  undergraduates
15:1 student/faculty ratio
24% of undergraduates study business

>>

Founded in 1919, John Brown University is a private institution, coed. Located on 200 acres in a rural community 25 miles from Fayetteville. Associate's and bachelor's degrees are offered.

ALTERNATIVE ADMISSIONS:

Contact: Don Crandall, Director of Admissions (501) 524-3131

John Brown University has a policy for alternative admissions students.

ADMISSION POLICIES:
- New and transfer students are eligible for alternative admissions, with a limit of 25 students. There is a wait list
- Requirements for admission as a freshman:
  300 — minimum verbal SAT
  340 — minimum math SAT
   12 — minimum ACT
      or
  2.1 — minimum GPA
Other considerations: essay/personal statement, letters of recommendation

- Requirements for admission as a transfer student:
  2.0 — minimum GPA
Other considerations: letters of recommendation

ACADEMIC COURSEWORK AND RELATED FEATURES:
- Support services: freshman orientation, academic advising, drug/alcohol counseling, psychological counseling, academic skills center, study technique workshops, career advising, peer counseling, health center, aptitude testing
- Students are not required to work with tutors
- Group and one-on-one tutoring by peer tutors as well as professional tutors in all academic areas
- Counseling is not required
- Students are assigned an academic adviser. None of the advisers serve alternative admissions students exclusively. Students meet with advisers 2 times per semester
- Placement testing is required in reading and writing
- Alternative admissions students do not take separate classes
- Students are limited to a credit load of 15 credits per semester through second semester of college

REQUIRED COURSES:
- Courses required of students who demonstrate deficiency:
  Developmental Reading
  Developmental English
- Minimum of 2.0 GPA required to stay at college; if below 2.0 GPA, a student must fill out a petition for readmission

PROFILE OF ALTERNATIVE ADMISSIONS STUDENTS:
- 30 alternative admissions students enrolled
- 83% of accepted students enrolled
- 94% enter as new students, 6% as transfer students
- 22% transfer to another college after freshman year, 30% transfer after sophomore year
- 3% minority, 57% female

Stacy Needle

- 23% state residents, no international students
- 6% 25 years or older
- 6% intercollegiate athletes
- 3% learning disabled
- 37% in top 50% of high school class
- 35% graduate within 4 years
- 38% graduate within 5 years

OTHER FEATURES/ACCOMMODATIONS:
- On-campus housing is available and is guaranteed for alternative admissions students
- A meal plan is available
- Financial aid is available

DEADLINES:
- Rolling admission
- February for financial aid
- March for reply date

KANSAS NEWMAN COLLEGE

>>>>>>>>>>>>>>>>>>>>>>>>>>>

Wichita, KS 67213
(316) 942-4291

_____

$5,390 Tuition and Fees
$2,616 Average Double Room and Meal Plan

356 full-time undergraduates, 495 part-time
  undergraduates
14:1 student/faculty ratio
45% of undergraduates study math/sciences

>>

Founded in 1933, Kansas Newman College is a private institution, coed, affiliated with the Roman Catholic church. Located on 51 acres in a large city. Associate's and bachelor's degrees are offered.

ALTERNATIVE ADMISSIONS:
Contact: Kendra Whitcomb, Director of Admissions
(316) 942-4291

Kansas Newman College has a policy for alternative admissions students.

ADMISSION POLICIES:
- New and transfer students are eligible for alternative admissions, with a limit of 15 students. There is no wait list
- Requirements for admission as a freshman:
  1.5 — minimum GPA
Other considerations: ACT scores
- Requirements for admission as a transfer student:
  1.5 — minimum GPA

ACADEMIC COURSEWORK AND RELATED FEATURES:
- Support services: freshman orientation, college survival skills, academic advising, career advising
- Students are not required to work with tutors
- One-on-one tutoring by peer tutors in most academic areas
- Counseling is not required
- Students are assigned an academic adviser. None of the advisers serve alternative admissions students exclusively
- Placement testing is required in English and math
- Alternative admissions students do not take separate classes
- Students are not limited to credit load

PROFILE OF ALTERNATIVE ADMISSIONS STUDENTS:
- 4 alternative admissions students enrolled
- 2% of accepted students enrolled
- 80% transfer to another college after freshman year
- 1% minority, 50% female
- 85% state residents, no international students
- None 25 years or older
- 1% intercollegiate athletes
- No learning disabled
- None in top 50% of high school class

OTHER FEATURES/ACCOMMODATIONS:
- On-campus housing is available and is guaranteed for alternative admissions students
- A meal plan is available
- Financial aid is available

DEADLINES:
- Rolling admission
- March 15 for financial aid

KENDALL COLLEGE

>>>>>>>>>>>>>>>>>>>>>>>>>>

Evanston, IL 60201
(708) 866-1300

$6,051 Tuition and Fees
$3,777 Average Double Room and Meal Plan

357 full-time undergraduates, 27 part-time
   undergraduates
15:1 student/faculty ratio
24% of undergraduates study business

>>

Founded in 1934, Kendall College is a private institu-
tion, coed, affiliated with the United Methodist church.
Located on 1½ acres in a town 10 miles from Chicago.
Associate's and bachelor's degrees are offered.

ALTERNATIVE ADMISSIONS:

Contact: Kathy McCarville, Coordinator of Freshman
Year Program (708) 866-1385

Kendall College has a structured program, Freshman
Year Program, initiated in 1975 for alternative admissions students. The formal program of studies begins
in the fall and lasts for 1 semester; however, students
can also enter the program in the spring and continue
for 1 semester.

ADMISSION POLICIES:

• New students are eligible for alternative admissions

• Requirements for admission as a freshman:
  380 — average verbal SAT
  380 — average math SAT
      or
   12 — minimum ACT

  1.5 — minimum GPA
Other considerations: high school rank, essay/personal
statement

ACADEMIC COURSEWORK AND RELATED FEATURES:

• Support services: freshman orientation, college survival skills, academic advising, drug/alcohol counseling, academic skills center, study technique
  workshops, career advising, peer counseling, aptitude testing
• Separate new-student orientation
• Students are not required to work with tutors
• Group and one-on-one tutoring by peer tutors as well
  as professional tutors in all academic areas

• Counseling is not required
• Students are assigned an academic adviser. Fifty per-
  cent of the advisers serve alternative admissions stu-
  dents exclusively. Students meet with advisers at
  least 2 times per semester
• Placement testing is required in reading and math
• A total of 23 full-time faculty at the institution
• Two faculty members assigned to the program, who
  are trained to work with alternative admissions stu-
  dents
• Students take classes with alternative admissions
  students
• Alternative admissions classes average 20 students
• Students are not limited to credit load

REQUIRED COURSES:

• Courses required of students who demonstrate defi-
  ciency:
  College Reading and Study Skills (credit-bearing)—
    alternative admissions students only
  College Writing (credit-bearing)—alternative admis-
    sions students only
  Fundamentals of Math (credit-bearing)—alternative
    admissions students only

• Remedial courses are calculated in GPA
• Minimum of 2.0 GPA required to stay in program; if
  below 2.0 GPA, a student is placed on academic probation

PROFILE OF ALTERNATIVE ADMISSIONS STUDENTS:

• 30 alternative admissions students enrolled
• 80% of accepted students enrolled
• 100% enter as new students
• 25% of the students transfer to another college after
  freshman year, 10% transfer after sophomore year
• 40% minority, 50% female
• 90% state residents, no international students
• 2% 25 years or older
• No intercollegiate athletes
• 15% learning disabled
• None in top 50% of high school class
• 20% graduate within 4 years

OTHER FEATURES/ACCOMMODATIONS:

• On-campus housing is available, but is not guaranteed
  for alternative admissions students
• A meal plan is available
• Financial aid is available

DEADLINES:

• Rolling admission
• June 1 for financial aid

Stacy Needle

KING COLLEGE

>>>>>>>>>>>>>>>>>>>>>>>>>>>>

Bristol, TN 37620
(615) 968-1787

$5,550 Tuition and Fees
$1,500 Average Double Room
$1,550 Average Meal Plan

512 full-time undergraduates, 21 part-time
    undergraduates
15:1 student/faculty ratio
30% of undergraduates study business

>>

Founded in 1867, King College is a private institution,
coed, affiliated with the Presbyterian church. Located
on 135 acres in a small city 30 miles from Johnson City.
Bachelor's degrees are offered.

ALTERNATIVE ADMISSIONS:

Contact: Edwin Seaver, Dean of Admissions (615) 968-
1787

King College has a policy for alternative admissions
students.

ADMISSION POLICIES:

- New students are eligible for alternative admissions

- Requirements for admission as a freshman:
    400 — minimum verbal SAT
    400 — minimum math SAT
    48 — minimum TSWE
       or
    17 — minimum ACT

    2.0 — minimum GPA
Other considerations: essay/personal statement

ACADEMIC COURSEWORK AND RELATED FEATURES:

- Support services: freshman orientation, college survival skills, academic advising, drug/alcohol counseling, psychological counseling, study technique
  workshops, career advising, aptitude testing
- Students are not required to work with tutors
- Group and one-on-one tutoring by peer tutors in all
  academic areas
- Counseling is not required
- Students are assigned an academic adviser. None of
  the advisers serve alternative admissions students
  exclusively. Students meet with advisers at least 3
  times per semester

- Placement testing is not required
- Alternative admissions students do not take separate
  classes

REQUIRED COURSES:

- Minimum of 1.6 GPA required to stay at college; if
  below 1.6 GPA, a student is placed on academic probation and offered special assistance

PROFILE OF ALTERNATIVE ADMISSIONS STUDENTS:

- 38 alternative admissions students enrolled

OTHER FEATURES/ACCOMMODATIONS:

- On-campus housing is available and is guaranteed for
  alternative admissions students
- A meal plan is available
- Financial aid is available

DEADLINES:

- Rolling admission
- March 15 for financial aid
- June 1 for reply date

LAMBUTH COLLEGE

>>>>>>>>>>>>>>>>>>>>>>>>>>>>>

Jackson, TN 38301
(901) 425-3223

$4,200 Tuition and Fees
$1,078 Average Double Room
$1,540 Average Meal Plan

637 full-time undergraduates, 130 part-time
    undergraduates
14:1 student/faculty ratio
20% of undergraduates study business

>>

Founded in 1843, Lambuth College is a private institution, coed, affiliated with the United Methodist church.
Located on 50 acres in a small city 75 miles from Memphis. Bachelor's degrees are offered.

ALTERNATIVE ADMISSIONS:

Contact: Nancy Tipton, Director of Admissions (901)
425-3223

Lambuth College has a policy for alternative admissions students.

ADMISSION POLICIES:

- New and transfer students are eligible for alternative admissions

- Admission considerations—new student: SAT or ACT scores, high school GPA, letters of recommendation

- Admission considerations—transfer student: GPA at previous institution, number of credits completed, letter of good standing from previous institution

ACADEMIC COURSEWORK AND RELATED FEATURES:

- Support services: freshman orientation, college survival skills, academic advising, psychological counseling, academic skills center, peer counseling, aptitude testing, extended time for tests
- Students are not required to work with tutors
- One-on-one tutoring by peer tutors as well as professional tutors in all academic areas
- Counseling is not required
- Students are assigned an academic adviser. None of the advisers serve alternative admissions students exclusively
- Placement testing is required in reading
- Students take 1 class with alternative admissions students only
- Alternative admissions classes average 20 students
- Students are not limited to credit load

REQUIRED COURSES:

- Courses required of students who demonstrate deficiency:
  College Reading Improvement

OTHER FEATURES/ACCOMMODATIONS:

- On-campus housing is available and is guaranteed for alternative admissions students
- On-campus housing is required of alternative admissions students
- A meal plan is available
- Financial aid is available

DEADLINES:

- Rolling admission
- March 15 for financial aid
- May 1 for reply date

LA ROCHE COLLEGE

>>>>>>>>>>>>>>>>>>>>>>>>>>>>

Pittsburgh, PA 15237
(412) 367-9241

$5,910 Tuition and Fees
$3,320 Average Double Room and Meal Plan

669 full-time undergraduates, 956 part-time undergraduates
17:1 student/faculty ratio
47% of undergraduates study arts/humanities

>>

Founded in 1963, La Roche College is a private institution, coed, affiliated with the Roman Catholic church. Located on 16 acres in a rural community. Bachelor's degrees are offered.

ALTERNATIVE ADMISSIONS:

Additional cost: $1,500 basic program fee
Contact: Richard Levitt, Director of Project Achievement and Pre-Session (412) 367-9300, Ext. 171

La Roche College has a structured summer program, Pre-Session, initiated in 1981 for alternative admissions students. The program begins in June and lasts for 6 weeks. Ninety-eight percent of the students complete the program in that time.

ADMISSION POLICIES:

- New students are eligible for alternative admissions, with a limit of 15 students. There is a wait list

- Requirements for admission as a freshman:
  393 — average verbal SAT
  333 — average math SAT
  1.8 — average GPA
Other considerations: high school rank, type of high school attended, difficulty of high school courses taken, interview with admissions counselor, age of applicant

ACADEMIC COURSEWORK AND RELATED FEATURES:

- Support services: college survival skills, academic advising, drug/alcohol counseling, psychological counseling, academic skills center, study technique workshops, career advising, peer counseling, extended time for tests, holistic student-development program
- Separate new-student orientation
- Students are not required to work with tutors
- Group and one-on-one tutoring by peer tutors as well as professional tutors in all academic areas

Stacy Needle

- Counseling is required
- Students are assigned an academic adviser. None of the advisers serve alternative admissions students exclusively
- Placement testing is required in reading, English, and math
- A total of 38 full-time faculty at the institution
- Four faculty members assigned to the program, who are trained to work with alternative admissions students
- Students take all of their classes with alternative admissions students
- Alternative admissions classes average 10 students
- Students are limited to a credit load of 12–13 credits per semester through spring semester of freshman year

REQUIRED COURSES:

- Remedial courses required:
  Learning Techniques—alternative admissions students only
  Reading Development—alternative admissions students only
  Written Communication Skills—alternative admissions students only
  Preparation for College Math—alternative admissions students only

- Remedial courses are calculated in GPA

PROFILE OF ALTERNATIVE ADMISSIONS STUDENTS:

- 100% enter as new students
- 12% of the students transfer to another college after freshman year, 6% transfer after sophomore year
- 12% minority, 65% female
- 94% state residents, no international students
- None 25 years or older
- No intercollegiate athletes
- No learning disabled
- None in top 50% of high school class
- 20% graduate within 4 years
- 50% graduate within 5 years

OTHER FEATURES/ACCOMMODATIONS:

- On-campus housing is available and is guaranteed for alternative admissions students
- On-campus housing is not required of alternative admissions students
- A meal plan is available
- Financial aid is available

DEADLINES:

- Rolling admission
- June 30 for financial aid
- June 21 for reply date

LINDENWOOD COLLEGE

>>>>>>>>>>>>>>>>>>>>>>>>>>>

St. Charles, MO 63301
(314) 949-2000

———

$7,000 Tuition and Fees
$1,750 Average Double Room
$1,750 Average Meal Plan

800 full-time undergraduates, 1,200 part-time
  undergraduates
14:1 student/faculty ratio
75% of undergraduates study business

>>

Founded in 1827, Lindenwood College is a private institution, coed, affiliated with the Presbyterian church. Located on 90 acres in a town. Associate's and bachelor's degrees are offered.

ALTERNATIVE ADMISSIONS:

Contact: Fred Remey, Dean of Student Life (314) 949-2000

Lindenwood College has a structured program, Consolidated Advising Program (C.A.P.), initiated in 1984 for alternative admissions students. The formal program of studies begins in the spring and lasts for 1 year; however, students can also enter the program in the spring and continue for 1 year. Ninety-seven percent of the students complete the program in that time.

ADMISSION POLICIES:

- New and transfer students are eligible for alternative admissions

- Requirements for admission as a freshman:
  18 — average ACT
  3.0 — average GPA
Other considerations: SAT scores (in place of ACT), high school rank, essay/personal statement

- Requirements for admission as a transfer student:
  2.0 — minimum GPA
Other considerations: essay/personal statement

ACADEMIC COURSEWORK AND RELATED FEATURES:

- Support services: freshman orientation, college survival skills, academic advising, drug/alcohol counseling, academic skills center, study technique workshops, career advising, peer counseling, extended time for tests

The Other Route into College

- Separate new-student orientation
- Students are not required to work with tutors
- Group and one-on-one tutoring by peer tutors as well as professional tutors
- Counseling is required
- Students are assigned an academic adviser
- Placement testing is required
- A total of 60 full-time faculty at the institution
- Special faculty assigned to the program, who are trained to work with alternative admissions students
- Alternative admissions students do not take separate classes
- Students are limited to a credit load of 12 credits per semester through first semester of program

PROFILE OF ALTERNATIVE ADMISSIONS STUDENTS:
- 31 alternative admissions students enrolled
- 7% of accepted students enrolled

OTHER FEATURES/ACCOMMODATIONS:
- On-campus housing is available, but is not guaranteed for alternative admissions students
- A meal plan is available
- Financial aid is available

DEADLINES:
- Rolling admission

LONG ISLAND UNIVERSITY/ BROOKLYN CAMPUS

>>>>>>>>>>>>>>>>>>>>>>>>>>>

Brooklyn, NY 11201
(718) 403-1011

$7,500 Tuition and Fees
$2,000 Average Double Room
$1,000 Average Meal Plan

2,988 full-time undergraduates, 919 part-time undergraduates

>>

Founded in 1926, Long Island University/Brooklyn Campus is a private institution, coed. Located on 22 acres in a city. Associate's and bachelor's degrees are offered.

Stacy Needle

ALTERNATIVE ADMISSIONS:
Contact: Richard Sunday, Assistant Director of Admissions (718) 403-1011

Long Island University/Brooklyn Campus has a policy for alternative admissions students.

ADMISSION POLICIES:
- New students are eligible for alternative admissions

- Admission based on individual criteria

ACADEMIC COURSEWORK AND RELATED FEATURES:
- Students are not required to work with tutors
- Counseling is available
- Alternative admissions students do not take separate classes
- Students are not limited to credit load

REQUIRED COURSES:
- Minimum of 2.0 GPA required to stay at college; if below 2.0 GPA, a student is placed on academic probation

PROFILE OF ALTERNATIVE ADMISSIONS STUDENTS:
- 15% of the accepted students enrolled

OTHER FEATURES/ACCOMMODATIONS:
- On-campus housing is available
- A meal plan is available

DEADLINES:
- Rolling admission

LONG ISLAND UNIVERSITY/C. W. POST CAMPUS

>>>>>>>>>>>>>>>>>>>>>>>>>>>

Brookville, NY 11548
(516) 299-2415

$8,520 Tuition and Fees
$2,380 Average Double Room
$1,660 Average Meal Plan

5,281 full-time undergraduates, 1,059 part-time undergraduates
17:1 student/faculty ratio

Founded in 1954, Long Island University/C. W. Post Campus is a private institution, coed. Located on 400 acres in a small city, 25 miles from New York City. Bachelor's degrees are offered.

ALTERNATIVE ADMISSIONS:

Contact: James Patterson, Coordinator of the Directed Studies Program (516) 299-2233

Long Island University/C. W. Post Campus has a structured program, Directed Studies Program, initiated in 1986 for alternative admissions students. The formal program of studies begins in the fall and lasts for 1 year. Seventy-five percent of the students complete the program in that time.

ADMISSION POLICIES:

- New students are eligible for alternative admissions, with a limit of 125 students. There is a wait list

- Requirements for admission as a freshman:
  400 — minimum verbal SAT
      or
  400 — minimum math SAT
  Top 60% of high school class

ACADEMIC COURSEWORK AND RELATED FEATURES:

- Support services: freshman orientation, college survival skills, academic advising, drug/alcohol counseling, psychological counseling, study technique workshops, career advising, peer counseling
- Separate new-student orientation
- Students are not required to work with tutors
- Peer counseling is required
- Students are assigned an academic adviser. None of the advisers serve alternative admissions students exclusively. Students meet with advisers 2 times per semester
- Placement testing is required in math and reading
- A total of 319 full-time faculty at the institution
- Approximately 15 faculty assigned to the program
- Students take all of their classes with alternative admissions students
- Alternative admissions classes average 18 students
- Students are limited to a credit load of 12 credits per semester through spring semester of freshman year

REQUIRED COURSES:

- Remedial courses required:
  Sociology I and II (credit-bearing)—alternative admissions students only
  History I and II (credit-bearing)—alternative admissions students only
  English I and II (credit-bearing)—alternative admissions students only
  Political Science I and II (credit-bearing)—alternative admissions students only
- Remedial courses are calculated in GPA
- Minimum of 2.0 GPA required to stay in program; if below 2.0 GPA, a student is academically dismissed

PROFILE OF ALTERNATIVE ADMISSIONS STUDENTS:

- 78 alternative admissions students enrolled
- 100% enter as new students
- 13% minority, 53% female
- 79% state residents, no international students
- None 25 years or older
- 11% in top 50% of high school class

OTHER FEATURES/ACCOMMODATIONS:

- On-campus housing is available, but is not guaranteed for alternative admissions students
- A meal plan is available
- Financial aid is available

DEADLINES:

- Rolling admission

LONG ISLAND UNIVERSITY/ SOUTHAMPTON CAMPUS

>>>>>>>>>>>>>>>>>>>>>>>>>

Southampton, NY 11968
(516) 283-4000

$8,450 Tuition and Fees
$2,380 Average Double Room
$2,250 Average Meal Plan

1,000 full-time undergraduates, 150 part-time undergraduates

>>

Founded in 1963, Long Island University/Southampton Campus is a private institution, coed. Located on 110 acres in a rural community 90 miles from New York City. Bachelor's degrees are offered.

The Other Route into College

ALTERNATIVE ADMISSIONS:

Contact: Carol Gilbert, Director of Admissions, (516) 283-4000

Long Island University/Southampton Campus has a structured program, Study Center, for alternative admissions students. The formal program of studies begins in the fall and lasts for 1 year. Ninety percent of the students complete the program in that time.

ADMISSION POLICIES:

- New students are eligible for alternative admissions

- Requirements for admission as a freshman:
  300 — minimum verbal SAT
  300 — minimum math SAT
Other considerations: interview with admissions counselor

ACADEMIC COURSEWORK AND RELATED FEATURES:

- Students are required to work with tutors
- Counseling is available
- Alternative admissions students do not take separate classes
- Students are limited to a credit load of 12 credits per semester through fall semester of freshman year

REQUIRED COURSES:

- Remedial courses required:
  Remedial Writing
  Algebra
  Remedial Reading

- Minimum of 1.8 GPA required to stay in program; if below 1.8 GPA, a student is placed on academic probation

PROFILE OF ALTERNATIVE ADMISSIONS STUDENTS:

- 30% graduate within 4 years
- 70% graduate within 5 years

OTHER FEATURES/ACCOMMODATIONS:

- On-campus housing is available
- A meal plan is available

LOUISIANA COLLEGE

>>>>>>>>>>>>>>>>>>>>>>>>>>>

Pineville, LA 71359
(318) 487-7386

$3,300 Tuition and Fees
$1,160 Average Double Room
$1,372 Average Meal Plan

876 full-time undergraduates, 197 part-time
  undergraduates
17:1 student/faculty ratio

>>

Founded in 1906, Louisiana College is a private institution, coed, affiliated with the Southern Baptist church. Located on 81 acres in a town. Associate's and bachelor's degrees are offered.

ALTERNATIVE ADMISSIONS:

Contact: Byron McGee, Director of Admissions (318) 487-7386

Louisiana College has a structured program, Provisional Acceptance, for alternative admissions students. The formal program of studies begins in the fall and lasts for 1 year.

ADMISSION POLICIES:

- New and transfer students are eligible for alternative admissions, with a limit of 10 students. There is a wait list

- Admission considerations—new student: type of high school attended, difficulty of high school courses taken, interview with admissions counselor, letters of recommendation

- Admission considerations—transfer student: GPA at previous institution, number of credits completed

ACADEMIC COURSEWORK AND RELATED FEATURES:

- Support services: freshman orientation, academic advising, drug/alcohol counseling, psychological counseling, career advising, health center, aptitude testing
- Students are not required to work with tutors
- One-on-one tutoring by peer tutors as well as professional tutors in math and English
- Counseling is required
- Students are assigned an academic adviser. Students meet with advisers 4–5 times per semester
- Placement testing is required

Stacy Needle

- Alternative admissions students do not take separate classes
- Students are not limited to credit load

PROFILE OF ALTERNATIVE ADMISSIONS STUDENTS:

- 12 alternative admissions students enrolled

OTHER FEATURES/ACCOMMODATIONS:

- On-campus housing is available, but is not guaranteed for alternative admissions students
- A meal plan is available
- Financial aid is available

DEADLINES:

- Rolling admission—2 weeks after application is sent, notification of admission
- May 1 for financial aid

MAGDALEN COLLEGE
>>>>>>>>>>>>>>>>>>>>>>>>>>

Bedford, NH 03102
(603) 669-7735

$4,950 Tuition and Fees
$3,000 Average Double Room and Meal Plan

55 full-time undergraduates, 3 part-time
   undergraduates
10:1 student/faculty ratio
100% of undergraduates study arts/humanities

>>

Founded in 1973, Magdalen College is a private institution, coed, affiliated with the Roman Catholic church. Located on 6 acres in a town 5 miles from Manchester. Associate's and bachelor's degrees are offered.

ALTERNATIVE ADMISSIONS:

Contact: Paul Sullivan, Director of Admissions (603) 669-7735

Magdalen College has a policy for alternative admissions students.

ADMISSION POLICIES:

- New and transfer students are eligible for alternative admissions

- Requirements for admission as a freshman:
   400 — minimum verbal SAT
   400 — minimum math SAT
   1.5 — minimum GPA
Other considerations: ACT scores (in place of SAT), interview with admissions counselor, essay/personal statement, letters of recommendation

- Admission considerations—transfer student: interview with admissions counselor, essay/personal statement, letters of recommendation

ACADEMIC COURSEWORK AND RELATED FEATURES:

- Support services: freshman orientation, college survival skills, academic advising, drug/alcohol counseling, women's center, psychological counseling, academic skills center, study technique workshops, career advising, peer counseling, health center
- Students are not required to work with tutors
- Counseling is not required
- Students are not assigned an academic adviser
- Placement testing is not required
- Alternative admissions students do not take separate classes
- Students are not limited to credit load

PROFILE OF ALTERNATIVE ADMISSIONS STUDENTS:

- 6 alternative admissions students enrolled
- 5% of accepted students enrolled
- 20% of the students transfer to another college after freshman year, 20% transfer after sophomore year

OTHER FEATURES/ACCOMMODATIONS:

- On-campus housing is available, but is not guaranteed for alternative admissions students
- A meal plan is available
- Financial aid is available

DEADLINES:

- Rolling admission
- July 30 for financial aid
- August 15 for reply date

MALONE COLLEGE

>>>>>>>>>>>>>>>>>>>>>>>>>>>

Canton, OH 44709
(216) 489-0800

$6,744 Tuition and Fees
$1,459 Average Double Room
$1,350 Average Meal Plan

1,075 full-time undergraduates, 250 part-time
  undergraduates
15:1 student/faculty ratio
35% of undergraduates study arts/humanities

>>

Founded in 1892, Malone College is a private institution, coed, affiliated with the Evangelical Friends
church. Located on 78 acres in a small city 20 miles
from Akron. Associate's and bachelor's degrees are
offered.

ALTERNATIVE ADMISSIONS:

Contact: Dr. Steve Diakoff, Coordinator of Entry Semester Program (216) 489-0800, Ext. 499

Malone College has a structured program, Entry Semester Program, initiated in 1982 for alternative admissions students. The formal program of studies begins
in the fall and lasts for 1 semester. Ninety-four percent
of the students complete the program in that time.

ADMISSION POLICIES:

- New students are eligible for alternative admissions,
  with a limit of 30 students. There is no wait list

- Requirements for admission as a freshman:
    13 — average ACT
    2.15 — average GPA
Other considerations: high school rank, difficulty of high
school courses taken, interview with admissions counselor, essay/personal statement, letters of recommendation

ACADEMIC COURSEWORK AND RELATED FEATURES:

- Support services: freshman orientation, college survival skills, academic advising, drug/alcohol counseling, psychological counseling, study technique
  workshops, career advising, health center, aptitude
  testing, extended time for tests
- Separate new-student orientation
- Students are not required to work with tutors

- Group and one-on-one tutoring by peer tutors as well
  as professional tutors in all academic areas
- Counseling is not required
- Students are assigned an academic adviser. None of
  the advisers serve alternative admissions students
  exclusively. Students meet with advisers 3–5 times
  per semester
- Placement testing is not required
- A total of 47 full-time faculty at the institution
- Five faculty members assigned to the program, who
  are trained to work with alternative admissions stu-
  dents
- Students take classes with alternative admissions
  students only
- Alternative admissions classes average 30 students
- Students are not limited to credit load

REQUIRED COURSES:

- Remedial courses required:
  Basic Science (credit-bearing)—alternative admis-
    sions students only
  Study Skills-Basic Psychology (credit-bearing)—al-
    ternative admissions students only
  Basic Mathematics (credit-bearing)—alternative ad-
    missions students only
  Basic Bible (credit-bearing)—alternative admissions
    students only
  Basic English (credit-bearing)—alternative admis-
    sions students only

- Remedial courses are calculated in GPA

PROFILE OF ALTERNATIVE ADMISSIONS STUDENTS:

- 19 alternative admissions students enrolled
- 100% of accepted students enrolled
- 100% enter as new students
- 16% minority, 53% female
- 95% state residents, no international students
- None 25 years or older
- 42% intercollegiate athletes, Division NAIA sports
  available:
  baseball, basketball, cross-country, golf, soccer, ten-
    nis, track and field, cheerleading (men)
  basketball, cross-country, tennis, track and field, vol-
    leyball, cheerleading (women)
- 20% in top 50% of high school class

OTHER FEATURES/ACCOMMODATIONS:

- On-campus housing is available and is guaranteed for
  alternative admissions students
- On-campus housing is required of alternative admissions students
- A meal plan is available. It is required of alternative
  admissions students
- Financial aid is available

Stacy Needle

- Rolling admission
- April 15 for financial aid

MANHATTAN COLLEGE

>>>>>>>>>>>>>>>>>>>>>>>>>>

Riverdale, NY 10471
(212) 920-0200

$9,000 Tuition and Fees
$4,500 Average Double Room and Meal Plan

3,200 full-time undergraduates, 800 part-time
   undergraduates
15:1 student/faculty ratio
30% of undergraduates study engineering

>>

Founded in 1863, Manhattan College is a private institution, coed. Located in a large city. Associate's and bachelor's degrees are offered.

ALTERNATIVE ADMISSIONS:

Contact: Brother Myles, Director of Project Challenge
(212) 920-0100

Manhattan College has a structured program, Project Challenge, initiated in 1975 for alternative admissions students. The formal program of studies begins in the fall.

ADMISSION POLICIES:

- New and transfer students are eligible for alternative admissions, with a limit of 50–60 students. There is no wait list

- Requirements for admission as a freshman:
   380 — average verbal SAT
   420 — average math SAT
   33 — average TSWE
Other considerations: high school GPA, high school rank, type of high school attended, difficulty of high school courses taken, interview with admissions counselor, essay/personal statement, letters of recommendation

- Requirements for admission as a transfer student:
   1.9 — minimum GPA
Other considerations: difficulty of coursework, type of college attended, number of credits completed (less than 30 credits), interview with admissions counselor, essay/personal statement, letters of recommendation

ACADEMIC COURSEWORK AND RELATED FEATURES:

- Support services: freshman orientation, college survival skills, academic advising, drug/alcohol counseling, women's center, psychological counseling, academic skills center, study technique workshops, career advising, peer counseling, health center, aptitude testing
- Separate new-student orientation
- Students are required to work with tutors 1–2 hours per week
- Group and one-on-one tutoring by peer tutors as well as professional tutors in all academic areas
- Academic counseling is required
- Students are assigned an academic adviser. Twenty percent of the advisers serve alternative admissions students exclusively. Students meet with advisers 15–20 times per semester
- Placement testing is required in writing, math, and grammar
- Fifteen to twenty faculty members assigned to the program, who are trained to work with alternative admissions students
- Students take classes with alternative admissions students only
- Alternative admissions classes average 15–25 students
- Students are limited to a credit load of 12 credits per semester until they attain a 2.5 GPA

REQUIRED COURSES:

- Courses required of students who demonstrate deficiency:
   Remedial English (noncredit)—alternative admissions students only
   Remedial Math (noncredit)—alternative admissions students only

PROFILE OF ALTERNATIVE ADMISSIONS STUDENTS:

- 55 alternative admissions students enrolled
- 15% of the accepted students enrolled
- 95% enter as new students, 5% as transfer students
- 1–2% transfer to another college after freshman year, 1–2% transfer after sophomore year
- 30% minority, 50% female
- 70% state residents, 1% international students
- None 25 years or older
- 1% intercollegiate athletes

The Other Route into College

- No learning disabled
- 35% in top 50% of high school class
- 50% graduate within 4 years

OTHER FEATURES/ACCOMMODATIONS:
- On-campus housing is available and is guaranteed for alternative admissions students
- A meal plan is available
- Financial aid is available

DEADLINES:
- Rolling admission
- March 1 for financial aid
- May 1 for reply date

The program is best suited for an individual who needs to improve his/her reading, math, and study skills.

MANSFIELD UNIVERSITY

>>>>>>>>>>>>>>>>>>>>>>>>>>>

Mansfield, PA 16933
(717) 662-4243

$2,400 In-State Tuition and Fees
$7,080 Out-of-State Tuition and Fees
$1,366 Average Double Room
$ 950 Average Meal Plan

2,600 full-time undergraduates, 400 part-time undergraduates
17:1 student/faculty ratio

>>

Founded in 1857, Mansfield University is a public institution, coed. Located on 300 acres in a rural community 25 miles from Corning, New York. Associate's and bachelor's degrees are offered.

ALTERNATIVE ADMISSIONS:
Additional cost: $1,100 basic program fee
Contact: Dr. Enrico Serine, Director of Academic Advising Center (717) 662-4824

Mansfield University has a structured summer program, Academic Opportunity Program, initiated in 1975 for alternative admissions students. The program be-gins in July and lasts for 6 weeks. Ninety-eight percent of the students complete the program in that time.

ADMISSION POLICIES:
- New students are eligible for alternative admissions, with a limit of 75–80 students. There is a wait list
- Admission considerations—new student: SAT scores, high school GPA, high school rank, difficulty of high school courses taken

ACADEMIC COURSEWORK AND RELATED FEATURES:
- Support services: freshman orientation, college survival skills, academic advising, drug/alcohol counseling, psychological counseling, academic skills center, study technique workshops, career advising, peer counseling, health center, aptitude testing
- Separate new-student orientation
- Students are required to work with tutors
- One-on-one tutoring by peer tutors as well as professional tutors in English and math
- Academic counseling is required
- Students are assigned an academic adviser. All advisers serve alternative admissions students exclusively. Students meet with advisers 4–6 times per semester
- Placement testing is required in math and writing
- A total of 168 full-time faculty at the institution
- Eight to ten faculty assigned to the program
- Students take all of their classes with alternative admissions students
- Alternative admissions classes average 25 students

REQUIRED COURSES:
- Remedial courses required:
  Basic Reading and Study Skills (credit-bearing)
  General Mathematics (credit-bearing)
  Basic Writing Skills (credit-bearing)

- Remedial courses are calculated in GPA
- Minimum of 2.0 GPA required to stay in program; if below 2.0 GPA, a student is placed on academic probation

PROFILE OF ALTERNATIVE ADMISSIONS STUDENTS:
- 128 alternative admissions students enrolled
- 65% of accepted students enrolled
- 100% enter as new students
- 5% minority, 55% female
- No international students
- 1% learning disabled

OTHER FEATURES/ACCOMMODATIONS:
- On-campus housing is available and is guaranteed for alternative admissions students

Stacy Needle

- A meal plan is available
- Financial aid is available

DEADLINES:
- Rolling admission
- April 1 for financial aid
- March for reply date

MARIAN COLLEGE OF FOND DU LAC

>>>>>>>>>>>>>>>>>>>>>>>>>>>>

Fond du Lac, WI 54935
(414) 923-7650

$6,200 Tuition and Fees
$2,800 Average Double Room and Meal Plan

650 full-time undergraduates, 150 part-time
    undergraduates
17:1 student/faculty ratio
30% of undergraduates study business

>>

Founded in 1936, Marian College of Fond du Lac is a private institution, coed, affiliated with the Roman Catholic church. Located on 50 acres in a small city 90 miles from Milwaukee. Bachelor's degrees are offered.

ALTERNATIVE ADMISSIONS:

Contact: Gretchen Gall, Coordinator of Academic Advising (414) 923-7600

Marian College of Fond du Lac has a structured summer program, Project Direct, initiated in 1986 for alternative admissions students. The program lasts 2 semesters. Ninety percent of the students complete the program in that time.

ADMISSION POLICIES:
- New and transfer students are eligible for alternative admissions
- Admission considerations—new student: ACT scores, high school GPA, high school rank, type of high school attended, difficulty of high school courses taken, interview with admissions counselor, letters of recommendation

- Requirements for admission as a transfer student: 2.0 — minimum GPA

Other considerations: number of credits completed, interview with admissions counselor, letters of recommendation

ACADEMIC COURSEWORK AND RELATED FEATURES:
- Support services: freshman orientation, college survival skills, academic advising, drug/alcohol counseling, psychological counseling, academic skills center, study technique workshops, career advising, peer counseling, health center, aptitude testing, extended time for tests
- Students are not required to work with tutors
- Group and one-on-one tutoring by peer tutors as well as professional tutors in all academic areas
- Academic counseling is required
- Students are assigned an academic adviser. All advisers serve alternative admissions students exclusively
- Placement testing is required in writing, algebra, and reading comprehension
- A total of 120 full-time faculty at the institution
- One faculty member assigned to the program, who is trained to work with alternative admissions students
- Alternative admissions students do not take separate classes

REQUIRED COURSES:
- Remedial courses required:
  Review of English (credit-bearing)
  Basic Algebra (credit-bearing)
  Dynamics of Reading (credit-bearing)

- Remedial courses are calculated in GPA

PROFILE OF ALTERNATIVE ADMISSIONS STUDENTS:
- 22 alternative admissions students enrolled
- 75% of accepted students enrolled
- 20% minority, 70% female
- 90% state residents, 5% international students
- 10% 25 years or older
- 10% intercollegiate athletes
- 25% learning disabled
- 30% in top 50% of high school class

OTHER FEATURES/ACCOMMODATIONS:
- On-campus housing is available, but is not guaranteed for alternative admissions students
- A meal plan is available
- Financial aid is available

DEADLINES:
- Rolling admission
- March 15 for financial aid

MARIETTA COLLEGE

>>>>>>>>>>>>>>>>>>>>>>>>>>>

Marietta, OH 45750
(614) 374-4600

$10,250 Tuition and Fees
$ 1,550 Average Double Room
$ 1,450 Average Meal Plan

1,097 full-time undergraduates, 176 part-time
   undergraduates
12:1 student/faculty ratio

>>

Founded in 1835, Marietta College is a private institution, coed. Located on 60 acres in a town, 115 miles
from Columbus. Bachelor's degrees are offered.

ALTERNATIVE ADMISSIONS:

Additional cost: $1,250 basic program fee
Contact: George Banziger, Director of Summer Sessions (614) 374-4723

Marietta College has a structured summer program,
Summer Success Program, initiated in 1977 for alternative admissions students. The program begins in June
and lasts for 5 weeks. Five percent of the students
complete the program in that time.

ADMISSION POLICIES:

- New students are eligible for alternative admissions,
  with a limit of 50 students. There is a wait list

- Requirements for admission as a freshman:
  400 — average verbal SAT
  470 — average math SAT
      or
   16 — average ACT

  2.5 — average GPA
Other considerations: extracurricular activities, essay/
personal statement, letters of recommendation

ACADEMIC COURSEWORK AND RELATED FEATURES:

- Support services: freshman orientation, college survival skills, academic advising, academic skills center,
  study technique workshops, career advising, health
  center, extended time for tests
- Students are not required to work with tutors
- Counseling is not required
- Placement testing is not required

- Four faculty members assigned to the program, who
  are trained to work with alternative admissions students
- Alternative admissions students do not take separate
  classes

REQUIRED COURSES:

English
History
College Study Skills

- Minimum of 2.0 GPA required to stay in program; if
  below 2.0 GPA, a student may not enroll for the fall
  semester

PROFILE OF ALTERNATIVE ADMISSIONS STUDENTS:

- 21 alternative admissions students enrolled
- 38% of the accepted students enrolled
- 100% enter as new students
- 2% of the students transfer to another college after
  freshman year, 3% transfer after sophomore year
- 3% minority, 40% female
- 40% state residents, no international students
- None 25 years or older
- 78% in top 50% of high school class
- 55% graduate within 4 years

OTHER FEATURES/ACCOMMODATIONS:

- On-campus housing is available and is guaranteed for
  alternative admissions students
- On-campus housing is required of alternative admissions students
- A meal plan is available. It is required of alternative
  admissions students
- Financial aid is available

DEADLINES:

- Rolling admission
- May 1 for financial aid
- May 1 for reply date

Stacy Needle

MARQUETTE UNIVERSITY

>>>>>>>>>>>>>>>>>>>>>>>>>

Milwaukee, WI 53233
(414) 288-7302

$7,500 Tuition and Fees
$3,740 Average Double Room
$3,320 Average Meal Plan

8,213 full-time undergraduates, 922 part-time
   undergraduates
14:1 student/faculty ratio

>>

Founded in 1881, Marquette University is a private
institution, coed, affiliated with the Roman Catholic
church. Located on 80 acres in a large city. Associate's
and bachelor's degrees are offered.

ALTERNATIVE ADMISSIONS:

Additional cost: $1,500 basic program fee
Contact: Dr. Robert DeRoche, Associate Director
of Continuing Education and Summer Sessions (414)
288-7163

Marquette University has a structured summer program, Freshman Frontier Program, initiated in 1970 for
alternative admissions students. The program begins in
July and lasts for 1 year (summer, fall, and spring
semesters). During the summer, students enroll in one
3-credit course in an area of past academic strength and
in two noncredit courses in areas of past academic
weakness.

ADMISSION POLICIES:

• New students are eligible for alternative admissions,
  with a limit of 350 students. There is no wait list

• Requirements for admission as a freshman:
   400 — minimum verbal SAT
   400 — minimum math SAT
      or
   2.0 — minimum ACT
Other considerations: high school GPA, high school
rank

ACADEMIC COURSEWORK AND RELATED FEATURES:

• Support services: freshman orientation, academic ad-
  vising, career advising, health center
• Separate new-student orientation
• Students are not required to work with tutors

• One-on-one tutoring by peer tutors in all academic
  areas
• Students are assigned an academic adviser. All advisers serve alternative admissions students exclusively. Students meet with advisers at least 3 times
  per semester
• Placement testing is not required
• A total of 567 full-time faculty at the institution
• Ten to fifteen faculty members assigned to the program
• Students take classes with alternative admissions
  students only
• Alternative admissions classes average 15 students
• In the fall, students are limited to a credit load of 13
  credits per semester through spring semester of
  freshman year

REQUIRED COURSES:

• Minimum of 2.0 GPA required to stay in program; if
  below 2.0 GPA, a student is placed on academic probation

PROFILE OF ALTERNATIVE ADMISSIONS STUDENTS:

• 159 alternative admissions students enrolled
• 45% of accepted students enrolled
• 100% enter as new students
• 10% minority, 51% female
• 29% state residents, 1% international students
• None 25 years or older
• 4% intercollegiate athletes
• 2% learning disabled
• 37% in top 50% of high school class
• 45% graduate within 4 years

OTHER FEATURES/ACCOMMODATIONS:

• On-campus housing is available and is guaranteed for
  alternative admissions students
• A meal plan is available
• Financial aid is available

DEADLINES:

• Rolling admission

The Other Route into College

MASTER'S COLLEGE

>>>>>>>>>>>>>>>>>>>>>>>>>>

Newhall, CA 91322
(805) 259-3540

$6,050 Tuition and Fees
$3,690 Average Double Room and Meal Plan

434 full-time undergraduates, 407 part-time
  undergraduates
17:1 student/faculty ratio

>>

Founded in 1927, the Master's College is a private institution, coed. Located on 110 acres in a small city 35 miles from Los Angeles. Bachelor's degrees are offered.

ALTERNATIVE ADMISSIONS:

Contact: Tom Halstead, Dean of The Master's Institute
(805) 259-3540

The Master's College has a structured program, The Master's Institute, initiated in 1985 for alternative admissions students. The formal program of studies begins in the fall and lasts for 1 year; however, students can also enter the program in the spring and continue for 1 year. Ninety percent of the students complete the program in that time.

ADMISSION POLICIES:

- New and transfer students are eligible for alternative admissions

- Admission considerations—new student: essay/personal statement, letters of recommendation

- Admission considerations—transfer student: essay/personal statement, letters of recommendation

ACADEMIC COURSEWORK AND RELATED FEATURES:

- Support services: freshman orientation, college survival skills, academic advising, drug/alcohol counseling, women's center, psychological counseling, academic skills center, study technique workshops, career advising, peer counseling, health center, aptitude testing
- Students are not required to work with tutors
- Group and one-on-one tutoring by peer tutors in all academic areas
- Counseling is not required

- Students are assigned an academic adviser. None of the advisers serve alternative admissions students exclusively. Students meet with advisers 4–5 times per semester
- Placement testing is not required
- Alternative admissions students do not take separate classes
- Students are not limited to credit load

REQUIRED COURSES:

Old Testament Survey (credit-bearing)
New Testament Survey (credit-bearing)
Christian Theology (credit-bearing)
Methods of Bible Study (credit-bearing)
Foundations of Christian Life (credit-bearing)

- Required courses are calculated in GPA

PROFILE OF ALTERNATIVE ADMISSIONS STUDENTS:

- 35 alternative admissions students enrolled
- 70% of the accepted students enrolled
- 90% enter as new students, 10% as transfer students
- 10% transfer to another college after freshman year, 20% transfer after sophomore year
- 10% minority, 23% female
- 80% state residents, 3% international students
- 23% 25 years or older
- No intercollegiate athletes
- 10% in top 50% of high school class
- 30% graduate within 4 years
- 40% graduate within 5 years

OTHER FEATURES/ACCOMMODATIONS:

- On-campus housing is available, but is not guaranteed for alternative admissions students
- A meal plan is available
- Financial aid is available

DEADLINES:

- Rolling admission
- March 31 for financial aid

Stacy Needle

MEMPHIS COLLEGE OF ART
>>>>>>>>>>>>>>>>>>>>>>>>>>>

Memphis, TN 38112
(901) 726-4085

$6,750 Tuition and Fees
$ 975 Average Double Room
$ 600 Average Meal Plan

250 full-time undergraduates
10:1 student/faculty ratio
100% of undergraduates study arts/humanities

>>

Founded in 1936, the Memphis College of Art is a
private institution, coed. Located on 250 acres in a large
city. Bachelor's degrees are offered.

ALTERNATIVE ADMISSIONS:

Contact: Christine Ware, Director of Admissions (901)
726-4085

The Memphis College of Art has a policy for alternative
admissions students.

ADMISSION POLICIES:

- New and transfer students are eligible for alternative
  admissions

- Admission considerations—freshman: SAT or ACT
  scores, portfolio

- Admission considerations—transfer student: portfolio

ACADEMIC COURSEWORK AND RELATED FEATURES:

- Support services: freshman orientation, college survival skills, academic advising, drug/alcohol counseling, career advising, peer counseling
- Students are not required to work with tutors
- Counseling is not required
- Students are assigned an academic adviser. None of
  the advisers serve alternative admissions students
  exclusively
- Placement testing is not required
- Alternative admissions students do not take separate
  classes
- Students are not limited to credit load, yet are encouraged to take a load of 12 credits per semester
  through first semester of college

REQUIRED COURSES:

- Minimum of 1.75 GPA required to stay at college; if
  below 1.75 GPA, a student is counseled about other
  educational options

PROFILE OF ALTERNATIVE ADMISSIONS STUDENTS:

- 20 alternative admissions students enrolled
- 70% of accepted students enrolled
- 99% enter as new students, 1% as transfer students
- 15% minority, 50% female
- 85% state residents, no international students
- 1% 25 years or older
- 50% learning disabled
- 50% in top 50% of high school class
- 50% graduate within 4 years

OTHER FEATURES/ACCOMMODATIONS:

- On-campus housing is available, but is not guaranteed
  for alternative admissions students
- A meal plan is available
- Financial aid is available

DEADLINES:

- Rolling admission
- March 31 for financial aid
- May 1 for reply date

The program is best suited for a student who has a
strong desire and interest in the visual arts.

MERCY COLLEGE
>>>>>>>>>>>>>>>>>>>>>>>>>>>

Dobbs Ferry, NY 10522
(914) 693-4500

$6,000 Tuition and Fees

3,243 full-time undergraduates, 2,027 part-time
   undergraduates
14:1 student/faculty ratio

>>

Founded in 1950, Mercy College is a private institution,
coed. Located on 40 acres in a town 15 miles from New
York City. Associate's and bachelor's degrees are offered.

ALTERNATIVE ADMISSIONS:

Contact: Ann Rice, Dean of Academic Advising (914) 693-4500, Ext. 217

Mercy College has a structured program, New York State High School Equivalency Diploma Program, initiated in 1975 for alternative admissions students. The formal program of studies begins in the fall and lasts for 1 year; however, students can also enter the program in the spring and continue for 1 year. Students receive a GED upon completion of their studies.

ADMISSION POLICIES:

• New students are eligible for alternative admissions

• Admission considerations: interview with admissions counselor

ACADEMIC COURSEWORK AND RELATED FEATURES:

• Support services: freshman orientation, college survival skills, academic advising, drug/alcohol counseling, psychological counseling, academic skills center, study technique workshops, career advising, peer counseling, health tutors, aptitude testing, extended time for tests
• Separate new-student orientation
• Students are not required to work with tutors
• Academic counseling is required
• Students are assigned an academic adviser. Students meet with advisers 4 times per semester
• Placement testing is required
• Alternative admissions students do not take separate classes
• Students are limited to a credit load of 12 credits per semester through second semester of program

REQUIRED COURSES:

• Remedial courses required:
   Basic Writing Skills (noncredit)
   English as a Second Language (noncredit)
   Computational Skills and Basic Algebra (noncredit)
   Reading Fundamentals and Reading Strategies (noncredit)

• Minimum of 2.0 GPA required to stay in program; if below 2.0 GPA, a student is brought up before the College Review Board

OTHER FEATURES/ACCOMMODATIONS:

• On-campus housing is not available for alternative admissions students
• A meal plan is not available
• Financial aid is available

Stacy Needle

DEADLINES:

• Rolling admission
• August 15 for financial aid
• August 22 for reply date

MERCYHURST COLLEGE

▶▶▶▶▶▶▶▶▶▶▶▶▶▶▶▶▶▶▶▶▶▶▶▶▶▶▶

Erie, PA 16546
(814) 825-0202

$7,495 Tuition and Fees
$1,375 Average Double Room
$1,500 Average Meal Plan

2,044 full-time undergraduates, 461 part-time undergraduates
19:1 student/faculty ratio
16% of undergraduates study business

▶▶

Founded in 1926, Mercyhurst College is a private institution, coed, affiliated with the Roman Catholic church. Located on 80 acres in a small city 90 miles from Buffalo, New York. Associate's and bachelor's degrees are offered.

ALTERNATIVE ADMISSIONS:

Contact: Dr. Timothy Wise, Director of Corry Center (814) 664-7510

Mercyhurst College has a structured program, Corry Foundations Program, initiated in 1988 for alternative admissions students. The formal program of studies begins in the fall and lasts for 9 months. Eighty percent of the students complete the program in that time.

ADMISSION POLICIES:

• New students are eligible for alternative admissions, with a limit of 40 students

• Requirements for admission as a freshman:
   310 — minimum verbal SAT
   330 — minimum math SAT
   1.5 — minimum GPA
Other considerations: TSWE scores, high school rank, interview with admissions counselor

ACADEMIC COURSEWORK AND RELATED FEATURES:

- Support services: freshman orientation, college survival skills, academic advising, drug/alcohol counseling, academic skills center, study technique workshops, health center
- Separate new-student orientation
- Students are required to work with tutors 10 hours per week
- Group and one-on-one tutoring by professional tutors in all academic areas
- Counseling is not required
- Students are assigned an academic adviser
- Placement testing is required in math, reading, and writing
- A total of 82 full-time faculty at the institution
- Six faculty members assigned to the program, who are trained to work with alternative admissions students
- Students take all of their classes with alternative admissions students
- Alternative admissions classes average 15 students
- Students are not limited to credit load

REQUIRED COURSES:

- Courses required of students who demonstrate deficiency:
  Developmental Reading (credit-bearing)—alternative admissions students only
  Developmental Math (credit-bearing)—alternative admissions students only
  Developmental Writing (credit-bearing)—alternative admissions students only

- Remedial courses are calculated in GPA
- Minimum of 2.0 GPA required to stay in program; if below 2.0 GPA, a student is academically dismissed

PROFILE OF ALTERNATIVE ADMISSIONS STUDENTS:

- 14 alternative admissions students enrolled
- 13% of accepted students enrolled
- 100% enter as new students
- 2% minority, 45% female
- 48% state residents, no international students
- None 25 years or older
- 5% intercollegiate athletes
- No learning disabled
- 1% in top 50% of high school class

OTHER FEATURES/ACCOMMODATIONS:

- On-campus housing is available and is guaranteed for alternative admissions students
- On-campus housing is required of alternative admissions students
- A meal plan is available. It is required of alternative admissions students
- Financial aid is available

DEADLINES:

- Rolling admission—3 weeks after application is sent, notification of admission
- May 1 for financial aid

MICHIGAN STATE UNIVERSITY

>>>>>>>>>>>>>>>>>>>>>>>>>>>>>

East Lansing, MI 48824
(517) 355-8332

$2,520 In-State Tuition and Fees
$7,200 Out-of-State Tuition and Fees
$ 911 Average Double Room
$ 544 Average Meal Plan

31,306 full-time undergraduates, 3,663 part-time undergraduates
22% of undergraduates study business

>>

Founded in 1855, Michigan State University is a public institution, coed. Located on 5,100 acres in a small city 80 miles from Detroit. Bachelor's degrees are offered.

ALTERNATIVE ADMISSIONS:

Contact: James Tate, Coordinator of College Achievement Admissions Program (517) 355-9266

Michigan State University has a structured program, College Achievement Admissions Program, initiated in 1963 for alternative admissions students. The formal program of studies begins in the fall and lasts for a minimum of 1 year.

ADMISSION POLICIES:

- New students are eligible for alternative admissions

- Requirements for admission as a freshman:
  300 — minimum verbal SAT
  300 — minimum math SAT
    or
   10 — minimum ACT

  2.4 — minimum GPA

Other considerations: high school rank, type of high school attended, difficulty of high school courses taken

ACADEMIC COURSEWORK AND RELATED FEATURES:

- Support services: freshman orientation, college survival skills, academic advising, drug/alcohol counseling, psychological counseling, academic skills center, study technique workshops, career advising, peer counseling, health center, aptitude testing
- Students are required to work with tutors 2 hours per week
- Group and one-on-one tutoring by peer tutors as well as professional tutors in science, math, English, and social studies
- Counseling is not required
- Students are assigned an academic adviser. Students meet with advisers 2 times per semester
- Placement testing is required
- Students are limited to a credit load of 12 credits per semester until they have completed 40 credit hours

REQUIRED COURSES:

Seminar (noncredit)—alternative admissions students only

- Courses required of students who demonstrate deficiency:
  Remedial Writing
  Remedial Arithmetic
  Remedial Algebra

PROFILE OF ALTERNATIVE ADMISSIONS STUDENTS:

- 399 alternative admissions students enrolled
- 98% minority, 61% female
- 92% state residents
- 100% in top 50% of high school class
- 20% graduate within 4 years

OTHER FEATURES/ACCOMMODATIONS:

- On-campus housing is available and is guaranteed for alternative admissions students
- On-campus housing is required of alternative admissions students
- A meal plan is available. It is required of alternative admissions students
- Financial aid is available

DEADLINES:

- Rolling admission—4–6 weeks after application is sent, notification of admission
- June for financial aid

MIDDLE TENNESSEE STATE UNIVERSITY

>>>>>>>>>>>>>>>>>>>>>>>>>>

Murfreesboro, TN 37132
(615) 898-2111

$1,232 In-State Tuition and Fees
$4,186 Out-of-State Tuition and Fees
$1,148 Average Double Room
$ 708 Average Meal Plan

9,926 full-time undergraduates, 1,934 part-time undergraduates
25:1 student/faculty ratio
25% of undergraduates study business

>>

Founded in 1911, Middle Tennessee State University is a public institution, coed. Located on 500 acres in a town 32 miles from Nashville. Associate's and bachelor's degrees are offered.

ALTERNATIVE ADMISSIONS:

Contact: Dr. Carol Bader, Chairman of Developmental Studies Program (615) 898-2568

Middle Tennessee State University has a structured program, Developmental Studies Program, initiated in 1985 for alternative admissions students. The formal program of studies begins in the fall and lasts for 1 year. Eighty-two percent of the students complete the program in that time.

ADMISSION POLICIES:

- New and transfer students are eligible for alternative admissions

- Requirements for admission as a freshman:
  18 — average ACT
Other considerations: SAT scores (in place of ACT), high school GPA

- Admission considerations—transfer student: GPA at previous institution, type of college attended, number of credits completed

ACADEMIC COURSEWORK AND RELATED FEATURES:

- Support services: freshman orientation, college survival skills, academic advising, women's center, academic skills center, study technique workshops, career advising, peer counseling, health center, aptitude testing

Stacy Needle

- Separate new-student orientation
- Students are not required to work with tutors
- Group and one-on-one tutoring by peer tutors as well as professional tutors in English and math
- Counseling is not required
- Students are assigned an academic adviser. All advisers serve alternative admissions students exclusively
- Placement testing is required
- A total of 433 full-time faculty at the institution
- Special faculty assigned to the program, who are trained to work with alternative admissions students
- Students take all of their classes with alternative admissions students only
- Alternative admissions classes average 20–25 students
- Courses are offered in the evening
- Students are not limited to credit load

REQUIRED COURSES:

- Remedial courses required:
  Basic Mathematics (credit-bearing)—alternative admissions students only
  Basic Reading (credit-bearing)—alternative admissions students only
  Basic Study Skills (credit-bearing)—alternative admissions students only
- Other required courses:
  Basic Geometry (credit-bearing)
  Developmental Reading (credit-bearing)
- Courses required of students who demonstrate deficiency:
  Developmental Writing (credit-bearing)
  Elementary Algebra (credit-bearing)
  Intermediate Algebra (credit-bearing)
  Basic Writing (credit-bearing)—alternative admissions students only
- Remedial courses are not calculated in GPA
- Required courses are not calculated in GPA
- Minimum of 2.0 GPA required to stay in program; a student who fails twice to attain a 2.0 GPA is academically suspended

OTHER FEATURES/ACCOMMODATIONS:

- On-campus housing is available, but is not guaranteed for alternative admissions students
- A meal plan is available
- Financial aid is available

DEADLINES:

- July 1 for admission
- May 15 for financial aid

MIDWESTERN STATE UNIVERSITY

>>>>>>>>>>>>>>>>>>>>>>>>>>>>>>

Wichita Falls, TX 76308-2099
(817) 696-6782

$ 834 In-State Tuition and Fees
$3,330 Out-of-State Tuition and Fees
$2,412 Average Double Room and Meal Plan

2,958 full-time undergraduates, 1,753 part-time undergraduates
25:1 student/faculty ratio
24% of undergraduates study business

>>

Founded in 1922, Midwestern State University is a public institution, coed. Located on 167 acres in a small city 130 miles from Dallas. Associate's and bachelor's degrees are offered.

ALTERNATIVE ADMISSIONS:

Contact: Shirley Wilson, Assistant to the Registrar (817) 696-6782

Midwestern State University has a policy for alternative admissions students.

ADMISSION POLICIES:

- New and transfer students are eligible for alternative admissions

- Requirements for admission as a freshman:
  500 — minimum combined verbal and math SAT
      or
   10 — minimum ACT
Other considerations: high school rank, 4 years of high school English (nonremedial), and 2 years of high school math (nonremedial)

- Admission considerations—transfer student: admission based on individual criteria

ACADEMIC COURSEWORK AND RELATED FEATURES:

- Support services: freshman orientation, academic advising, drug/alcohol counseling, career advising, peer counseling, health center, aptitude testing
- Students are not required to work with tutors
- Counseling is not required
- Students are assigned an academic adviser
- Placement testing is required

The Other Route into College

- Alternative admissions students do not take separate classes
- Students are limited to a credit load of 12–14 credits per semester until they satisfactorily complete 24 credit hours

REQUIRED COURSES:
- Courses required of students who demonstrate deficiency:
  Freshman Seminar

OTHER FEATURES/ACCOMMODATIONS:
- On-campus housing is available, but is not guaranteed for alternative admissions students
- A meal plan is available

DEADLINES:
- Rolling admission
- May 1 for financial aid

MILWAUKEE SCHOOL OF ENGINEERING

>>>>>>>>>>>>>>>>>>>>>>>>>>>

Milwaukee, WI 53201-0644
(414) 277-7200

———

$7,800 Tuition and Fees
$1,620 Average Double Room
$1,080 Average Meal Plan

1,800 full-time undergraduates, 900 part-time undergraduates
17:1 student/faculty ratio
90% of undergraduates study engineering

>>

Founded in 1903, Milwaukee School of Engineering is a private institution, coed. Located on 12 acres in a large city. Associate's and bachelor's degrees are offered.

ALTERNATIVE ADMISSIONS:

Contact: Jean Snyder, Director of Learning Resource Center (414) 277-7266

Milwaukee School of Engineering has a structured program, Transition Track Program, initiated in 1988 for alternative admissions students. The formal program of studies begins in the fall and lasts for 1 year. Eighty-five percent of the students complete the program in that time.

ADMISSION POLICIES:
- New and transfer students are eligible for alternative admissions, with a limit of 70 students. There is no wait list

- Requirements for admission as a freshman:
  20 — average ACT
  2.0 — average GPA
Other considerations: high school rank, difficulty of high school courses taken, interview with admissions counselor, essay/personal statement

- Requirements for admission as a transfer student:
  2.0 — average GPA
Other considerations: difficulty of coursework, interview with admissions counselor, essay/personal statement

ACADEMIC COURSEWORK AND RELATED FEATURES:
- Support services: freshman orientation, college survival skills, academic advising, psychological counseling, academic skills center, study technique workshops, career advising, peer counseling, health center, aptitude testing, extended time for tests (if learning disabled)
- Separate new-student orientation
- Students are required to work with tutors approximately 2–5 hours per week
- Group and one-on-one tutoring by peer tutors as well as professional tutors
- Academic counseling is required
- Students are assigned an academic adviser. Students meet with advisers at least 2 times per semester
- Placement testing is required in reading, physics, grammar, and math
- A total of 110 full-time faculty at the institution
- Four faculty members assigned to the program, who are trained to work with alternative admissions students
- Students are limited to a credit load of 12–15 credits per semester through second semester of program

REQUIRED COURSES:
- Minimum of 2.0 GPA required to stay in program; if below 2.0 GPA, a student is placed on academic probation

PROFILE OF ALTERNATIVE ADMISSIONS STUDENTS:
- 63 alternative admissions students enrolled

Stacy Needle

OTHER FEATURES/ACCOMMODATIONS:
- On-campus housing is available, but is not guaranteed to alternative admissions students
- A meal plan is available
- Financial aid is available

DEADLINES:
- Rolling admission

MOLLOY COLLEGE

>>>>>>>>>>>>>>>>>>>>>>>>>>>>

Rockville Centre, NY 11570
(516) 678-5000, Ext. 240

$7,000 Tuition and Fees

1,500 full-time undergraduates
20:1 student/faculty ratio

>>

Founded in 1955, Molloy College is a private institution, coed, affiliated with the Roman Catholic church. Located on 25 acres in a town 20 miles from New York City. Associate's and bachelor's degrees are offered.

ALTERNATIVE ADMISSIONS:

Contact: Pamela Branham, Director of Albertus Magnus Program (516) 678-5000

Molloy College has a structured program, Albertus Magnus Program, initiated in 1986 for alternative admissions students. The formal program of studies begins in the summer and lasts for 3 semesters (summer, fall, and spring). Seventy percent of the students complete the program in that time.

ADMISSION POLICIES:
- New and transfer students are eligible for alternative admissions

- Requirements for admission as a freshman:
   340 — minimum verbal SAT
   300 — minimum math SAT
   1.9 — minimum GPA
Other considerations: type of high school attended, difficulty of high school courses taken, interview with admissions counselor, essay/personal statement, letters of recommendation, minority status, state residence

- Requirements for admission as a transfer student:
   2.0 — minimum GPA
Other considerations: difficulty of coursework, type of college attended, number of credits completed, interview with admissions counselor, essay/personal statement, letters of recommendation, age of applicant, state residence

ACADEMIC COURSEWORK AND RELATED FEATURES:
- Support services: freshman orientation, college survival skills, academic advising, women's center, psychological counseling, academic skills center, study technique workshops, career advising, peer counseling, extended time for tests
- Separate new-student orientation
- Students are not required to work with tutors
- Group and one-on-one tutoring by peer tutors as well as professional tutors in all academic areas
- Academic counseling is required
- Students are assigned an academic adviser
- Placement testing is required
- A total of 158 full-time faculty at the institution
- Two faculty members assigned to the program
- Students take an average of 20%–50% of their classes with alternative admissions students only
- Alternative admissions classes average 15 students
- Students are not limited to credit load

REQUIRED COURSES:
College Composition (credit-bearing)—alternative admissions students only
Critical Reading (credit-bearing)—alternative admissions students only
Voice and Diction (credit-bearing)
Critical Thinking (credit-bearing)—alternative admissions students only
- Courses required of students who demonstrate deficiency:
   Language Arts Skills Development (noncredit)—alternative admissions students only
   Introduction to College Composition (credit-bearing)—alternative admissions students only
   College Preparatory (noncredit)—alternative admissions students only

- Remedial courses are calculated in GPA

PROFILE OF ALTERNATIVE ADMISSIONS STUDENTS:
- 1% of students transfer to another college after freshman year, 5% transfer after sophomore year
- 100% state residents

The Other Route into College

OTHER FEATURES/ACCOMMODATIONS:
- On-campus housing is not available for alternative admissions students
- A meal plan is not available
- Financial aid is available

DEADLINES:
- Rolling admission—5 days after application is sent, notification of admission

MOREHEAD STATE UNIVERSITY

>>>>>>>>>>>>>>>>>>>>>>>>>>

Morehead, KY 40351
(606) 783-2000

$1,190 In-State Tuition and Fees
$3,319 Out-of-State Tuition and Fees
$1,060 Average Double Room
$1,310 Average Meal Plan

5,962 full-time undergraduates, 5,376 part-time undergraduates
21:1 student/faculty ratio

>>

Founded in 1922, Morehead State University is a public institution, coed. Located on 1,044 acres in a town 65 miles from Lexington. Associate's and bachelor's degrees are offered.

ALTERNATIVE ADMISSIONS:

Contact: Dr. Dan Connell, Director of Academic Services Center (606) 783-2005

Morehead State University has a structured program, Provisional Studies Program, initiated in 1987 for alternative admissions students. The formal program of studies begins in the fall and lasts for 1 year; however, students can also enter the program in the spring and continue for 1 year. Fifty percent of the students complete the program in that time.

ADMISSION POLICIES:
- New students are eligible for alternative admissions

- Requirements for admission as a freshman:
  10 — average ACT
  2.0 — average GPA

Other considerations: interview with admissions counselor

ACADEMIC COURSEWORK AND RELATED FEATURES:
- Support services: freshman orientation, college survival skills, academic advising, drug/alcohol counseling, psychological counseling, academic skills center, study technique workshops, career advising, peer counseling, health center, aptitude testing
- Separate new-student orientation
- Students are not required to work with tutors
- One-on-one tutoring by peer tutors in math, English, sociology, data processing, and other academic areas
- Academic counseling is required
- Students are not assigned an academic adviser
- Placement testing is required
- Students are limited to a credit load of 15 credits per semester

REQUIRED COURSES:
Career Planning (credit-bearing)
Study Skills (credit-bearing)
Use of Libraries (credit-bearing)
Orientation to University Life (credit-bearing)
- Courses required of students who demonstrate deficiency:
  Reading Enrichment (credit-bearing)—alternative admissions students only
  Developmental Writing (credit-bearing)—alternative admissions students only
  Arithmetic (credit-bearing)—alternative admissions students only

- Remedial courses are calculated in GPA
- Required courses are calculated in GPA

OTHER FEATURES/ACCOMMODATIONS:
- On-campus housing is available, but is not guaranteed for alternative admissions students
- A meal plan is available

Stacy Needle

MORGAN STATE UNIVERSITY

>>>>>>>>>>>>>>>>>>>>>>>>>>

Baltimore, MD 21239
(301) 444-3000

$1,922 In-State Tuition and Fees
$3,832 Out-of-State Tuition and Fees
$2,000 Average Double Room
$1,716 Average Meal Plan

2,960 full-time undergraduates, 644 part-time
  undergraduates
17:1 student/faculty ratio
39% of undergraduates study business

>>

Founded in 1867, Morgan State University is a public
institution, coed. Located on 122 acres in a large city.
Bachelor's degrees are offered.

ALTERNATIVE ADMISSIONS:

Contact: Sidney Edwards, Director of Academic Development (301) 444-3032

Morgan State University has a structured summer program, Provisional Admit Program, initiated in 1987 for
alternative admissions students. The program begins in
June and lasts for 8 weeks. Ninety-eight percent of the
students complete the program in that time.

ADMISSION POLICIES:

- New and transfer students are eligible for alternative
  admissions, with a limit of 200 students. There is a
  wait list

- Requirements for admission as a freshman:
  660 — minimum combined verbal and math SAT
  2.0 — minimum GPA
- Other considerations: ACT scores (in place of SAT)

- Admission considerations—transfer student: GPA at
  previous institution, type of college attended, number of credits completed (less than 32 credits), age
  of applicant, state residence

ACADEMIC COURSEWORK AND RELATED FEATURES:

- Support services: freshman orientation, college survival skills, academic advising, drug/alcohol counseling, psychological counseling, career advising, peer
  counseling, health center
- Students are not required to work with tutors

- Students are assigned an academic adviser
- Placement testing is required in reading, math, and
  English
- Students take all of their classes with alternative
  admissions students only
- Alternative admissions classes average 15 students

REQUIRED COURSES:

- Courses required of students who demonstrate defi-
  ciency:
  Developmental Reading (credit-bearing)—alterna-
    tive admissions students only
  Basic Math (credit-bearing)—alternative admissions
    students only
  Introduction to Composition (credit-bearing)—alter-
    native admissions students only

- Remedial courses are calculated in GPA
- Minimum of 2.0 GPA required to stay in program; if
  below 2.0 GPA, a student is academically dismissed

PROFILE OF ALTERNATIVE ADMISSIONS STUDENTS:

- 114 alternative admissions students enrolled
- 85% of accepted students enrolled
- 100% minority, 65% female
- 68% state residents
- None 25 years or older
- No intercollegiate athletes
- 20% in top 50% of high school class

OTHER FEATURES/ACCOMMODATIONS:

- On-campus housing is available, but is not guaranteed
  for alternative admissions students
- A meal plan is available
- Financial aid is available

DEADLINES:

- Rolling admission
- March 1 for financial aid

The Other Route into College

MOUNT MARTY COLLEGE

>>>>>>>>>>>>>>>>>>>>>>>>>>>

Yankton, SD 57078
(605) 668-1499

$5,775 Tuition and Fees
$2,460 Average Double Room and Meal Plan

470 full-time undergraduates, 401 part-time
   undergraduates
11:1 student/faculty ratio

>>

Founded in 1936, Mount Marty College is a private
institution, coed, affiliated with the Roman Catholic
church. Located on 80 acres in a small city 65 miles
from Sioux City, Iowa. Associate's and bachelor's degrees are offered.

ALTERNATIVE ADMISSIONS:

Contact: S. Pierre Roberts, Academic Adviser (605)
668-1595

Mount Marty College has a structured program, initiated in 1986 for alternative admissions students. The
formal program of studies begins in the fall and lasts for
a minimum of 1 semester.

ADMISSION POLICIES:

• New and transfer students are eligible for alternative
  admissions

• Requirements for admission as a freshman:
     8 — minimum ACT
     1.5 — minimum GPA
Other considerations: SAT scores (in place of ACT)

• Requirements for admission as a transfer student:
  1.35 — average GPA

ACADEMIC COURSEWORK AND RELATED FEATURES:

• Support services: freshman orientation, college survival skills, academic advising, academic skills center,
  career advising
• Students are not required to work with tutors
• Counseling is not required
• Students are assigned an academic adviser. None of
  the advisers serve alternative admissions students
  exclusively. Students meet with advisers 2–3 times
  per semester
• Placement testing is not required

• Alternative admissions students do not take separate
  classes
• Students are limited to a credit load of 14 credits per
  semester until they attain a 2.0 GPA

PROFILE OF ALTERNATIVE ADMISSIONS STUDENTS:

• 13 alternative admissions students enrolled
• 70% of accepted students enrolled
• 9% minority, 56% female
• 67% state residents, no international students
• 18% 25 years or older
• No intercollegiate athletes
• No learning disabled
• None in top 50% of high school class
• 25% graduate within 4 years
• 33% graduate within 5 years

OTHER FEATURES/ACCOMMODATIONS:

• On-campus housing is available and is guaranteed for
  alternative admissions students
• A meal plan is available
• Financial aid is available

DEADLINES:

• Rolling admission
• March 1 for financial aid

NAZARETH COLLEGE OF ROCHESTER

>>>>>>>>>>>>>>>>>>>>>>>>>>>

Rochester, NY 14610
(716) 586-2525

$7,400 Tuition and Fees
$1,900 Average Double Room
$1,900 Average Meal Plan

1,480 full-time undergraduates, 505 part-time
   undergraduates
14:1 student/faculty ratio

>>

Founded in 1924, Nazareth College of Rochester is a
private institution, coed. Located on 75 acres in a small
city. Bachelor's degrees are offered.

Stacy Needle

ALTERNATIVE ADMISSIONS:

Contact: Thomas DaRin, Director of Admissions (716) 586-2525

Nazareth College of Rochester has a policy for alternative admissions students.

ADMISSION POLICIES:

- New students are eligible for alternative admissions, with a limit of 80 students. There is no wait list

- Requirements for admission as a freshman:
  450 — average verbal SAT
  400 — average math SAT
  or
  19 — average ACT

  2.5 — average GPA

Other considerations: high school rank, essay/personal statement, letters of recommendation

ACADEMIC COURSEWORK AND RELATED FEATURES:

- Support services: freshman orientation, college survival skills, academic advising, drug/alcohol counseling, women's center, psychological counseling, academic skills center, study technique workshops, career advising, peer counseling, health center, aptitude testing, extended time for tests
- Students are not required to work with tutors
- Group and one-on-one tutoring by peer tutors as well as professional tutors in all academic areas
- Students are assigned an academic adviser. None of the advisers serve alternative admissions students exclusively. Students meet with advisers 2 times per semester
- Placement testing is required in math and writing
- A total of 120 full-time faculty at the institution
- Two faculty members assigned to the program, who are trained to work with alternative admissions students
- Students take an average of 20% of their classes with alternative admissions students only
- Alternative admissions classes average 20 students
- Students are limited to a credit load of 13 credits per semester through fall semester of freshman year

REQUIRED COURSES:

- Courses required of students who demonstrate deficiency:
  Study Skills (noncredit)—alternative admissions students only

PROFILE OF ALTERNATIVE ADMISSIONS STUDENTS:

- 40 alternative admissions students enrolled
- 50% of accepted students enrolled

- 100% enter as new students
- 15% of the students transfer to another college after freshman year, 15% transfer after sophomore year
- 8% minority, 50% female
- 80% state residents, no international students
- None 25 years or older
- 20% intercollegiate athletes, Division III sports available:
  soccer, basketball, swimming, tennis, golf, lacrosse (men)
  soccer, basketball, swimming, tennis, golf, softball, volleyball (women)
- 80% in top 50% of high school class
- 40% graduate within 4 years

OTHER FEATURES/ACCOMMODATIONS:

- On-campus housing is available
- A meal plan is available
- Financial aid is available

DEADLINES:

- Rolling admission
- March 30 for financial aid
- May 1 for reply date

NEBRASKA WESLEYAN UNIVERSITY

>>>>>>>>>>>>>>>>>>>>>>>>>>

Lincoln, NE 68504
(402) 465-2218

$7,188 Tuition and Fees
$2,570 Average Double Room
$2,850 Average Meal Plan

1,286 full-time undergraduates, 290 part-time undergraduates
13:1 student/faculty ratio

>>

Founded in 1887, Nebraska Wesleyan University is a private institution, coed, affiliated with the United Methodist church. Located on 50 acres in a small city, 50 miles from Omaha. Associate's and bachelor's degrees are offered.

The Other Route into College

ALTERNATIVE ADMISSIONS:

Contact: Kendal Sieg, Director of Admissions (402) 465-2218

Nebraska Wesleyan University has a policy for alternative admissions students.

ADMISSION POLICIES:

- New and transfer students are eligible for alternative admissions

- Requirements for admission as a freshman:
  14 — average ACT
Other considerations: high school GPA, high school rank, type of high school attended

- Admission considerations—transfer student: GPA at previous institution

ACADEMIC COURSEWORK AND RELATED FEATURES:

- Support services: freshman orientation, academic advising, psychological counseling, career advising, health center
- Students are not required to work with tutors
- Counseling is not required
- Students are assigned an academic adviser. None of the advisers serve alternative admissions students exclusively
- Placement testing is not required
- Alternative admissions students do not take separate classes
- Students are limited to a credit load of 13 credits per semester through fall semester of freshman year

REQUIRED COURSES:

- Minimum of 1.6 GPA required to stay at college; if below 1.6 GPA, a student is placed on academic probation

PROFILE OF ALTERNATIVE ADMISSIONS STUDENTS:

- 14 alternative admissions students enrolled
- 45% of accepted students enrolled
- 28% minority, 50% female
- 100% state residents
- 35% intercollegiate athletes, Division III sports available:
  football, basketball, baseball, indoor track, track, cross-country, tennis (men)
  volleyball, basketball, softball, indoor track, track, cross-country, tennis (women)
- No learning disabled
- None in top 50% of high school class

OTHER FEATURES/ACCOMMODATIONS:

- On-campus housing is available and is guaranteed for alternative admissions students

- A meal plan is available. It is required of alternative admissions students
- Financial aid is available

DEADLINES:

- March 1 for admission; after March 1, applications are reviewed on a space-available basis
- April 1 for notification of acceptance

NEUMANN COLLEGE

>>>>>>>>>>>>>>>>>>>>>>>>>>

Aston, PA 19014
(215) 459-0905

$6,790 Tuition and Fees

465 full-time undergraduates, 599 part-time
  undergraduates
12:1 student/faculty ratio
39% of undergraduates study arts/letters

>>

Founded in 1965, Neumann College is a private institution, coed, affiliated with the Roman Catholic church. Located on 20 acres in a town 12 miles from Philadelphia. Associate's and bachelor's degrees are offered.

ALTERNATIVE ADMISSIONS:

Contact: Sister Marcus Streibig (215) 459-0905

Neumann College has a structured program, Program for Academic Competence and Enrichment (P.A.C.E.), initiated in 1983 for alternative admissions students. The formal program of studies begins in the fall and lasts for 1 year.

ADMISSION POLICIES:

- New students are eligible for alternative admissions, with a limit of 15–20 students. There is a wait list

- Requirements for admission as a freshman:
  300 — minimum verbal SAT
  300 — minimum math SAT
- Other considerations: high school GPA, high school rank, interview with admissions counselor

ACADEMIC COURSEWORK AND RELATED FEATURES:

- Support services: freshman orientation, college survival skills, academic advising, drug/alcohol counsel-

Stacy Needle

ing, psychological counseling, academic skills center, study technique workshops, career advising, health center
- Separate new-student orientation
- Students are required to work with tutors
- One-on-one tutoring by peer tutors as well as professional tutors in math, reading, study skills, and writing
- Counseling is not required
- Students are assigned an academic adviser. Five percent of the advisers serve alternative admissions students exclusively. Students meet with advisers at least 2 times per semester
- Placement testing is required in essay writing, math, and reading
- A total of 44 full-time faculty at the institution
- Special faculty assigned to the program
- Students take an average of 25% of their classes with alternative admissions students only
- Alternative admissions classes average 15 students
- Students are limited to a credit load of 13 credits per semester through spring semester of freshman year

REQUIRED COURSES:

- Remedial courses required:
  Study Skills (credit-bearing)—alternative admissions students only
  Reading Lab (credit-bearing)—alternative admissions students only
- Other required courses
  Reading for the Disciplined (credit-bearing)
  General Psychology (credit-bearing)
  The American Heritage (credit-bearing)
  Introduction to Effective Writing (credit-bearing)
- Courses required of students who demonstrate deficiency:
  Successful Writing (credit-bearing)
  Developmental Algebra (credit-bearing)

- Remedial courses are calculated in GPA
- Required courses are calculated in GPA
- Minimum of 2.0 GPA required to stay in program; if below 2.0 GPA, a student is placed on academic probation

PROFILE OF ALTERNATIVE ADMISSIONS STUDENTS:

- 14 alternative admissions students enrolled
- 17% of accepted students enrolled
- 100% enter as new students
- 7% minority, 78% female
- 93% state residents, no international students
- None 25 years or older
- No intercollegiate athletes

- No learning disabled
- 57% in top 50% of high school class

OTHER FEATURES/ACCOMMODATIONS:
- On-campus housing is not available
- A meal plan is not available

DEADLINES:
- Rolling admission
- March 1 for financial aid
- May 1 for reply date

NEW ENGLAND COLLEGE

>>>>>>>>>>>>>>>>>>>>>>>>>>>

Henniker, NH 03242
(603) 428-2223

$9,790 Tuition and Fees
$4,200 Average Double Room and Meal Plan

960 full-time undergraduates, 60 part-time undergraduates
17:1 student/faculty ratio
45% of undergraduates study business

>>

Founded in 1946, New England College is a private institution, coed. Located on 220 acres in a rural community 17 miles from Concord. Bachelor's degrees are offered.

ALTERNATIVE ADMISSIONS:

Contact: Jolene Greene, Director of Admissions (603) 428-2223

New England College has a policy, Summer Seminar, initiated in 1979, for alternative admissions students.

ADMISSION POLICIES:
- New and transfer students are eligible for alternative admissions, with a limit of 50 students. There is a wait list

The Other Route into College

- Requirements for admission as a freshman:
  - 420 — average verbal SAT
  - 400 — average math SAT
  - or
  - 18 — average ACT

Other considerations: high school GPA, high school rank, type of high school attended, difficulty of high school courses taken, essay/personal statement, letters of recommendation

- Requirements for admission as a transfer student:
  - 2.0 — minimum GPA

Other considerations: difficulty of coursework, number of credits completed (less than 30 credits)

ACADEMIC COURSEWORK AND RELATED FEATURES:

- Placement testing is not required

OTHER FEATURES/ACCOMMODATIONS:

- On-campus housing is available for alternative admissions students
- A meal plan is available

DEADLINES:

- Rolling admission—3–4 weeks after application is sent, notification of admission
- April 15 for financial aid
- May 1 for reply date

NEW HAMPSHIRE COLLEGE

>>>>>>>>>>>>>>>>>>>>>>>>>>>

Manchester, NH 03104
(603) 645-9611

$8,840 Tuition and Fees
$2,400 Average Double Room
$1,980 Average Meal Plan

1,500 full-time undergraduates, 25 part-time
  undergraduates
22:1 student/faculty ratio
100% of undergraduates study business

>>

Founded in 1932, New Hampshire College is a private institution, coed. Located on 700 acres in a small city 50 miles from Boston, Massachusetts. Associate's and bachelor's degrees are offered.

ALTERNATIVE ADMISSIONS:

Additional cost: $2,160 basic program fee
Contact: Dr. Francis Doucette, Director of Learning Center (603) 645-9606

New Hampshire College has a structured summer program, Freshmen Entrance Program, for alternative admissions students. The program begins in July and lasts for 6 weeks. This college preparatory program focuses on basic skills.

ADMISSION POLICIES:

- New students are eligible for alternative admissions
- Admission considerations: SAT scores, high school GPA, type of high school attended, difficulty of high school courses taken, letters of recommendation

ACADEMIC COURSEWORK AND RELATED FEATURES:

- Support services: freshman orientation, college survival skills, academic advising, drug/alcohol counseling, psychological counseling, academic skills center, study technique workshops, career advising, peer counseling, health center, aptitude testing, extended time for tests
- Separate new-student orientation
- Students are not required to work with tutors
- Group and one-on-one tutoring by peer tutors as well as professional tutors
- Counseling is not required
- Students are assigned an academic adviser. None of the advisers serve alternative admissions students exclusively
- Placement testing is not required
- A total of 58 full-time faculty at the institution
- Approximately 1 faculty member assigned to the program, who is trained to work with alternative admissions students

PROFILE OF ALTERNATIVE ADMISSIONS STUDENTS:

- 19 alternative admissions students enrolled
- 100% enter as new students
- 20% minority, 40% female
- 25% state residents, no international students
- None 25 years or older
- No intercollegiate athletes
- None in top 50% of high school class
- 45% graduate within 4 years

Stacy Needle

110

OTHER FEATURES/ACCOMMODATIONS:

- On-campus housing is available and is guaranteed for alternative admissions students
- A meal plan is available
- Financial aid is available

DEADLINES:

- Rolling admission
- March 15 for financial aid
- June 15 for reply date

The program is best suited for a student with a marginal high school record.

NEW YORK UNIVERSITY

>>>>>>>>>>>>>>>>>>>>>>>>>>>

New York, NY 10011
(212) 998-4500

$13,335 Tuition and Fees
$ 6,132 Average Double Room and Meal Plan

10,000 full-time undergraduates, 1,000 part-time undergraduates
13:1 student/faculty ratio

>>

Founded in 1831, New York University is a private institution, coed. Located in a large city. Associate's and bachelor's degrees are offered.

ALTERNATIVE ADMISSIONS:

Contact: Steven Curry, Director of General Studies Program (212) 998-7120

New York University has a structured program, General Studies Program, initiated in 1972 for alternative admissions students. The formal program of studies begins in the fall and lasts for 2 years. Eighty percent of the students complete the program in that time. Students receive an associate's degree upon completion of their studies.

ADMISSION POLICIES:

- New students are eligible for alternative admissions, with a limit of 750–800 students. There is no wait list

- Requirements for admission as a freshman:
  475 — average verbal SAT
  510 — average math SAT
  2.8 — average GPA
Other considerations: high school rank, type of high school attended, difficulty of high school courses taken, interview with admissions counselor, essay/personal statement, letters of recommendation

ACADEMIC COURSEWORK AND RELATED FEATURES:

- Support services: freshman orientation, academic advising, drug/alcohol counseling, women's center, psychological counseling
- Separate new-student orientation
- Students are not required to work with tutors
- Counseling is not required
- Students are assigned an academic adviser
- Placement testing is not required
- A total of 2,520 full-time faculty at the institution
- Eighty faculty members assigned to the program
- Students take all of their classes with alternative admissions students
- Alternative admissions classes average 24 students

PROFILE OF ALTERNATIVE ADMISSIONS STUDENTS:

- 380 alternative admissions students enrolled
- 51% of accepted students enrolled
- 65%–75% graduate within 4 years

OTHER FEATURES/ACCOMMODATIONS:

- On-campus housing is available and is guaranteed for alternative admissions students
- A meal plan is available
- Financial aid is available

DEADLINES:

- February 1 for admission; after February 1, applications are reviewed on a space-available basis
- January 1 for financial aid
- April 1 for notification of admission
- May 1 for reply date

The program is best suited for a well-prepared student who does not require remedial coursework.

NORTH CAROLINA SCHOOL OF THE ARTS

>>>>>>>>>>>>>>>>>>>>>>>>>>

Winston-Salem, NC 27117
(919) 770-3291

$1,191 In-State Tuition and Fees
$5,523 Out-of-State Tuition and Fees
$1,250 Average Double Room
$1,477 Average Meal Plan

485 full-time undergraduates, 15 part-time
  undergraduates
7:1 student/faculty ratio
100% of undergraduates study arts/humanities

>>

Founded in 1965, North Carolina School of the Arts is
a public institution, coed. Located on 45 acres in a large
city. Associate's and bachelor's degrees are offered.

ALTERNATIVE ADMISSIONS:

Contact: Edward Brake, Director of Admissions (919)
770-3291

North Carolina School of the Arts has a policy for alternative admissions students.

ADMISSION POLICIES:

- New and transfer students are eligible for alternative
  admissions

- Admission considerations—freshman: type of
  courses taken, audition/portfolio

- Admission considerations—transfer student: audi-
  tion/portfolio

ACADEMIC COURSEWORK AND RELATED FEATURES:

- Support services: freshman orientation, academic advising, drug/alcohol counseling, academic skills center, career advising, peer counseling, health center,
  aptitude testing
- Students are not required to work with tutors
- Group and one-on-one tutoring by professional tutors in English and math
- Counseling is not required
- Students are assigned an academic adviser. None of
  the advisers serve alternative admissions students
  exclusively. Students meet with advisers 1 time per
  semester
- Placement testing is not required

- Alternative admissions students do not take separate
  classes
- Students are not limited to credit load

PROFILE OF ALTERNATIVE ADMISSIONS STUDENTS:

- 99% enter as new students, 1% as transfer students
- 14% minority, 50% female
- 50% state residents, 8% international students
- None 25 years or older
- No intercollegiate athletes
- No learning disabled
- 75% in top 50% of high school class
- 45% graduate within 4 years
- 46% graduate within 5 years

OTHER FEATURES/ACCOMMODATIONS:

- On-campus housing is available, but is not guaranteed
  for alternative admissions students
- A meal plan is available
- Financial aid is available

DEADLINES:

- Rolling admission
- April 1 for financial aid
- May 30 for reply date

The program is best suited for a student whose academic record does not meet the regular admission requirements, yet has exceptional artistic talent or
potential.

NORTHEASTERN UNIVERSITY

>>>>>>>>>>>>>>>>>>>>>>>>>>>>

Boston, MA 02115
(617) 437-5634

$9,458 Tuition and Fees
$3,180 Average Double Room
$2,790 Average Meal Plan

15,497 full-time undergraduates, 12,072 part-time
  undergraduates
29:1 student/faculty ratio
29% of undergraduates study engineering

Stacy Needle

112

>>

Founded in 1898, Northeastern University is a private institution, coed. Located on 55 acres in a large city. Associate's and bachelor's degrees are offered.

ALTERNATIVE ADMISSIONS:

Contact: Richard Wilson, Program Manager of Alternative Freshman Year Program (617) 437-5643

Northeastern University has a structured program, Alternative Freshman Year Program, initiated in 1974 for alternative admissions students. The formal program of studies begins in the fall and lasts for 1 year; however, students can also enter the program in the winter and continue for 1 year. Approximately 60% of the students complete the program in that time.

ADMISSION POLICIES:

• New students are eligible for alternative admissions

• Requirements for admission as a freshman:
    353 — average verbal SAT
    376 — average math SAT
    1.77 — average GPA
Other considerations: high school rank, type of high school attended, difficulty of high school courses taken, extracurricular activities, community service/volunteer work, essay/personal statement

ACADEMIC COURSEWORK AND RELATED FEATURES:

• Support services: freshman orientation, college survival skills, academic advising, drug/alcohol counseling, psychological counseling, academic skills center, study technique workshops, career advising, health center, aptitude testing, extended time for tests
• Separate new-student orientation
• Students are required to work with tutors 2 hours per week
• Group tutoring by professional tutors in math, English, history, and reading
• Academic and personal counseling is required
• Students are assigned an academic adviser. All advisers serve alternative admissions students exclusively. Students meet with advisers 5–6 times per semester
• Placement testing is required in English and math
• A total of 763 full-time faculty at the institution
• Approximately 80 faculty members assigned to the program, who are trained to work with alternative admissions students
• Students take an average of 85% of their classes with alternative admissions students only
• Alternative admissions classes average 20 students
• Students are not limited to credit load

REQUIRED COURSES:

• Remedial courses required:
    Math Preliminaries I (credit-bearing)—alternative admissions students only
    Math Preliminaries II (credit-bearing)—alternative admissions students only
• Other required courses:
    Intensive Language Skills (credit-bearing)—alternative admissions students only
    Fundamentals of English (credit-bearing)—alternative admissions students only
    History of Civilization (credit-bearing)—alternative admissions students only

• Required courses are calculated in GPA

PROFILE OF ALTERNATIVE ADMISSIONS STUDENTS:

• 586 alternative admissions students enrolled
• 49% of accepted students enrolled
• 20% graduate within 5 years
• 25% graduate within 6 years

OTHER FEATURES/ACCOMMODATIONS:

• On-campus housing is available and is guaranteed for alternative admissions students
• A meal plan is available
• Financial aid is not available

DEADLINES:

• Rolling admission
• May 1 for reply date

The program is best suited for a student who has fulfilled a complete college preparatory program in high school, yet did not achieve above-average grades and/or did not work up to his/her full potential.

NORTHERN ARIZONA UNIVERSITY

>>>>>>>>>>>>>>>>>>>>>>>>>>>>

Flagstaff, AZ 86011-4084
(602) 523-5511

$1,412 In-State Tuition and Fees
$5,004 Out-of-State Tuition and Fees
$1,260 Average Double Room
$1,272 Average Meal Plan

The Other Route into College

11,029 full-time undergraduates, 1,549 part-time
  undergraduates
23:1 student/faculty ratio
49% of undergraduates study arts/humanities/sciences

>>

Founded in 1899, Northern Arizona University is a public institution, coed. Located on 730 acres in a small city 140 miles from Phoenix. Bachelor's degrees are offered.

ALTERNATIVE ADMISSIONS:

Additional cost: $450 basic program fee
Contact: Beverly Grace-Odeleye, Director of Multicultural Student Center (602) 523-5656

Northern Arizona University has a structured summer program, Structured Transition and Academic Readiness (S.T.A.R.), initiated in 1988 for alternative admissions students. The program begins in early June and lasts 6 weeks. The student takes 1 class in Communications and the other in Basic Skills. One hundred percent of the students complete the program in 6 weeks.

ADMISSION POLICIES:

• New students are eligible for alternative admissions

• Admission based on individual criteria

ACADEMIC COURSEWORK AND RELATED FEATURES:

• Support services: freshman orientation, college survival skills, academic advising, drug/alcohol counseling, psychological counseling, academic skills center, study technique workshops, peer counseling, health center
• Separate new-student orientation
• Students are not required to work with tutors
• Group and one-on-one tutoring by peer tutors as well as professional tutors in most academic areas
• Counseling is not required
• Students are assigned an academic adviser
• Placement testing is required in English and math
• Alternative admissions students do not take separate classes

OTHER FEATURES/ACCOMMODATIONS:

• On-campus housing is available and is guaranteed for alternative admissions students
• On-campus housing is required of alternative admissions students
• A meal plan is available. It is required of alternative admissions students
• Financial aid is available

Stacy Needle

114

The program is best suited for a student from a multicultural background who needs assistance in completing a college degree.

NORTHWEST MISSOURI STATE UNIVERSITY

>>>>>>>>>>>>>>>>>>>>>>>>>>>>

Maryville, MO 64468
(816) 562-1562

$1,320 In-State Tuition and Fees
$2,400 Out-of-State Tuition and Fees
$1,150 Average Double Room and Meal Plan

4,292 full-time undergraduates, 482 part-time
  undergraduates
25:1 student/faculty ratio
34% of undergraduates study education

>>

Founded in 1905, Northwest Missouri State University is a public institution, coed. Located on 166 acres in a rural community 45 miles from St. Joseph. Bachelor's degrees are offered.

ALTERNATIVE ADMISSIONS:

Contact: Dale Montague, Director of Admissions (816) 562-1562

Northwest Missouri State University has a policy for alternative admissions students.

ADMISSION POLICIES:

• New and transfer students are eligible for alternative admissions

• Requirements for admission as a freshman:
  19.4 — average ACT
Other considerations: high school GPA, high school rank, letters of recommendation

• Requirements for admission as a transfer student:
  2.0 — minimum GPA
Other considerations: letters of recommendation

ACADEMIC COURSEWORK AND RELATED FEATURES:

- Support services: freshman orientation, college survival skills, academic advising, drug/alcohol counseling, psychological counseling, academic skills center, study technique workshops, career advising, peer counseling, health center, aptitude testing, extended time for tests
- Placement testing is required
- Alternative admissions students do not take separate classes
- Students are limited to a credit load of 13 credits per semester until they attain a 2.0 GPA

REQUIRED COURSES:

- Remedial courses required:
  Reading (noncredit)
  Math (noncredit)
  English (noncredit)

OTHER FEATURES/ACCOMMODATIONS:

- On-campus housing is available and is guaranteed for alternative admissions students
- A meal plan is available

DEADLINES:

- Rolling admission

NOTRE DAME COLLEGE OF OHIO

>>>>>>>>>>>>>>>>>>>>>>>>>>>

Cleveland, OH 44121
(216) 382-9806

$5,750 Tuition and Fees
$2,930 Average Double Room
$1,840 Average Meal Plan

208 full-time undergraduates, 546 part-time undergraduates
12:1 student/faculty ratio
34% of undergraduates study business

>>

Founded in 1922, Notre Dame College of Ohio is a private institution, women only, affiliated with the Roman Catholic church. Located on 53 acres in a town. Associate's and bachelor's degrees are offered.

ALTERNATIVE ADMISSIONS:

Contact: Jerri Marsee, Director of Admissions (216) 382-9806

Notre Dame College of Ohio has a structured program, Conditional Admission, initiated in 1922 for alternative admissions students. The formal program of studies begins in the fall and lasts for 1 year. Ninety percent of the students complete the program in that time.

ADMISSION POLICIES:

- New students are eligible for alternative admissions

- Requirements for admission as a freshman:
  340 — minimum verbal SAT
  310 — minimum math SAT
      or
   12 — minimum ACT

  1.8 — minimum GPA

Other considerations: high school rank, letters of recommendation

ACADEMIC COURSEWORK AND RELATED FEATURES:

- Support services: freshman orientation, academic advising, academic skills center, study technique workshops, career advising, health center
- Students are not required to work with tutors
- One-on-one tutoring by peer tutors as well as professional tutors in all academic areas
- Counseling is not required
- Students are assigned an academic adviser. None of the advisers serve alternative admissions students exclusively. Students meet with advisers approximately 4 times per semester
- Placement testing is required in math, English, and foreign language
- Alternative admissions students do not take separate classes
- Students are limited to a credit load of 12 credits per semester

REQUIRED COURSES:

- Minimum of 2.0 GPA required to stay in program; if below 2.0 GPA, a student is academically suspended

PROFILE OF ALTERNATIVE ADMISSIONS STUDENTS:

- 19 alternative admissions students enrolled
- 70% of accepted students enrolled
- 100% enter as new students
- 100% female
- 86% state residents, no international students
- None 25 years or older
- No intercollegiate athletes
- None in top 50% of high school class

The Other Route into College

OTHER FEATURES/ACCOMMODATIONS:
- On-campus housing is available, but is not guaranteed for alternative admissions students
- A meal plan is available
- Financial aid is available

DEADLINES:
- Rolling admission
- March 1 for financial aid

OAKLAND CITY COLLEGE

>>>>>>>>>>>>>>>>>>>>>>>>>>>>

Oakland City, IN 47660
(812) 749-1222

$5,990 Tuition and Fees
$ 850 Average Double Room
$1,580 Average Meal Plan

550 full-time undergraduates, 100 part-time
   undergraduates
14:1 student/faculty ratio
45% of undergraduates study business

>>

Founded in 1885, Oakland City College is a private institution, coed, affiliated with the General Baptist church. Located on 10 acres in a rural community 30 miles from Evansville. Associate's and bachelor's degrees are offered.

ALTERNATIVE ADMISSIONS:

Contact: Dr. Bernard Marley, Associate Professor of Education (812) 749-1222, Ext. 272

Oakland City College has a structured program, Project Opportunity, initiated in 1985 for alternative admissions students. The formal program of studies begins in the fall and lasts for 1 year.

ADMISSION POLICIES:
- New and transfer students are eligible for alternative admissions
- Admission considerations—freshman: SAT or ACT scores, high school GPA, high school rank
- Admission considerations—transfer student: GPA at previous institution

ACADEMIC COURSEWORK AND RELATED FEATURES:
- Support services: freshman orientation, academic advising
- Students are required to work with tutors 5 hours per week
- Group and one-on-one tutoring by peer tutors as well as professional tutors in all academic areas
- Personal and career counseling is required
- Students are assigned an academic adviser. Fifty percent of the advisers serve alternative admissions students exclusively. Students meet with advisers 2 times per semester
- Placement testing is required in reading, English, and math
- A total of 44 full-time faculty at the institution
- Four faculty members assigned to the program, who are trained to work with alternative admissions students
- Students take an average of 75% of their classes with alternative admissions students only
- Alternative admissions classes average 6–8 students
- Students are not limited to credit load

REQUIRED COURSES:

College Reading Skills (credit-bearing)—alternative admissions students only
- Courses required of students who demonstrate deficiency:
  Basic Study Skills (credit-bearing)—alternative admissions students only
  Basic English Skills (credit-bearing)—alternative admissions students only
  Fundamentals of Math (credit-bearing)—alternative admissions students only
  Fundamentals of Reading (credit-bearing)—alternative admissions students only

- Remedial courses are calculated in GPA
- Required courses are calculated in GPA
- Minimum of 1.5 GPA required to stay in program

PROFILE OF ALTERNATIVE ADMISSIONS STUDENTS:
- 8 alternative admissions students enrolled
- No minority, 50% female
- 75% state residents, 20% international students
- None 25 years or older
- No intercollegiate athletes
- No learning disabled
- None in top 50% of high school class
- 50% graduate within 4 years
- 20% graduate within 5 years

Stacy Needle

OTHER FEATURES/ACCOMMODATIONS:
- On-campus housing is available, but is not guaranteed for alternative admissions students
- A meal plan is available
- Financial aid is available

DEADLINES:
- Rolling admission
- March 1 for financial aid

OAKWOOD COLLEGE
>>>>>>>>>>>>>>>>>>>>>>>>>>

Huntsville, AL 35896
(205) 726-7030

$5,351 Tuition and Fees
$3,051 Average Double Room and Meal Plan

1,159 full-time undergraduates, 77 part-time
  undergraduates
13:1 student/faculty ratio
27% of undergraduates study math/sciences

>>

Founded in 1896, Oakwood College is a private institution, coed, affiliated with the Seventh-day Adventist church. Located on 1,185 acres in a town. Associate's and bachelor's degrees are offered.

ALTERNATIVE ADMISSIONS:
Contact: Linda Webb, Director of Developmental Learning Resource Center (205) 726-7145

Oakwood College has a structured program, Scholarship Improvement Program, for alternative admissions students. The formal program of studies begins in the fall.

ADMISSION POLICIES:
- New and transfer students are eligible for alternative admissions

- Admission considerations—new student: ACT scores, high school GPA, letters of recommendation, age of applicant

- Admission considerations—transfer student: GPA at previous institution, number of credits completed, letters of recommendation, age of applicant

ACADEMIC COURSEWORK AND RELATED FEATURES:
- Support services: freshman orientation, college survival skills, academic advising, drug/alcohol counseling, psychological counseling, academic skills center, career advising, health center, aptitude testing
- Students are required to work with tutors
- Group and one-on-one tutoring by peer tutors in all academic areas
- Counseling is not required
- Students are assigned an academic adviser
- Placement testing is required
- Students are limited to a credit load of 14 credits per semester until they attain a 2.0 GPA

REQUIRED COURSES:
- Remedial courses required:
  Basic Math
  Basic English
  Developmental Reading
  Study Skills

- Remedial courses are not calculated in GPA
- Minimum of 1.5 GPA required to stay in program; if below 1.5 GPA, a student has an additional quarter to attain a 1.5 GPA before he/she is academically dismissed

OTHER FEATURES/ACCOMMODATIONS:
- On-campus housing is available and is guaranteed for alternative admissions students
- A meal plan is available
- Financial aid is available

DEADLINES:
- Rolling admission
- April 15 for financial aid

OKLAHOMA CITY UNIVERSITY
>>>>>>>>>>>>>>>>>>>>>>>>>>>

Oklahoma City, OK 73106
(405) 521-5050

$4,558 Tuition and Fees
$1,380 Average Double Room
$1,680 Average Meal Plan

The Other Route into College

1,061 full-time undergraduates, 512 part-time
  undergraduates
21:1 student/faculty ratio

>>

Founded in 1904, Oklahoma City University is a private
institution, coed, affiliated with the Methodist church.
Located on 64 acres in a large city. Bachelor's degrees
are offered.

ALTERNATIVE ADMISSIONS:

Contact: Linda Vater, Director of Admissions (405)
521-5050

Oklahoma City University has a policy for alternative
admissions students.

ADMISSION POLICIES:

- New and transfer students are eligible for alternative
  admissions

- Admission considerations—new student: SAT or
  ACT scores, high school GPA, interview with admissions counselor, essay/personal statement, letters of
  recommendation

- Admission considerations—transfer student: GPA at
  previous institution, type of college attended, number of credits completed, interview with admissions
  counselor, essay/personal statement, letters of
  recommendation

ACADEMIC COURSEWORK AND RELATED FEATURES:

- Separate new-student orientation
- Placement testing is required
- Alternative admissions students do not take separate
  classes
- Students are not limited to credit load

OTHER FEATURES/ACCOMMODATIONS:

- On-campus housing is available, but is not guaranteed
  for alternative admissions students
- A meal plan is available

DEADLINES:

- Rolling admission

OLD DOMINION UNIVERSITY

>>>>>>>>>>>>>>>>>>>>>>>>>>>

Norfolk, VA 23529-0050
(804) 683-3637

_____

$2,462 In-State Tuition and Fees
$4,982 Out-of-State Tuition and Fees
$4,052 Average Double Room and Meal Plan

9,778 full-time undergraduates, 1,964 part-time
  undergraduates
19:1 student/faculty ratio

>>

Founded in 1930, Old Dominion University is a public
institution, coed. Located on 146 acres in a small city.
Bachelor's degrees are offered.

ALTERNATIVE ADMISSIONS:

Contact: Dr. Richard Parrent, Director of Admissions
(804) 683-3637

Old Dominion University has a structured program,
Academic Opportunity Program, for alternative admissions students. The formal program of studies begins
in the fall and lasts for 1 semester; however, students
can also enter the program in the spring and continue
for 1 semester.

ADMISSION POLICIES:

- New students are eligible for alternative admissions,
  with a limit of 500 students. There is no wait list

- Admission considerations—freshman: SAT scores,
  high school GPA, high school rank

ACADEMIC COURSEWORK AND RELATED FEATURES:

- Support services: freshman orientation, academic advising, women's center, psychological counseling, academic skills center, study technique workshops,
  career advising, peer counseling, health center, extended time for tests
- Separate new-student orientation
- Students are not required to work with tutors
- One-on-one tutoring by peer tutors as well as professional tutors in most academic areas
- Academic counseling is required
- Students are assigned an academic adviser. All advisers serve alternative admissions students exclusively. Students meet with advisers 1 time per
  semester

Stacy Needle

- Placement testing is required in math, reading, and writing
- Alternative admissions students do not take separate classes
- Students are not limited to credit load

REQUIRED COURSES:

- Courses required of students who demonstrate deficiency:
  Developmental Math
  Developmental Writing
  Developmental Reading

OTHER FEATURES/ACCOMMODATIONS:

- On-campus housing is available and is guaranteed for alternative admissions students
- A meal plan is available

DEADLINES:

- Rolling admission—4–6 weeks after application is sent, notification of admission
- January 1 for financial aid

The program is best suited for a student with a strong GPA but lower than recommended standardized test scores.

PACE UNIVERSITY
>>>>>>>>>>>>>>>>>>>>>>>>>>>

New York, NY 10038
(212) 346-1323

$7,880 Tuition and Fees
$2,800 Average Double Room
$1,200 Average Meal Plan

3,090 full-time undergraduates, 3,813 part-time undergraduates

>>

Founded in 1906, Pace University is a private institution, coed. Located in a large city. Associate's and bachelor's degrees are offered.

ALTERNATIVE ADMISSIONS:

Contact: Elizabeth Lee, Director of Challenge to Achievement at Pace (212) 346-1894

Pace University has a structured program, Challenge to Achievement at Pace (C.A.P.), for alternative admissions students. The formal program of studies begins in the fall and lasts for 1 year. Eighty-five percent of the students complete the program in that time.

ADMISSION POLICIES:

- New students are eligible for alternative admissions, with a limit of 250–300 students. There is a wait list
- Admission considerations—new students: SAT scores, high school GPA, high school rank, type of high school attended, letters of recommendation

ACADEMIC COURSEWORK AND RELATED FEATURES:

- Support services: freshman orientation, college survival skills, academic advising, drug/alcohol counseling, psychological counseling, academic skills center, study technique workshops, career advising, peer counseling, health center
- Students are not required to work with tutors
- One-on-one tutoring by peer tutors in all academic areas
- Counseling is not required
- Students are assigned an academic adviser
- Placement testing is required
- Special faculty assigned to the program
- Students take an average of 15% of their classes with alternative admissions students
- Alternative admissions classes average 17–20 students

REQUIRED COURSES:

- Minimum of 2.0 GPA required to stay in program; if below 2.0 GPA, a student is placed on academic probation

PROFILE OF ALTERNATIVE ADMISSIONS STUDENTS:

- 317 alternative admissions students enrolled

OTHER FEATURES/ACCOMMODATIONS:

- On-campus housing is available, but is not guaranteed for alternative admissions students
- A meal plan is available
- Financial aid is available

DEADLINES:

- Rolling admission
- March 15 for financial aid

PACE UNIVERSITY, PLEASANTVILLE/ BRIARCLIFF CAMPUS

>>>>>>>>>>>>>>>>>>>>>>>>>>>

Pleasantville, NY 10570
(914) 773-3746

$7,840 Tuition and Fees
$2,800 Average Double Room
$1,200 Average Meal Plan

3,000 full-time undergraduates, 1,000 part-time
undergraduates

>>

Founded in 1906, Pace University, Pleasantville/Briar-cliff Campus is a private institution, coed. Located on 220 acres in a town 30 miles from New York City. Associate's and bachelor's degrees are offered.

ALTERNATIVE ADMISSIONS:

Contact: Dr. Ruth Ann Thompson, Coordinator of Challenge to Achievement at Pace (914) 773-3666

Pace University, Pleasantville/Briarcliff Campus has a structured program, Challenge to Achievement at Pace (C.A.P.), initiated in 1986 for alternative admissions students. The formal program of studies begins in the fall and lasts for 2 semesters. Seventy-five percent of the students complete the program in that time.

ADMISSION POLICIES:

- New students are eligible for alternative admissions, with a limit of 90 students. There is no wait list

- Requirements for admission as a freshman:
  350 — minimum verbal SAT
  300 — minimum math SAT
Other considerations: high school GPA, difficulty of high school courses taken, letters of recommendation

ACADEMIC COURSEWORK AND RELATED FEATURES:

- Support services: freshman orientation, college survival skills, academic advising, drug/alcohol counseling, psychological counseling, academic skills center, study technique workshops, career advising, health center, aptitude testing
- Separate new-student orientation
- Students are required to work with tutors
- One-on-one tutoring by peer tutors as well as professional tutors

- Counseling is required
- Students are assigned an academic adviser. All advisers serve alternative admissions students exclusively. Students meet with advisers at least 3 times per semester.
- Placement testing is required in logic relations, math, and writing/reading
- Fifteen to twenty faculty members assigned to the program
- Students take an average of 75% of their classes with alternative admissions students
- Alternative admissions classes average 20–22 students
- Students are not limited to credit load

REQUIRED COURSES:

- Remedial courses required:
  Mathematical Reasoning (noncredit)—alternative admissions students only

- Minimum of 2.0 GPA required to stay in program; if below 2.0 GPA, a student is placed on academic probation

PROFILE OF ALTERNATIVE ADMISSIONS STUDENTS:

- 86 alternative admissions students enrolled
- 76% of the accepted students enrolled
- 100% enter as new students
- 10%–12% of the students transfer to another college after freshman year
- 9% minority, 47% female
- 70% state residents, no international students
- None 25 years or older
- 3% intercollegiate athletes
- No learning disabled
- 60% in top 50% of high school class

OTHER FEATURES/ACCOMMODATIONS:

- On-campus housing is available, but is not guaranteed for alternative admissions students
- A meal plan is available
- Financial aid is available

DEADLINES:

- Rolling admission
- March 15 for financial aid

Stacy Needle

PENNSYLVANIA STATE UNIVERSITY

>>>>>>>>>>>>>>>>>>>>>>>>>>>

University Park, PA 16802
(814) 865-5471

$3,754 In-State Tuition and Fees
$7,900 Out-of-State Tuition and Fees
$3,330 Average Double Room and Meal Plan

29,654 full-time undergraduates, 1,859 part-time
undergraduates

>>

Founded in 1855, Pennsylvania State University is a
public institution, coed. Located in a town 90 miles from
Harrisburg. Associate's and bachelor's degrees are offered.

ALTERNATIVE ADMISSIONS:

Contact: Scott Healy, Director of Admissions (814) 865-
5471

Pennsylvania State University has a policy, Provisional
Admission, for alternative admissions students.

ADMISSION POLICIES:

• New students are eligible for alternative admissions

• Admission based on individual criteria

ACADEMIC COURSEWORK AND RELATED FEATURES:

• Support services: freshman orientation, college survival skills, academic advising, drug/alcohol counseling, women's center, psychological counseling,
academic skills center, study technique workshops,
peer counseling, health center, aptitude testing
• Placement testing is required in English and math
• Alternative admissions students do not take separate
classes
• Students are not limited to credit load

PROFILE OF ALTERNATIVE ADMISSIONS STUDENTS:

• 1,800 alternative admissions students enrolled
• 70% of the accepted students enrolled

OTHER FEATURES/ACCOMMODATIONS:

• On-campus housing is not available for alternative
admissions students
• A meal plan is not available
• Financial aid is available

DEADLINES:

• November 30 for admission; after November 30, applications are accepted on a space-available basis.
• January 1–February 15 for financial aid

PENNSYLVANIA STATE UNIVERSITY AT ERIE, THE BEHREND COLLEGE

>>>>>>>>>>>>>>>>>>>>>>>>>>>

Erie, PA 16563
(814) 898-6100

$3,754 In-State Tuition and Fees
$7,900 Out-of-State Tuition and Fees
$1,480 Average Double Room
$1,770 Average Meal Plan

2,216 full-time undergraduates, 361 part-time
undergraduates
17:1 student/faculty ratio

>>

Founded in 1948, Pennsylvania State University at
Erie, The Behrend College is a public institution, coed.
Located on 700 acres in a small city 130 miles from
Pittsburgh. Associate's and bachelor's degrees are of-
fered.

ALTERNATIVE ADMISSIONS:

Contact: Patricia Bailey, Director of Admissions (814)
898-6100

Pennsylvania State University at Erie, The Behrend
College has a policy for alternative admissions students.

ADMISSION POLICIES:

• New and transfer students are eligible for alternative
admissions

• Admission considerations—new student: SAT
scores, high school GPA

• Requirements for admission as a transfer student:
2.0 — minimum GPA

The Other Route into College

ACADEMIC COURSEWORK AND RELATED FEATURES:

- Support services: freshman orientation, academic advising, drug/alcohol counseling, psychological counseling, academic skills center, career advising, peer counseling, health center
- Students are not required to work with tutors
- Group and one-on-one tutoring by peer tutors as well as professional tutors in all academic areas
- Counseling is not required
- Students are assigned an academic adviser
- Alternative admissions students do not take separate classes
- Students are not limited to credit load

PROFILE OF ALTERNATIVE ADMISSIONS STUDENTS:

- 14% minority, 9% female
- 100% state residents, no international students

OTHER FEATURES/ACCOMMODATIONS:

- On-campus housing is not available for alternative admissions students
- A meal plan is not available
- Financial aid is available

DEADLINES:

- Rolling admission—6–8 weeks after application is sent, notification of admission
- February 15 for financial aid

PRESCOTT COLLEGE

>>>>>>>>>>>>>>>>>>>>>>>>>>>

Prescott, AZ 86301
(602) 778-2090

$6,200 Tuition and Fees

160 full-time undergraduates, 15 part-time
   undergraduates
9:1 student/faculty ratio
30% of undergraduates study math/sciences

>>

Founded in 1966, Prescott College is a private institution, coed. Located on 2 acres in a town 100 miles from Phoenix. Bachelor's degrees are offered.

Stacy Needle

ALTERNATIVE ADMISSIONS:

Contact: Derek Peterson, Assistant Director of Admissions (602) 778-2090

Prescott College has a structured program, College of Second Chance, initiated in 1972 for alternative admissions students. The formal program of studies begins in the fall and lasts for 1 year. Eighty percent of the students complete the program in that time.

ADMISSION POLICIES:

- New and transfer students are eligible for alternative admissions, with a limit of 15 students. There is a wait list

- Requirements for admission as a freshman:
  1.8 — average GPA
Other considerations: high school rank, type of high school attended, difficulty of high school courses taken, interview with admissions counselor, essay/personal statement, letters of recommendation

- Requirements for admission as a transfer student:
  1.2 — minimum GPA
Other considerations: number of credits completed, community service/volunteer work, interview with admissions counselor, essay/personal statement, letters of recommendation

ACADEMIC COURSEWORK AND RELATED FEATURES:

- Support services: freshman orientation, college survival skills, academic advising, drug/alcohol counseling, academic skills center, study technique workshops, career advising, extended time for tests
- Students are not required to work with tutors
- Group and one-on-one tutoring by peer tutors in all academic areas
- Counseling is not required
- Students are assigned an academic adviser. Sixty-five percent of the advisers serve alternative admissions students exclusively. Students meet with advisers 5–10 times per semester
- Placement testing is required in English and math
- Alternative admissions students do not take separate classes
- Students are not limited to credit load

REQUIRED COURSES:

- Courses required of students who demonstrate deficiency:
  Writing Workshop
  Math Workshop

- Minimum of 2.0 GPA required to stay in program; if below 2.0 GPA, a student is placed on academic probation

PROFILE OF ALTERNATIVE ADMISSIONS STUDENTS:

- 15 alternative admissions students enrolled
- 85% of the accepted students enrolled
- 30% enter as new students, 70% as transfer students
- 3% minority, 47% female
- 3% state residents, 6% international students
- 22% 25 years or older
- 15% learning disabled
- 65% in top 50% of high school class

OTHER FEATURES/ACCOMMODATIONS:

- On-campus housing is not available for alternative admissions students
- A meal plan is not available
- Financial aid is available

DEADLINES:

- Rolling admission
- April 15 for financial aid
- June 21 for reply date

The program is best suited for a mature, self-motivated, creative person.

QUINNIPIAC COLLEGE

>>>>>>>>>>>>>>>>>>>>>>>>>

Hamden, CT 06518
(203) 281-8600

$8,910 Tuition and Fees
$4,170 Average Double Room and Meal Plan

2,032 full-time undergraduates, 752 part-time
   undergraduates
13:1 student/faculty ratio

>>

Founded in 1929, Quinnipiac College is a private institution, coed. Located on 160 acres in a town 15 miles from New Haven. Associate's and bachelor's degrees are offered.

ALTERNATIVE ADMISSIONS:

Contact: David Cole, Director of Academic Assistance Program (203) 288-5251, Ext. 356

Quinnipiac College has a structured program, Academic Assistance Program, initiated in 1971 for alternative admissions students. The formal program of studies

begins in the fall and lasts for 1 year; however, students can also enter the program in the spring and continue for 1 year. Approximately 85% of the students complete the program in that time.

ADMISSION POLICIES:

- New students are eligible for alternative admissions, with a limit of 130 students. There is no wait list
- Requirements for admission as a freshman:
  360 — average verbal SAT
  380 — average math SAT
  2.0 — average GPA
Other considerations: TSWE scores, high school rank, essay/personal statement, letters of recommendation

ACADEMIC COURSEWORK AND RELATED FEATURES:

- Support services: freshman orientation, college survival skills, academic advising, drug/alcohol counseling, women's center, psychological counseling, career advising, peer counseling, health center, aptitude testing
- Students are encouraged to work with tutors 1–2 hours per week
- One-on-one tutoring by peer tutors in accounting, biology, English, math, and Spanish
- Counseling is not required
- Students are assigned an academic adviser
- Placement testing is required in English and math
- A total of 150 full-time faculty at the institution
- Six to eight faculty assigned to the program
- Alternative admissions students do not take separate classes

REQUIRED COURSES:

- Courses required of students who demonstrate deficiency:
  Pre-College English (credit-bearing)
  Pre-College Math (credit-bearing)
- Remedial courses are calculated in GPA
- Minimum of 2.0 GPA required to stay in program; if below 2.0 GPA, a student is academically dismissed

PROFILE OF ALTERNATIVE ADMISSIONS STUDENTS:

- 129 alternative admissions students enrolled
- 35% of the accepted students enrolled
- 100% enter as new students
- 10% transfer to another college after freshman year, 20% transfer after sophomore year
- None 25 years or older

OTHER FEATURES/ACCOMMODATIONS:

- On-campus housing is available and is guaranteed for alternative admissions students

The Other Route into College

- A meal plan is available
- Financial aid is available

DEADLINES:

- Rolling admission
- March 1 for financial aid
- May 1 for reply date

RAMAPO COLLEGE OF NEW JERSEY

>>>>>>>>>>>>>>>>>>>>>>>>>>

Mahwah, NJ 07430
(201) 529-7600

$2,200 In-State Tuition and Fees
$2,800 Out-of-State Tuition and Fees
$2,700 Average Double Room
$1,200 Average Meal Plan

2,412 full-time undergraduates, 1,879 part-time
   undergraduates
20:1 student/faculty ratio
30% of undergraduates study business

>>

Founded in 1968, Ramapo College of New Jersey is a public institution, coed. Located on 350 acres in a town 25 miles from New York City. Bachelor's degrees are offered.

ALTERNATIVE ADMISSIONS:

Contact: Nancy Jaeger, Associate Director of Admissions (201) 529-7600

Ramapo College of New Jersey has a policy for alternative admissions students.

ADMISSION POLICIES:

- New students are eligible for alternative admissions, with a limit of approximately 50 students. There is no wait list
- Requirements for admission as a freshman:
   400 — average verbal SAT
   420 — average math SAT
   2.25 — average GPA
Other considerations: TSWE scores, type of high school attended, difficulty of high school courses taken, interview with admissions counselor, essay/personal statement

ACADEMIC COURSEWORK AND RELATED FEATURES:

- Support services: freshman orientation, college survival skills, academic advising, drug/alcohol counseling, women's center, psychological counseling, academic skills center, study technique workshops, career advising, peer counseling, health center, aptitude testing, extended time for tests
- Students are not required to work with tutors
- Group and one-on-one tutoring by peer tutors as well as professional tutors in all academic areas
- Counseling is not required
- Students are assigned an academic adviser. None of the advisers serve alternative admissions students exclusively
- Alternative admissions students do not take separate classes

REQUIRED COURSES:

- Courses required of students who demonstrate deficiency:
Remedial Math
Remedial English

PROFILE OF ALTERNATIVE ADMISSIONS STUDENTS:

- 50 alternative admissions students enrolled
- 90% of accepted students enrolled
- 100% enter as new students
- 25% minority, 50% female
- 100% state residents
- None 25 years or older
- 40% intercollegiate athletes, Division III sports available:
basketball, baseball, football, tennis, golf, soccer (men)
basketball, volleyball, tennis, softball (women)
- 20% learning disabled
- 20% in top 50% of high school class
- 55% graduate within 4 years
- 25% graduate within 5 years

OTHER FEATURES/ACCOMMODATIONS:

- On-campus housing is available, but is not guaranteed for alternative admissions students
- A meal plan is available
- Financial aid is available

DEADLINES:

- Rolling admission
- May 1 for financial aid
- May 1 for reply date

Stacy Needle

RHODE ISLAND COLLEGE

>>>>>>>>>>>>>>>>>>>>>>>>>

Providence, RI 02908
(401) 456-8234

$1,412 In-State Tuition and Fees
$4,040 Out-of-State Tuition and Fees
$1,800 Average Double Room
$2,150 Average Meal Plan

2,548 full-time undergraduates, 1,492 part-time
  undergraduates

>>

Founded in 1854, Rhode Island College is a public institution, coed. Located on 125 acres in a town. Associate's and bachelor's degrees are offered.

ALTERNATIVE ADMISSIONS:

Contact: Patricia Marzzacco, Coordinator of Recruit-
ment (401) 456-8234

Rhode Island College has a structured summer program, Performance Based Admissions, for alternative
admissions students.

ADMISSION POLICIES:

• New students are eligible for alternative admissions

• Admission based on individual criteria

ACADEMIC COURSEWORK AND RELATED FEATURES:

• Counseling is available
• Alternative admissions students do not take separate
  classes

REQUIRED COURSES:

• Minimum of 2.0 GPA required to stay in program; if
  below 2.0 GPA, a student may not enroll for the fall
  semester

PROFILE OF ALTERNATIVE ADMISSIONS STUDENTS:

• 69% graduate within 4 years

OTHER FEATURES/ACCOMMODATIONS:

• On-campus housing is available
• A meal plan is available

RIDER COLLEGE

>>>>>>>>>>>>>>>>>>>>>>>>>

Lawrenceville, NJ 08648
(609) 896-5041

$9,160 Tuition and Fees
$2,050 Average Double Room
$1,950 Average Meal Plan

3,000 full-time undergraduates, 1,100 part-time
  undergraduates
16:1 student/faculty ratio
50% of undergraduates study business

>>

Founded in 1865, Rider College is a private institution,
coed. Located on 340 acres in a town 3 miles from
Trenton. Associate's and bachelor's degrees are offered.

ALTERNATIVE ADMISSIONS:

Additional cost: $900–$1,400 basic program fee
Contact: Susan Christian, Director of Admissions (609)
896-5041

Rider College has a structured summer program, Summer Trial, for alternative admissions students. The program begins in either June or July and lasts for 6 weeks.
A student must complete 2 courses as well as study
skills seminars. Ninety percent of the students complete the program in 6 weeks.

ADMISSION POLICIES:

• New students are eligible for alternative admissions,
  with a limit of approximately 50 students. There is no
  wait list

• Requirements for admission as a freshman:
   420 — average verbal SAT
   420 — average math SAT
   40 — average TSWE
   2.0 — average GPA
Other considerations: high school rank, type of high
school attended, interview with admissions counselor,
letters of recommendation, alumni affiliation/recom-
mendation, athletic ability

ACADEMIC COURSEWORK AND RELATED FEATURES:

• Support services: freshman orientation, academic advising, drug/alcohol counseling, psychological counseling, academic skills center, study technique
  workshops, career advising, peer counseling, health
  center, aptitude testing

The Other Route into College

- Separate new-student orientation
- Students are not required to work with tutors
- Group and one-on-one tutoring by peer tutors in all academic areas
- Counseling is not required
- Students are assigned an academic adviser
- Placement testing is required in English and math
- Alternative admissions students do not take separate classes

REQUIRED COURSES:

- Remedial courses required:
  Pre-Composition (credit-bearing)

- Remedial courses are calculated in GPA

PROFILE OF ALTERNATIVE ADMISSIONS STUDENTS:

- 50 alternative admissions students enrolled
- 60% of the accepted students enrolled
- 100% enter as new students
- 15% of the students transfer to another college after freshman year, 25% transfer after sophomore year
- 10% minority, 50% female
- 75% state residents, no international students
- None 25 years or older
- 5% intercollegiate athletes
- 5%–10% learning disabled
- 33% in top 50% of high school class
- 60% graduate within 4 years

OTHER FEATURES/ACCOMMODATIONS:

- On-campus housing is available and is guaranteed for alternative admissions students
- A meal plan is available
- Financial aid is available

DEADLINES:

- Rolling admission
- March 1 for financial aid

ROBERT MORRIS COLLEGE

>>>>>>>>>>>>>>>>>>>>>>>>>>>

Coraopolis, PA 15108
(412) 262-8206

$4,200 Tuition and Fees
$1,500 Average Double Room and Meal Plan

Stacy Needle

2,987 full-time undergraduates, 2,096 part-time undergraduates

>>

Founded in 1921, Robert Morris College is a private institution, coed. Located on 230 acres in a town 17 miles from Pittsburgh. Associate's and bachelor's degrees are offered.

ALTERNATIVE ADMISSIONS:

Contact: R.E. Sukitsch, Dean of Enrollment (412) 262-8206

Robert Morris College has a structured program, Guided Studies, for alternative admissions students. The formal program of studies begins in the fall and lasts for a minimum of 1 semester.

ADMISSION POLICIES:

- New students are eligible for alternative admissions

- Requirements for admission as a freshman:
  1.75–2.00—minimum GPA

ACADEMIC COURSEWORK AND RELATED FEATURES:

- Students are not required to work with tutors
- Counseling is available
- Alternative admissions students do not take separate classes
- Students are limited to a credit load of 12 credits per semester

PROFILE OF ALTERNATIVE ADMISSIONS STUDENTS:

- 65% of the accepted students enrolled
- 48% graduate within 4 years

OTHER FEATURES/ACCOMMODATIONS:

- On-campus housing is available
- A meal plan is available

DEADLINES:

- Rolling admission

ROBERTS WESLEYAN COLLEGE

>>>>>>>>>>>>>>>>>>>>>>>>>>>

Rochester, NY 14624-1997
(716) 594-9471

$7,374 Tuition and Fees
$1,096 Average Double Room
$1,554 Average Meal Plan

667 full-time undergraduates, 77 part-time
   undergraduates
13:1 student/faculty ratio

>>

Founded in 1866, Roberts Wesleyan College is a private institution, coed, affiliated with the Free Methodist Church of North America. Located on 75 acres in a large city. Associate's and bachelor's degrees are offered.

ALTERNATIVE ADMISSIONS:

Contact: Barry Smith, Director of Admissions (716) 594-9471

Roberts Wesleyan College has a structured program, Conditional Acceptance, initiated in 1984 for alternative admissions students. The formal program of studies begins in the fall and lasts for 1 semester; however, students can also enter the program in the spring and continue for 1 semester.

ADMISSION POLICIES:

- New and transfer students are eligible for alternative admissions

- Admission considerations—new student: SAT or ACT scores, high school GPA, high school rank, difficulty of high school courses taken, essay/personal statement, letters of recommendation

- Admission considerations—transfer student: GPA at previous institution, number of credits completed, essay/personal statement, letters of recommendation

ACADEMIC COURSEWORK AND RELATED FEATURES:

- Support services: freshman orientation, college survival skills, academic advising, drug/alcohol counseling, psychological counseling, academic skills center, study technique workshops, career advising, health center, aptitude testing

- Students are required to work with tutors
- Group and one-on-one tutoring by peer tutors as well as professional tutors
- Counseling is not required
- Students are assigned an academic adviser. Students meet with advisers 15 times per semester
- Placement testing is required in reading, English, and math
- A total of 42 full-time faculty at the institution
- Three faculty members assigned to the program, who are trained to work with alternative admissions students
- Alternative admissions students do not take separate classes

REQUIRED COURSES:

- Remedial courses required:
  Math Essentials (noncredit)
  English Essentials (noncredit)

PROFILE OF ALTERNATIVE ADMISSIONS STUDENTS:

- 10% of the accepted students enrolled

OTHER FEATURES/ACCOMMODATIONS:

- On-campus housing is available for alternative admissions students
- A meal plan is available
- Financial aid is available

DEADLINES:

- Rolling admission—2 weeks after application is sent, notification of admission
- March 15 for financial aid

ROCHESTER INSTITUTE OF TECHNOLOGY

>>>>>>>>>>>>>>>>>>>>>>>>>>>

Rochester, NY 14623
(716) 475-6631

$9,972 Tuition and Fees
$2,355 Average Double Room
$2,115 Average Meal Plan

The Other Route into College

8,500 full-time undergraduates, 1,000 part-time
  undergraduates
17:1 student/faculty ratio
20% of undergraduates study engineering

>>

Founded in 1829, Rochester Institute of Technology is
a private institution, coed. Located on 1,300 acres in a
town. Associate's and bachelor's degrees are offered.

ALTERNATIVE ADMISSIONS:

Additional cost: $1,292 basic program fee
Contact: Irene Payne, Associate Director of Learning
Development Center (716) 475-6942

Rochester Institute of Technology has a structured
summer program, College Anticipation Program, initiated in 1975 for alternative admissions students. The
program begins in July and lasts for 5 weeks. The College Anticipation Program is an individualized plan of
academic skills development along with one or more
college credit courses.

ADMISSION POLICIES:

• New students are eligible for alternative admissions

• Admission considerations: SAT or ACT scores, high
  school GPA, high school rank, type of high school
  attended, difficulty of high school courses taken,
  essay/personal statement

• Admission to the College Anticipation Program is
  open to students who have graduated from an accred-
  ited high school

ACADEMIC COURSEWORK AND RELATED FEATURES:

• Support services: freshman orientation, college sur-
  vival skills, academic advising, academic skills center,
  study technique workshops, aptitude testing
• Students are not required to work with tutors
• Personal and career counseling is recommended
• Students are assigned an academic adviser
• Placement testing is not required
• A total of 565 full-time faculty at the institution
• Four to five faculty assigned to the program, who
  are trained to work with alternative admissions stu-
  dents

REQUIRED COURSES:

• Remedial courses required:
  Math Skills (noncredit)
  Reading Skills (noncredit)
  Writing Skills (noncredit)
  Study Skills Workshops (noncredit)

• Other required courses:
  Self-Awareness Personal Management (noncredit)
  Creative Problem Solving (noncredit)
  Self-Awareness/Goal Setting (noncredit)
  Persuasive Presentation (noncredit)

OTHER FEATURES/ACCOMMODATIONS:

• On-campus housing is available for alternative admissions students
• A meal plan is available

DEADLINES:

• Rolling admission

The program is best suited for a student who needs to
strengthen his/her self-motivation, self-discipline, and
self-confidence.

ROCKHURST COLLEGE
>>>>>>>>>>>>>>>>>>>>>>>>>>>

Kansas City, MO 64110
(816) 926-4100

$6,850 Tuition and Fees
$3,260 Average Double Room and Meal Plan

1,169 full-time undergraduates, 674 part-time
  undergraduates
20:1 student/faculty ratio

>>

Founded in 1910, Rockhurst College is a private institution, coed, affiliated with the Roman Catholic church.
Located on 25 acres in a large city. Bachelor's degrees
are offered.

ALTERNATIVE ADMISSIONS:

Contact: Michaela Zahner, Assistant Dean of College of
Arts and Sciences (816) 926-4075

Rockhurst College has a structured program, Freshman
Incentive Program, initiated in 1974 for alternative admissions students. The formal program of studies begins in the fall and lasts for 1 year. Seventy to
seventy-five percent of the students complete the program in that time.

Stacy Needle

ADMISSION POLICIES:

- New students are eligible for alternative admissions

- Requirements for admission as a freshman:
  16 — average ACT
Other considerations: SAT scores (in place of ACT), high school rank, letters of recommendation

ACADEMIC COURSEWORK AND RELATED FEATURES:

- Support services: freshman orientation, college survival skills, academic advising, drug/alcohol counseling, psychological counseling, academic skills center, study technique workshops, career advising, health center, aptitude testing
- Students are not required to work with tutors
- One-on-one tutoring by peer tutors as well as professional tutors in English, math, and science
- Counseling is not required
- Students are assigned an academic adviser. Students meet with advisers 7 times per semester
- A total of 96 full-time faculty at the institution
- Five faculty members assigned to the program, who are trained to work with alternative admissions students
- Students take an average of 40% of their classes with alternative admissions students only
- Alternative admissions classes average 20 students
- Students are not limited to credit load

REQUIRED COURSES:

- Remedial courses required:
  Study Skills (credit-bearing)—alternative admissions students only

- Remedial courses are calculated in GPA

PROFILE OF ALTERNATIVE ADMISSIONS STUDENTS:

- 20 alternative admissions students enrolled
- 65% of the accepted students enrolled
- 100% enter as new students
- 37% minority, 52% female
- 56% state residents
- 11% intercollegiate athletes
- 41% in top 50% of high school class

OTHER FEATURES/ACCOMMODATIONS:

- On-campus housing is available, but is not guaranteed for alternative admissions students
- A meal plan is available
- Financial aid is available

DEADLINES:

- Rolling admission
- April 1 for financial aid
- August 15 for reply date

RUSSELL SAGE COLLEGE

>>>>>>>>>>>>>>>>>>>>>>>>>>

Troy, NY 12180
(518) 270-2217

$8,970 Tuition and Fees
$3,900 Average Double Room and Meal Plan

1,060 full-time undergraduates, 160 part-time
  undergraduates

>>

Founded in 1916, Russell Sage College is a private institution, women only. Located on 8 acres in a small city 10 miles from Albany. Bachelor's degrees are offered.

ALTERNATIVE ADMISSIONS:

Contact: Susan Kiernan, Director of Admissions (518) 270-2217

Russell Sage College has a structured program, Sage Study Program, for alternative admissions students.

ADMISSION POLICIES:

- New students are eligible for alternative admissions

- Admission based on individual criteria

ACADEMIC COURSEWORK AND RELATED FEATURES:

- Students are not required to work with tutors
- Counseling is available
- Alternative admissions students do not take separate classes
- Students are limited to a credit load of 12 credits per semester through spring semester of freshman year

PROFILE OF ALTERNATIVE ADMISSIONS STUDENTS:

- 25% of the accepted students enrolled
- 75% graduate within 4 years

OTHER FEATURES/ACCOMMODATIONS:

- On-campus housing is available
- A meal plan is available

DEADLINES:

- Rolling admission

SACRED HEART UNIVERSITY

>>>>>>>>>>>>>>>>>>>>>>>>>>>

Fairfield, CT 06606
(203) 371-7880

$7,100 Tuition and Fees

1,665 full-time undergraduates, 2,164 part-time
  undergraduates

>>

Sacred Heart University is a private institution, coed,
affiliated with the Roman Catholic church. Located on
53 acres in a town. Associate's and bachelor's degrees
are offered.

ALTERNATIVE ADMISSIONS:

Contact: Diane Hanrahan, Admissions Counselor (203)
371-7880

Sacred Heart University has a structured program, Developmental Studies Program, for alternative admissions students. The formal program of studies begins
in the fall and lasts for 1 semester. Eighty percent of
the students complete the program in that time.

ADMISSION POLICIES:

• New students are eligible for alternative admissions

• Requirements for admission as a freshman:
  600 — minimum combined verbal and math SAT
• Other considerations: interview with admissions
  counselor

ACADEMIC COURSEWORK AND RELATED FEATURES:

• Students are required to work with tutors
• Counseling is available
• Alternative admissions students do not take separate
  classes
• Students are limited to a credit load of 12 credits per
  semester through spring semester of freshman year

REQUIRED COURSES:

• Remedial courses required:
  Basic English

• Minimum of 2.0 GPA required to stay in program; if
  below 2.0 GPA, a student is placed on academic
  probation

PROFILE OF ALTERNATIVE ADMISSIONS STUDENTS:

• 91% of the accepted students enrolled
• 70% graduate within 4 years

Stacy Needle

130

OTHER FEATURES/ACCOMMODATIONS:

• On-campus housing is not available
• A meal plan is not available

DEADLINES:

• Rolling admission

ST. CLOUD STATE UNIVERSITY

>>>>>>>>>>>>>>>>>>>>>>>>>>>>

St. Cloud, MN 56301-4498
(612) 255-2244

$1,536 In-State Tuition and Fees
$2,472 Out-of-State Tuition and Fees
$2,115 Average Double Room and Meal Plan

13,500 full-time undergraduates, 3,000 part-time
  undergraduates
22:1 student/faculty ratio
26% of undergraduates study business

>>

Founded in 1869, St. Cloud State University is a public
institution, coed. Located on 92 acres in a small city.
Bachelor's degrees are offered.

ALTERNATIVE ADMISSIONS:

Contact: Susan McGrath, Assistant to the Vice Presi-
dent/Coordinator of Division of General Studies (612)
255-4910

St. Cloud State University has a structured program,
Division of General Studies, initiated in 1982 for alternative admissions students. The formal program of
studies begins in the fall and lasts for 1 year; however,
students can also enter the program in the winter and
continue for 1 year. Sixty-five percent of the students
complete the program in that time.

ADMISSION POLICIES:

• New students are eligible for alternative admissions,
  with a limit of 250 students. There is no wait list

• Admission considerations: high school rank

ACADEMIC COURSEWORK AND RELATED FEATURES:

• Support services: freshman orientation, college survival skills, academic advising, drug/alcohol counsel-

ing, women's center, psychological counseling, academic skills center, study technique workshops, career advising, peer counseling, health center, aptitude testing

- Placement testing is required
- Students are not required to work with tutors
- Counseling is not required
- Students are assigned an academic adviser. Ninety percent of the advisers serve alternative admissions students exclusively. Students meet with advisers a minimum of 2 times per semester
- Placement testing is not required
- A total of 600 full-time faculty at the institution
- One faculty member assigned to the program, who is trained to work with alternative admissions students
- Students take an average of 50% of their classes with alternative admissions students only
- Alternative admissions classes average 25 students
- Students are not limited to credit load

REQUIRED COURSES:

- Managing the College Experience (credit-bearing)
- Required courses are not calculated in GPA

PROFILE OF ALTERNATIVE ADMISSIONS STUDENTS:

- 225 alternative admissions students enrolled
- 90% of the accepted students enrolled
- 100% enter as new students
- 10% of the students transfer to another college after freshman year, 10% transfer after sophomore year
- 30% minority, 40% female
- 80% state residents, no international students
- None 25 years or older
- 25% intercollegiate athletes, Division II sports available:
  football, hockey, cross-country, baseball, track, swimming, diving, tennis, basketball, wrestling, golf (men)
  volleyball, golf, cross-country, tennis, track, softball, basketball, swimming, diving (women)
- 1% learning disabled
- None in top 50% of high school class

OTHER FEATURES/ACCOMMODATIONS:

- On-campus housing is available, but is not guaranteed for alternative admissions students
- A meal plan is available
- Financial aid is available

DEADLINES:

- December 1 for admission; after December 1, applications are reviewed on a space-available basis
- January 1 for financial aid

SAINT JOSEPH COLLEGE

>>>>>>>>>>>>>>>>>>>>>>>>>>>>

West Hartford, CT 06117
(203) 232-4571, Ext. 216

$8,900 Tuition and Fees
$4,000 Average Double Room and Meal Plan

505 full-time undergraduates, 181 part-time undergraduates

>>

Founded in 1932, Saint Joseph College is a private institution, women only, affiliated with the Roman Catholic church. Located on 84 acres in a town. Bachelor's degrees are offered.

ALTERNATIVE ADMISSIONS:

Contact: Carolyn Rock, Assistant Director of Admissions (203) 232-4571, Ext. 216

Saint Joseph College has a policy for alternative admissions students.

ADMISSION POLICIES:

- New students are eligible for alternative admissions
- Admission considerations: SAT scores, high school GPA, high school rank, interview with admissions counselor, letters of recommendation.

ACADEMIC COURSEWORK AND RELATED FEATURES:

- Students are not required to work with tutors
- Counseling is available
- Alternative admissions students do not take separate classes
- Students are limited to a credit load of 12 credits per semester through fall or spring semester of freshman year, depending on academic progress

OTHER FEATURES/ACCOMMODATIONS:

- On-campus housing is available
- A meal plan is available

DEADLINES:

- Rolling admission

SAINT LEO COLLEGE

>>>>>>>>>>>>>>>>>>>>>>>>>>

Saint Leo, FL 33574
(904) 588-8283

$7,132 Tuition and Fees
$1,400 Average Double Room
$1,860 Average Meal Plan

956 full-time undergraduates, 89 part-time
   undergraduates
17:1 student/faculty ratio
48% of undergraduates study business

>>

Founded in 1889, Saint Leo College is a private institution, coed, affiliated with the Roman Catholic church. Located on 64 acres in a rural community 25 miles from Tampa. Associate's and bachelor's degrees are offered.

ALTERNATIVE ADMISSIONS:

Contact: Dr. Mark Edmonds, Director of Learning Assistance Services (904) 588-8466

Saint Leo College has a structured program, Developmental Studies, initiated in 1978 for alternative admissions students. The formal program of studies begins in the fall and lasts for 1 semester. Seventy-five to eighty percent of the students complete the program in that time.

ADMISSION POLICIES:

• New students are eligible for alternative admissions, with a limit of 175 students. There is no wait list

• Requirements for admission as a freshman:
   300 — minimum verbal SAT
   300 — minimum math SAT
   30 — minimum TSWE
Other considerations: high school GPA, high school rank, difficulty of high school courses taken, essay/personal statement, letters of recommendation

ACADEMIC COURSEWORK AND RELATED FEATURES:

• Support services: freshman orientation, college survival skills, academic advising
• Students are required to work with tutors ½ hour per week
• One-on-one tutoring by professional tutors in English and math
• Counseling is not required

• Students are assigned an academic adviser. None of the advisers serve alternative admissions students exclusively. Students meet with advisers 1–2 times per semester
• Placement testing is required in English and math
• A total of 53 full-time faculty at the institution
• Eleven faculty members assigned to the program, who are trained to work with alternative admissions students
• Alternative admissions students do not take separate classes
• Students are not limited to credit load

REQUIRED COURSES:

Introduction to College (credit-bearing)
• Courses required of students who demonstrate deficiency:
   Developmental Reading (credit-bearing)
   Developmental Writing (credit-bearing)
   Developmental Math (credit-bearing)

• Remedial courses are calculated in GPA
• Required courses are calculated in GPA
• Minimum of 1.5 GPA required to stay in program; if below 1.5 GPA, a student is academically dismissed

PROFILE OF ALTERNATIVE ADMISSIONS STUDENTS:

• 50% graduate within 4 years

OTHER FEATURES/ACCOMMODATIONS:

• On-campus housing is available, but is not guaranteed for alternative admissions students
• A meal plan is available
• Financial aid is available

DEADLINES:

• Rolling admission
• April 1 for financial aid
• May 1 for reply date

The program is best suited for an underprepared student who is motivated to work in order to learn the requisite skills necessary to succeed in college.

Stacy Needle

SAINT MARY'S COLLEGE OF MINNESOTA

>>>>>>>>>>>>>>>>>>>>>>>>>>

Winona, MN 55987
(507) 457-1SMC

$7,940 Tuition and Fees
$1,560 Average Double Room
$1,300 Average Meal Plan

1,300 full-time undergraduates, 25 part-time
   undergraduates
15:1 student/faculty ratio
25% of undergraduates study math/sciences

>>

Founded in 1912, Saint Mary's College of Minnesota is a private institution, coed, affiliated with the Roman Catholic church. Located on 400 acres in a town. Bachelor's degrees are offered.

ALTERNATIVE ADMISSIONS:

Contact: Tony Piscitiello, Vice President for Admission
(800) 635-5987

Saint Mary's College of Minnesota has a structured program, St. Thomas Aquinas Program, initiated in 1986 for alternative admissions students. The formal program of studies begins in the fall and lasts for 1 year. Ninety percent of the students complete the program in that time.

ADMISSION POLICIES:

- New students are eligible for alternative admissions

- Requirements for admission as a freshman:
   14 — minimum ACT
   1.8 — minimum GPA
Other considerations: SAT scores (in place of ACT), high school rank, type of high school attended, difficulty of high school courses taken, essay/personal statement

ACADEMIC COURSEWORK AND RELATED FEATURES:

- Support services: freshman orientation, college survival skills, academic advising, drug/alcohol counseling, women's center, psychological counseling, academic skills center, study technique workshops, career advising, peer counseling, health center, aptitude testing, extended time for tests

- Students are required to work with tutors 3–4 times per week
- Group and one-on-one tutoring by peer tutors as well as professional tutors in all academic areas
- Counseling is not required
- Students are assigned an academic adviser. None of the advisers serve alternative admissions students exclusively. Students meet with advisers 6–7 times per semester
- Placement testing is required
- A total of 82 full-time faculty at the institution
- Two faculty members assigned to the program, who are trained to work with alternative admissions students
- Students are not limited to credit load

REQUIRED COURSES:

- Remedial courses required:
   Writing Skills (credit-bearing)
   Math (credit-bearing)

- Remedial courses are calculated in GPA
- Minimum of 1.8 GPA required to stay in program; if below 1.8 GPA, a student is placed on academic probation

PROFILE OF ALTERNATIVE ADMISSIONS STUDENTS:

- 40 alternative admissions students enrolled
- 75% of the accepted students enrolled
- 100% enter as new students
- 5%–6% of the students transfer to another college after freshman year, 10% transfer after sophomore year
- 5% minority, 50% female
- 50% state residents, no international students
- None 25 years or older
- 20% intercollegiate athletes, Division III sports available:
   cross-country, soccer, golf, ice hockey, basketball, cross-country skiing, baseball, tennis (men)
   cross-country, volleyball, soccer, golf, basketball, cross-country skiing, softball, tennis (women)
- 50% learning disabled
- 10% in top 50% of high school class
- 50% graduate within 4 years

OTHER FEATURES/ACCOMMODATIONS:

- On-campus housing is available and is guaranteed for alternative admissions students
- On-campus housing is required of alternative admissions students
- A meal plan is available. It is required of alternative admissions students
- Financial aid is available

The Other Route into College

DEADLINES:
- Rolling admission
- April 1 for financial aid
- May 1 for reply date

SAINT PETER'S COLLEGE

>>>>>>>>>>>>>>>>>>>>>>>>>

Jersey City, NJ 07306-5944
(201) 915-9213

$7,113 Tuition and Fees
$2,520 Average Double Room
$1,836 Average Meal Plan

2,182 full-time undergraduates, 1,249 part-time undergraduates

>>

Founded in 1872, Saint Peter's College is a private institution, coed, affiliated with the Roman Catholic church. Located on 8 acres in a small city. Associate's and bachelor's degrees are offered.

ALTERNATIVE ADMISSIONS:

Contact: Dr. Richard Petriello, Director of Admissions, (201) 915-9213

Saint Peter's College has a structured program, The Entering Student Support Program (E.S.S.P.), for alternative admissions students. The formal program of studies begins in the fall and lasts for 1 year. Seventy-five percent of the students complete the program in that time.

ADMISSION POLICIES:
- New students are eligible for alternative admissions

- Requirements for admission as a freshman:
  700 — minimum combined verbal and math SAT
  2.0 — minimum GPA
Other considerations: high school rank, interview with admissions counselor, letters of recommendation

ACADEMIC COURSEWORK AND RELATED FEATURES:
- Students are not required to work with tutors
- Counseling is available

- Students take classes with alternative admissions students only
- Alternative admissions classes average 18 students
- Students are limited to a credit load of 12 credits per semester through spring semester of freshman year

REQUIRED COURSES:
- Minimum of 1.8 GPA required to stay in program; if below 1.8 GPA, a student is placed on academic probation

PROFILE OF ALTERNATIVE ADMISSIONS STUDENTS:
- 53% of the accepted students enrolled
- 60% graduate within 4 years

OTHER FEATURES/ACCOMMODATIONS:
- On-campus housing is available
- A meal plan is available

DEADLINES:
- Rolling admission

SAINT VINCENT COLLEGE

>>>>>>>>>>>>>>>>>>>>>>>>>>

Latrobe, PA 15650
(412) 537-4540

$7,409 Tuition and Fees
$1,444 Average Double Room
$1,680 Average Meal Plan

978 full-time undergraduates, 215 part-time undergraduates
15:1 student/faculty ratio
30% of undergraduates study business

>>

Founded in 1846, Saint Vincent College is a private institution, coed, affiliated with the Roman Catholic church. Located on 100 acres in a town 35 miles from Pittsburgh. Bachelor's degrees are offered.

ALTERNATIVE ADMISSIONS:

Additional cost: $2,201 basic program fee
Contact: Br. David Kelly, Director of Opportunity Program (412) 537-9761

Stacy Needle

Saint Vincent College has a structured summer program, Opportunity Program, initiated in 1974 for alternative admissions students. The program begins in June and lasts for 6 weeks. Ninety-eight percent of the students complete the program in that time.

ADMISSION POLICIES:

• New students are eligible for alternative admissions, with a limit of 40 students. There is a wait list

• Admission considerations: high school GPA, high school rank, type of high school attended, difficulty of high school courses taken, interview with admissions counselor

ACADEMIC COURSEWORK AND RELATED FEATURES:

• Support services: freshman orientation, college survival skills, academic advising, drug/alcohol counseling, psychological counseling, academic skills center, study technique workshops, career advising, health center, aptitude testing, extended time for tests (if learning disabled)
• Separate new-student orientation
• Students are required to work with tutors 10 hours per week
• Group and one-on-one tutoring by peer tutors
• Academic counseling is required
• Students are assigned an academic adviser. Seventy-five percent of the advisers serve alternative admissions students exclusively
• Placement testing is required in reading, English, and math
• A total of 65 full-time faculty at the institution
• Seven faculty members assigned to the program
• Students take all of their classes with alternative admissions students
• Alternative admissions classes average 20 students
• Students are limited to a credit load of 12 credits per semester through fall semester of freshman year

REQUIRED COURSES:

• Remedial courses required:
  Introduction to Freshman Studies (credit-bearing)—alternative admissions students only
  Grammar and Composition (credit-bearing)—alternative admissions students only
  Basic Math (credit-bearing)—alternative admissions students only
  Math Overview (credit-bearing)—alternative admissions students only

• Remedial courses are calculated in GPA
• Minimum of 2.0 GPA required to stay in program

PROFILE OF ALTERNATIVE ADMISSIONS STUDENTS:
• 41 alternative admissions students enrolled
• 100% enter as new students
• 1% minority, 50% female
• None 25 years or older
• 1% intercollegiate athletes
• 35% graduate within 4 years
• 50% graduate within 5 years

OTHER FEATURES/ACCOMMODATIONS:
• On-campus housing is available and is guaranteed for alternative admissions students
• A meal plan is available. It is required of alternative admissions students
• Financial aid is available

DEADLINES:
• Rolling admission
• May 1 for financial aid

The program is best suited for a student who has ability, but is unfocused or lacks direction.

SAM HOUSTON STATE UNIVERSITY
>>>>>>>>>>>>>>>>>>>>>>>>>

Huntsville, TX 77341
(409) 294-1056

$ 916–$1,060 In-State Tuition and Fees
$3,412–$4,180 Out-of-State Tuition and Fees
$1,200 Average Double Room
$1,340 Average Meal Plan

8,330 full-time undergraduates, 1,714 part-time undergraduates
26:1 student/faculty ratio

>>

Founded in 1879, Sam Houston State University is a public institution, coed. Located on 1,254 acres in a small city 70 miles from Houston. Bachelor's degrees are offered.

ALTERNATIVE ADMISSIONS:

Contact: H. A. Bass, Director of Admissions (409) 294-1056

The Other Route into College

Sam Houston State University has a structured summer program, Summer Admissions Program, initiated in 1976 for alternative admissions students. The program begins in June and lasts for 2 summer terms. Fifty percent of the students complete the program in that time.

ADMISSION POLICIES:

- New students are eligible for alternative admissions

- Requirements for admission as a freshman:
  400 — minimum verbal SAT
  400 — minimum math SAT
  or
  18 — average ACT
Other considerations: high school rank, type of high school attended

ACADEMIC COURSEWORK AND RELATED FEATURES:

- Support services: freshman orientation, academic advising, psychological counseling, career advising, health center, aptitude testing
- Students are not required to work with tutors
- Group and one-on-one tutoring by professional tutors in math, history, and English
- Counseling is not required
- Students are not assigned an academic adviser
- Placement testing is required
- Alternative admissions students do not take separate classes

REQUIRED COURSES:

- Minimum of 2.0 GPA required to stay in program; if below 2.0 GPA, a student may not enroll for the fall semester

OTHER FEATURES/ACCOMMODATIONS:

- On-campus housing is available, but is not guaranteed for alternative admissions students
- A meal plan is available

SCHOOL OF THE ART INSTITUTE OF CHICAGO

>>>>>>>>>>>>>>>>>>>>>>>>>>>>

Chicago, IL 60603
(312) 899-5219

$9,300 Tuition and Fees

1,230 full-time undergraduates, 257 part-time undergraduates
12:1 student/faculty ratio
100% of undergraduates study arts/humanities

>>

Founded in 1866, the School of the Art Institute of Chicago is a private institution, coed. Located in a large city. Bachelor's degrees are offered.

ALTERNATIVE ADMISSIONS:

Contact: Barbara Guenther, (312) 899-5100

The School of the Art Institute of Chicago has a structured program, Freshman Access Program, initiated in 1987 for alternative admissions students. The formal program of studies begins in the fall and lasts for 1 year; however, students can also enter the program in the spring and continue for 1 year.

ADMISSION POLICIES:

- New and transfer students are eligible for alternative admissions

- Admission considerations—new student: SAT or ACT scores, high school GPA, essay/personal statement, letters of recommendation
  Students with SAT verbal scores below 420, ACT scores below 18, and/or poor academic record are eligible for Freshman Access Program

- Admission considerations—transfer student: GPA at previous institution, essay/personal statement, letters of recommendation

ACADEMIC COURSEWORK AND RELATED FEATURES:

- Support services: freshman orientation, college survival skills, academic advising, psychological counseling, academic skills center, career advising, peer counseling, aptitude testing
- Students are not required to work with tutors
- One-on-one tutoring by peer tutors as well as professional tutors in English

Stacy Needle

- Academic counseling is required
- Students are not assigned an academic adviser
- Placement testing is required in reading and writing
- A total of 90 full-time faculty at the institution
- Three faculty members assigned to the program, who are trained to work with alternative admissions students
- Students take classes with alternative admissions students only
- Alternative admissions classes average 20 students
- Students are not limited to credit load

REQUIRED COURSES:
- Courses required of students who demonstrate deficiency:
  Reading—alternative admissions students only
  Writing—alternative admissions students only

- Remedial courses are calculated in GPA
- Minimum of 2.0 GPA required to stay in program; if below 2.0 GPA, a student is placed on academic probation

PROFILE OF ALTERNATIVE ADMISSIONS STUDENTS:
- 40 alternative admissions students enrolled
- 80% of the accepted students enrolled
- 80% enter as new students, 20% as transfer students
- 28% minority, 3% international students
- 10% learning disabled
- 75% graduate within 4 years

OTHER FEATURES/ACCOMMODATIONS:
- On-campus housing is not available for alternative admissions students
- A meal plan is not available
- Financial aid is available

DEADLINES:
- Rolling admission
- August 1 for financial aid

The program is best suited for a student interested in art, yet has a weak academic background.

SETON HILL COLLEGE
>>>>>>>>>>>>>>>>>>>>>>>>>>>>>

Greensburg, PA 15601
(412) 838-4255

$7,500 Tuition and Fees
$3,280 Average Double Room and Meal Plan

550 full-time undergraduates, 320 part-time undergraduates

>>

Founded in 1883, Seton Hill College is a private institution, women only, affiliated with the Roman Catholic church. Located on 205 acres in a town 30 miles from Pittsburgh. Bachelor's degrees are offered.

ALTERNATIVE ADMISSIONS:

Contact: Barbara Strickler, Director of Admissions
(412) 838-4255

Seton Hill College has a structured summer program, Opportunity Program, for alternative admissions students. The program lasts for 6 weeks. Ninety-five percent of the students complete the program in that time.

ADMISSION POLICIES:
- New students are eligible for alternative admissions, with a limit of 30 students

- Admission considerations: interview with admissions counselor, letters of recommendation

ACADEMIC COURSEWORK AND RELATED FEATURES:
- Students are required to work with tutors
- Counseling is available
- Alternative admissions students do not take separate classes

REQUIRED COURSES:
- Minimum of 2.0 GPA required to stay in program; if below 2.0 GPA, a student may not enroll for the fall semester

PROFILE OF ALTERNATIVE ADMISSIONS STUDENTS:
- 92% graduate within 4 years

OTHER FEATURES/ACCOMMODATIONS:
- On-campus housing is available
- A meal plan is available

DEADLINES:
- Rolling admission

The Other Route into College

SIENA HEIGHTS COLLEGE

>>>>>>>>>>>>>>>>>>>>>>>>>>>

Adrian, MI 49221
(517) 263-0731

$5,640 Tuition and Fees
$3,300 Average Double Room and Meal Plan

1,000 full-time undergraduates
15:1 student/faculty ratio
18% of undergraduates study arts/humanities

>>

Founded in 1919, Siena Heights College is a private institution, coed, affiliated with the Roman Catholic church. Located on 140 acres in a small city 40 miles from Ann Arbor. Associate's and bachelor's degrees are offered.

ALTERNATIVE ADMISSIONS:

Contact: Mary Boylan, Director of Admissions (517) 263-0731

Siena Heights College has a structured program, On-Condition Admit, initiated in 1981 for alternative admissions students. The formal program of studies begins in the fall and lasts for 1 semester.

ADMISSION POLICIES:

- New students are eligible for alternative admissions

- Admission considerations: SAT or ACT scores, high school GPA, interview with admissions counselor, essay/personal statement, minority status

ACADEMIC COURSEWORK AND RELATED FEATURES:

- Support services: freshman orientation, college survival skills, academic advising, drug/alcohol counseling, psychological counseling, academic skills center, study technique workshops, career advising, peer counseling, health center, aptitude testing, extended time for tests
- Separate new-student orientation
- Students are not required to work with tutors
- Group and one-on-one tutoring by peer tutors as well as professional tutors in all academic areas
- Counseling is not required
- Students are assigned an academic adviser
- A total of 12 full-time faculty at the institution
- Special faculty assigned to the program, who are trained to work with alternative admissions students

- Students take an average of 50% of their classes with alternative admissions students
- Alternative admissions classes average 16 students
- Courses are also offered in the evening

REQUIRED COURSES:

- Remedial courses required:
  English (credit-bearing)—alternative admissions students only
  Decisions and Dilemmas (credit-bearing)—alternative admissions students only
  Reading (credit-bearing)—alternative admissions students only
  Math (credit-bearing)—alternative admissions students only
- Remedial courses are calculated in GPA

PROFILE OF ALTERNATIVE ADMISSIONS STUDENTS:

- 30 alternative admissions students enrolled
- 90% of the accepted students enrolled
- 100% enter as new students

OTHER FEATURES/ACCOMMODATIONS:

- On-campus housing is available, but is not guaranteed for alternative admissions students
- A meal plan is available
- Financial aid is available

DEADLINES:

- Rolling admission
- March 15 for financial aid
- June for reply date

SIERRA NEVADA COLLEGE

>>>>>>>>>>>>>>>>>>>>>>>>>>>

Incline Village, NV 89450-4269
(702) 831-1314

$6,150 Tuition and Fees
$2,000 Average Double Room

170 full-time undergraduates
12:1 student/faculty ratio
54% of undergraduates study business

Stacy Needle

>>

Founded in 1969, Sierra Nevada College is a private institution, coed. Located on 20 acres in a small city 35 miles from Reno. Bachelor's degrees are offered.

ALTERNATIVE ADMISSIONS:

Contact: Bradford Beckwith, Director of Admissions (702) 831-1314

Sierra Nevada College has a policy for alternative admissions students.

ADMISSION POLICIES:

- New and transfer students are eligible for alternative admissions

- Requirements for admission as a freshman:
  400 — average verbal SAT
  415 — average math SAT
  2.75 — average GPA
Other considerations: ACT scores (in place of SAT), essay/personal statement, letters of recommendation

- Requirements for admission as a transfer student:
  2.0 — minimum GPA
Other considerations: essay/personal statement

ACADEMIC COURSEWORK AND RELATED FEATURES:

- Placement testing is required in math and English
- Alternative admissions students do not take separate classes
- Students are limited to a credit load of 12 credits per semester until they attain a 2.0 GPA

REQUIRED COURSES:

- Courses required of students who demonstrate deficiency:
  Introduction to Writing
  Introduction to Math
- Minimum of 2.0 GPA required to stay at college; if below 2.0 GPA, a student is placed on academic probation

PROFILE OF ALTERNATIVE ADMISSIONS STUDENTS:

- 16 alternative admissions students enrolled
- 10% of the accepted students enrolled
- 60% enter as new students, 40% as transfer students
- 2% of the students transfer to another college after freshman year, 3% transfer after sophomore year
- 1% minority, 45% female
- 5% state residents, 1% international students
- 35% 25 years or older
- 3% intercollegiate athletes
- No learning disabled
- 75% in top 50% of high school class

OTHER FEATURES/ACCOMMODATIONS:

- On-campus housing is available, but is not guaranteed for alternative admissions students
- A meal plan is not available
- Financial aid is available

DEADLINES:

- Rolling admission—2 weeks after application is sent, notification of admission
- April 1 for financial aid
- June 1 for reply date

SIOUX FALLS COLLEGE

>>>>>>>>>>>>>>>>>>>>>>>>>>>>

Sioux Falls, SD 57105
(605) 331-6600

$6,210 Tuition and Fees
$1,100 Average Double Room
$1,371 Average Meal Plan

560 full-time undergraduates, 145 part-time undergraduates
14:1 student/faculty ratio
26% of undergraduates study business

>>

Founded in 1883, Sioux Falls College is a private institution, coed, affiliated with the American Baptist church. Located on 12 acres in a small city. Associate's and bachelor's degrees are offered.

ALTERNATIVE ADMISSIONS:

Contact: John French, Director of Admissions (605) 331-6600

Sioux Falls College has a policy for alternative admissions students.

ADMISSION POLICIES:

- New students are eligible for alternative admissions

- Requirements for admission as a freshman:
  19 — average ACT
  2.32 — average GPA

The Other Route into College

Other considerations: SAT scores (in place of ACT), high school rank, difficulty of high school courses taken, interview with admissions counselor, essay/personal statement, letters of recommendation

ACADEMIC COURSEWORK AND RELATED FEATURES:

- Support services: freshman orientation, college survival skills, academic advising, drug/alcohol counseling, women's center, psychological counseling, academic skills center, study technique workshops, career advising, peer counseling, health center, aptitude testing
- Students are not required to work with tutors
- Counseling is not required
- Students are assigned an academic adviser. Students meet with advisers 1–2 times per semester
- Alternative admissions students do not take separate classes

REQUIRED COURSES:

- Minimum of 1.5 GPA required to stay at college; if below 1.5 GPA, a student is placed on academic probation

OTHER FEATURES/ACCOMMODATIONS:

- On-campus housing is available and is guaranteed for alternative admissions students
- A meal plan is available

DEADLINES:

- February 1 for admission
- April 1 for financial aid

SOUTHERN ILLINOIS UNIVERSITY AT CARBONDALE

>>>>>>>>>>>>>>>>>>>>>>>>>>>

Carbondale, IL 62901
(618) 536-4405

$2,166 In-State Tuition and Fees
$5,287 Out-of-State Tuition and Fees
$2,636 Average Double Room and Meal Plan

Stacy Needle

140

17,818 full-time undergraduates, 2,308 part-time undergraduates
18:1 student/faculty ratio
19% of undergraduates study education

>>

Founded in 1869, Southern Illinois University at Carbondale is a public institution, coed. Located on 7,253 acres in a town 90 miles from St. Louis, Missouri. Associate's and bachelor's degrees are offered.

ALTERNATIVE ADMISSIONS:

Contact: Yvonne Williams, Acting Director (618) 536-6646

Southern Illinois University at Carbondale has a structured program, Center for Basic Studies, initiated in 1973 for alternative admissions students. The formal program of studies begins in the fall and lasts for approximately 1 year.

ADMISSION POLICIES:

- New students are eligible for alternative admissions, with a limit of 600 students. There is a wait list

- Requirements for admission as a freshman:
    - 10 — minimum ACT
    - 2.0 — minimum GPA
Other considerations: SAT scores (in place of ACT), high school rank, difficulty of high school courses taken, interview with admissions counselor

ACADEMIC COURSEWORK AND RELATED FEATURES:

- Support services: freshman orientation, college survival skills, academic advising, women's center, psychological counseling, academic skills center, study technique workshops, career advising, health center
- Separate new-student orientation
- Students are not required to work with tutors
- One-on-one tutoring by peer tutors in English, speech, math, history, and social studies
- Counseling is not required
- Students are assigned an academic adviser. All advisers serve alternative admissions students exclusively. Students meet with advisers at least 2 times per semester
- Placement testing is required in math, English, reading, and speech
- Students take classes with alternative admissions students
- Alternative admissions classes average 20 students
- Students are limited to a credit load of 14 credits per semester through spring semester of freshman year

REQUIRED COURSES:

Study Skills

- Minimum of 2.0 GPA required to stay in program; if below 2.0 GPA, a student is placed on academic probation

PROFILE OF ALTERNATIVE ADMISSIONS STUDENTS:

- 16% of the accepted students enrolled
- 100% enter as new students
- 32% minority, 58% female
- None 25 years or older
- No learning disabled
- 32% in top 50% of high school class
- 11% graduate within 4 years

OTHER FEATURES/ACCOMMODATIONS:

- On-campus housing is available, but is not guaranteed for alternative admissions students
- A meal plan is available
- Financial aid is available

DEADLINES:

- Rolling admission—6–8 weeks after application is sent, notification of admission
- April 1 for financial aid

SOUTHERN NAZARENE UNIVERSITY

>>>>>>>>>>>>>>>>>>>>>>>>>>>

Bethany, OK 73008
(405) 491-6324

$1,728–$2,160 Tuition and Fees
$1,354 Average Double Room
$1,408 Average Meal Plan

1,129 full-time undergraduates, 197 part-time undergraduates

>>

Founded in 1899, Southern Nazarene University is a private institution, coed, affiliated with the Church of the Nazarene. Located on 40 acres in a small city. Associate's and bachelor's degrees are offered.

ALTERNATIVE ADMISSIONS:

Contact: Susan Middendorf, Director of Admissions
(405) 491-6324

Southern Nazarene University has a policy for alternative admissions students.

ADMISSION POLICIES:

- New and transfer students are eligible for alternative admissions
- Admission considerations—new student: ACT scores, high school GPA, interview with admissions counselor
- Admission considerations—transfer student: GPA at previous institution, number of credits completed, interview with admissions counselor

ACADEMIC COURSEWORK AND RELATED FEATURES:

- Support services: freshman orientation, college survival skills, academic advising, psychological counseling, study technique workshops, career advising, peer counseling
- Students are not required to work with tutors
- One-on-one tutoring by peer tutors
- Students are assigned an academic adviser. None of the advisers serve alternative admissions students exclusively
- Placement testing is required
- Alternative admissions students do not take separate classes
- Students are not limited to credit load

OTHER FEATURES/ACCOMMODATIONS:

- On-campus housing is available and is guaranteed for alternative admissions students
- A meal plan is available. It is required of alternative admissions students
- Financial aid is available

The Other Route into College

SOUTHERN VERMONT COLLEGE

>>>>>>>>>>>>>>>>>>>>>>>>>>

Bennington, VT 05201
(802) 442-3137

$5,850 Tuition and Fees
$1,590 Average Double Room
$1,690 Average Meal Plan

405 full-time undergraduates, 209 part-time
   undergraduates
16:1 student/faculty ratio

>>

Founded in 1926, Southern Vermont College is a private institution, coed. Located on 370 acres in a town 30 miles from Albany, New York. Associate's and bachelor's degrees are offered.

ALTERNATIVE ADMISSIONS:

Contact: Ann Madden-Kirvin, Director of Admissions
(802) 442-3137

Southern Vermont College has a structured program, Conditional Acceptance, initiated in 1989 for alternative admissions students. The formal program of studies begins in the fall and lasts a minimum of 1 semester.

ADMISSION POLICIES:

• New and transfer students are eligible for alternative admissions

• Admission considerations—new student: high school GPA, high school rank, essay/personal statement, letters of recommendation

• Admission considerations—transfer student: GPA at previous institution, essay/personal statement, letters of recommendation

ACADEMIC COURSEWORK AND RELATED FEATURES:

• Support services: freshman orientation, academic advising, drug/alcohol counseling, psychological counseling, academic skills center, study technique workshops, career advising
• Students are required to work with tutors
• Group and one-on-one tutoring by peer tutors in all academic areas
• Counseling is not required
• Students are assigned an academic adviser

• Placement testing is required in composition, math, and reading
• Alternative admissions students do not take separate classes
• Students are limited to a credit load of 12 credits per semester until a satisfactory GPA is attained

REQUIRED COURSES:

• Remedial courses required:
  Study Skills (noncredit)

OTHER FEATURES/ACCOMMODATIONS:

• On-campus housing is available and is guaranteed for alternative admissions students
• A meal plan is available
• Financial aid is available

DEADLINES:

• Rolling admission

SOUTHWEST STATE UNIVERSITY

>>>>>>>>>>>>>>>>>>>>>>>>>>

Marshall, MN 56258
(507) 537-6286

$ 980–$1,225 In-State Tuition and Fees
$1,521–$1,902 Out-of-State Tuition and Fees
$1,500 Average Double Room
$ 790 Average Meal Plan

2,125 full-time undergraduates, 516 part-time
   undergraduates
19:1 student/faculty ratio

>>

Founded in 1963, Southwest State University is a public institution, coed. Located on 250 acres in a rural community 90 miles from Sioux Falls, South Dakota. Associate's and bachelor's degrees are offered.

ALTERNATIVE ADMISSIONS:

Contact: Philip Coltart, Director of Admissions (507) 537-6286

Southwest State University has a policy for alternative admissions students.

Stacy Needle

ADMISSION POLICIES:

- New and transfer students are eligible for alternative admissions

- Requirements for admission as a freshman:
  18 — average ACT
Other considerations: high school GPA, high school rank

- Admission considerations—transfer student: GPA at previous institution, type of college attended, number of credits completed

ACADEMIC COURSEWORK AND RELATED FEATURES:

- Support services: freshman orientation, college survival skills, academic advising, drug/alcohol counseling, women's center, psychological counseling, academic skills center, study technique workshops, career advising, peer counseling, health center, aptitude testing, extended time for tests
- Students are not required to work with tutors
- Counseling is not required
- Students are assigned an academic adviser. None of the advisers serve alternative admissions students exclusively
- Placement testing is not required
- Alternative admissions students do not take separate classes
- Students are limited to a credit load of 12 credits per semester through fall semester of freshman year

PROFILE OF ALTERNATIVE ADMISSIONS STUDENTS:

- 130 alternative admissions students enrolled
- 12% of the accepted students enrolled

OTHER FEATURES/ACCOMMODATIONS:

- On-campus housing is available, but is not guaranteed for alternative admissions students
- A meal plan is available

DEADLINES:

- Rolling admission

SOUTHWEST TEXAS STATE UNIVERSITY

>>>>>>>>>>>>>>>>>>>>>>>>>>>

San Marcos, TX 78666
(512) 245-2364

$ 982 In-State Tuition and Fees
$4,102 Out-of-State Tuition and Fees
$2,706 Average Double Room
$1,080 Average Meal Plan

14,631 full-time undergraduates, 3,415 part-time
  undergraduates
25:1 student/faculty ratio
24% of undergraduates study business

>>

Founded in 1903, Southwest Texas State University is a public institution, coed. Located on 1,091 acres in a town 30 miles from Austin. Associate's and bachelor's degrees are offered.

ALTERNATIVE ADMISSIONS:

Contact: Colleen Willard, Associate Director of Admissions (512) 245-2803

Southwest Texas State University has a structured summer program, Summer Conditional, for alternative admissions students. The program begins in June and lasts for 2½ months. Fifty-four percent of the students complete the program in that time.

ADMISSION POLICIES:

- New students are eligible for alternative admissions

- Requirements for admission as a freshman:
  600 — minimum combined verbal and math SAT
      or
   16 — minimum ACT
Other considerations: high school rank, age of applicant (under 21 years old)

ACADEMIC COURSEWORK AND RELATED FEATURES:

- Support services: freshman orientation, college survival skills, academic advising, drug/alcohol counseling, psychological counseling, academic skills center, study technique workshops, career advising, peer counseling, health center, aptitude testing
- Separate new-student orientation
- Students are not required to work with tutors
- Group and one-on-one tutoring by peer tutors as well as professional tutors

The Other Route into College

- Academic counseling is required
- Students are not assigned an academic adviser
- Placement testing is not required
- A total of 726 full-time faculty at the institution
- Two faculty members assigned to the program, who are trained to work with alternative admissions students
- Alternative admissions students do not take separate classes

REQUIRED COURSES:
- Remedial courses required:
  Pre-College Algebra (credit-bearing)
  Basic Reading/Writing (credit-bearing)

- Remedial courses are calculated in GPA
- Minimum of 2.0 GPA required to stay in program; if below 2.0 GPA, a student may not enroll for fall semester

PROFILE OF ALTERNATIVE ADMISSIONS STUDENTS:
- 166 alternative admissions students enrolled
- 58% of the accepted students enrolled

OTHER FEATURES/ACCOMMODATIONS:
- On-campus housing is available and is guaranteed for alternative admissions students
- On-campus housing is required of alternative admissions students
- A meal plan is available. It is required of alternative admissions students
- Financial aid is available

DEADLINES:
- May 15 for admission
- March 15 for financial aid
- May 15 for notification of admission

SPRING ARBOR COLLEGE
>>>>>>>>>>>>>>>>>>>>>>>>>>>

Spring Arbor, MI 49283
(517) 750-1200

$6,946 Tuition and Fees
$1,048 Average Double Room
$1,485 Average Meal Plan

Stacy Needle

602 full-time undergraduates, 180 part-time undergraduates
13:1 student/faculty ratio
27% of undergraduates study education

>>

Founded in 1873, Spring Arbor College is a private institution, coed, affiliated with the Free Methodist church. Located on 70 acres in a rural community 8 miles from Jackson. Associate's and bachelor's degrees are offered.

ALTERNATIVE ADMISSIONS:

Contact: Carolee Hamilton, Director of Learning Skills Center (517) 750-1200, Ext. 235

Spring Arbor College has a structured program, Conditional Admission, for alternative admissions students. The formal program of studies begins in the fall and lasts for 1–2 semesters; however, students can also enter the program in the spring and continue for 1–2 semesters.

ADMISSION POLICIES:
- New and transfer students are eligible for alternative admissions

- Requirements for admission as a freshman:
  12 — average ACT
  2.36 — average GPA
Other considerations: SAT scores (in place of ACT), essay/personal statement

- Requirements for admission as a transfer student:
  1.31 — minimum GPA
Other considerations: difficulty of coursework, type of college attended, number of credits completed

ACADEMIC COURSEWORK AND RELATED FEATURES:
- Support services: freshman orientation, college survival skills, academic advising, psychological counseling, academic skills center, career advising, health center, aptitude testing
- Students are not required to work with tutors
- Group and one-on-one tutoring in math, English, reading, and study skills
- Counseling is not required
- Students are assigned an academic adviser. None of the advisers serve alternative admissions students exclusively
- A total of 63 full-time faculty at the institution
- Two faculty members assigned to the program, who are trained to work with alternative admissions students

- Students are limited to a credit load of 13 credits per semester through second semester of program

REQUIRED COURSES:

- Reading Improvement/Study (credit-bearing)—alternative admissions students only
- Courses required of students who demonstrate deficiency:
  Math Lab (noncredit)—alternative admissions students only
  English Lab (noncredit)—alternative admissions students only
  Basic Composition

- Required courses are not calculated in GPA
- Minimum of 1.6 GPA required to stay in program; if below 1.6 GPA, a student is placed on academic probation

PROFILE OF ALTERNATIVE ADMISSIONS STUDENTS:

- 25 alternative admissions students enrolled
- 66% of the accepted students enrolled
- 20% minority, 40% female
- 96% state residents
- 28% intercollegiate athletes, Division NAIA sports available:
  baseball, basketball, cross-country, golf, soccer, tennis, track (men)
  basketball, cross-country, softball, tennis, track, volleyball (women)
- 4% learning disabled
- 29% in top 50% of high school class

OTHER FEATURES/ACCOMMODATIONS:

- On-campus housing is available and is guaranteed for alternative admissions students
- A meal plan is available
- Financial aid is available

DEADLINES:

- Rolling admission
- January 31 for financial aid

SPRING HILL COLLEGE

>>>>>>>>>>>>>>>>>>>>>>>>>>>>>

Mobile, AL 36608
(205) 460-2130

$8,250 Tuition and Fees
$2,000 Average Double Room
$1,870 Average Meal Plan

1,261 full-time undergraduates, 39 part-time undergraduates
14:1 student/faculty ratio
36% of undergraduates study business

>>

Founded in 1830, Spring Hill College is a private institution, coed, affiliated with the Roman Catholic church. Located on 500 acres in a large city. Bachelor's degrees are offered.

ALTERNATIVE ADMISSIONS:

Additional cost: $1,700 basic program fee
Contact: Elbert Lalande, Director of Student Development (205) 460-2351

Spring Hill College has a structured summer program, Summer Development Session, initiated in 1981 for alternative admissions students. The program begins in mid-June and lasts for 6 weeks. Ninety-five percent of the students complete the program in that time.

ADMISSION POLICIES:

- New students are eligible for alternative admissions, with a limit of 30 students. There is no wait list

- Requirements for admission as a freshman:
  817 — average combined verbal and math SAT
  or
  17 — average ACT
  2.2 — average GPA
  Other considerations: type of high school attended, difficulty of high school courses taken, letters of recommendation

ACADEMIC COURSEWORK AND RELATED FEATURES:

- Support services: freshman orientation, college survival skills, academic advising, psychological counseling, academic skills center, study technique workshops, career advising, peer counseling, health center
- Students are not required to work with tutors

The Other Route into College

- One-on-one tutoring by professional tutors in English, math, and reading
- Academic and personal counseling is required
- Students are assigned an academic adviser. None of the advisers serve alternative admissions students exclusively. Students meet with advisers approximately 7 times per semester
- Placement testing is required in English, math, and reading
- A total of 68 full-time faculty at the institution
- Six faculty members assigned to the program, who are trained to work with alternative admissions students
- Students take an average of 70% of their classes with alternative admissions students only
- Alternative admissions classes average 12 students
- Students are limited to a credit load of 12 credits per semester through spring semester of freshman year

REQUIRED COURSES:
- Remedial courses required:
  Study Skills (credit-bearing)—alternative admissions students only
  English (credit-bearing)—alternative admissions students only
- Other required courses:
  Math (credit-bearing)
  Reading (credit-bearing)—alternative admissions students only
- Remedial courses are not calculated in GPA
- Required courses are not calculated in GPA
- Minimum of 2.0 GPA required to stay in program; if below 2.0 GPA, a student is academically dismissed

PROFILE OF ALTERNATIVE ADMISSIONS STUDENTS:
- 90 alternative admissions students enrolled
- 40% of the accepted students enrolled
- 100% enter as new students
- 5% of the students transfer to another college after freshman year, 10% transfer after sophomore year
- 3% minority, 47% female
- 3% state residents, no international students
- None 25 years or older
- No intercollegiate athletes
- 10% learning disabled
- 6% in top 50% of high school class
- 65% graduate within 5 years

OTHER FEATURES/ACCOMMODATIONS:
- On-campus housing is available and is guaranteed for alternative admissions students
- A meal plan is available

Stacy Needle

DEADLINES:
- Rolling admission
- May 1 for financial aid
- June 1 for reply date

STATE UNIVERSITY OF NEW YORK AT ALBANY

>>>>>>>>>>>>>>>>>>>>>>>>>>

Albany, NY 12222
(518) 442-5435

———

$1,350 In-State Tuition and Fees
$4,700 Out-of-State Tuition and Fees
$2,000 Average Double Room
$1,100 Average Meal Plan

10,626 full-time undergraduates, 497 part-time undergraduates
18:1 student/faculty ratio
42% of undergraduates study social sciences

>>

Founded in 1844, State University of New York at Albany is a public institution, coed. Located on 350 acres in a large city. Bachelor's degrees are offered.

ALTERNATIVE ADMISSIONS:

Contact: R. Thomas Flemming, Associate Director of Admissions (518) 442-5435

State University of New York at Albany has a structured program, Talented Student Admission Program, initiated in 1972 for alternative admissions students. The formal program of studies begins in the fall and lasts for 4 years.

ADMISSION POLICIES:
- New students are eligible for alternative admissions, with a limit of 180 students. There is no wait list

- Requirements for admission as a freshman:
  400 — minimum verbal SAT
  400 — minimum math SAT
Other considerations: ACT scores (in place of SAT), high school GPA, high school rank, type of high school

attended, difficulty of high school courses taken, essay/personal statement, letters of recommendation, state residence

ACADEMIC COURSEWORK AND RELATED FEATURES:
- Support services: freshman orientation, college survival skills, academic advising, drug/alcohol counseling, women's center, psychological counseling, academic skills center, career advising, peer counseling, health center, aptitude testing
- Students are not required to work with tutors
- One-on-one tutoring by peer tutors as well as professional tutors in all academic areas
- Counseling is not required
- Students are assigned an academic adviser. None of the advisers serve alternative admissions students exclusively
- Placement testing is not required
- Alternative admissions students do not take separate classes
- Students are not limited to credit load

PROFILE OF ALTERNATIVE ADMISSIONS STUDENTS:
- 90 alternative admissions students enrolled
- 54% of the accepted students enrolled
- 100% enter as new students

OTHER FEATURES/ACCOMMODATIONS:
- On-campus housing is available and is guaranteed for alternative admissions students
- A meal plan is available
- Financial aid is available

DEADLINES:
- February 15 for admission
- April 1 for notification of admission
- May 1 for reply date

The program is best suited for a solid academic student whose GPA is low because of overcommitment to an exceptional talent and/or extraordinary ability.

STATE UNIVERSITY OF NEW YORK AT STONY BROOK
>>>>>>>>>>>>>>>>>>>>>>>>>>

Stony Brook, NY 11794-1901
(516) 632-6868

$1,500 In-State Tuition and Fees
$4,855 Out-of-State Tuition and Fees
$2,360 Average Double Room
$1,474 Average Meal Plan

9,636 full-time undergraduates, 1,632 part-time undergraduates
15:1 student/faculty ratio
15% of undergraduates study social sciences

>>

Founded in 1957, the State University of New York at Stony Brook is a public institution, coed. Located on 1,100 acres in a town 60 miles from New York City. Bachelor's degrees are offered.

ALTERNATIVE ADMISSIONS:
Contact: Theresa La Rocca-Meyer, Dean of Admissions and Enrollment Planning (516) 632-6868

The State University of New York at Stony Brook has a policy for alternative admissions students.

ADMISSION POLICIES:
- New students are eligible for alternative admissions

- Requirements for admission as a freshman:
    470 — average verbal SAT
    540 — average math SAT
Other considerations: high school GPA, letters of recommendation

ACADEMIC COURSEWORK AND RELATED FEATURES:
- Support services: freshman orientation, academic advising, women's center, psychological counseling, health center
- Students are not required to work with tutors
- Counseling is not required
- Placement testing is required in math and writing
- Alternative admissions students do not take separate classes
- Students are not limited to credit load

The Other Route into College

PROFILE OF ALTERNATIVE ADMISSIONS STUDENTS:

- 608 alternative admissions students enrolled
- 36% of the accepted students enrolled
- 100% enter as new students
- 27% minority, 41% female
- 92% state residents, 1% international students
- .2% 25 years or older
- No intercollegiate athletes
- No learning disabled
- 71% in top 50% of high school class

OTHER FEATURES/ACCOMMODATIONS:

- On-campus housing is available and is guaranteed for alternative admissions students
- A meal plan is available
- Financial aid is available

DEADLINES:

- Rolling admission
- March 1 for financial aid
- May 1 for reply date

The program is best suited for a student who shows potential in his/her later high school years.

STATE UNIVERSITY OF NEW YORK COLLEGE AT BROCKPORT

>>>>>>>>>>>>>>>>>>>>>>>>>>

Brockport, NY 14420
(716) 395-2751

$1,511 In-State Tuition and Fees
$4,700 Out-of-State Tuition and Fees
$1,920 Average Double Room
$1,510 Average Meal Plan

5,349 full-time undergraduates, 1,439 part-time undergraduates
19:1 student/faculty ratio
47% of undergraduates study social sciences

>>

Founded in 1867, State University of New York College at Brockport is a public institution, coed. Located on 597 acres in a town 16 miles from Rochester. Bachelor's degrees are offered.

Stacy Needle

ALTERNATIVE ADMISSIONS:

Additional cost: $1,053 basic program fee
Contact: Dr. Thomas Bonner, Dean of General Education (716) 395-2291

The State University of New York College at Brockport has a structured summer program, Transition Program, initiated in 1980 for alternative admissions students. The program begins in July and lasts for 5 weeks. Ninety-five percent of the students complete the program in that time.

ADMISSION POLICIES:

- New students are eligible for alternative admissions, with a limit of 150 students. There is no waiting list

- Requirements for admission as a freshman:
  427 — average verbal SAT
  487 — average math SAT
Other considerations: high school GPA

ACADEMIC COURSEWORK AND RELATED FEATURES:

- Support services: freshman orientation, college survival skills, academic advising, drug/alcohol counseling, psychological counseling, academic skills center, study technique workshops, career advising, peer counseling, health center, aptitude testing, extended time for tests
- Separate new-student orientation
- Students are required to work with tutors 5 hours per week
- Group and one-on-one tutoring by peer tutors as well as professional tutors
- Counseling is not required
- Students are assigned an academic adviser. None of the advisers serve alternative admissions students exclusively
- Placement testing is not required
- A total of 308 full-time faculty at the institution
- Twenty-one faculty members assigned to the program, who are trained to work with alternative admissions students
- Students take all of their classes with alternative admissions students only
- Alternative admissions classes average 25–30 students
- Students are limited to a credit load of 13 credits per semester through spring semester of freshman year

REQUIRED COURSES:

- Minimum of 2.0 GPA required to stay in program; if below 2.0 GPA, a student is placed on academic probation

PROFILE OF ALTERNATIVE ADMISSIONS STUDENTS:
- 150 alternative admissions students enrolled
- 100% enter as new students
- 100% state residents, no international students
- None 25 years or older
- 1% learning disabled
- None in top 50% of high school class
- 40% graduate within 4 years

OTHER FEATURES/ACCOMMODATIONS:
- On-campus housing is available and is guaranteed for alternative admissions students
- A meal plan is available
- Financial aid is available

DEADLINES:
- Rolling admission
- March 1 for financial aid

The program is best suited for a student who was an underachiever in high school.

STATE UNIVERSITY OF NEW YORK COLLEGE AT BUFFALO

>>>>>>>>>>>>>>>>>>>>>>>>>>

Buffalo, NY 14222
(716) 878-4017

$1,455 In-State Tuition and Fees
$4,700 Out-of-State Tuition and Fees
$1,990 Average Double Room
$1,490 Average Meal Plan

8,199 full-time undergraduates, 2,485 part-time undergraduates
21:1 student/faculty ratio

>>

Founded in 1871, State University of New York College at Buffalo is a public institution, coed. Located on 110 acres in a large city. Bachelor's degrees are offered.

ALTERNATIVE ADMISSIONS:

Contact: Deborah Renzi, Director of Admissions (716) 878-4017

The State University of New York College at Buffalo has a policy, Special Consideration, initiated in 1986 for alternative admissions students.

ADMISSION POLICIES:
- New students are eligible for alternative admissions, with a limit of 48 students. There is no wait list
- Admission considerations: high school GPA, high school rank, interview with admissions counselor, essay/personal statement, letters of recommendation

ACADEMIC COURSEWORK AND RELATED FEATURES:
- Support services: freshman orientation, college survival skills, academic advising, drug/alcohol counseling, psychological counseling, academic skills center, study technique workshops, career advising, health center, aptitude testing
- Students are not required to work with tutors
- Group and one-on-one tutoring by peer tutors as well as professional tutors in all academic areas
- Counseling is not required
- Students are assigned an academic adviser. None of the advisers serve alternative admissions students exclusively
- Placement testing is required in English and math
- Alternative admissions students do not take separate classes
- Students are limited to a credit load of 12 credits per semester through spring semester of freshman year

REQUIRED COURSES:
- Minimum of 2.0 GPA required to stay at college; if below 2.0 GPA, a student is placed on academic probation

PROFILE OF ALTERNATIVE ADMISSIONS STUDENTS:
- 24 alternative admissions students enrolled

OTHER FEATURES/ACCOMMODATIONS:
- On-campus housing is available, but is not guaranteed for alternative admissions students
- A meal plan is available
- Financial aid is available

DEADLINES:
- Rolling admission
- May for reply date

The Other Route into College

STATE UNIVERSITY OF NEW YORK COLLEGE AT GENESEO

>>>>>>>>>>>>>>>>>>>>>>>>>>

Geneseo, NY 14454
(716) 245-5571

_____

$1,350 In-State Tuition and Fees
$4,700 Out-of-State Tuition and Fees
$1,972 Average Double Room
$1,100 Average Meal Plan

4,788 full-time undergraduates, 104 part-time
  undergraduates
18:1 student/faculty ratio
20% of undergraduates study math/sciences

>>

Founded in 1867, State University of New York College at Geneseo is a public institution, coed. Located on 220 acres in a town 25 miles from Rochester. Bachelor's degrees are offered.

ALTERNATIVE ADMISSIONS:

Contact: Dr. Ramon Rocha, Assistant to the Vice President for Minority Affairs (716) 245-5620

State University of New York College at Geneseo has a structured program, Transitional Opportunity Program (T.O.P.), initiated in 1986 for alternative admissions students. The formal program of studies begins in the fall and lasts for 4 years. Students receive a bachelor's degree upon completion of their studies.

ADMISSION POLICIES:

- New students are eligible for alternative admissions, with a limit of 25 students. There is no wait list

- Requirements for admission as a freshman:
    470 — average verbal SAT
    517 — average math SAT
      or
    20 — average ACT
Other considerations: high school GPA, high school rank, essay/personal statement, minority status

ACADEMIC COURSEWORK AND RELATED FEATURES:

- Support services: freshman orientation, college survival skills, academic advising, drug/alcohol counseling, women's center, psychological counseling, academic skills center, study technique workshops, career advising, peer counseling, health center, aptitude testing
- Students are not required to work with tutors
- Group and one-on-one tutoring by peer tutors as well as professional tutors in all academic areas
- Counseling is not required
- Students are assigned an academic adviser. None of the advisers serve alternative admissions students exclusively
- Placement testing is required in math and writing
- Alternative admissions students do not take separate classes
- Students are limited to a credit load of 12 credits per semester through fall semester of freshman year

REQUIRED COURSES:

- Courses required of students who demonstrate deficiency:
  Basic Skills English
  Essential Math for College Students

PROFILE OF ALTERNATIVE ADMISSIONS STUDENTS:

- 25 alternative admissions students enrolled
- 40% of the accepted students enrolled
- 100% enter as new students
- 100% minority, 60% female
- 96% state residents, no international students
- None 25 years or older
- 8% intercollegiate athletes
- No learning disabled
- 90% in top 50% of high school class

OTHER FEATURES/ACCOMMODATIONS:

- On-campus housing is available and is guaranteed for alternative admissions students
- On-campus housing is required of alternative admissions students
- A meal plan is available. It is required of alternative admissions students
- Financial aid is available

DEADLINES:

- January 15 for admission; after January 15, applications are reviewed on a space-available basis
- February 15 for financial aid
- March 15 for notification of admission
- May 1 for reply date

The program is best suited for a student who, although motivated, may need special support services and workshops to encourage success.

Stacy Needle

TAMPA COLLEGE
>>>>>>>>>>>>>>>>>>>>>>>>>>>>>>

Tampa, FL 33614
(813) 879-6000

$4,200 Tuition and Fees

600 full-time undergraduates, 200 part-time
   undergraduates
25:1 student/faculty ratio
90% of undergraduates study business

>>

Founded in 1890, Tampa College is a private institution,
coed. Located on 3 acres in a large city. Associate's and
bachelor's degrees are offered.

ALTERNATIVE ADMISSIONS:

Contact: Sharon Occhipiati, Coordinator of General Education (813) 879-6000

Tampa College has a structured program, Ability to
Benefit, initiated in 1988 for alternative admissions students. The formal program of studies begins in the fall
and lasts for 3–12 months; however, students can also
enter the program in the spring and continue for 3–12
months.

ADMISSION POLICIES:

- New and transfer students are eligible for alternative
admissions

- Admission considerations—new student: interview
with admissions counselor

- Requirements for admission as a transfer student:
1.5 — minimum GPA
Other considerations: interview with admissions counselor

ACADEMIC COURSEWORK AND RELATED FEATURES:

- Support services: freshman orientation, college survival skills, academic advising, academic skills center,
study technique workshops, career advising, peer
counseling, aptitude testing
- Separate new-student orientation
- Students are not required to work with tutors
- One-on-one tutoring by peer tutors as well as professional tutors in math, English, reading, and accounting
- Academic and placement counseling is not required
- Students are assigned an academic adviser. All of the

advisers serve alternative admissions students exclu-
sively. Students meet with advisers several times
per semester
- Placement testing is required
- A total of 8 full-time faculty at the institution
- One faculty member assigned to the program, who is
trained to work with alternative admissions students
- Students take classes with alternative admissions
students
- Alternative admissions classes average 12–20 stu-
dents
- Courses are also offered in the evening
- Students are not limited to credit load

REQUIRED COURSES:

- Courses required of students who demonstrate deficiency:
Basic Mathematics (credit-bearing)—alternative admissions students only
Basic English Studies (credit-bearing)—alternative
admissions students only
Basic Reading (credit-bearing)—alternative admissions students only
College Success Seminar (credit-bearing)

PROFILE OF ALTERNATIVE ADMISSIONS STUDENTS:

- 15 alternative admissions students enrolled
- 100% of the accepted students enrolled
- 95% enter as new students, 5% as transfer students
- 10% of the students transfer to another college after
freshman year, 2% transfer after sophomore year
- 10% minority, 10% female
- 100% state residents, no international students
- 30% 25 years or older
- No intercollegiate athletes
- None learning disabled
- None in top 50% of high school class
- 80% graduate within 4 years
- 10% graduate within 5 years

OTHER FEATURES/ACCOMMODATIONS:

- On-campus housing is not available
- A meal plan is not available
- Financial aid is available

The Other Route into College

TENNESSEE TECHNOLOGICAL UNIVERSITY

>>>>>>>>>>>>>>>>>>>>>>>>>>>>

Cookeville, TN 38505
(615) 372-3888

$ 679 In-State Tuition and Fees
$2,156 Out-of-State Tuition and Fees
$ 625 Average Double Room
$ 575 Average Meal Plan

6,195 full-time undergraduates, 806 part-time
  undergraduates
19:1 student/faculty ratio
28% of undergraduates study engineering

>>

Founded in 1915, Tennessee Technological University
is a public institution, coed. Located on 240 acres in a
small city 80 miles from Nashville. Bachelor's degrees
are offered.

ALTERNATIVE ADMISSIONS:

Contact: Dr. James Perry, Director of Admissions (615)
372-3888

Tennessee Technological University has a structured
program, Regulated Admissions, initiated in 1986 for
alternative admissions students. The formal program of
studies begins in the fall; however, students can also
enter the program in the spring.

ADMISSION POLICIES:

- New and transfer students are eligible for alternative
  admissions, with a limit of 250 students. There is no
  wait list

- Admission considerations—new student: ACT
  scores, high school GPA, type of high school attended, difficulty of high school courses taken, letters
  of recommendation

- Admission considerations—transfer student: GPA at
  previous institution, type of college attended, number of credits completed (less than 24 credits)

ACADEMIC COURSEWORK AND RELATED FEATURES:

- Support services: freshman orientation, college survival skills, academic advising, drug/alcohol counseling, psychological counseling, academic skills center,

study technique workshops, career advising, peer
counseling, health center, aptitude testing, extended
time for tests
- Separate new-student orientation
- Students are not required to work with tutors
- Academic and career counseling is required
- Students are assigned an academic adviser. Students
  meet with advisers 2 times per semester
- Placement testing is required
- A total of 377 full-time faculty at the institution
- Special faculty assigned to the program, who are
  trained to work with alternative admissions students
- Alternative admissions students do not take separate
  classes
- Students are limited to a credit load of 16 credits per
  semester until they show satisfactory competencies
  in deficient areas

REQUIRED COURSES:

- Minimum of 2.0 GPA required to stay in program; if
  below 2.0 GPA, a student must apply for permission
  to remain in the program

OTHER FEATURES/ACCOMMODATIONS:

- On-campus housing is available for alternative admis-
  sions students
- A meal plan is available
- Financial aid is available

DEADLINES:

- Rolling admission
- April 15 for financial aid

TEXAS A&I UNIVERSITY

>>>>>>>>>>>>>>>>>>>>>>>>>>>>

Kingsville, TX 78363
(512) 595-3907

$ 900 In-State Tuition and Fees
$4,000 Out-of-State Tuition and Fees
$2,300 Average Double Room and Meal Plan

3,474 full-time undergraduates, 974 part-time
  undergraduates
19:1 student/faculty ratio

Stacy Needle

152

Founded in 1925, Texas A&I University is a public institution, coed. Located on 246 acres in a rural community 40 miles from Corpus Christi. Bachelor's degrees are offered.

ALTERNATIVE ADMISSIONS:

Contact: Dr. Gary Low, Director of Counseling (512) 595-3991

Texas A&I University has a structured program, Individual Approval, for alternative admissions students. The formal program of studies begins in the fall and lasts for approximately 1 year; however, students can also enter the program in the spring and continue for approximately 1 year.

ADMISSION POLICIES:

• New students are eligible for alternative admissions

• Requirements for admission as a freshman:
  300–350 — average verbal SAT
  300–350 — average math SAT
  or
  12–15 — average ACT
Other considerations: high school rank

ACADEMIC COURSEWORK AND RELATED FEATURES:

• Support services: freshman orientation, college survival skills, academic advising, drug/alcohol counseling, psychological counseling, academic skills center, study technique workshops, career advising, peer counseling, health center, aptitude testing
• Separate new-student orientation
• Students are not required to work with tutors
• Group and one-on-one tutoring by peer tutors as well as professional tutors in math, English, and science
• Group counseling is required
• Students are assigned an academic adviser
• Placement testing is required
• A total of 234 full-time faculty at the institution
• Special faculty assigned to the program
• Students take all of their classes with alternative admissions students only
• Alternative admissions classes average 25 students
• Students are limited to a credit load of 14 credits per semester through first semester of program

REQUIRED COURSES:

• Remedial courses required:
  Developmental Algebra (credit-bearing)—alternative admissions students only
  Developmental Math (credit-bearing)—alternative admissions students only
  Developmental Reading (credit-bearing)—alternative admissions students only
  Developmental Writing (credit-bearing)—alternative admissions students only
• Remedial courses are calculated in GPA
• Minimum of 2.0 GPA required to stay in program; if below 2.0 GPA, a student is placed on academic probation

OTHER FEATURES/ACCOMMODATIONS:

• On-campus housing is available and is guaranteed for alternative admissions students
• A meal plan is available
• Financial aid is available

DEADLINES:

• Rolling admission

TEXAS A&M UNIVERSITY

>>>>>>>>>>>>>>>>>>>>>>>>>>>>

College Station, TX 77843
(409) 845-1031

$ 432–$576 In-State Tuition and Fees
$2,928–$3,904 Out-of-State Tuition and Fees
$1,450 Average Double Room
$1,641 Average Meal Plan

29,578 full-time undergraduates, 2,265 part-time undergraduates
21:1 student/faculty ratio
23% of undergraduates study engineering

>>

Founded in 1876, Texas A&M University is a public institution, coed. Located on 5,142 acres in a town 90 miles from Houston. Bachelor's degrees are offered.

ALTERNATIVE ADMISSIONS:

Contact: Kriss Boyd, Director of General Studies (409) 845-5916

Texas A&M University has a structured summer program, Provisional Admissions Program, for alternative admissions students. The program begins in June and lasts for 10 weeks. A student must take 3 courses in

The Other Route into College

such academic fields as English, history, and political science. Sixty-five to seventy percent of the students complete the program in 10 weeks.

ADMISSION POLICIES:

- New students are eligible for alternative admissions, with a limit of 300 students. There is no wait list

- Admission based on individual criteria

ACADEMIC COURSEWORK AND RELATED FEATURES:

- Support services: college survival skills, academic advising, drug/alcohol counseling, psychological counseling, career advising, health center, aptitude testing
- Separate new-student orientation
- Students are not required to work with tutors
- Counseling is not required
- Students are assigned an academic adviser
- Placement testing is not required
- Alternative admissions students do not take separate classes

REQUIRED COURSES:

- Minimum of 2.0 GPA required to stay in program; if below 2.0 GPA, a student may not enroll for the fall semester

PROFILE OF ALTERNATIVE ADMISSIONS STUDENTS:

- 287 alternative admissions students enrolled
- 85% of the accepted students enrolled
- 100% enter as new students
- 14% minority, 40% female
- 90% state residents
- None 25 years or older
- No intercollegiate athletes
- 55% in top 50% of high school class
- 20% graduate within 4 years
- 40% graduate within 5 years

OTHER FEATURES/ACCOMMODATIONS:

- On-campus housing is available and is guaranteed for alternative admissions students
- A meal plan is available
- Financial aid is available

DEADLINES:

- Rolling admission
- February 1 for financial aid

TEXAS WESLEYAN UNIVERSITY

>>>>>>>>>>>>>>>>>>>>>>>>>>>

Fort Worth, TX 76105
(817) 531-4422

$5,200 Tuition and Fees
$1,150 Average Double Room
$1,310 Average Meal Plan

989 full-time undergraduates, 311 part-time undergraduates
14:1 student/faculty ratio
34% of undergraduates study business

>>

Founded in 1890, Texas Wesleyan University is a private institution, coed, affiliated with the United Methodist church. Located on 74 acres in a large city. Bachelor's degrees are offered.

ALTERNATIVE ADMISSIONS:

Contact: Timothy Martinez, Director of Admissions
(817) 531-4422

Texas Wesleyan University has a structured summer program, Summer Trial Admissions, initiated in 1981 for alternative admissions students. The program begins in June and lasts for 4 weeks.

ADMISSION POLICIES:

- New students are eligible for alternative admissions

- Admission considerations—new student: SAT or ACT scores, high school GPA, high school rank

ACADEMIC COURSEWORK AND RELATED FEATURES:

- Support services: freshman orientation, college survival skills, academic advising, drug/alcohol counseling, psychological counseling, academic skills center, study technique workshops, career advising, peer counseling, health center, aptitude testing, extended time for tests
- Students are not required to work with tutors
- Counseling is not required
- Students are assigned an academic adviser
- Students are limited to a credit load of 12 credits per semester through spring semester of freshman year

REQUIRED COURSES:

- Remedial courses required:
  Skills Development (credit-bearing)—alternative admissions students only

Stacy Needle

- Remedial courses are not calculated in GPA
- Minimum of 2.0 GPA required to stay in program

OTHER FEATURES/ACCOMMODATIONS:
- On-campus housing is available, but is not guaranteed for alternative admissions students
- A meal plan is available

DEADLINES:
- Rolling admission
- April 15 for financial aid
- April 15 for reply date

THIEL COLLEGE
>>>>>>>>>>>>>>>>>>>>>>>>>

Greenville, PA 16125
(412) 588-7700, Ext. 483

$7,730 Tuition and Fees
$3,800 Average Double Room and Meal Plan

774 full-time undergraduates, 168 part-time undergraduates

>>

Founded in 1866, Thiel College is a private institution, coed, affiliated with the Evangelical Lutheran Church in America. Located on 135 acres in a rural community 70 miles from Pittsburgh. Bachelor's degrees are offered.

ALTERNATIVE ADMISSIONS:

Contact: James Enrietti, Director of Admissions (412) 588-7700, Ext. 483

Thiel College has a structured program, Thiel Academic Assistance Program, for alternative admissions students. The formal program of studies begins in the fall and lasts for a minimum of 1 semester.

ADMISSION POLICIES:
- New students are eligible for alternative admissions, with a limit of 40 students
- Admission considerations: high school GPA, extracurricular activities, letters of recommendation

ACADEMIC COURSEWORK AND RELATED FEATURES:
- Counseling is available
- Alternative admissions students do not take separate classes
- Students are limited to a credit load of 12 credits per semester through fall semester of freshman year

REQUIRED COURSES:
- Remedial courses required:
  Remedial English
  Remedial Math

PROFILE OF ALTERNATIVE ADMISSIONS STUDENTS:
- 50% of the accepted students enrolled

OTHER FEATURES/ACCOMMODATIONS:
- On-campus housing is available
- A meal plan is available

DEADLINES:
- Rolling admission

TOUGALOO COLLEGE
>>>>>>>>>>>>>>>>>>>>>>>>>

Tougaloo, MS 39174
(601) 977-7700

$3,518 Tuition and Fees
$ 950 Average Double Room
$ 600 Average Meal Plan

787 full-time undergraduates, 161 part-time undergraduates
15:1 student/faculty ratio

>>

Founded in 1869, Tougaloo College is a private institution, coed, affiliated with the United Church of Christ. Located on 1,265 acres in a small city 1 mile from Jackson. Associate's and bachelor's degrees are offered.

ALTERNATIVE ADMISSIONS:

Contact: Carolyn Evans, Director of Admissions (601) 977-7700

Tougaloo College has a policy for alternative admissions students.

The Other Route into College

ADMISSION POLICIES:

- New students are eligible for alternative admissions
- Admission considerations: SAT or ACT scores, high school GPA

ACADEMIC COURSEWORK AND RELATED FEATURES:

- Support services: freshman orientation, college survival skills, academic advising, drug/alcohol counseling, women's center, psychological counseling, academic skills center, study technique workshops, career advising, peer counseling, health center, aptitude testing, extended time for tests
- Students are not required to work with tutors
- Counseling is not required
- Students are assigned an academic adviser. None of the advisers serve alternative admissions students exclusively
- Placement testing is required in English, math, and reading
- Alternative admissions students do not take separate classes
- Students are limited to a credit load of 12 credits per semester through fall semester of freshman year

OTHER FEATURES/ACCOMMODATIONS:

- On-campus housing is available for alternative admissions students
- A meal plan is available
- Financial aid is available

TRINITY COLLEGE

>>>>>>>>>>>>>>>>>>>>>>>>>>

Washington, DC 20017
(202) 939-5040

$9,425 Tuition and Fees
$2,660 Average Double Room
$3,040 Average Meal Plan

400 full-time undergraduates, 452 part-time undergraduates
11:1 student/faculty ratio

>>

Founded in 1897, Trinity College is a private institution, women only, affiliated with the Roman Catholic church. Located on 26 acres in a large city. Bachelor's degrees are offered.

Stacy Needle

ALTERNATIVE ADMISSIONS:

Contact: Donna Quinn, Director of Admissions (202) 939-5040

Trinity College has a policy, Reduced Course Load Admissions, for alternative admissions students.

ADMISSION POLICIES:

- New students are eligible for alternative admissions
- Requirements for admission as a freshman:
  400 — minimum verbal SAT
  400 — minimum math SAT
  2.0 — minimum GPA

Other considerations: high school rank, type of high school attended, difficulty of high courses taken, essay/personal statement, letters of recommendation

ACADEMIC COURSEWORK AND RELATED FEATURES:

- Support services: freshman orientation, college survival skills, academic advising, psychological counseling, academic skills center, career advising, health center
- Students are not required to work with tutors
- Counseling is not required
- Students are assigned an academic adviser. None of the advisers serve alternative admissions students exclusively
- Placement testing is not required
- Alternative admissions students do not take separate classes
- Students are limited to a credit load of 12 credits per semester through fall semester of freshman year

REQUIRED COURSES:

- Minimum of 2.0 GPA required to stay at college; if below 2.0 GPA, a student is placed on academic probation

PROFILE OF ALTERNATIVE ADMISSIONS STUDENTS:

- 21 alternative admissions students enrolled
- 100% enter as new students
- 100% female
- None 25 years or older
- 75% graduate within 4 years

OTHER FEATURES/ACCOMMODATIONS:

- On-campus housing is available and is guaranteed for alternative admissions students
- On-campus housing is required of alternative admissions students
- A meal plan is available. It is required of alternative admissions students
- Financial aid is available

DEADLINES:
- Rolling admission
- March 1 for financial aid

The program is best suited for a young woman who shows motivation and serious intent to compensate for a weaker academic record.

UNION COLLEGE
>>>>>>>>>>>>>>>>>>>>>>>>>>>>

Barbourville, KY 40906
(606) 546-4223

$4,970 Tuition and Fees
$2,320 Average Double Room and Meal Plan

659 full-time undergraduates, 136 part-time
  undergraduates
15:1 student/faculty ratio
45% of undergraduates study business

>>

Founded in 1879, Union College is a private institution, coed, affiliated with the United Methodist church. Located on 110 acres in a town 100 miles from Lexington. Associate's and bachelor's degrees are offered.

ALTERNATIVE ADMISSIONS:

Contact: Donald Hapward, Director of Admissions
(606) 546-4223

Union College has a policy for alternative admissions students.

ADMISSION POLICIES:
- New students are eligible for alternative admissions

- Requirements for admission as a freshman:
    8 — minimum ACT
Other considerations: high school GPA, essay/personal statement

- Students not meeting regular admissions criteria may write a letter of appeal to the Admissions Committee.

ACADEMIC COURSEWORK AND RELATED FEATURES:
- Support services: freshman orientation, college survival skills, academic advising, drug/alcohol counseling, academic skills center, career advising, peer counseling, aptitude testing

- Students are required to work with tutors 2–3 hours per week
- Group and one-on-one tutoring by peer tutors in all academic areas
- Counseling is not required
- Students are assigned an academic adviser. None of the advisers serve alternative admissions students exclusively. Students meet with advisers a minimum of 2 times per semester
- Placement testing is required in English, math, and reading
- Alternative admissions students do not take separate classes
- Students are limited to a credit load of 12 credits per semester through fall semester of freshman year

REQUIRED COURSES:
- Remedial courses required:
  Study Skills (credit-bearing)
- Courses required of students who demonstrate deficiency:
  College Reading (credit-bearing)
  Developmental Math (credit-bearing)
  Developmental English (credit-bearing)

PROFILE OF ALTERNATIVE ADMISSIONS STUDENTS:
- 20 alternative admissions students enrolled
- 98% of the accepted students enrolled
- 100% enter as new students
- 13% minority, 47% female
- 98% state residents, no international students
- None 25 years or older
- 13% intercollegiate athletes
- No learning disabled

OTHER FEATURES/ACCOMMODATIONS:
- On-campus housing is available and is guaranteed for alternative admissions students
- A meal plan is available
- Financial aid is available

DEADLINES:
- Rolling admission
- March 15 for financial aid

The Other Route into College

UNITY COLLEGE

>>>>>>>>>>>>>>>>>>>>>>>>>>

Unity, ME 04988
(207) 948-3131

$4,946 In-State Tuition and Fees
$6,128 Out-of-State Tuition and Fees
$3,521 Average Double Room and Meal Plan

302 full-time undergraduates

>>

Founded in 1965, Unity College is a private institution, coed. Located on 185 acres in a rural community. Associate's and bachelor's degrees are offered.

ALTERNATIVE ADMISSIONS:

Addtional cost: $850 basic program fee
Contact: John Craig, Dean for Enrollment Services
(207) 948-3131

Unity College has a structured summer program, Summer Institute, for alternative admissions students. The program lasts for 4 weeks. This program offers entering students the opportunity to strengthen their basic academic skills and get an introduction to college life. One hundred percent of the students complete the program in that time.

ADMISSION POLICIES:

• New students are eligible for alternative admissions

• Requirements for admission as a freshman:
  250 — minimum verbal SAT
  250 — minimum math SAT

ACADEMIC COURSEWORK AND RELATED FEATURES:

• Students are required to work with tutors
• Counseling is available
• Alternative admissions students do not take separate classes

REQUIRED COURSES:

• Remedial courses required:
  Basic Writing Workshop
  Basic Math Workshop
• Other required courses:
  New-Student Orientation
  Freshman Seminar
  Introduction to Natural History

Stacy Needle

PROFILE OF ALTERNATIVE ADMISSIONS STUDENTS:

• 47% of the accepted students enrolled
• 85% graduate within 4 years
• 5% graduate within 5 years

OTHER FEATURES/ACCOMMODATIONS:

• On-campus housing is available
• A meal plan is available

DEADLINES:

• Rolling admission

UNIVERSITY OF ALABAMA

>>>>>>>>>>>>>>>>>>>>>>>>>>

Tuscaloosa, AL 35487-0312
(205) 348-5666

$ 862 In-State Tuition and Fees
$2,130 Out-of-State Tuition and Fees
$ 795 Average Double Room
$ 695 Average Meal Plan

15,296 full-time undergraduates, 2,854 part-time
   undergraduates
21:1 student/faculty ratio
30% of undergraduates study business

>>

Founded in 1831, the University of Alabama is a public institution, coed. Located on 1,000 acres in a small city. Bachelor's degrees are offered.

ALTERNATIVE ADMISSIONS:

Contact: Bobby Ray Hicks, Associate Director of Admission Services (205) 348-5666

The University of Alabama has a structured summer program, Summer/Spring Trial, initiated in 1985 for alternative admissions students. The program begins in June and lasts for 10 weeks. One hundred percent of the students complete the program in that time.

ADMISSION POLICIES:

• New students are eligible for alternative admissions

- Requirements for admission as a freshman:
  720 — minimum combined verbal and math SAT
      or
  16 — minimum ACT

  2.0 — minimum GPA

ACADEMIC COURSEWORK AND RELATED FEATURES:

- Support services: freshman orientation, college survival skills, academic advising, drug/alcohol counseling, women's center, psychological counseling, academic skills center, study technique workshops, career advising, peer counseling, health center, aptitude testing, extended time for tests
- Separate new-student orientation
- Students are not required to work with tutors
- Group and one-on-one tutoring by peer tutors as well as professional tutors in most academic areas
- Counseling is not required
- Students are assigned an academic adviser
- Placement testing is required
- Alternative admissions students do not take separate classes

REQUIRED COURSES:

Academic Potential (credit-bearing)

- Required courses are not calculated in GPA
- Minimum of 2.0 GPA required to stay in the program; if below 2.0 GPA, a student may not return for the fall semester

OTHER FEATURES/ACCOMMODATIONS:

- On-campus housing is available, but is not guaranteed for alternative admissions students
- A meal plan is available
- Financial aid is available

DEADLINES:

- Rolling admission
- March for financial aid
- May for reply date

UNIVERSITY OF ALASKA FAIRBANKS

>>>>>>>>>>>>>>>>>>>>>>>>>>>

Fairbanks, AK 99775
(907) 474-7521

$1,512 In-State Tuition and Fees
$3,120 Out-of-State Tuition and Fees
$1,040 Average Double Room
$1,450 Average Meal Plan

3,223 full-time undergraduates, 4,509 part-time
  undergraduates
11:1 student/faculty ratio
12% of undergraduates study social sciences

>>

Founded in 1917, the University of Alaska Fairbanks is a public institution, coed. Located on 2,250 acres in a small city. Associate's and bachelor's degrees are offered.

ALTERNATIVE ADMISSIONS:

Contact: James Mansfield, Director of Admissions (907) 474-7521

The University of Alaska Fairbanks has a policy for alternative admissions students.

ADMISSION POLICIES:

- New and transfer students are eligible for alternative admissions

- Admission considerations—new student: SAT or ACT scores

- Admission considerations—transfer student: GPA at previous institution

ACADEMIC COURSEWORK AND RELATED FEATURES:

- Support services: freshman orientation, college survival skills, academic advising, drug/alcohol counseling, women's center, psychological counseling, academic skills center, study technique workshops, career advising, peer counseling, health center, aptitude testing
- Separate new-student orientation
- Students are not required to work with tutors
- Group and one-on-one tutoring by peer tutors as well as professional tutors in all academic areas
- Counseling is not required

The Other Route into College

- Students are assigned an academic adviser
- Placement testing is required
- Alternative admissions students do not take separate classes
- Students are not limited to credit load

REQUIRED COURSES:
- Courses required of students who demonstrate deficiency:
  Elementary Exposition (credit-bearing)
  Elementary Algebra (credit-bearing)
  Math Lab (credit-bearing)
  Intermediate Algebra (credit-bearing)

- Remedial courses are calculated in GPA
- Minimum of 2.0 GPA required to stay at college; if below 2.0 GPA, a student is placed on academic probation

PROFILE OF ALTERNATIVE ADMISSIONS STUDENTS:
- 324 alternative admissions students enrolled
- 26% of accepted students enrolled
- 50% female
- 99% state residents, no international students
- 14% 25 years or older
- No intercollegiate athletes

OTHER FEATURES/ACCOMMODATIONS:
- On-campus housing is available, but is not guaranteed for alternative admissions students
- A meal plan is available
- Financial aid is available

DEADLINES:
- Rolling admission
- May 1 for financial aid

The program is best suited for a student who needs to improve his/her academic skills.

UNIVERSITY OF ARKANSAS AT LITTLE ROCK

>>>>>>>>>>>>>>>>>>>>>>>>>>>>>

Little Rock, AR 72204
(501) 569-3127

———

$1,474 In-State Tuition and Fees
$2,040 Out-of-State Tuition and Fees

5,247 full-time undergraduates, 4,158 part-time undergraduates
16:1 student/faculty ratio
15% of undergraduates study business

>>

Founded in 1927, the University of Arkansas at Little Rock is a public institution, coed. Located in a small city. Associate's and bachelor's degrees are offered.

ALTERNATIVE ADMISSIONS:

Contact: Sue Pine, Director of Admissions (501) 569-3127

The University of Arkansas at Little Rock has a structured program, Conditional Admission, for alternative admissions students. The formal program of studies begins in the fall and lasts for 1 year; however, students can also enter the program in the spring and continue for 1 year.

ADMISSION POLICIES:
- New and transfer students are eligible for alternative admissions

- Admission considerations—new student: SAT or ACT scores, high school GPA

- Admission considerations—transfer student: GPA at previous institution

ACADEMIC COURSEWORK AND RELATED FEATURES:
- Support services: freshman orientation, college survival skills, academic advising, drug/alcohol counseling, psychological counseling, academic skills center, study technique workshops, career advising, health center
- Students are not required to work with tutors
- One-on-one tutoring by peer tutors as well as professional tutors
- Counseling is not required
- Students are not assigned an academic adviser

Stacy Needle

- Placement testing is required in English, math, and reading
- Students are not limited to credit load

REQUIRED COURSES:
- Courses required of students who demonstrate deficiency:
  Elementary Algebra (credit-bearing)
  Intermediate Algebra (credit-bearing)
  Composition Fundamentals (credit-bearing)
  College Reading (credit-bearing)

- Remedial courses are not calculated in GPA
- Minimum of 1.7 GPA required to stay in program; if below 1.7 GPA, a student is academically suspended

OTHER FEATURES/ACCOMMODATIONS:
- On-campus housing is not available
- A meal plan is not available
- Financial aid is available

DEADLINES:
- Rolling admission
- May 1 for financial aid

UNIVERSITY OF BRIDGEPORT

>>>>>>>>>>>>>>>>>>>>>>>>>>>>

Bridgeport, CT 06601
(203) 576-4552

$10,166 Tuition and Fees
$ 4,828 Average Double Room and Meal Plan

2,027 full-time undergraduates, 997 part-time
  undergraduates
13:1 student/faculty ratio
26% of undergraduates study business

>>

Founded in 1927, the University of Bridgeport is a private institution, coed. Located on 86 acres in a small city. Associate's and bachelor's degrees are offered.

ALTERNATIVE ADMISSIONS:
Contact: George Blake, Director of Basic Studies (203) 576-4239

The University of Bridgeport has a structured program, Basic Studies, initiated in 1972 for alternative admissions students. The formal program of studies begins in the fall and lasts for 2–4 semesters; however, a student can also enter the program in the spring and continue for 2–4 semesters.

ADMISSION POLICIES:
- New and transfer students are eligible for alternative admissions, with a limit of 140 students. There is no wait list

- Admission considerations—new student: SAT or ACT scores, high school GPA, interview with faculty member or director of program, essay/personal statement, letters of recommendation

- Requirements for admission as a transfer student:
  1.8 — minimum GPA
- Other considerations: number of credits completed (less than 15 credits), interview with admissions counselor, essay/personal statement, letters of recommendation

ACADEMIC COURSEWORK AND RELATED FEATURES:
- Support services: freshman orientation, college survival skills, academic advising, drug/alcohol counseling, psychological counseling, academic skills center, study technique workshops, career advising, health center, aptitude testing, extended time for tests
- Students are required to work with tutors
- Group and one-on-one tutoring by peer tutors as well as professional tutors
- Counseling is not required
- Students are assigned an academic adviser. All advisers serve alternative admissions students exclusively
- Placement testing is required in math and reading/writing
- A total of 194 full-time faculty at the institution
- Eleven faculty members assigned to the program
- Students take an average of 50% of their classes with alternative admissions students
- Alternative admissions classes average 15–20 students
- Students are not limited to credit load

REQUIRED COURSES:
- Courses required of students who demonstrate deficiency:
  Elementary Algebra (noncredit)—alternative admissions students only
  Study Skills (noncredit)—alternative admissions students only

The Other Route into College

- Minimum of 1.5 GPA (after first semester) required to stay in program; if below 1.5 GPA, a student may be terminated

PROFILE OF ALTERNATIVE ADMISSIONS STUDENTS:
- 140 alternative admissions students enrolled
- 36% of the accepted students enrolled
- 99% enter as new students, 1% as transfer students
- 5%–10% of the students transfer to another college after freshman year, 5%–10% transfer after sophomore year
- 49% minority
- No international students
- 5% 25 years or older
- 5% intercollegiate athletes
- 15% learning disabled
- 30% in top 50% of high school class
- 40% graduate within 5 years

OTHER FEATURES/ACCOMMODATIONS:
- On-campus housing is available and is guaranteed for alternative admissions students
- A meal plan is available
- Financial aid is available

DEADLINES:
- Rolling admission
- April 1 for financial aid
- May 1 for reply date

UNIVERSITY OF CALIFORNIA AT SANTA BARBARA

>>>>>>>>>>>>>>>>>>>>>>>>>>>

Santa Barbara, CA 93106
(805) 961-2881

$1,578 In-State Tuition and Fees
$5,699 Out-of-State Tuition and Fees
$5,260 Average Double Room and Meal Plan

16,853 full-time undergraduates
19:1 student/faculty ratio
20% of undergraduates study math/sciences

Stacy Needle

>>

Founded in 1891, the University of California at Santa Barbara is a public institution, coed. Located on 815 acres in a small city. Bachelor's degrees are offered.

ALTERNATIVE ADMISSIONS:
Contact: William Villa, Director of Admissions (805) 961-2881

The University of California at Santa Barbara has a policy for alternative admissions students.

ADMISSION POLICIES:
- New and transfer students are eligible for alternative admissions
- Admission considerations—new student: SAT or ACT scores, high school GPA, essay/personal statement
- Requirements for admission as a transfer student: 2.4 — minimum GPA
Other considerations: number of credits completed

ACADEMIC COURSEWORK AND RELATED FEATURES:
- Support services: freshman orientation, college survival skills, academic advising, drug/alcohol counseling, women's center, psychological counseling, academic skills center, study technique workshops, career advising, peer counseling, health center, aptitude testing
- Students are not required to work with tutors
- Group and one-on-one tutoring by peer tutors as well as professional tutors
- Students are not assigned an academic adviser
- Placement testing is required
- Alternative admissions students do not take separate classes
- Students are not limited to credit load

REQUIRED COURSES:
- Minimum of 2.0 GPA required to stay at college; if below 2.0 GPA, a student is placed on academic probation

PROFILE OF ALTERNATIVE ADMISSIONS STUDENTS:
- 540 alternative admissions students enrolled
- 52% of the accepted students enrolled
- 61% enter as new students, 39% as transfer students
- 67% minority, 55% female
- 95% state residents
- 16% 25 years or older
- 13% graduate within 4 years
- 37% graduate within 5 years

OTHER FEATURES/ACCOMMODATIONS:
- On-campus housing is available, but is not guaranteed for alternative admissions students
- A meal plan is available

DEADLINES:
- Rolling admission
- March 2 for financial aid
- May 1 for reply date

ACADEMIC COURSEWORK AND RELATED FEATURES:
- Placement testing is not required
- Alternative admissions students do not take separate classes

REQUIRED COURSES:
- Minimum of 2.0 GPA required to stay at college; if below 2.0 GPA, a student is placed on academic probation

OTHER FEATURES/ACCOMMODATIONS:
- On-campus housing is not available
- A meal plan is not available

UNIVERSITY OF COLORADO AT DENVER
>>>>>>>>>>>>>>>>>>>>>>>>>>

Denver, CO 80204
(303) 556-2704

_____

$1,488 In-State Tuition and Fees
$6,170 Out-of-State Tuition and Fees

3,013 full-time undergraduates, 2,544 part-time
   undergraduates
11:1 student/faculty ratio
24% of undergraduates study arts/humanities

>>

Founded in 1957, the University of Colorado at Denver is a public institution, coed. Located on 171 acres in a large city. Bachelor's degrees are offered.

ALTERNATIVE ADMISSIONS:

Contact: Danny Martinez, Executive Director of Student Retention Services (303) 556-4721

The University of Colorado at Denver has a policy, Educational Opportunity Program, initiated in 1973 for alternative admissions students.

ADMISSION POLICIES:
- New students are eligible for alternative admissions, with a limit of approximately 165 students. There is a wait list
- Requirements for admission as a freshman:
    17 — average ACT
    2.5 — average GPA
Other considerations: SAT scores (in place of ACT), high school rank

UNIVERSITY OF DETROIT
>>>>>>>>>>>>>>>>>>>>>>>>>>

Detroit, MI 48221
(313) 927-1245

_____

$8,280 Tuition and Fees
$1,696 Average Double Room
$1,650 Average Meal Plan

2,106 full-time undergraduates, 1,330 part-time
   undergraduates
30:1 student/faculty ratio
30% of undergraduates study arts/humanities

>>

Founded in 1877, the University of Detroit is a private institution, coed, affiliated with the Roman Catholic church. Located on 70 acres in a large city. Bachelor's degrees are offered.

ALTERNATIVE ADMISSIONS:

Contact: Kathleen Bush, Director of Support Services and Special Admissions (313) 927-1245

The University of Detroit has a structured program, Project 100/Challenge, initiated in 1981 for alternative admissions students. The formal program of studies begins in the fall and lasts for a minimum of 2 semesters.

The Other Route into College

ADMISSION POLICIES:

- New students are eligible for alternative admissions

- Requirements for admission as a freshman:
  12 — minimum ACT
  2.75 — minimum GPA
  Other considerations: SAT scores (in place of ACT), interview with admissions counselor, state residence

ACADEMIC COURSEWORK AND RELATED FEATURES:

- Support services: freshman orientation, academic advising, psychological counseling, academic skills center, study technique workshops, career advising
- Students are required to work with tutors 5 hours per week
- Group and one-on-one tutoring by peer tutors as well as professional tutors in math, English, business, social sciences, and physical sciences
- Counseling is not required
- Students are assigned an academic adviser. All advisers serve alternative admissions students exclusively
- Placement testing is required in math, chemistry, and language
- Alternative admissions students do not take separate classes

REQUIRED COURSES:

- Reading Efficiency (credit-bearing)
- Basic Techniques of Math (credit-bearing)

- Required courses are calculated in GPA

PROFILE OF ALTERNATIVE ADMISSIONS STUDENTS:

- 82 alternative admissions students enrolled
- 100% of the accepted students enrolled
- 100% enter as new students
- 3% of the students transfer to another college after freshman year, 5% transfer after sophomore year
- 60% minority, 65% female
- 98% state residents, 1% international students
- None 25 years or older
- 3% intercollegiate athletes
- No learning disabled
- 30% in top 50% of high school class
- 55% graduate within 4 years

OTHER FEATURES/ACCOMMODATIONS:

- On-campus housing is available and is guaranteed for alternative admissions students
- A meal plan is available
- Financial aid is available

DEADLINES:

- Rolling admission

Stacy Needle

UNIVERSITY OF DUBUQUE

>>>>>>>>>>>>>>>>>>>>>>>>>>>>

Dubuque, IA 52001
(319) 589-3200

$7,125 Tuition and Fees
$1,325 Average Double Room
$1,325 Average Meal Plan

646 full-time undergraduates, 234 part-time undergraduates
16:1 student/faculty ratio
28% of undergraduates study business

>>

Founded in 1852, the University of Dubuque is a private institution, coed, affiliated with the Presbyterian church. Located on 56 acres in a small city. Associate's and bachelor's degrees are offered.

ALTERNATIVE ADMISSIONS:

Contact: Ron Cronacher, Director of Admissions (319) 589-3200

The University of Dubuque has a policy for alternative admissions students.

ADMISSION POLICIES:

- New and transfer students are eligible for alternative admissions, with a limit of 40 students. There is a wait list

- Admission considerations—new student: SAT or ACT scores, high school rank

- Admission considerations—transfer student: GPA at previous institution, number of credits completed (less than 18 credits), essay/personal statement

ACADEMIC COURSEWORK AND RELATED FEATURES:

- Support services: freshman orientation, academic advising, drug/alcohol counseling, psychological counseling, academic skills center, study technique workshops, career advising, peer counseling, health center, extended time for tests
- Students are required to work with tutors
- One-on-one tutoring by peer tutors in business, computers, math, reading, and writing skills
- Students are assigned an academic adviser. None of the advisers serve alternative admissions students exclusively. Students meet with advisers at least 2 times per semester

- Placement testing is required
- Students take an average of 35% of their classes with alternative admissions students
- Alternative admission classes average 20 students

REQUIRED COURSES:
- Freshman Seminar
- Courses required of students who demonstrate deficiency:
  Preparatory English (credit-bearing)
  Reading and Study Skills (credit-bearing)
  Introduction to Algebra (credit-bearing)
- Remedial courses are calculated in GPA

PROFILE OF ALTERNATIVE ADMISSIONS STUDENTS:
- 35% female
- 60% state residents, 17% international students
- 45% in top 50% of high school class

OTHER FEATURES/ACCOMMODATIONS:
- On-campus housing is available and is guaranteed for alternative admissions students
- A meal plan is available
- Financial aid is available

DEADLINES:
- Rolling admission
- March 30 for financial aid

UNIVERSITY OF FINDLAY

>>>>>>>>>>>>>>>>>>>>>>>>>

Findlay, OH 45840
(419) 424-4540

$3,658 Tuition and Fees
$ 775 Average Double Room
$ 818 Average Meal Plan

1,342 full-time undergraduates, 733 part-time
  undergraduates
16:1 student/faculty ratio

>>

Founded in 1882, the University of Findlay is a private institution, coed, affiliated with Church of God. Located on 25 acres in a small city 35 miles from Toledo. Associate's and bachelor's degrees are offered.

ALTERNATIVE ADMISSIONS:
Contact: Donna Smith, Director of Supporting Skills System (419) 424-4697

The University of Findlay has a structured program, Foundations Program, initiated in 1981 for alternative admissions students. The formal program of studies begins in the fall and lasts for 1 year. Seventy-five percent of the students complete the program in that time.

ADMISSION POLICIES:
- New and transfer students are eligible for alternative admissions, with a limit of 50 students. There is a wait list

- Requirements for admission as a freshman:
  240 — minimum verbal SAT
  240 — minimum math SAT
      or
    7 — minimum ACT

  1.4 — minimum GPA
Other considerations: high school counselor recommendation

- Requirements for admission as a transfer student:
  1.4 — minimum GPA
Other considerations: interview with admissions counselor

ACADEMIC COURSEWORK AND RELATED FEATURES:
- Support services: freshman orientation, college survival skills, academic advising, psychological counseling, academic skills center, career advising, health center, extended time for tests
- Students are not required to work with tutors
- Group and one-on-one tutoring by peer tutors
- Counseling is not required
- Students are assigned an academic adviser. All advisers serve alternative admissions students exclusively. Students meet with advisers 3 times per semester
- Placement testing is required in reading
- A total of 80 full-time faculty at the institution
- Four faculty members assigned to the program, who are trained to work with alternative admissions students
- Students take an average of 40% of their classes with alternative admissions students only
- Alternative admissions classes average 26 students
- Students are not limited to credit load

The Other Route into College

REQUIRED COURSES:

- Remedial courses required:
  Writing and Reading Review (credit-bearing)
  Fundamentals of Math
- Other required courses:
  Foundations Seminar (credit-bearing)—alternative
  admissions students only
- Courses required of students who demonstrate deficiency:
  Reading Improvement

- Remedial courses are calculated in GPA
- Required courses are calculated in GPA
- Minimum of 1.1 GPA required to stay in program; if
  below 1.1 GPA, a student is academically dismissed

PROFILE OF ALTERNATIVE ADMISSIONS STUDENTS:

- 56 alternative admissions students enrolled
- 60% of the accepted students enrolled
- 16% minority, 17% female
- 90% state residents, no international students
- None 25 years or older
- 40% intercollegiate athletes, Division NAIA sports
  available:
  football, cross-country, soccer, basketball, swimming, diving, wrestling, tennis, golf, baseball (men)
  volleyball, cross-country, soccer, basketball, swimming, diving, tennis, softball (women)
- 3% learning disabled
- None in top 50% of high school class
- 22% graduate within 4 years
- 31% graduate within 5 years

OTHER FEATURES/ACCOMMODATIONS:

- On-campus housing is available and is guaranteed for
  alternative admissions students
- On-campus housing is required of alternative admissions students
- A meal plan is available. It is required of alternative
  admissions students
- Financial aid is available

DEADLINES:

- Rolling admission
- April 1 for financial aid
- June 30 for reply date

The program is best suited for a student who has a
strong desire to attend college, yet has poor grades.

Stacy Needle

UNIVERSITY OF HARTFORD

>>>>>>>>>>>>>>>>>>>>>>>>>>

West Hartford, CT 06117
(203) 243-4296

$10,992 Tuition and Fees
$ 2,894 Average Double Room
$ 1,872 Average Meal Plan

4,156 full-time undergraduates, 1,668 part-time
  undergraduates
11:1 student/faculty ratio
29% of undergraduates study arts/humanities

>>

Founded in 1877, the University of Hartford is a private
institution, coed. Located on 300 acres in a town. Associate's and bachelor's degrees are offered.

ALTERNATIVE ADMISSIONS:

Additional cost: $250 basic program fee
Contact: Joseph Burke, Dean of College of Basic Studies (203) 243-4018

The University of Hartford has a structured program,
College of Basic Studies, initiated in 1968 for alternative admissions students. The formal program of studies begins in the fall and lasts for 2 years.
Approximately 80% of the students complete the program in that time. Students receive an associate's degree upon the completion of their studies.

ADMISSION POLICIES:

- New students are eligible for alternative admissions

- Admission based on individual criteria

ACADEMIC COURSEWORK AND RELATED FEATURES:

- Support services: freshman orientation, college survival skills, academic advising, drug/alcohol counseling, psychological counseling, academic skills center, study technique workshops, career advising, peer counseling, health center, aptitude testing, extended time for tests
- Separate new-student orientation
- Placement testing is required in reading and math
- Students take all of their classes with alternative admissions students
- Alternative admissions classes average 20–25 students

REQUIRED COURSES:

English Composition (credit-bearing)—alternative admissions students only

Mathematics (credit-bearing)—alternative admissions students only

Western Civilization (credit-bearing)—alternative admissions students only

Study Skills (credit-bearing)—alternative admissions students only

Biology (credit-bearing)—alternative admissions students only

- Required courses are calculated in GPA
- Minimum of 2.0 GPA required to stay in program; if below 2.0 GPA, a student is placed on academic probation

PROFILE OF ALTERNATIVE ADMISSIONS STUDENTS:

- 75% graduate within 4 years

OTHER FEATURES/ACCOMMODATIONS:

- On-campus housing is available for alternative admissions students
- A meal plan is available

DEADLINES:

- Rolling admission
- May 1 for reply date

The program is best suited for a student who has experienced difficulty in meeting the demands of a college preparatory program in high school, but exhibits the potential and motivation necessary for success at the college level. Integrated into the program, a student will learn to develop fundamental learning habits.

Note: The above information was compiled from the University of Hartford's *Undergraduate Bulletin.*

UNIVERSITY OF HARTFORD

>>>>>>>>>>>>>>>>>>>>>>>>>>>

West Hartford, CT 06117
(203) 243-4296

___

$10,992 Tuition and Fees
$ 2,894 Average Double Room
$ 1,872 Average Meal Plan

4,156 full-time undergraduates, 1,668 part-time undergraduates
11:1 student/faculty ratio
29% of undergraduates study arts/humanities

>>

Founded in 1877, the University of Hartford is a private institution, coed. Located on 300 acres in a town. Associate's and bachelor's degrees are offered.

ALTERNATIVE ADMISSIONS:

Additional cost: $1,875 basic program fee
Contact: Richard Lugli, Associate Professor of Government (203) 243-4878

The University of Hartford has a structured summer program, Pre-College Summer Institute, initiated in 1967 for alternative admissions students. The program begins in July and lasts for 5 weeks. This is an intensive academic experience designed to ease the transition to the college experience by strengthening reading, writing, and math skills. Ninety-eight percent of the students complete the program in 5 weeks.

ADMISSION POLICIES:

- New students are eligible for alternative admissions, with a limit of 60 students. There is no wait list

- Requirements for admission as a freshman:
    - 350 — minimum verbal SAT
    - 350 — minimum math SAT
    - 35 — minimum TSWE
    - 2.0 — minimum GPA

Other considerations: high school rank, essay/personal statement

ACADEMIC COURSEWORK AND RELATED FEATURES:

- Support services: freshman orientation, college survival skills, academic advising, drug/alcohol counseling, psychological counseling, academic skills center, study technique workshops, career advising, peer counseling, health center, aptitude testing, extended time for tests
- Separate new-student orientation
- Students are not required to work with tutors
- One-on-one tutoring by peer tutors as well as professional tutors in math, English, reading, and study skills
- Counseling is not required
- Students are assigned an academic adviser. All advisers serve alternative admissions students exclusively. Students meet with advisers 5–10 times per summer session
- Placement testing is required in math

The Other Route into College

- Students take all of their classes with alternative admissions students
- Alternative admissions classes average 10 students
- Students are limited to a credit load of 13 credits per semester through fall semester of freshman year

REQUIRED COURSES:

- Remedial courses required:
  English Composition (noncredit)—alternative admissions students only
  Pre-College Math (noncredit)—alternative admissions students only
  College Reading and Study Skills (credit-bearing)—alternative admissions students only
  Western Civilization to 1648 (credit-bearing)

PROFILE OF ALTERNATIVE ADMISSIONS STUDENTS:

- 62 alternative admissions students enrolled
- 92% of the accepted students enrolled
- 100% enter as new students
- 1% minority, 50% female
- 10%–12% state residents, 1% international students
- None 25 years or older
- 1% intercollegiate athletes
- 12–15% learning disabled
- 3% in top 50% of high school class

OTHER FEATURES/ACCOMMODATIONS:

- On-campus housing is available and is guaranteed for alternative admissions students
- A meal plan is available
- Financial aid is not available

DEADLINES:

- Rolling admission
- May 1 for reply date

The program is best suited for a student who has taken a good academic program in high school with a varied level of success and is prepared to work very hard to improve his/her study habits.

UNIVERSITY OF HAWAII AT HILO

>>>>>>>>>>>>>>>>>>>>>>>>>>

Hilo, HI 96720-4091
(808) 933-3414

$　400 In-State Tuition and Fees
$2,460 Out-of-State Tuition and Fees
$　980 Average Double Room
$1,312 Average Meal Plan

2,366 full-time undergraduates, 1,264 part-time undergraduates
10:1 student/faculty ratio
13% of undergraduates study business

>>

Founded in 1970, the University of Hawaii at Hilo is a public institution, coed. Located on 137 acres in a small city. Associate's and bachelor's degrees are offered.

ALTERNATIVE ADMISSIONS:

Contact: Kathy Hammes, Acting Admissions Coordinator (808) 933-3325

The University of Hawaii at Hilo has a policy for alternative admissions students.

ADMISSION POLICIES:

- New and transfer students are eligible for alternative admissions

- Requirements for admission as a freshman:
  400 — average verbal SAT
  400 — average math SAT
  or
  19 — average ACT

  2.0 — average GPA

- Requirements for admission as a transfer student:
  2.0 — average GPA
Other considerations: number of credits completed, age of applicant

ACADEMIC COURSEWORK AND RELATED FEATURES:

- Support services: freshman orientation, college survival skills, academic advising, drug/alcohol counseling, psychological counseling, academic skills center, study technique workshops, career advising, peer counseling, health center, aptitude testing
- Students are not required to work with tutors

Stacy Needle

- Group and one-on-one tutoring by peer tutors
- Counseling is not required
- Students are not assigned an academic adviser
- Placement testing is required in algebra, math, reading, and writing
- Students are not limited to credit load

REQUIRED COURSES:
- Courses required of students who demonstrate deficiency:
  Remedial Reading and Study Skills
  Basic Writing
  Basic Math
  Basic Algebra

OTHER FEATURES/ACCOMMODATIONS:
- On-campus housing is available, but is not guaranteed for alternative admissions students
- A meal plan is available
- Financial aid is available

DEADLINES:
- Rolling admission
- March 1 for financial aid

UNIVERSITY OF LA VERNE
>>>>>>>>>>>>>>>>>>>>>>>>>>>

La Verne, CA 91750
(714) 593-3511, Ext. 4026

$9,145 Tuition and Fees
$1,764 Average Double Room
$1,710 Average Meal Plan

1,532 full-time undergraduates, 1,694 part-time undergraduates
17:1 student/faculty ratio

>>

Founded in 1891, the University of La Verne is a private institution, coed, affiliated with the Church of the Brethren. Located on 27 acres in a town 35 miles from Los Angeles. Associate's and bachelor's degrees are offered.

ALTERNATIVE ADMISSIONS:
Contact: John Gingrich, Dean of Arts and Sciences (714) 593-3511, Ext. 4680

The University of La Verne has a structured program, Learning Enhancement Program, initiated in 1988 for alternative admissions students. The formal program of studies begins in the fall and lasts for 1 semester; however, students can also enter the program in the spring and continue for 1 semester.

ADMISSION POLICIES:
- New and transfer students are eligible for alternative admissions, with a limit of 54 students. There is a wait list
- Requirements for admission as a freshman:
  333 — average verbal SAT
  384 — average math SAT
  36 — average TSWE
  or
  15 — minimum ACT

  2.44 — average GPA
  Other considerations: difficulty of high school courses taken, interview with admissions counselor, essay/personal statement, letters of recommendation

- Admission considerations—transfer student: GPA at previous institution, difficulty of coursework, type of college attended, number of credits completed, interview with admissions counselor, essay/personal statement, letters of recommendation

ACADEMIC COURSEWORK AND RELATED FEATURES:
- Support services: freshman orientation, college survival skills, academic advising, drug/alcohol counseling, psychological counseling, academic skills center, study technique workshops, career advising, health center, aptitude testing
- Students are required to work with tutors 1 hour per week
- One-on-one tutoring by professional tutors in all academic areas
- Academic counseling is required
- Students are assigned an academic adviser. Students meet with advisers 3 times per semester
- Placement testing is not required
- A total of 212 full-time faculty at the institution
- Three faculty members assigned to the program, who are trained to work with alternative admissions students
- Alternative admissions students do not take separate classes
- Students are limited to a credit load of 14 credits per semester through first semester of program

The Other Route into College

REQUIRED COURSES:

Learning Enrichment Seminar (credit-bearing)

- Required courses are not calculated in GPA
- Minimum of 2.0 GPA required to stay in program; if below 2.0 GPA, a student is placed on academic probation

PROFILE OF ALTERNATIVE ADMISSIONS STUDENTS:

- 95 alternative admissions students enrolled
- 56% of the accepted students enrolled
- 27% female

OTHER FEATURES/ACCOMMODATIONS:

- On-campus housing is available, but is not guaranteed for alternative admissions students
- A meal plan is available
- Financial aid is available

DEADLINES:

- Rolling admission
- March 1 for financial aid
- May 1 for reply date

UNIVERSITY OF MAINE

>>>>>>>>>>>>>>>>>>>>>>>>>>>>>

Orono, ME 04469
(207) 581-1561

$2,120 In-State Tuition and Fees
$5,450 Out-of-State Tuition and Fees
$3,600 Average Double Room and Meal Plan

7,781 full-time undergraduates, 1,999 part-time undergraduates

>>

Founded in 1865, the University of Maine is a public institution, coed. Located on 3,295 acres in a rural community 8 miles from Bangor. Associate's and bachelor's degrees are offered.

ALTERNATIVE ADMISSIONS:

Contact: Cindy Mitchell, Assistant Director of Enrollment Management (207) 581-1561

Stacy Needle

The University of Maine has a structured program, Liberal Studies, for alternative admissions students. The formal program of studies begins in the fall and lasts for 2 years. Fifteen to twenty percent of the students complete the program in that time.

ADMISSION POLICIES:

- New students are eligible for alternative admissions
- Admission based on individual criteria

ACADEMIC COURSEWORK AND RELATED FEATURES:

- Students are not required to work with tutors
- Counseling is available
- Students take classes with alternative admissions students only
- Alternative admissions classes average 22 students
- Students are not limited to credit load

PROFILE OF ALTERNATIVE ADMISSIONS STUDENTS:

- 44% of the accepted students enrolled

OTHER FEATURES/ACCOMMODATIONS:

- On-campus housing is available
- A meal plan is available

DEADLINES:

- March 1 for admission

UNIVERSITY OF MAINE AT FARMINGTON

>>>>>>>>>>>>>>>>>>>>>>>>>>>>>

Farmington, ME 04938
(207) 778-9521

$1,710 In-State Tuition and Fees
$4,140 Out-of-State Tuition and Fees
$1,600 Average Double Room
$1,400 Average Meal Plan

1,630 full-time undergraduates, 728 part-time undergraduates

>>

The University of Maine at Farmington is a public institution, coed. Located on 32 acres in a rural community 30 miles from Augusta. Associate's and bachelor's degrees are offered.

ALTERNATIVE ADMISSIONS:

Contact: James Collins, Associate Director of Admissions (207) 778-9521

The University of Maine at Farmington has a structured program, Program of Basic Studies, for alternative admissions students. The formal program of studies begins in the fall and lasts for 1 year. Seventy-five percent of the students complete the program in that time.

ADMISSION POLICIES:

• New students are eligible for alternative admissions, with a limit of 45 students

• Admission considerations: student must be handicapped, first generation in college, or low income

ACADEMIC COURSEWORK AND RELATED FEATURES:

• Students are required to work with tutors
• Counseling is available
• Students take classes with alternative admissions students only
• Alternative admissions classes average 12 students
• Students are limited to a credit load of 12 credits per semester through spring semester of freshman year

REQUIRED COURSES:

• Remedial courses required:
Study Skills
Math
Reading Skills

PROFILE OF ALTERNATIVE ADMISSIONS STUDENTS:

• 87% of the accepted students enrolled
• 25%–30% graduate within 4 years
• 3%–5% graduate within 5 years

OTHER FEATURES/ACCOMMODATIONS:

• On-campus housing is available
• A meal plan is available

DEADLINES:

• Rolling admission

UNIVERSITY OF MAINE AT FORT KENT

>>>>>>>>>>>>>>>>>>>>>>>>>>>

Fort Kent, ME 04743
(207) 834-3162, Ext. 135

$1,368–$1,710 In-State Tuition and Fees
$3,312–$4,140 Out-of-State Tuition and Fees
$ 3,075 Average Double Room and Meal Plan

276 full-time undergraduates, 399 part-time
undergraduates
9:1 student/faculty ratio

>>

Founded in 1878, the University of Maine at Fort Kent is a public institution, coed. Located on 52 acres in a town. Associate's and bachelor's degrees are offered.

ALTERNATIVE ADMISSIONS:

Contact: Jerry Nadeau, Director of Admissions (207) 834-3162, Ext. 135

The University of Maine at Fort Kent has a policy for alternative admissions students.

ADMISSION POLICIES:

• New and transfer students are eligible for alternative admissions

• Admission based on individual criteria

ACADEMIC COURSEWORK AND RELATED FEATURES:

• Support services: freshman orientation, drug/alcohol counseling, psychological counseling, academic skills center, career advising, peer counseling
• Students are not required to work with tutors
• Group and one-on-one tutoring by peer tutors as well as professional tutors in all academic areas
• Counseling is not required
• Students are assigned an academic adviser
• Placement testing is required in math, reading, and writing

REQUIRED COURSES:

• Courses required of students who demonstrate deficiency:
Writing Skills
Math Skills
Learning Skills

The Other Route into College

171

OTHER FEATURES/ACCOMMODATIONS:

- On-campus housing is available, but is not guaranteed for alternative admissions students
- A meal plan is available

DEADLINES:

- Rolling admission

UNIVERSITY OF MAINE AT MACHIAS

>>>>>>>>>>>>>>>>>>>>>>>>>>>

Machias, ME 04654
(207) 255-3313, Ext. 318

$1,710 In-State Tuition and Fees
$4,140 Out-of-State Tuition and Fees
$3,045 Average Double Room and Meal Plan

570 full-time undergraduates, 330 part-time
   undergraduates

>>

Founded in 1909, the University of Maine at Machias is a public institution, coed. Located on 47 acres in a rural community 90 miles from Bangor. Associate's and bachelor's degrees are offered.

ALTERNATIVE ADMISSIONS:

Contact: David Baldwin, Director of Admissions (207) 255-3133, Ext. 318

The University of Maine at Machias has a policy, Curriculum of Basic Studies, for alternative admissions students.

ADMISSION POLICIES:

- New students are eligible for alternative admissions

- Admission based on individual criteria

ACADEMIC COURSEWORK AND RELATED FEATURES:

- Students are required to work with tutors
- Counseling is available
- Alternative admissions students do not take separate classes
- Students are limited to a credit load of 13 credits per semester through fall semester of freshman year

REQUIRED COURSES:

- Minimum of 2.0 GPA required to stay at college; if below 2.0 GPA, a student is placed on academic probation

OTHER FEATURES/ACCOMMODATIONS:

- On-campus housing is available
- A meal plan is available

DEADLINES:

- Rolling admission

UNIVERSITY OF MAINE AT PRESQUE ISLE

>>>>>>>>>>>>>>>>>>>>>>>>>>

Presque Isle, ME 04769
(207) 764-0311

$1,710 In-State Tuition and Fees
$4,140 Out-of-State Tuition and Fees
$3,088 Average Double Room and Meal Plan

684 full-time undergraduates, 605 part-time
   undergraduates
11:1 student/faculty ratio
35% of undergraduates study education

>>

Founded in 1908, the University of Maine at Presque Isle is a public institution, coed. Located on 150 acres in a small city 156 miles from Bangor. Associate's and bachelor's degrees are offered.

ALTERNATIVE ADMISSIONS:

Contact: Frances Kehoe, Director of Enrollment Management (207) 764-0311

The University of Maine at Presque Isle has a policy for alternative admissions students.

ADMISSION POLICIES:

- New and transfer students are eligible for alternative admissions

Stacy Needle

172

- Requirements for admission as a freshman:
  350 — minimum verbal SAT
  350 — minimum math SAT
  30 — minimum TSWE
  2.0 — minimum GPA

- Requirements for admission as a transfer student:
  2.0 — minimum GPA
Other considerations: difficulty of coursework

ACADEMIC COURSEWORK AND RELATED FEATURES:
- Support services: freshman orientation, academic advising, drug/alcohol counseling, women's center, academic skills center, study technique workshops, career advising, health center, aptitude testing
- Students are required to work with tutors
- Group and one-on-one tutoring by peer tutors in all academic areas
- Students are assigned an academic adviser. None of the advisers serve alternative admissions students exclusively. Students meet with advisers 2–3 times per semester
- Placement testing is required in English, reading, algebra, and arithmetic
- Students take classes with alternative admissions students only
- Alternative admissions classes average 10–15 students
- Courses are also offered in the evening
- Students are limited to a credit load of 12 credits per semester through second semester of college

REQUIRED COURSES:
- Courses required of students who demonstrate deficiency:
  Basic Studies: English (credit-bearing)
  Basic Studies: Reading (credit-bearing)
  Basic Studies: Math (credit-bearing)

- Remedial courses are calculated in GPA

PROFILE OF ALTERNATIVE ADMISSIONS STUDENTS:
- 150 alternative admissions students enrolled
- 90% of the accepted students enrolled
- 75% enter as new students, 25% as transfer students
- 5% minority, 55% female
- 90% state residents, 1% international students
- 45% 25 years or older
- 5% intercollegiate athletes
- 10% learning disabled

OTHER FEATURES/ACCOMMODATIONS:
- On-campus housing is available and is guaranteed for alternative admissions students

- A meal plan is available
- Financial aid is available

DEADLINES:
- Rolling admission
- August 1 for financial aid

UNIVERSITY OF MASSACHUSETTS AT BOSTON
>>>>>>>>>>>>>>>>>>>>>>>>>>>

Boston, MA 02125
(617) 287-6100

$1,000 In-State Tuition and Fees
$3,500 Out-of-State Tuition and Fees

12,000 full-time and part-time undergraduates

>>

Founded in 1974, the University of Massachusetts at Boston is a public institution, coed. Located in a large city. Bachelor's degrees are offered.

ALTERNATIVE ADMISSIONS:
Contact: Miguel Alvarez, Assistant Director of Admissions (617) 287-6100

The University of Massachusetts at Boston has a structured summer program, Developmental Studies Program, for alternative admissions students. The program begins in June and lasts for 6 weeks. Ninety-two percent of the students complete the program in that time.

ADMISSION POLICIES:
- New students are eligible for alternative admissions, with a limit of 250–300 students. There is no wait list

- Requirements for admission as a freshman:
  300 — minimum verbal SAT
  300 — minimum math SAT
  35 — minimum TSWE
Other considerations: high school GPA, high school rank, state residence

The Other Route into College

ACADEMIC COURSEWORK AND RELATED FEATURES:

- Support services: freshman orientation, college survival skills, academic advising, career advising, peer counseling, health center
- Separate new-student orientation
- Students are not required to work with tutors
- One-on-one tutoring by peer tutors as well as professional tutors
- Academic counseling is required
- Students are assigned an academic adviser
- Placement testing is required
- Alternative admissions students do not take separate classes

PROFILE OF ALTERNATIVE ADMISSIONS STUDENTS:

- 257 alternative admissions students enrolled
- 46% minority, 57% female
- 100% state residents
- 24% 25 years or older

OTHER FEATURES/ACCOMMODATIONS:

- On-campus housing is not available for alternative admissions students
- A meal plan is not available
- Financial aid is available

DEADLINES:

- Rolling admission—2–3 weeks after application is sent, notification of admission
- May 1 for financial aid

The program is best suited for a student who needs to develop his/her math and verbal skills.

UNIVERSITY OF MICHIGAN

>>>>>>>>>>>>>>>>>>>>>>>>>>>

Ann Arbor, MI 48109
(313) 764-7433

$ 2,152 In-State Tuition and Fees
$10,880 Out-of-State Tuition and Fees
$ 1,892 Average Double Room
$ 1,747 Average Meal Plan

Stacy Needle

11,085 full-time undergraduates, 10,303 part-time undergraduates
13:1 student/faculty ratio
52% of undergraduates study arts/humanities

>>

Founded in 1817, the University of Michigan is a public institution, coed. Located on 2,700 acres in a small city 55 miles from Detroit. Bachelor's degrees are offered.

ALTERNATIVE ADMISSIONS:

Contact: Patricia Caldwell, Senior Admissions Counselor (313) 764-7433

The University of Michigan has a structured program, Educational Opportunities for Non-Traditional Students, initiated in 1976 for alternative admissions students. The formal program of studies begins in the fall and lasts for 4 years; however, students can also enter the program in the spring and continue for 4 years. Students receive a bachelor's degree upon completion of their studies.

ADMISSION POLICIES:

- New and transfer students are eligible for alternative admissions

- Admission considerations—new student: interview with admissions counselor, essay/personal statement, letters of recommendation, age of applicant

- Admission considerations—transfer student: interview with admissions counselor, essay/personal statement, letters of recommendation, age of applicant

ACADEMIC COURSEWORK AND RELATED FEATURES:

- Support services: freshman orientation, college survival skills, academic advising, drug/alcohol counseling, psychological counseling, academic skills center, study technique workshops, career advising, peer counseling, health center, aptitude testing
- Students are not required to work with tutors
- Group and one-on-one tutoring by peer tutors in all academic areas
- Counseling is required
- Placement testing is required
- Alternative admissions students do not take separate classes
- Students are not limited to credit load

REQUIRED COURSES:

- Minimum of 2.0 GPA required to stay in program; if below 2.0 GPA, a student is placed on academic probation

PROFILE OF ALTERNATIVE ADMISSIONS STUDENTS:

- 20 alternative admissions students enrolled
- 100% of the accepted students enrolled
- 55% enter as new students, 45% as transfer students
- 5% minority, 60% female
- 80% state residents, 1% international students
- 100% 25 years or older
- 40% graduate within 4 years
- 60% graduate within 5 years

OTHER FEATURES/ACCOMMODATIONS:

- On-campus housing is available, but is not guaranteed for alternative admissions students
- A meal plan is available
- Financial aid is available

DEADLINES:

- Rolling admission
- February 15 for financial aid
- May 1 for reply date

The program is best suited for an individual out of high school at least 3 years.

UNIVERSITY OF NEBRASKA–LINCOLN

>>>>>>>>>>>>>>>>>>>>>>>>>>>

Lincoln, NE 68588-0415
(402) 472-3620

$1,810 In-State Tuition and Fees
$4,435 Out-of-State Tuition and Fees
$2,430 Average Double Room and Meal Plan

16,155 full-time undergraduates, 3,600 part-time undergraduates
18:1 student/faculty ratio
21% of undergraduates study arts/humanities

>>

Founded in 1869, the University of Nebraska–Lincoln is a public institution, coed. Located on 569 acres in a small city. Bachelor's degrees are offered.

ALTERNATIVE ADMISSIONS:

Contact: Robert Zetocha, Assistant Director of Admissions (402) 472-3620

The University of Nebraska–Lincoln has a structured program, Conditional Admission, initiated in 1986 for alternative admissions students. The formal program begins in the fall and lasts approximately 1 year; however, students can also enter the program in the spring and continue for approximately 1 year.

ADMISSION POLICIES:

- New students are eligible for alternative admissions

- Requirements for admission as a freshman:
  341 — average verbal SAT
  363 — average math SAT
  or
  13 — average ACT

Other considerations: high school rank, type of high school attended, type of courses taken (3 years of English and 1 year of algebra)

ACADEMIC COURSEWORK AND RELATED FEATURES:

- Support services: freshman orientation, college survival skills, academic advising, drug/alcohol counseling, women's center, psychological counseling, academic skills center, study technique workshops, career advising, peer counseling, health center, aptitude testing, extended time for tests
- Students are not required to work with tutors
- One-on-one tutoring by peer tutors
- Counseling is not required
- Students are assigned an academic adviser. None of the advisers serve alternative admissions students exclusively. Students meet with advisers at least 1 time per semester
- Placement testing is not required
- Alternative admissions students do not take separate classes
- Students are not limited to credit load

REQUIRED COURSES:

- Remedial courses required:
  Intermediate Algebra (noncredit)

PROFILE OF ALTERNATIVE ADMISSIONS STUDENTS:

- 178 alternative admissions students enrolled
- 75% of the accepted students enrolled
- 100% enter as new students
- 13% minority, 48% female
- 7% 25 years or older
- 4% intercollegiate athletes
- 2% learning disabled
- None in top 50% of high school class

OTHER FEATURES/ACCOMMODATIONS:

- On-campus housing is available and is guaranteed for alternative admissions students

The Other Route into College

- A meal plan is available
- Financial aid is available

DEADLINES:
- Rolling admission
- March 1 for financial aid
- August 15 for reply date

UNIVERSITY OF NEVADA AT LAS VEGAS

>>>>>>>>>>>>>>>>>>>>>>>>>>>

Las Vegas, NV 89014
(702) 739-3443

$ 960–$1,200 In-State Tuition and Fees
$2,460–$2,700 Out-of-State Tuition and Fees
$ 4,082 Average Double Room and Meal Plan

7,922 full-time undergraduates, 5,061 part-time
   undergraduates
5:1 student/faculty ratio

>>

Founded in 1957, the University of Nevada at Las Vegas is a public institution, coed. Located on 335 acres in a small city. Bachelor's degrees are offered.

ALTERNATIVE ADMISSIONS:

Contact: Dr. Jim Kitchen, Director of Academic Advising (702) 739-3627

The University of Nevada at Las Vegas has a structured program, Academic Advising Center/Alternate Criteria, initiated in 1981 for alternative admissions students. The formal program of studies begins in the fall and lasts for a minimum of 1 semester.

ADMISSION POLICIES:
- New and transfer students are eligible for alternative admissions

- Requirements for admission as a freshman:
   620 — Average combined verbal and math SAT
        or
   16 — average ACT
   1.98 — average GPA

- Requirements for admission as a transfer student:
   1.82 — average GPA
Other considerations: type of college attended, number of credits completed

ACADEMIC COURSEWORK AND RELATED FEATURES:
- Support services: freshman orientation, college survival skills, academic advising, psychological counseling, academic skills center, career advising, peer counseling, health center, aptitude testing, extended time for tests
- Students are not required to work with tutors
- One-on-one tutoring by peer tutors as well as professional tutors in all academic areas
- Counseling is not required
- Students are assigned an academic adviser
- Placement testing is required
- Alternative admissions students do not take separate classes
- Students are not limited to credit load

PROFILE OF ALTERNATIVE ADMISSIONS STUDENTS:
- 97 alternative admissions students enrolled
- 96% of the accepted students enrolled
- 59% enter as new students, 41% as transfer students
- 51% state residents, 8% international students
- 12% 25 years or older
- No intercollegiate athletes
- 8% learning disabled

OTHER FEATURES/ACCOMMODATIONS:
- On-campus housing is available, but is not guaranteed for alternative admissions students
- A meal plan is available
- Financial aid is available

DEADLINES:
- Rolling admission
- February 1 for financial aid

Stacy Needle

UNIVERSITY OF NEW ENGLAND

>>>>>>>>>>>>>>>>>>>>>>>>>>>

Biddeford, ME 04005
(207) 283-0171

$7,950 Tuition and Fees
$3,830 Average Double Room and Meal Plan

560 full-time undergraduates, 60 part-time
  undergraduates

>>

Founded in 1953, the University of New England is a
private institution, coed. Located on 122 acres in a rural
community 16 miles from Portland. Associate's and
bachelor's degrees are offered.

ALTERNATIVE ADMISSIONS:

Contact: Bob Pecchia, Associate Director of Admissions (207) 283-0171

The University of New England has a structured program, Conditional Accept, for alternative admissions
students. The formal program of studies begins in the
fall and lasts for 1 semester.

ADMISSION POLICIES:

• New students are eligible for alternative admissions,
  with a limit of 30 students

• Admission considerations: SAT scores, interview
  with admissions counselor, type of classes taken

ACADEMIC COURSEWORK AND RELATED FEATURES:

• Students are required to work with tutors
• Counseling is available
• Alternative admissions students do not take separate
  classes
• Students are limited to a credit load of 12–15 credits
  per semester through fall semester of freshman year

REQUIRED COURSES:

• Minimum of 2.0 GPA required to stay in program; if
  below 2.0 GPA, a student is placed on academic probation

PROFILE OF ALTERNATIVE ADMISSIONS STUDENTS:

• 70% of the accepted students enrolled

OTHER FEATURES/ACCOMMODATIONS:

• On-campus housing is available
• A meal plan is available

DEADLINES:

• Rolling admission

UNIVERSITY OF NORTH CAROLINA AT WILMINGTON

>>>>>>>>>>>>>>>>>>>>>>>>>>>

Wilmington, NC 28403-3297
(919) 395-3243

$ 476 In-State Tuition and Fees
$2,395 Out-of-State Tuition and Fees
$1,650 Average Double Room
$1,106 Average Meal Plan

5,537 full-time undergraduates, 751 part-time
  undergraduates
16:1 student/faculty ratio
21% of undergraduates study business

>>

Founded in 1947, the University of North Carolina at
Wilmington is a public institution, coed. Located on 650
acres in a large city 123 miles from Raleigh. Bachelor's
degrees are offered.

ALTERNATIVE ADMISSIONS:

Contact: Anne Collins, Assistant Director of Admissions (919) 395-3133

The University of North Carolina at Wilmington has a
structured program, Unclassified Student Program, initiated in 1975 for alternative admissions students. The
formal program of studies begins in the fall and lasts for
1–2 semesters; however, students can also enter the
program in the spring and continue for 1–2 semesters.

ADMISSION POLICIES:

• New and transfer students are eligible for alternative
  admissions

The Other Route into College

- Requirements for admission as a freshman:
  - 700 — minimum combined verbal and math SAT
  - or
  - 15 — minimum ACT
  - 2.0 — average GPA
- A high school graduate who has not attended an institution of higher education and has been graduated at least 2 years may apply for admission as an unclassified student
- Requirements for admission as a transfer student:
  - 2.0 — minimum GPA

Other considerations: number of credits completed (less than 24 credits)
- A transfer student who has not enrolled in an institution of higher education for at least 1 year and who has not been academically suspended within the last 3 years may apply for admission as an unclassified student

ACADEMIC COURSEWORK AND RELATED FEATURES:
- Support services: freshman orientation, college survival skills, academic advising, drug/alcohol counseling, psychological counseling, study technique workshops, career advising, health center, aptitude testing
- Students are not required to work with tutors
- Group and one-on-one tutoring by peer tutors as well as professional tutors in English and math
- Counseling is not required
- Students are assigned an academic adviser. None of the advisers serve alternative admissions students exclusively. Students meet with advisers at least 2 times per semester
- Alternative admissions students do not take separate classes

REQUIRED COURSES:
- Minimum of 2.0 GPA required to stay in program; if below 2.0 GPA, a student is placed on academic probation

OTHER FEATURES/ACCOMMODATIONS:
- On-campus housing is available, but is not guaranteed for alternative admissions students
- A meal plan is available
- Financial aid is available

DEADLINES:
- December 1 and February 15 for admission
- April 15 for financial aid
- February 15 and April 15 for notification of admission
- May 1 for reply date

The program is best suited for an adult student (over 30 years old) returning to college.

Stacy Needle

UNIVERSITY OF NORTHERN IOWA

>>>>>>>>>>>>>>>>>>>>>>>>>>>

Cedar Falls, IA 50614
(319) 273-2281

$1,690 In-State Tuition and Fees
$4,346 Out-of-State Tuition and Fees
$2,158 Average Double Room and Meal Plan

8,979 full-time undergraduates, 1,538 part-time undergraduates
17:1 student/faculty ratio
30% of undergraduates study business

>>

Founded in 1876, the University of Northern Iowa is a public institution, coed. Located on 723 acres in a small city 7 miles from Waterloo. Bachelor's degrees are offered.

ALTERNATIVE ADMISSIONS:
Contact: Jack L. Wielengn, Director of Admissions
(319) 273-2281

The University of Northern Iowa has a policy for alternative admissions students.

ADMISSION POLICIES:
- New and transfer students are eligible for alternative admissions

- Requirements for admission as a freshman:
  - 21 — average ACT

Other considerations: high school rank

- Requirements for admission as a transfer student:
  - 2.0 — minimum GPA

ACADEMIC COURSEWORK AND RELATED FEATURES:
- Support services: freshman orientation, college survival skills, academic advising, drug/alcohol counseling, psychological counseling, academic skills center, study technique workshops, career advising, peer counseling, health center, aptitude testing
- Students are not required to work with tutors
- Group and one-on-one tutoring by peer as well as professional tutors in most academic areas
- Counseling is not required
- Students are assigned an academic adviser. None of the advisers serve alternative admissions students exclusively

- Placement testing is not required
- Alternative admissions students do not take separate classes

REQUIRED COURSES:
- Remedial courses required:
  College Preparatory English (noncredit)
  Elementary Algebra (noncredit)

PROFILE OF ALTERNATIVE ADMISSIONS STUDENTS:
- 202 alternative admissions students enrolled
- 11% of the accepted students enrolled
- 11% minority, 50% female
- 90% state residents, no international students
- 10% 25 years or older
- 11% intercollegiate athletes
- No learning disabled
- None in top 50% of high school class
- 33% graduate within 5 years

OTHER FEATURES/ACCOMMODATIONS:
- On-campus housing is available, but is not guaranteed for alternative admissions students
- A meal plan is available
- Financial aid is available

DEADLINES:
- Rolling admission—2 weeks after application is sent, notification of admission
- March 15 for financial aid

UNIVERSITY OF OREGON
>>>>>>>>>>>>>>>>>>>>>>>>>

Eugene, OR 97403
(503) 346-3201

$1,832 In-State Tuition and Fees
$5,093 Out-of-State Tuition and Fees
$3,333 Average Double Room and Meal Plan

12,573 full-time undergraduates, 1,866 part-time undergraduates
16:1 student/faculty ratio
53% of undergraduates study arts and sciences

>>
Founded in 1876, the University of Oregon is a public institution, coed. Located on 250 acres in a small city 150 miles from Portland. Bachelor's degrees are offered.

ALTERNATIVE ADMISSIONS:
Contact: James Buch, Director of Admissions (503) 346-3201

The University of Oregon has a policy for alternative admissions students.

ADMISSION POLICIES:
- New students are eligible for alternative admissions

- Requirements for admission as a freshman:
  350 — minimum verbal SAT
  350 — minimum math SAT
  30 — minimum TSWE
  2.5 — minimum GPA
  Other considerations: ACT scores (in place of SAT)

ACADEMIC COURSEWORK AND RELATED FEATURES:
- Support services: freshman orientation, college survival skills, academic advising, drug/alcohol counseling, women's center, psychological counseling, academic skills center, study technique workshops, career advising, peer counseling, health center, aptitude testing, extended time for tests
- Students are not required to work with tutors
- Group and one-on-one tutoring by peer tutors as well as professional tutors in math and writing
- Counseling is not required
- Students are assigned an academic adviser. None of the advisers serve alternative admissions students exclusively
- Placement testing is not required
- Alternative admissions students do not take separate classes
- Students are not limited to credit load

PROFILE OF ALTERNATIVE ADMISSIONS STUDENTS:
- 72 alternative admissions students enrolled
- 5% of the accepted students enrolled
- 2% minority, 50% female
- 3% intercollegiate athletes

OTHER FEATURES/ACCOMMODATIONS:
- On-campus housing is available, but is not guaranteed for alternative admissions students
- A meal plan is available

DEADLINES:
- Rolling admission
- March 1 for financial aid

The Other Route into College

UNIVERSITY OF PITTSBURGH

>>>>>>>>>>>>>>>>>>>>>>>>>>>>

Pittsburgh, PA 15260
(412) 624-PITT

$3,820 In-State Tuition and Fees
$7,840 Out-of-State Tuition and Fees
$1,936 Average Double Room
$1,328 Average Meal Plan

13,396 full-time undergraduates, 5,465 part-time
  undergraduates

>>

Founded in 1787, the University of Pittsburgh is a public institution, coed. Located in a large city. Bachelor's
degrees are offered.

ALTERNATIVE ADMISSIONS:

Additional cost: $1,500–$2,125 basic program fee
Contact: Anne Rawlinson, Co-Director of Special Student Programs (412) 624-6789

The University of Pittsburgh has a structured summer
program, Summer Transitional Educational Program
(S.T.E.P.), initiated in 1988 for alternative admissions
students. The program begins in June and lasts for 7½
weeks.

ADMISSION POLICIES:

- New students are eligible for alternative admissions,
  with a limit of 60 students. There is no wait list

- Admission considerations—new student: SAT
  scores, high school rank, essay/personal statement

ACADEMIC COURSEWORK AND RELATED FEATURES:

- Support services: freshman orientation, college survival skills, academic advising, drug/alcohol counseling, women's center, psychological counseling,
  academic skills center, study technique workshops,
  career advising, peer counseling, health center
- Separate new-student orientation
- Students are not required to work with tutors
- Group and one-on-one tutoring by peer tutors as well
  as professional tutors in math and English composition
- Counseling is not required

- Students are assigned an academic adviser. None of
  the advisers serve alternative admissions students
  exclusively. Students meet with advisers 2 times per
  semester
- Placement testing is required in algebra and composition
- A total of 2,430 full-time faculty at the institution
- Fifteen faculty members assigned to the program,
  who are trained to work with alternative admissions
  students
- Students are not limited to credit load

REQUIRED COURSES:

- Courses required of students who demonstrate defi-
  ciency:
  College Algebra
  Basic Writing

- Minimum of 2.0 GPA required to stay in program; if
  below 2.0 GPA, a student may not enroll for the fall
  semester

OTHER FEATURES/ACCOMMODATIONS:

- On-campus housing is available, but is not guaranteed
  for alternative admissions students
- A meal plan is available
- Financial aid is available

DEADLINES:

- Rolling admission
- March 1 for financial aid
- May 1 for reply date

The program is best suited for a student who has the
potential to do college-level work, but has one or two
weaknesses in his/her background.

UNIVERSITY OF REDLANDS

>>>>>>>>>>>>>>>>>>>>>>>>>>>>

Redlands, CA 92373-0999
(714) 335-4074

$11,890 Tuition and Fees
$ 2,600 Average Double Room
$ 2,140 Average Meal Plan

Stacy Needle

180

1,259 full-time undergraduates, 84 part-time
   undergraduates
13:1 student/faculty ratio

>>

Founded in 1907, the University of Redlands is a private institution, coed. Located on 130 acres in a town 20 miles from San Bernardino. Bachelor's degrees are offered.

ALTERNATIVE ADMISSIONS:

Contact: Paul Driscoll, Director of Admissions (714) 335-4074

The University of Redlands has a policy for alternative admissions students.

ADMISSION POLICIES:

• New and transfer students are eligible for alternative admissions

• Requirements for admission as a freshman:
   425 — average verbal SAT
   468 — average math SAT
   44 — average TSWE
      or
   17 — average ACT

   2.75 — average GPA
Other considerations: high school rank, type of high school attended, difficulty of high school courses taken, extracurricular activities, community service/volunteer work, essay/personal statement, letters of recommendation

• Requirements for admission as a transfer student:
   2.99 — average GPA
Other considerations: difficulty of coursework, type of college attended, number of credits completed (less than 60 credits), essay/personal statement, letters of recommendation

ACADEMIC COURSEWORK AND RELATED FEATURES:

• Support services: freshman orientation, college survival skills, academic advising, drug/alcohol counseling, women's center, psychological counseling, academic skills center, study technique workshops, career advising, peer counseling, health center
• Students are not required to work with tutors
• Group and one-on-one tutoring by peer tutors in most academic areas
• Counseling is not required
• Students are assigned an academic adviser

• Placement testing is not required
• Alternative admissions students do not take separate classes

REQUIRED COURSES:

• Minimum of 2.0 GPA required to stay at college; if below 2.0 GPA, a student is placed on academic probation

PROFILE OF ALTERNATIVE ADMISSIONS STUDENTS:

• 41 alternative admissions students enrolled
• 11% of the accepted students enrolled

OTHER FEATURES/ACCOMMODATIONS:

• On-campus housing is available and is guaranteed for alternative admissions students
• A meal plan is available
• Financial aid is available

DEADLINES:

• Rolling admission
• March 1 for financial aid
• May 1 for reply date

UNIVERSITY OF SOUTH ALABAMA
>>>>>>>>>>>>>>>>>>>>>>>>>>>

Mobile, AL 36688
(205) 460-6141

$1,875 In-State Tuition and Fees
$2,575 Out-of-State Tuition and Fees
$1,283 Average Double Room
$1,365 Average Meal Plan

6,660 full-time undergraduates, 2,384 part-time
   undergraduates
20:1 student/faculty ratio
21% of undergraduates study business

>>

Founded in 1963, the University of South Alabama is a public institution, coed. Located on 1,585 acres in a small city. Bachelor's degrees are offered.

The Other Route into College

ALTERNATIVE ADMISSIONS:

Contact: Dr. Sylvia Spann, Department Chairperson
(205) 460-7155

The University of South Alabama has a structured program, Developmental Studies Program, initiated in 1981 for alternative admissions students. The formal program of studies begins in the fall and lasts for approximately 4 quarters; however, students can enter the program in the spring and continue for approximately 4 quarters.

ADMISSION POLICIES:

- New and transfer students are eligible for alternative admissions

- Requirements for admission as a freshman:
    13 — average ACT
    1.89 — average GPA
Other considerations: interview with admissions counselor, essay/personal statement

- Requirements for admission as a transfer student:
    1.41 — average GPA
Other considerations: number of credits completed

ACADEMIC COURSEWORK AND RELATED FEATURES:

- Support services: freshman orientation, college survival skills, academic advising, study technique workshops, career advising, aptitude testing
- Separate new-student orientation
- Students are required to work with tutors 1 hour per week
- Group and one-on-one tutoring by professional tutors in writing and math
- Academic and personal counseling is required
- Students are assigned an academic adviser. All advisers serve alternative admissions students exclusively. Students meet with advisers 2 times per quarter
- Placement testing is required in math
- A total of 605 full-time faculty at the institution
- Four faculty members assigned to the program
- Students take an average of 65% of their classes with alternative admissions students
- Alternative admissions classes average 15 students
- Courses are also offered in the evening

REQUIRED COURSES:

Math (credit-bearing)
Writing (credit-bearing)
Study Skills (credit-bearing)
Seminar (credit-bearing)

- Remedial courses are calculated in GPA

PROFILE OF ALTERNATIVE ADMISSIONS STUDENTS:

- 114 alternative admissions students enrolled
- 52% of the accepted students enrolled
- 96% enter as new students, 4% as transfer students
- 21% minority, 54% female
- 86% state residents, 1% international students
- 6% 25 years or older

OTHER FEATURES/ACCOMMODATIONS:

- On-campus housing is available, but is not guaranteed for alternative admissions students
- A meal plan is available
- Financial aid is available

DEADLINES:

- Rolling admission
- April for financial aid
- September 10 for reply date

UNIVERSITY OF SOUTH CAROLINA
>>>>>>>>>>>>>>>>>>>>>>>>>>

Columbia, SC 29208
(803) 777-7700

$2,448 In-State Tuition and Fees
$5,548 Out-of-State Tuition and Fees
$2,790 Average Double Room and Meal Plan

12,919 full-time undergraduates, 3,043 part-time
    undergraduates
16:1 student/faculty ratio
28% of undergraduates study business

>>

Founded in 1801, the University of South Carolina is a public institution, coed. Located on 242 acres in a small city. Bachelor's degrees are offered.

ALTERNATIVE ADMISSIONS:

Contact: James Burns, Director of Provisional Year
(803) 777-2554

The University of South Carolina has a structured program, Provisional Year, initiated in 1984 for alternative admissions students. The formal program of studies

Stacy Needle

begins in the fall and lasts for 1 year. Approximately 68% of the students complete the program in that time.

ADMISSION POLICIES:

- New students are eligible for alternative admissions, with a limit of 150 students. There is no wait list

- Requirements for admission as a freshman:
340–420 — average verbal SAT
375–480 — average math SAT
Other considerations: high school GPA, high school rank

ACADEMIC COURSEWORK AND RELATED FEATURES:

- Support services: freshman orientation, college survival skills, academic advising, drug/alcohol counseling, women's center, psychological counseling, academic skills center, career advising, peer counseling, health center
- Students are not required to work with tutors
- Counseling is not required
- Students are assigned an academic adviser. All advisers serve alternative admissions students exclusively
- A total of 1,069 full-time faculty at the institution
- Nine faculty members assigned to the program, who are trained to work with alternative admissions students
- Students take all of their classes with alternative admissions students
- Alternative admissions classes average 25 students
- Students are not limited to credit load

REQUIRED COURSES:

English (credit-bearing)—alternative admissions students only
Social Science (credit-bearing)—alternative admissions students only
History (credit-bearing)—alternative admissions students only
Math (credit-bearing)—alternative admissions students only
Science (credit-bearing)—alternative admissions students only

- Required courses are calculated in GPA
- Minimum of 2.0 GPA required to stay in program; if below 2.0 GPA, a student must leave the University of South Carolina

PROFILE OF ALTERNATIVE ADMISSIONS STUDENTS:

- 252 alternative admissions students enrolled
- 100% enter as new students
- 50% state residents, no international students
- None 25 years or older
- 6% intercollegiate athletes

- 26% graduate within 4 years
- 21% graduate within 5 years

OTHER FEATURES/ACCOMMODATIONS:

- On-campus housing is available, but is not guaranteed for alternative admissions students
- A meal plan is available
- Financial aid is available

DEADLINES:

- Rolling admission
- April 1 for financial aid

UNIVERSITY OF SOUTH CAROLINA AT AIKEN

>>>>>>>>>>>>>>>>>>>>>>>>>>>>>

Aiken, SC 29801
(803) 648-6851

$1,770 In-State Tuition and Fees
$3,540 Out-of-State Tuition and Fees
$2,390 Average Double Room and Meal Plan

1,797 full-time undergraduates, 931 part-time undergraduates
12:1 student/faculty ratio

>>

Founded in 1961, the University of South Carolina at Aiken is a public institution, coed. Located on 144 acres in a small city. Associate's and bachelor's degrees are offered.

ALTERNATIVE ADMISSIONS:

Contact: Randy Duckett, Director of Admissions (803) 648-6851

The University of South Carolina at Aiken has a policy for alternative admissions students.

ADMISSION POLICIES:

- New and transfer students are eligible for alternative admissions

- Admission considerations—new student: SAT scores, essay/personal statement, letters of recommendation

The Other Route into College

- Admission considerations—transfer student: GPA at previous institution, essay/personal statement, letters of recommendation

ACADEMIC COURSEWORK AND RELATED FEATURES:

- Support services: freshman orientation, college survival skills, academic advising, drug/alcohol counseling, psychological counseling, academic skills center, study technique workshops, career advising, aptitude testing
- Students are not required to work with tutors
- Group and one-on-one tutoring by peer tutors as well as professional tutors
- Counseling is not required
- Students are assigned an academic adviser. None of the advisers serve alternative admissions students exclusively
- Placement testing is required in English, foreign language, and math
- Alternative admissions students do not take separate classes
- Students are not limited to credit load

REQUIRED COURSES:

- Courses required of students who demonstrate deficiency:
  Basic Writing
  An Introduction to Elementary Mathematics

PROFILE OF ALTERNATIVE ADMISSIONS STUDENTS:

- 60 alternative admissions students enrolled
- 98% of accepted students enrolled
- No international students

OTHER FEATURES/ACCOMMODATIONS:

- On-campus housing is available, but is not guaranteed for alternative admissions students
- A meal plan is available
- Financial aid is available

DEADLINES:

- Rolling admission
- March 15 for financial aid

UNIVERSITY OF SOUTH CAROLINA-COASTAL CAROLINA COLLEGE

>>>>>>>>>>>>>>>>>>>>>>>>>>>>

Conway, SC 29526
(803) 349-2026

$1,750 In-State Tuition and Fees
$3,890 Out-of-State Tuition and Fees
$2,200 Average Double Room and and Meal Plan

2,922 full-time undergraduates, 1,179 part-time
  undergraduates
23:1 student/faculty ratio
31% of undergraduates study business

>>

Founded in 1954, Coastal Carolina College is a public institution, coed. Located on 208 acres in a small city 9 miles from Myrtle Beach. Associate's and bachelor's degrees are offered.

ALTERNATIVE ADMISSIONS:

Contact: Dr. Susan Webb, Director of Advising and Freshman Programs (803) 349-2087

Coastal Carolina College has a structured summer program, Summer Admissions Program, initiated in 1988 for alternative admissions students. The program begins in July and lasts for 5 weeks. Fifty percent of the students complete the program in that time.

ADMISSION POLICIES:

- New students are eligible for alternative admissions

- Requirements for admission as a freshman:
  310 — average verbal SAT
  334 — average math SAT
Other considerations: ACT scores (in place of SAT), high school GPA, high school rank, state residence

ACADEMIC COURSEWORK AND RELATED FEATURES:

- Support services: freshman orientation, college survival skills, academic advising, drug/alcohol counseling, psychological counseling, academic skills center, study technique workshops, career advising, peer counseling, health center, aptitude testing
- Separate new-student orientation
- Students are not required to work with tutors

Stacy Needle

- Group and one-on-one tutoring by peer tutors in math, English, and foreign language
- Counseling is not required
- Students are assigned an academic adviser. None of the advisers serve alternative admissions students exclusively. Students meet with advisers at least 1 time per semester
- Placement testing is required in English, math, and foreign language
- Students take all of their classes with alternative admissions students
- Alternative admissions classes average 20 students

PROFILE OF ALTERNATIVE ADMISSIONS STUDENTS:
- 8 alternative admissions students enrolled
- 35% of accepted students enrolled
- 100% enter as new students
- 100% state residents

OTHER FEATURES/ACCOMMODATIONS:
- On-campus housing is available, but is not guaranteed for alternative admissions students
- A meal plan is available

DEADLINES:
- Rolling admission
- April 1 for financial aid

UNIVERSITY OF SOUTHERN MAINE
>>>>>>>>>>>>>>>>>>>>>>>>>>>

Gorham, ME 04038
(207) 780-5215

$1,830 In-State Tuition and Fees
$5,160 Out-of-State Tuition and Fees
$1,800 Average Double Room
$1,760 Average Meal Plan

3,854 full-time undergraduates, 4,757 part-time undergraduates

>>

The University of Southern Maine is a public institution, coed. Located on 125 acres in a town. Associate's and bachelor's degrees are offered.

ALTERNATIVE ADMISSIONS:
Contact: Deborah Daeris, Admissions Counselor (207) 780-5215

The University of Southern Maine has a structured program, Admissions with Conditions, for alternative admissions students. The formal program of studies begins in the fall and lasts for approximately 2 semesters.

ADMISSION POLICIES:
- New students are eligible for alternative admissions
- Admission based on individual criteria

ACADEMIC COURSEWORK AND RELATED FEATURES:
- Students are not required to work with tutors
- Counseling is available
- Alternative admissions students do not take separate classes
- Students are limited to a credit load of 12 credits per semester through fall semester of freshman year

REQUIRED COURSES:
- Remedial courses required:
  Remedial English
  Remedial Math

PROFILE OF ALTERNATIVE ADMISSIONS STUDENTS:
- 63% of the accepted students enrolled

OTHER FEATURES/ACCOMMODATIONS:
- On-campus housing is available
- A meal plan is available

DEADLINES:
- Rolling admission

UNIVERSITY OF SOUTHERN MISSISSIPPI

>>>>>>>>>>>>>>>>>>>>>>>>>>

Hattiesburg, MS 39406
(601) 266-5555

$1,834 In-State Tuition and Fees
$3,016 Out-of-State Tuition and Fees
$1,146 Average Double Room
$ 965 Average Meal Plan

8,238 full-time undergraduates, 1,141 part-time
  undergraduates
16:1 student/faculty ratio
26% of undergraduates study liberal arts

>>

Founded in 1910, the University of Southern Mississippi is a public institution, coed. Located on 840 acres
in a small city. Bachelor's degrees are offered.

ALTERNATIVE ADMISSIONS:

Contact: Wayne Pyle, Director of Admissions (601)
266-5555

The University of Southern Mississippi has a policy for
alternative admissions students.

ADMISSION POLICIES:

• New students are eligible for alternative admissions

• Requirements for admission as a freshman:
    13 — minimum ACT
    2.0 — minimum GPA

ACADEMIC COURSEWORK AND RELATED FEATURES:

• Support services: freshman orientation, academic ad-
  vising, psychological counseling, career advising,
  health center, aptitude testing
• Students are not required to work with tutors
• Counseling is not required
• Students are not assigned an academic adviser
• Placement testing is not required
• Alternative admissions students do not take separate
  classes
• Students are not limited to credit load

REQUIRED COURSES:

• Remedial courses required:
  Developmental Reading (noncredit)

Developmental Math (noncredit)
Developmental English (noncredit)

PROFILE OF ALTERNATIVE ADMISSIONS STUDENTS:

• 58 alternative admissions students enrolled
• 100% of the accepted students enrolled
• 100% enter as new students

OTHER FEATURES/ACCOMMODATIONS:

• On-campus housing is available, but is not guaranteed
  for alternative admissions students
• A meal plan is available
• Financial aid is available

DEADLINES:

• June 5 for admission
• March 30 for financial aid

UNIVERSITY OF TEXAS AT AUSTIN

>>>>>>>>>>>>>>>>>>>>>>>>>>>

Austin, TX 78712
(512) 471-7601

$ 900 In-State Tuition and Fees
$4,026 Out-of-State Tuition and Fees
$3,083 Average Double Room and Meal Plan

38,118 full-time undergraduates
22:1 student/faculty ratio
31% of undergraduates study arts/humanities

>>

Founded in 1883, the University of Texas at Austin is
a public institution, coed. Located on 300 acres in a
small city 70 miles from San Antonio. Bachelor's degrees are offered.

ALTERNATIVE ADMISSIONS:

Contact: Neal Hartman, Associate Director of Admissions (512) 471-7601

The University of Texas at Austin has a structured
program, Provisional Admission Program, initiated in
1965 for alternative admissions students. The program
begins in June and lasts for approximately 6 weeks.
Forty-five percent of the students complete the program in that time.

Stacy Needle

186

ADMISSION POLICIES:

• New students are eligible for alternative admissions

• Admission considerations: SAT or ACT scores, high school rank, state residence

ACADEMIC COURSEWORK AND RELATED FEATURES:

• Support services: freshman orientation, college survival skills, academic advising, study technique workshops, peer counseling, health center, aptitude testing
• Separate new-student orientation
• Students are not required to work with tutors
• Group and one-on-one tutoring by peer tutors as well as professional tutors in all academic areas
• Counseling is not required
• Students are assigned an academic adviser. Students meet with advisers 1–4 times per semester
• Placement testing is required in English, math, and foreign language
• Alternative admissions students do not take separate classes
• Students are not limited to credit load

REQUIRED COURSES:

Rhetoric and Composition (credit-bearing)
College Algebra or Elementary Functions and Coordinate Geometry (credit-bearing)
Social Science (credit-bearing)
Natural Science (credit-bearing)

• Required courses are calculated in GPA

PROFILE OF ALTERNATIVE ADMISSIONS STUDENTS:

• 350 alternative admissions students enrolled
• 5% minority
• 100% state residents, no international students
• None 25 years or older
• No intercollegiate athletes
• No learning disabled

OTHER FEATURES/ACCOMMODATIONS:

• On-campus housing is available, but is not guaranteed for alternative admissions students
• A meal plan is available

DEADLINES:

• Rolling admission
• March 1 for financial aid

UNIVERSITY OF WASHINGTON

>>>>>>>>>>>>>>>>>>>>>>>>>>>>>

Seattle, WA 98195
(206) 543-9686

$1,827 In-State Tuition and Fees
$5,082 Out-of-State Tuition and Fees
$1,764 Average Double Room
$1,200 Average Meal Plan

20,079 full-time undergraduates, 4,193 part-time undergraduates
12:1 student/faculty ratio
13% of undergraduates study social sciences

>>

Founded in 1861, the University of Washington is a public institution, coed. Located on 694 acres in a large city. Bachelor's degrees are offered.

ALTERNATIVE ADMISSIONS:

Contact: Enrique Morales, Director of Admissions, Office of Minority Affairs (206) 543-6598

The University of Washington has a structured program, Educational Opportunity Program, initiated in 1969 for alternative admissions students. The formal program of studies begins in the fall and lasts for 4 years. Students receive a bachelor's degree upon completion of their studies.

ADMISSION POLICIES:

• New and transfer students are eligible for alternative admissions

• Requirements for admission as a freshman:
  450 — average verbal SAT
  400 — average math SAT
  2.95 — average GPA
Other considerations: difficulty of high school courses taken; student must be a minority or first generation in college

• Requirements for admission as a transfer student:
  2.0 — minimum GPA
Other considerations: type of college attended, state residence

ACADEMIC COURSEWORK AND RELATED FEATURES:

• Support services: freshman orientation, college survival skills, academic advising, women's center, psy-

The Other Route into College

chological counseling, academic skills center, study technique workshops, career advising, health center, aptitude testing
- Separate new-student orientation
- Students are not required to work with tutors
- Group and one-on-one tutoring by peer tutors as well as professional tutors in all natural and social sciences
- Academic and career counseling is required
- Students are assigned an academic adviser. All advisers serve alternative admissions students exclusively. Students meet with advisers 1–3 times per quarter
- Placement testing is required in English and math
- Students take an average of 34% of their classes with alternative admissions students only
- Alternative admissions classes average 30–40 students

REQUIRED COURSES:

- Remedial courses required:
  English Composition (credit-bearing)—alternative admissions students only
  Beginning Algebra (credit-bearing)—alternative admissions students only
  Intermediate Algebra (credit-bearing)—alternative admissions students only
  Introduction to Elementary Functions (credit-bearing)—alternative admissions students only

- Remedial courses are calculated in GPA
- Minimum of 2.0 GPA required to stay in program; if below 2.0 GPA, a student is subject to academic probation or dismissal

PROFILE OF ALTERNATIVE ADMISSIONS STUDENTS:

- 743 alternative admissions students enrolled
- 71% of the accepted students enrolled
- 65% enter as new students, 35% as transfer students
- 92% minority, 45% female
- 88% state residents, no international students
- 15% 25 years or older
- No intercollegiate athletes
- 1% learning disabled
- 65% in top 50% of high school class
- 30% graduate within 4 years
- 40% graduate within 5 years

OTHER FEATURES/ACCOMMODATIONS:

- On-campus housing is available, but is not guaranteed for alternative admissions students
- A meal plan is available
- Financial aid is available

DEADLINES:

- New students—February 1, transfer students—July 1 for admission
- March 1 for financial aid
- August 15 for reply date

UNIVERSITY OF WISCONSIN AT GREEN BAY

>>>>>>>>>>>>>>>>>>>>>>>>>>>>

Green Bay, WI 54311-7001
(414) 465-2111

$ 840 In-State Tuition and Fees
$2,521 Out-of-State Tuition and Fees
$1,085 Average Double Room
$1,000 Average Meal Plan

3,597 full-time undergraduates, 1,394 part-time undergraduates
16:1 student/faculty ratio
31% of undergraduates study social sciences

>>

Founded in 1968, the University of Wisconsin at Green Bay is a public institution, coed. Located on 700 acres in a rural community. Associate's and bachelor's degrees are offered.

ALTERNATIVE ADMISSIONS:

Contact: Michael Marinetti, Director of Educational Opportunity Program (414) 465-2671

The University of Wisconsin at Green Bay has a structured program, Educational Opportunity Program, initiated in 1972 for alternative admissions students. The formal program of studies begins in the fall and lasts for 3 semesters; however, students can also enter the program in the spring and continue for 3 semesters. Eighty percent of the students complete the program in that time.

ADMISSION POLICIES:

- New students are eligible for alternative admissions, with a limit of 40 students. There is a wait list
- Admission considerations: high school GPA, high school rank, interview with admissions counselor

Stacy Needle

ACADEMIC COURSEWORK AND RELATED FEATURES:

- Support services: freshman orientation, college survival skills, academic advising, drug/alcohol counseling, women's center, psychological counseling, academic skills center, study technique workshops, career advising, peer counseling, health center, aptitude testing, extended time for tests
- Separate new-student orientation
- Students are not required to work with tutors
- Group and one-on-one tutoring by peer tutors as well as professional tutors in all academic areas
- Counseling is not required
- Students are assigned an academic adviser. All advisers serve alternative admissions students exclusively. Students meet with advisers 5 times per semester
- Placement testing is required in English, math, and reading
- A total of 158 full-time faculty at the institution
- Seven faculty members assigned to the program, who are trained to work with alternative admissions students
- Students take an average of 50% of their classes with alternative admissions students only
- Alternative admissions classes average 18 students
- Students are limited to a credit load of 12 credits per semester through second semester of program

REQUIRED COURSES:

- Courses required of students who demonstrate deficiency:
  Study Skills Laboratories (credit-bearing)—alternative admissions students only
  College Reading Skills (credit-bearing)—alternative admissions students only
  Elementary Algebra (credit-bearing)
  Fundamentals of Writing (credit-bearing)
- Remedial courses are not calculated in GPA

OTHER FEATURES/ACCOMMODATIONS:

- On-campus housing is available, but is not guaranteed for alternative admissions students
- A meal plan is available
- Financial aid is available

DEADLINES:

- Rolling admission
- April for financial aid
- June for reply date

UNIVERSITY OF WISCONSIN AT MILWAUKEE

>>>>>>>>>>>>>>>>>>>>>>>>>>>>>>

Milwaukee, WI 53201
(414) 229-3800

$2,053 In-State Tuition and Fees
$3,093 Out-of-State Tuition and Fees
$1,444 Average Double Room
$1,600 Average Meal Plan

12,309 full-time undergraduates, 8,377 part-time
  undergraduates
19:1 student/faculty ratio

>>

Founded in 1956, the University of Wisconsin at Milwaukee is a public institution, coed. Located on 93 acres in a large city 90 miles from Chicago. Bachelor's degrees are offered.

ALTERNATIVE ADMISSIONS:

Contact: Robert Kaleta, Director of Department of Learning Skills and Educational Opportunity (414) 229-5135

The University of Wisconsin at Milwaukee has a structured program, Department of Learning Skills and Educational Opportunity, initiated in 1968 for alternative admissions students. The formal program of studies begins in the fall and lasts for a minimum of 5 semesters; however, students can also enter the program in the spring and continue for a minimum of 5 semesters.

ADMISSION POLICIES:

- New and transfer students are eligible for alternative admissions

- Requirements for admission as a freshman:
    11 — average ACT
    2.0 — average GPA
  Other considerations: high school rank, interview with admissions counselor

- Admission considerations—transfer student: GPA at previous institution, number of credits completed (less than 30 credits), interview with admissions counselor

The Other Route into College

ACADEMIC COURSEWORK AND RELATED FEATURES:

- Support services: freshman orientation, college survival skills, academic advising, drug/alcohol counseling, psychological counseling, academic skills center, study technique workshops, career advising, health center, aptitude testing, extended time for tests (if learning disabled)
- Separate new-student orientation
- Students are required to work with tutors
- Group and one-on-one tutoring by peer tutors in all academic areas
- Academic counseling is required
- Students are assigned an academic adviser. All advisers serve alternative admissions students exclusively
- Placement testing is required in reading, math, and English
- A total of 1,200 full-time faculty at the institution
- Nine faculty members assigned to the program, who are trained to work with alternative admissions students
- Students take an average of 50% of their classes with alternative admissions students only
- Alternative admissions classes average 20–25 students
- Students are limited to a credit load of 9–12 credits per semester until academic performance indicates ability to succeed with a full credit load

REQUIRED COURSES:

- Courses required of students who demonstrate deficiency:
  Study Skills (credit-bearing)
  Foundation Course in Math (noncredit)
  Reading (credit-bearing)
  English Composition (noncredit)

PROFILE OF ALTERNATIVE ADMISSIONS STUDENTS:

- 1,200 alternative admissions students enrolled
- 80%–85% of accepted students enrolled
- 86% enter as new students, 14% as transfer students
- 50% minority, 55% female
- 12% 25 years or older
- 2% learning disabled
- 16% in top 50% of high school class

OTHER FEATURES/ACCOMMODATIONS:

- On-campus housing is available, but is not guaranteed for alternative admissions students
- A meal plan is available
- Financial aid is available

DEADLINES:

- Rolling admission
- March 1 for financial aid

Stacy Needle

The program is best suited for an educationally disadvantaged student who needs basic skills review.

UNIVERSITY OF WISCONSIN/PARKSIDE

>>>>>>>>>>>>>>>>>>>>>>>>>>>

Kenosha, WI 53141
(414) 553-2355

$1,698 In-State Tuition and Fees
$5,098 Out-of-State Tuition and Fees
$1,786 Average Double Room
$ 970 Average Meal Plan

3,500 full-time undergraduates, 1,800 part-time
  undergraduates
35:1 student/faculty ratio
50% of undergraduates study business

>>

Founded in 1968, the University of Wisconsin/Parkside is a public institution, coed. Located on 700 acres in a small city 9 miles from Racine. Bachelor's degrees are offered.

ALTERNATIVE ADMISSIONS:

Contact: Carol Cashen, Director of Learning Assistance and Counseling (414) 553-2608

The University of Wisconsin/Parkside has a structured program, Prescriptive Advising, initiated in 1986 for alternative admissions students. The formal program of studies begins in the fall and lasts until the student attains a 2.0 GPA.

ADMISSION POLICIES:

- New and transfer students are eligible for alternative admissions

- Admission considerations—new student: SAT or ACT scores, high school rank, difficulty of high school courses taken, minority status, age of applicant

- Admission considerations—transfer student: GPA at previous institution, number of credits completed

ACADEMIC COURSEWORK AND RELATED FEATURES:

- Students are not required to work with tutors
- Counseling is not required
- Students are assigned an academic adviser. Students meet with advisers 6 times per semester
- Placement testing is required in English and math
- Alternative admissions students do not take separate classes
- Students are limited to a credit load of 12 credits per semester until student attains a 2.0 GPA

REQUIRED COURSES:

- Courses required of students who demonstrate deficiency:
  Essential Math Skills (credit-bearing)
  Elementary Algebra (credit-bearing)
  Intermediate Algebra (credit-bearing)
  Developmental Reading (credit-bearing)
  Reading Improvement (credit-bearing)
- Remedial courses required:
  Composition Preparation (credit-bearing)
- Remedial courses are calculated in GPA

OTHER FEATURES/ACCOMMODATIONS:

- On-campus housing is available, but is not guaranteed for alternative admissions students
- A meal plan is available

DEADLINES:

- Rolling admission
- April for financial aid

UNIVERSITY OF WYOMING

>>>>>>>>>>>>>>>>>>>>>>>>>

Laramie, WY 82071
(307) 766-5160

$1,003 In-State Tuition and Fees
$3,039 Out-of-State Tuition and Fees
$1,226 Average Double Room
$1,734 Average Meal Plan

8,963 full-time undergraduates, 1,810 part-time undergraduates
16:1 student/faculty ratio
25% of undergraduates study arts/humanities

>>

Founded in 1886, the University of Wyoming is a public institution, coed. Located on 735 acres in a town 127 miles from Denver, Colorado. Bachelor's degrees are offered.

ALTERNATIVE ADMISSIONS:

Contact: Dr. Richard Davis, Director of Admissions (307) 766-5160

The University of Wyoming has a policy for alternative admissions students.

ADMISSION POLICIES:

- New and transfer students are eligible for alternative admissions

- Admission considerations—new student: SAT or ACT scores, high school GPA, type of high school attended, age of applicant

- Admission considerations—transfer student: GPA at previous institution, type of college attended, number of credits completed, age of applicant

ACADEMIC COURSEWORK AND RELATED FEATURES:

- Support services: freshman orientation, college survival skills, academic advising, drug/alcohol counseling, women's center, psychological counseling, academic skills center, study technique workshops, career advising, peer counseling, health center, aptitude testing, extended time for tests
- Students are not required to work with tutors
- Counseling is not required
- Students are assigned an academic adviser. None of the advisers serve alternative admissions students exclusively. Students meet with advisers 2 times per semester
- Placement testing is required in math
- Alternative admissions students do not take separate classes
- Students are limited to a credit load of 12 credits per semester through first semester of college

REQUIRED COURSES:

- Courses required of students who demonstrate deficiency:
  Remedial Math (noncredit)

OTHER FEATURES/ACCOMMODATIONS:

- On-campus housing is available, but is not guaranteed for alternative admissions students
- A meal plan is available

The Other Route into College

DEADLINES:

- Rolling admission
- March 1 for financial aid

The program is best suited for a student who is over 25 years old and out of high school for a minimum of 3 years.

UPSALA COLLEGE

>>>>>>>>>>>>>>>>>>>>>>>>>

East Orange, NJ 07019
(201) 266-7191

$8,795 Tuition and Fees
$1,890 Average Double Room
$2,040 Average Meal Plan

789 full-time undergraduates, 446 part-time
   undergraduates

>>

Founded in 1893, Upsala College is a private institution, coed, affiliated with the Evangelical Lutheran Church in America. Located on 45 acres in a town. Bachelor's degrees are offered.

ALTERNATIVE ADMISSIONS:

Contact: Robert Nilan, Director of Admissions (201) 266-7191

Upsala College has a structured program, Challenge, for alternative admissions students. The formal program of studies begins in the fall and lasts for 1 year. Seventy-five percent of the students complete the program in that time.

ADMISSION POLICIES:

- New students are eligible for alternative admissions, with a limit of 30 students

- Requirements for admission as a freshman: 650 — minimum combined verbal and math SAT

ACADEMIC COURSEWORK AND RELATED FEATURES:

- Students are not required to work with tutors
- Counseling is available

Stacy Needle

192

- Students take classes with alternative admissions students only
- Alternative admissions classes average 15 students

REQUIRED COURSES:

Freshman Seminar

- Minimum of 2.0 GPA required to stay in program; if below 2.0 GPA, a student is placed on academic probation

PROFILE OF ALTERNATIVE ADMISSIONS STUDENTS:

- 50% of the accepted students enrolled
- 50% graduate within 4 years

OTHER FEATURES/ACCOMMODATIONS:

- On-campus housing is available
- A meal plan is available

DEADLINES:

- Rolling admission

VALDOSTA STATE COLLEGE

>>>>>>>>>>>>>>>>>>>>>>>>>>

Valdosta, GA 31698
(912) 333-5791

$1,530 In-State Tuition and Fees
$3,891 Out-of-State Tuition and Fees
$ 825 Average Double Room
$1,245 Average Meal Plan

3,876 full-time undergraduates, 1,900 part-time
   undergraduates
22:1 student/faculty ratio

>>

Founded in 1913, Valdosta State College is a public institution, coed. Located on 170 acres in a small city 120 miles from Jacksonville, Florida. Associate's and bachelor's degrees are offered.

ALTERNATIVE ADMISSIONS:

Contact: Dr. Joe Daniels, Developmental Studies (912) 333-5934

Valdosta State College has a structured program, Developmental Studies, for alternative admissions students. The formal program of studies begins in the fall and lasts for 1 year; however, students can also enter the program in the spring and continue for 1 year.

ADMISSION POLICIES:

- New and transfer students are eligible for alternative admissions

- Requirements for admission as a freshman:
  280 — minimum verbal SAT
  250 — minimum math SAT
  2.0 — minimum GPA
Other considerations: ACT scores (in place of SAT)

- Requirements for admission as a transfer student:
  1.8 — minimum GPA
Other considerations: difficulty of coursework, number of credits completed (less than 20 credits)

ACADEMIC COURSEWORK AND RELATED FEATURES:

- Support services: freshman orientation, college survival skills, academic advising, drug/alcohol counseling, women's center, psychological counseling, career advising, peer counseling, health center
- Students are not required to work with tutors
- Students are assigned an academic adviser
- Placement testing is required
- A total of 260 full-time faculty at the institution
- Special faculty assigned to the program, who are trained to work with alternative admissions students
- Students take classes with alternative admissions students only
- Alternative admissions classes average 28 students
- Courses are also offered in the evening
- Students are not limited to credit load

PROFILE OF ALTERNATIVE ADMISSIONS STUDENTS:

- 551 alternative admissions students enrolled

OTHER FEATURES/ACCOMMODATIONS:

- On-campus housing is available, but is not guaranteed for alternative admissions students
- A meal plan is available
- Financial aid is available

DEADLINES:

- Rolling admission
- May 1 for financial aid

VIRGINIA COMMONWEALTH UNIVERSITY

>>>>>>>>>>>>>>>>>>>>>>>>>>>

Richmond, VA 23284
(804) 367-1222

$2,547 In-State Tuition and Fees
$6,042 Out-of-State Tuition and Fees
$1,933 Average Double Room
$1,410 Average Meal Plan

10,114 full-time undergraduates, 4,994 part-time undergraduates
13:1 student/faculty ratio
23% of undergraduates study arts/humanities

>>

Founded in 1838, Virginia Commonwealth University is a public institution, coed. Located on 34 acres in a large city. Bachelor's degrees are offered.

ALTERNATIVE ADMISSIONS:

Additional cost: $913.50 basic program fee (in-state)
$2,227.50 basic program fee (out-of-state)
Contact: Dr. Quincy Moore, Director of The Office of Academic Support (804) 367-1650

Virginia Commonwealth University has a structured summer program, Office of Academic Support, initiated in 1971 for alternative admissions students. The program begins in mid-June and lasts for 7 weeks. Ninety-nine percent of the students complete the program in that time.

ADMISSION POLICIES:

- New students are eligible for alternative admissions, with a limit of 200 students. There is no wait list

- Requirements for admission as a freshman:
  319 — average verbal SAT
  354 — average math SAT
  2.5 — average GPA
Other considerations: difficulty of high school courses taken; student must be a minority, first generation in college, or low income

ACADEMIC COURSEWORK AND RELATED FEATURES:

- Support services: freshman orientation, college survival skills, academic advising, drug/alcohol counseling, psychological counseling, academic skills center,

The Other Route into College

study technique workshops, career advising, peer counseling, health center, aptitude testing
- Separate new-student orientation
- Students are not required to work with tutors
- Group and one-on-one tutoring by peer tutors in all academic areas
- Academic, personal, and career counseling is required
- Students are assigned an academic adviser
- Placement testing is required in English and math
- Alternative admissions students do not take separate classes
- Alternative admissions classes average 15–20 students
- Students are limited to a credit load of 15 credits per semester through spring semester of sophomore year

REQUIRED COURSES:
- Courses required of students who demonstrate deficiency:
  Remedial Level English
  Remedial Level Math

PROFILE OF ALTERNATIVE ADMISSIONS STUDENTS:
- 159 alternative admissions students enrolled
- 44% of the accepted students enrolled
- 100% enter as new students
- 88% minority, 79% female
- 95% state residents, no international students
- None 25 years or older
- 1% intercollegiate athletes

OTHER FEATURES/ACCOMMODATIONS:
- On-campus housing is available for all students
- A meal plan is available
- Financial aid is available

DEADLINES:
- February 1 for admission; after February 1, applications are reviewed on a space-available basis
- February 1 for financial aid
- April 1 for notification of admission
- May 1 for reply date

The program is best suited for a highly motivated student who has taken a college preparatory curriculum in high school.

WAYNESBURG COLLEGE
>>>>>>>>>>>>>>>>>>>>>>>>>>

Waynesburg, PA 15370
(412) 852-3248

$6,816 Tuition and Fees
$1,380 Average Double Room
$1,400 Average Meal Plan

972 full-time undergraduates, 37 part-time
  undergraduates
15:1 student/faculty ratio
27% of undergraduates study business

>>

Founded in 1849, Waynesburg College is a private institution, coed, affiliated with the Presbyterian church. Located on 30 acres in a small city 60 miles from Pittsburgh. Associate's and bachelor's degrees are offered.

ALTERNATIVE ADMISSIONS:
Contact: Charles Beiter, Jr., Director of ACT 101 (412) 852-3261

Waynesburg College has a structured program, Academic Support Program, initiated in 1976 for alternative admissions students. The formal program of studies begins in the fall and lasts for 4 years. Approximately 50% of the students complete the program in that time. Students receive a bachelor's degree upon completion of their studies.

ADMISSION POLICIES:
- New and transfer students are eligible for alternative admissions
- Admission considerations—new student: SAT or ACT scores, high school GPA, high school rank, state residence
- Admission considerations—transfer student: GPA at previous institution

ACADEMIC COURSEWORK AND RELATED FEATURES:
- Support services: freshman orientation, college survival skills, drug/alcohol counseling, academic skills center, study technique workshops, career advising, health center, extended time for tests
- Separate new-student orientation
- Students are not required to work with tutors

Stacy Needle

194

- Group and one-on-one tutoring by peer tutors as well as professional tutors in all academic areas
- Counseling is required
- Students are assigned an academic adviser. Students meet with advisers approximately 4 times per semester
- Placement testing is required in math, reading, and written expression/essay
- Alternative admissions students do not take separate classes
- Students are not limited to credit load

REQUIRED COURSES:

Study Skills (credit-bearing)
- Courses required of students who demonstrate deficiency:
  Introduction to Writing
  Basic Concepts

- Required courses are calculated in GPA

PROFILE OF ALTERNATIVE ADMISSIONS STUDENTS:

- 195 alternative admissions students enrolled
- 65% of the accepted students enrolled

OTHER FEATURES/ACCOMMODATIONS:

- On-campus housing is available and is guaranteed for alternative admissions students
- On-campus housing is required of alternative admissions students
- A meal plan is available. It is required of alternative admissions students
- Financial aid is available

DEADLINES:

- Rolling admission
- May 1 for financial aid

WEBBER COLLEGE

>>>>>>>>>>>>>>>>>>>>>>>>

Babson Park, FL 33827
(813) 638-1431, Ext. 10

$5,190 Tuition and Fees
$ 420 Average Double Room
$ 870 Average Meal Plan

242 full-time undergraduates, 61 part-time undergraduates
15:1 student/faculty ratio
100% of undergraduates study business

>>

Founded in 1927, Webber College is a private institution, coed. Located on 110 acres in a rural community 6 miles from Lake Wales. Associate's and bachelor's degrees are offered.

ALTERNATIVE ADMISSIONS:

Contact: Cheryl Massey, Director of Admissions (813) 638-1431

Webber College has a policy for alternative admissions students.

ADMISSION POLICIES:

- New and transfer students are eligible for alternative admissions

- Requirements for admission as a freshman:
  350 — average verbal SAT
  320 — average math SAT
     or
   14 — average ACT

  2.2 — average GPA
Other considerations: difficulty of high school courses taken, essay/personal statement, letters of recommendation

- Requirements for admission as a transfer student:
  2.0 — minimum GPA
Other considerations: essay/personal statement, letters of recommendation

ACADEMIC COURSEWORK AND RELATED FEATURES:

- Support services: freshman orientation, academic advising, drug/alcohol counseling, study technique workshops, health center
- Students are not required to work with tutors
- One-on-one tutoring by peer tutors in all academic areas
- Counseling is not required
- Students are assigned an academic adviser. None of the advisers serve alternative admissions students exclusively
- Placement testing is required in reading, English, and math
- Students take an average of 20% of their classes with alternative admissions students
- Alternative admissions classes average 10 students
- Students are limited to a 15-credit load per semester until they attain a 2.0 GPA

The Other Route into College

REQUIRED COURSES:
- Minimum of 1.8 GPA required to stay at college; if below 1.8 GPA, a student is placed on academic probation

PROFILE OF ALTERNATIVE ADMISSIONS STUDENTS:
- 23 alternative admissions students
- 90% of the accepted students enrolled
- 80% enter as new students, 20% as transfer students
- 2% minority, 3% female
- 2% state residents, 1% international students
- None 25 years or older
- 3% intercollegiate athletes
- 1% learning disabled
- 75% graduate within 4 years
- 25% graduate within 5 years

OTHER FEATURES/ACCOMMODATIONS:
- On-campus housing is available and is guaranteed for alternative admissions students
- A meal plan is available
- Financial aid is available

DEADLINES:
- Rolling admission
- August 1 for financial aid
- August 15 for reply date

WEST CHESTER UNIVERSITY
>>>>>>>>>>>>>>>>>>>>>>>>>>>

West Chester, PA 19383
(215) 436-3411

$2,178 In-State Tuition and Fees
$4,034 Out-of-State Tuition and Fees
$2,956 Average Double Room and Meal Plan

7,544 full-time undergraduates, 2,217 part-time undergraduates
19:1 student/faculty ratio
18% of undergraduates study education

Stacy Needle

196

>>

Founded in 1871, West Chester University is a public institution, coed. Located on 385 acres in a town 25 miles from Philadelphia. Associate's and bachelor's degrees are offered.

ALTERNATIVE ADMISSIONS:
Additional cost: $1,200–$1,300 basic program fee
Contact: Dr. Peter Kyper, Director of Academic Development Program (215) 436-3505

West Chester University has a structured program, Academic Development Program, initiated in 1981 for alternative admissions students. The program begins in late June and lasts for 6 weeks.

ADMISSION POLICIES:
- New students are eligible for alternative admissions

- Requirements for admission as a freshman:
  - 300 — minimum verbal SAT
  - 300 — minimum math SAT
  - 35 — minimum TSWE
  - 2.0 — minimum GPA

Other considerations: essay/personal statement, letters of recommendation

ACADEMIC COURSEWORK AND RELATED FEATURES:
- Support services: freshman orientation, college survival skills, academic advising, drug/alcohol counseling, women's center, psychological counseling, academic skills center, study technique workshops, career advising, peer counseling, health center, aptitude testing
- Separate new-student orientation
- Students are required to work with tutors
- Group and one-on-one tutoring by peer tutors as well as professional tutors in all academic areas
- Counseling is required
- Students are assigned an academic adviser
- Placement testing is required in English and math
- A total of 518 full-time faculty at the institution
- Fifteen faculty members assigned to the program, who are trained to work with alternative admissions students
- Students take classes with alternative admissions students only
- Alternative admissions classes average 15 students

REQUIRED COURSES:
- Courses required of students who demonstrate deficiency:
  Basic Writing (credit-bearing)—alternative admissions students only

Remedial Reading and Study Skills (credit-bearing)—alternative admissions students only

Fundamentals of Speech (credit-bearing)—alternative admissions students only

Preparatory Math (credit-bearing)—alternative admissions students only
> or

Fundamentals of Algebra (credit-bearing)—alternative admissions students only

- Minimum of 1.8 GPA required to stay in program; if below 1.8 GPA, a student is placed on academic probation

PROFILE OF ALTERNATIVE ADMISSIONS STUDENTS:

- 139 alternative admissions students enrolled
- 100% enter as new students
- 50% minority
- 75% state residents, no international students
- 90% in top 50% of high school class
- 40%–50% graduate within 5 years

OTHER FEATURES/ACCOMMODATIONS:

- On-campus housing is available and is guaranteed for alternative admissions students
- A meal plan is available
- Financial aid is available

DEADLINES:

- Rolling admission

The program is best suited for a motivated, eager-to-learn student who is receptive to the notion that remedial study is required for success.

WEST TEXAS STATE UNIVERSITY

>>>>>>>>>>>>>>>>>>>>>>>>>>

Canyon, TX 79016
(806) 656-2020

$ 824 In-State Tuition and Fees
$3,320 Out-of-State Tuition and Fees
$1,200 Average Double Room
$1,246 Average Meal Plan

3,345 full-time undergraduates, 1,017 part-time undergraduates
19:1 student/faculty ratio

>>

Founded in 1910, West Texas State University is a public institution, coed. Located on 120 acres in a town 10 miles from Amarillo. Bachelor's degrees are offered.

ALTERNATIVE ADMISSIONS:

Contact: Lila Vars, Director of Admissions (806) 656-2020

West Texas State University has a structured program, Student Success Program, initiated in 1988 for alternative admissions students. The formal program of studies begins in the fall and lasts for 1 year. Fifty percent of the students complete the program in that time.

ADMISSION POLICIES:

- New and transfer students are eligible for alternative admissions

- Requirements for admission as a freshman:
  300 — minimum verbal SAT
  300 — minimum math SAT
     or
   12 — minimum ACT
Other considerations: high school rank, type of high school attended

- Admission considerations—transfer student: GPA at previous institution, number of credits completed

ACADEMIC COURSEWORK AND RELATED FEATURES:

- Support services: freshman orientation, college survival skills, academic advising, drug/alcohol counseling, psychological counseling, study technique workshops, career advising, peer counseling, health center, aptitude testing
- Students are not required to work with tutors
- One-on-one tutoring by peer tutors as well as professional tutors
- Counseling is not required
- Students are assigned an academic adviser
- Placement testing is not required
- A total of 313 full-time faculty at the institution
- Eight faculty members assigned to the program, who are trained to work with alternative admissions students
- Alternative admissions students do not take separate classes

REQUIRED COURSES:

- Remedial courses required:
  Elementary Group Dynamics (credit-bearing)
  Remedial English (noncredit)
  Remedial Math I and II (noncredit)

The Other Route into College

- Minimum of 1.5 GPA required to stay in program; if below 1.5 GPA, a student is placed on academic probation

OTHER FEATURES/ACCOMMODATIONS:
- On-campus housing is available and is guaranteed for alternative admissions students
- A meal plan is available

WESTERN ILLINOIS UNIVERSITY

>>>>>>>>>>>>>>>>>>>>>>>>>>

Macomb, IL 61455
(309) 298-1891

$2,032 In-State Tuition and Fees
$4,192 Out-of-State Tuition and Fees
$2,445 Average Double Room and Meal Plan

12,000 full-time undergraduates
17:1 student/faculty ratio

>>

Founded in 1899, Western Illinois University is a public institution, coed. Located on 1,050 acres in a rural community 65 miles from Peoria. Bachelor's degrees are offered.

ALTERNATIVE ADMISSIONS:

Contact: Marsha Kozlowski, Acting Director (309) 298-1871

Western Illinois University has a structured program, Office of Academic Services, initiated in 1972 for alternative admissions students. The formal program of studies begins in the fall and lasts for 2–4 semesters; however, students can also enter in the spring and continue for 2–4 semesters.

ADMISSION POLICIES:
- New students are eligible for alternative admissions, with a limit of 400 students. There is a wait list

- Requirements for admission as a freshman:
  10 — minimum ACT
Other considerations: high school rank, difficulty of high school courses taken, state residence

ACADEMIC COURSEWORK AND RELATED FEATURES:
- Support services: freshman orientation, college survival skills, academic advising, drug/alcohol counseling, women's center, psychological counseling, academic skills center, study technique workshops, career advising, health center, aptitude testing
- Separate new-student orientation
- Students are required to work with tutors 1–10 hours per week
- Group and one-on-one tutoring by peer tutors
- Counseling is not required
- Students are assigned an academic adviser. All advisers serve alternative admissions students exclusively. Students meet with advisers 5–10 times per semester
- Placement testing is required
- Alternative admissions students do not take separate classes
- Students are not limited to credit load

REQUIRED COURSES:
- Minimum of 1.75 GPA required to stay in program; if below 1.75 GPA, a student is academically dismissed

PROFILE OF ALTERNATIVE ADMISSIONS STUDENTS:
- 350 alternative admissions students enrolled
- 90% of the accepted students enrolled
- 100% enter as new students
- 5% of the students transfer to another college after freshman year
- 37% minority, 60% female
- 100% state residents, no international students
- 1% 25 years or older
- 5% intercollegiate athletes
- 1% learning disabled
- 30% in top 50% of high school class

OTHER FEATURES/ACCOMMODATIONS:
- On-campus housing is available and is guaranteed for alternative admissions students
- A meal plan is available
- Financial aid is available

DEADLINES:
- Rolling admission

Stacy Needle

WESTERN KENTUCKY UNIVERSITY

>>>>>>>>>>>>>>>>>>>>>>>>>>>>

Bowling Green, KY 42101
(502) 745-2551

$1,160 In-State Tuition and Fees
$3,280 Out-of-State Tuition and Fees
$ 870 Average Double Room

9,430 full-time undergraduates, 2,579 part-time
  undergraduates
18:1 student/faculty ratio
22% of undergraduates study math/sciences

>>

Founded in 1906, Western Kentucky University is a
public institution, coed. Located on 223 acres in a small
city. Associate's and bachelor's degrees are offered.

ALTERNATIVE ADMISSIONS:

Contact: Cheryl Chambless, Director of Admissions
(502) 745-2551

Western Kentucky University has a policy for alternative admissions students.

ADMISSION POLICIES:

- New and transfer students are eligible for alternative
  admissions

- Requirements for admission as a freshman:
    14 — average ACT
  Other considerations: high school GPA

- Requirements for admission as a transfer student:
    1.7 — minimum GPA

ACADEMIC COURSEWORK AND RELATED FEATURES:

- Support services: freshman orientation, academic ad-
  vising, psychological counseling, study technique
  workshops, career advising, health center, aptitude
  testing
- Separate new-student orientation
- Students are not required to work with tutors
- Academic counseling is required
- Students are assigned an academic adviser. Students
  meet with advisers at least 1 time per semester
- Placement testing is not required
- Alternative admissions students do not take separate
  classes
- Students are not limited to credit load

REQUIRED COURSES:

- Minimum of 2.0 GPA required to stay in college; if
  below 2.0 GPA, a student is placed on academic probation

PROFILE OF ALTERNATIVE ADMISSIONS STUDENTS:

- 240 alternative admissions students enrolled
- 100% of the accepted students enrolled
- 53% enter as new students, 47% as transfer students
- 5% of the students transfer to another college after
  freshman year, 6% transfer after sophomore year
- 28% minority, 54% female
- 90% state residents, 1% international students
- 53% 25 years or older
- No intercollegiate athletes

OTHER FEATURES/ACCOMMODATIONS:

- On-campus housing is available, but is not guaranteed
  for alternative admissions students
- A meal plan is not available
- Financial aid is available

DEADLINES:

- Rolling admission
- April 15 for financial aid

WESTERN MICHIGAN UNIVERSITY

>>>>>>>>>>>>>>>>>>>>>>>>>>>

Kalamazoo, MI 49008
(616) 387-1000

$2,130 In-State Tuition and Fees
$5,040 Out-of-State Tuition and Fees
$1,288 Average Double Room
$1,872 Average Meal Plan

14,658 full-time undergraduates, 4,045 part-time
  undergraduates
18:1 student/faculty ratio
28% of undergraduates study business

>>

Founded in 1903, Western Michigan University is a
public institution, coed. Located on 390 acres in a small
city. Bachelor's degrees are offered.

The Other Route into College

ALTERNATIVE ADMISSIONS:

Contact: Pat Thompson, Director of Alpha Student Development Program (616) 387-3321

Western Michigan University has a structured program, Alpha Student Development Program, for alternative admissions students. The formal program of studies begins in the fall and lasts for 1 year. Seventy-five percent of the students complete the program in that time.

ADMISSION POLICIES:

- New students are eligible for alternative admissions, with a limit of 150 students. There is no wait list

- Requirements for admission as a freshman:
  18 — minimum ACT
  2.0 — minimum GPA

ACADEMIC COURSEWORK AND RELATED FEATURES:

- Support services: freshman orientation, college survival skills, academic advising, drug/alcohol counseling, women's center, psychological counseling, academic skills center, study technique workshops, career advising, peer counseling, health center, aptitude testing
- Students are not required to work with tutors
- Group and one-on-one tutoring by peer tutors as well as professional tutors
- Academic, career, and personal counseling is required
- Students are assigned an academic adviser. All advisers serve alternative admissions students exclusively. Students meet with advisers 1–2 times per semester
- Placement testing is required in math, reading, and writing
- Alternative admissions students do not take separate classes
- Students are limited to a credit load of 15 credits per semester through spring semester of freshman year

REQUIRED COURSES:

- Courses required of students who demonstrate deficiency:
  General Math (credit-bearing)
  Elective Reading for College (credit-bearing)
  Basic Writing Skills (credit-bearing)

- Remedial courses are calculated in GPA
- Minimum of 2.0 GPA required to stay in program

PROFILE OF ALTERNATIVE ADMISSIONS STUDENTS:

- 166 alternative admissions students enrolled
- 100% enter as new students
- 4% minority, 50% female
- None 25 years or older
- 10% intercollegiate athletes

OTHER FEATURES/ACCOMMODATIONS:

- On-campus housing is available and is guaranteed for alternative admissions students
- A meal plan is available
- Financial aid is available

DEADLINES:

- Rolling admission

WESTERN MICHIGAN UNIVERSITY
>>>>>>>>>>>>>>>>>>>>>>>>>>>>

Kalamazoo, MI 49008
(616) 387-1000

$2,130 In-State Tuition and Fees
$5,040 Out-of-State Tuition and Fees
$1,288 Average Double Room
$1,872 Average Meal Plan

14,658 full-time undergraduates, 4,045 part-time undergraduates
18:1 student/faculty ratio
28% of undergraduates study business

>>

Founded in 1903, Western Michigan University is a public institution, coed. Located on 390 acres in a small city. Bachelor's degrees are offered.

ALTERNATIVE ADMISSIONS:

Additional cost: $1,300 basic program fee
Contact: Hal Bates, Director of Martin Luther King Program (616) 387-3322

Western Michigan University has a structured summer program, Martin Luther King Program, initiated in 1968 for alternative admissions students. The program begins in June and lasts for 8 weeks. Fifty-five percent of the students complete the program in that time.

Stacy Needle

ADMISSION POLICIES:

- New students are eligible for alternative admissions, with a limit of 100 students. There is no wait list

- Requirements for admission as a freshman:
  10 — minimum ACT
  1.8 — Minimum GPA
  Other considerations: minority status

ACADEMIC COURSEWORK AND RELATED FEATURES:

- Support services: freshman orientation, college survival skills, academic advising, drug/alcohol counseling, women's center, psychological counseling, academic skills center, study technique workshops, career advising, peer counseling, health center, aptitude testing, extended time for tests
- Separate new-student orientation
- Students are required to work with tutors 4–6 hours per week
- Group and one-on-one tutoring by peer tutors in all academic areas
- Academic counseling is required
- Students are assigned an academic adviser. Students meet with advisers 4 times per semester
- Placement testing is required in math, reading, and writing
- A total of 794 full-time faculty at the institution
- Special faculty assigned to the program, who are trained to work with alternative admissions students
- Students take classes with alternative admissions students only
- Alternative admissions classes average 25 students
- Students are limited to a credit load of 12–14 credits per semester through spring semester of freshman year

REQUIRED COURSES:

- Remedial courses required:
  Reading (credit-bearing)—alternative admissions students only
  Writing (credit-bearing)—alternative admissions students only
  Math (credit-bearing)
- Other required courses:
  Freshman Seminar (credit-bearing)—alternative admissions students only
  College Writing (credit-bearing)

- Remedial courses are calculated in GPA
- Required courses are calculated in GPA
- Minimum of 2.0 GPA required to stay in program; if below 2.0 GPA, a student is placed on academic probation

PROFILE OF ALTERNATIVE ADMISSIONS STUDENTS:

- 101 alternative admissions students enrolled
- 90% of the accepted students enrolled
- 100% enter as new students
- 90% minority, 45% female
- 85% state residents, 55% international students
- None 25 years or older
- 10% intercollegiate athletes
- 1% learning disabled
- None in top 50% of high school class
- 17% graduate within 5 years

OTHER FEATURES/ACCOMMODATIONS:

- On-campus housing is available and is guaranteed for alternative admissions students
- A meal plan is available
- Financial aid is available

DEADLINES:

- Rolling admission

WESTERN OREGON STATE COLLEGE

>>>>>>>>>>>>>>>>>>>>>>>>>>>

Monmouth, OR 97361
(503) 838-8211

$1,685 In-State Tuition and Fees
$4,476 Out-of-State Tuition and Fees
$2,667 Average Double Room and Meal Plan

3,549 full-time undergraduates, 431 part-time undergraduates
19:1 student/faculty ratio
45% of undergraduates study liberal arts

>>

Founded in 1856, Western Oregon State College is a public institution, coed. Located on 132 acres in a rural community 15 miles from Salem. Associate's and bachelor's degrees are offered.

ALTERNATIVE ADMISSIONS:

Contact: Janine Allen, Director of Enrollment Management (503) 838-8211

Western Oregon State College has a policy for alternative admissions students.

The Other Route into College

ADMISSION POLICIES:

- New students are eligible for alternative admissions

- Admission considerations—new student: SAT or ACT scores, high school GPA, essay/personal statement, letters of recommendation

ACADEMIC COURSEWORK AND RELATED FEATURES:

- Support services: freshman orientation, college survival skills, academic advising, drug/alcohol counseling, psychological counseling, academic skills center, study technique workshops, career advising, peer counseling, health center, aptitude testing
- Students are not required to work with tutors
- Group and one-on-one tutoring by peer tutors as well as professional tutors in all academic areas
- Counseling is not required
- Students are assigned an academic adviser. Students meet with advisers at least 1 time per semester
- Placement testing is not required
- Alternative admissions students do not take separate classes
- Students are not limited to credit load

PROFILE OF ALTERNATIVE ADMISSIONS STUDENTS:

- 5% of the accepted students enrolled

OTHER FEATURES/ACCOMMODATIONS:

- On-campus housing is available and is guaranteed for alternative admissions students
- On-campus housing is required of alternative admissions students
- A meal plan is available. It is required of alternative admissions students
- Financial aid is available

DEADLINES:

- Rolling admission
- March 1 for financial aid

WESTMAR COLLEGE

>>>>>>>>>>>>>>>>>>>>>>>>>

Le Mars, IA 51031
(712) 546-5444

$7,492 Tuition and Fees
$1,312 Average Double Room
$1,629 Average Meal Plan

Stacy Needle

566 full-time undergraduates, 28 part-time undergraduates
14:1 student/faculty ratio
40% of undergraduates study business

>>

Founded in 1890, Westmar College is a private institution, coed. Located on 82 acres in a town 25 miles from Sioux City. Bachelor's degrees are offered.

ALTERNATIVE ADMISSIONS:

Contact: Dr. Jim Utesch, Director of Admissions (712) 546-5444

Westmar College has a policy for alternative admissions students.

ADMISSION POLICIES:

- New and transfer students are eligible for alternative admissions

- Requirements for admission as a freshman:
  13 — minimum ACT
  1.75 — minimum GPA
Other considerations: interview with admissions counselor

- Admission considerations—transfer student: admission based on individual criteria

ACADEMIC COURSEWORK AND RELATED FEATURES:

- Support services: freshman orientation, college survival skills, academic advising, psychological counseling, academic skills center, career advising, peer counseling, health center, aptitude testing, extended time for tests
- Students are not required to work with tutors
- Group and one-on-one tutoring by peer tutors in all academic areas
- Counseling is not required
- Students are assigned an academic adviser. None of the advisers serve alternative admissions students exclusively. Students meet with advisers 4 times per semester
- Placement testing is required in English and math
- Alternative admissions students do not take separate classes
- Students are limited to a credit load of 13 credits per semester through first semester of college

REQUIRED COURSES:

- Courses required of students who demonstrate deficiency:
  Basic Skills Math (credit-bearing)
  Developmental English (credit-bearing)

- Remedial courses are calculated in GPA

PROFILE OF ALTERNATIVE ADMISSIONS STUDENTS:

- 18 alternative admissions students enrolled
- 70% of the accepted students enrolled

OTHER FEATURES/ACCOMMODATIONS:

- On-campus housing is available and is guaranteed for alternative admissions students
- A meal plan is available
- Financial aid is available

DEADLINES:

- Rolling admission
- April 1 for financial aid

WHITWORTH COLLEGE

>>>>>>>>>>>>>>>>>>>>>>>>>>

Spokane, WA 99251
(509) 466-3212

$9,090 Tuition and Fees
$1,541 Average Double Room
$1,884 Average Meal Plan

1,350 full-time undergraduates, 650 part-time
 undergraduates
15:1 student/faculty ratio

>>

Founded in 1890, Whitworth College is a private institution, coed, affiliated with the Presbyterian church. Located on 200 acres in a large city 275 miles from Seattle. Bachelor's degrees are offered.

ALTERNATIVE ADMISSIONS:

Contact: Gail Berg, Director of Career/Life Advising
(509) 466-3271

Whitworth College has a structured program, Provisional Admission, initiated in 1986 for alternative admissions students. The formal program of studies begins in the fall and lasts for 1 semester. Sixty-seven percent of the students complete the program in that time.

ADMISSION POLICIES:

- New students are eligible for alternative admissions, with a limit of 30 students. There is a wait list

- Requirements for admission as a freshman:
  350 — minimum verbal SAT
  350 — minimum math SAT
  2.2 — minimum GPA
  Other considerations: ACT scores (in place of SAT), high school rank, essay/personal statement, letters of recommendation

ACADEMIC COURSEWORK AND RELATED FEATURES:

- Support services: freshman orientation, college survival skills, academic advising, drug/alcohol counseling, psychological counseling, academic skills center, study technique workshops, career advising, peer counseling, health center, aptitude testing
- Separate new-student orientation
- Students are required to work with tutors 3 hours per week
- Group and one-on-one tutoring by peer tutors in math, science, and English
- Counseling is not required
- Students are assigned an academic adviser. Fifty percent of the advisers serve alternative admissions students exclusively. Students meet with advisers at least 6 times per semester
- Placement testing is required
- A total of 87 full-time faculty at the institution
- Five faculty members assigned to the program, who are trained to work with alternative admissions students
- Alternative admissions students do not take separate classes
- Students are not limited to credit load

REQUIRED COURSES:

United States History to 1865 (credit-bearing)
Personal Financial Affairs (credit-bearing)
Reading Literature (credit-bearing)
Social Reality (credit-bearing)

- Required courses are calculated in GPA
- Minimum of 2.25 GPA required to stay in program; if below 2.25 GPA, a student is academically dismissed

PROFILE OF ALTERNATIVE ADMISSIONS STUDENTS:

- 30 alternative admissions students enrolled
- 47% of the accepted students enrolled
- 100% enter as new students
- 1% minority, 30% female
- 50% state residents, no international students
- None 25 years or older
- 10% intercollegiate athletes
- 10% learning disabled
- None in top 50% of high school class

The Other Route into College

OTHER FEATURES/ACCOMMODATIONS:

- On-campus housing is available and is guaranteed for alternative admissions students
- On-campus housing is required of alternative admissions students
- A meal plan is available. It is required of alternative admissions students
- Financial aid is available

DEADLINES:

- March 1 for admission; after March 1, applications are reviewed on a space-available basis
- February 1 for financial aid
- April for notification of admission
- May 1 for reply date

WILLIAM WOODS COLLEGE

>>>>>>>>>>>>>>>>>>>>>>>>>>

Fulton, MO 65251
(314) 642-2251

$6,800 Tuition and Fees
$1,250 Average Double Room
$1,450 Average Meal Plan

710 full-time undergraduates, 30 part-time
   undergraduates
13:1 student/faculty ratio

>>

Founded in 1870, William Woods College is a private institution, women only, affiliated with the Disciples of Christ church. Located on 160 acres in a town. Bachelor's degrees are offered.

ALTERNATIVE ADMISSIONS:

Contact: Jack Dudley, Director of Academic Support Services (314) 642-2251

William Woods College has a structured program for alternative admissions students. The formal program of studies begins in the fall and lasts for 1 year.

ADMISSION POLICIES:

- New and transfer students are eligible for alternative admissions

- Requirements for admission as a freshman:
  449 — average verbal SAT
  451 — average math SAT
    or
  19 — average ACT

  2.88 — minimum GPA

Other considerations: high school rank, type of high school attended, difficulty of high school courses taken, interview with admissions counselor, essay/personal statement, letters of recommendation

- Admission considerations—transfer student: GPA at previous institution, type of college attended, number of credits completed, interview with admissions counselor, essay/personal statement, letters of recommendation

ACADEMIC COURSEWORK AND RELATED FEATURES:

- Support services: freshman orientation, college survival skills, academic advising, drug/alcohol counseling, women's center, psychological counseling, academic skills center, study technique workshops, career advising, peer counseling, health center, aptitude testing
- Separate new-student orientation
- Students are not required to work with tutors
- One-on-one tutoring by peer tutors in all academic areas
- Students are assigned an academic adviser. All advisers serve alternative admissions students exclusively. Students meet with advisers 6–10 times per semester
- Placement testing is not required
- A total of 50 full-time faculty at the institution
- One faculty member assigned to the program, who is trained to work with alternative admissions students
- Students take classes with alternative admissions students only
- Alternative admissions classes average 20 students
- Courses are also offered in the evening

REQUIRED COURSES:

- Remedial courses required:
  Introduction to English Composition (credit-bearing)
  Freshmen Seminar (credit-bearing)—alternative admissions students only

- Remedial courses are calculated in GPA

PROFILE OF ALTERNATIVE ADMISSIONS STUDENTS:

- 35 alternative admissions students enrolled
- 88% enter as new students, 12% as transfer students
- 100% female
- 42% state residents, no international students

Stacy Needle

- 35% graduate within 4 years
- 15% graduate within 5 years

OTHER FEATURES/ACCOMMODATIONS:
- On-campus housing is available and is guaranteed for alternative admissions students
- A meal plan is available
- Financial aid is available

DEADLINES:
- Rolling admission
- May 1 for reply date

XAVIER UNIVERSITY
>>>>>>>>>>>>>>>>>>>>>>>>>>>

Cincinnati, OH 45207
(513) 745-3301

$7,650 Tuition and Fees
$1,860 Average Double Room
$1,740 Average Meal Plan

2,700 full-time undergraduates, 1,200 part-time
   undergraduates
16:1 student/faculty ratio

>>

Founded in 1831, Xavier University is a private institution, coed, affiliated with the Roman Catholic church. Located on 86 acres in a large city. Associate's and bachelor's degrees are offered.

ALTERNATIVE ADMISSIONS:

Additional Cost: $1,700 basic program fee
Contact: Doris Jackson, Director of Academic Advising/ Summer Bridge Program (513) 745-3489

Xavier University has a structured summer program, Summer Bridge Program, initiated in 1982 for alternative admissions students. The program begins in June and lasts for 6 weeks. One hundred percent of the students complete the program in that time.

ADMISSION POLICIES:
- New students are eligible for alternative admissions, with a limit of 30 students. There is a wait list

- Requirements for admission as a freshman:
  450 — average verbal SAT
  497 — average math SAT
      or
  22 — average ACT

  2.15 — average GPA
  Other considerations: high school rank, type of high school attended

ACADEMIC COURSEWORK AND RELATED FEATURES:
- Support services: freshman orientation, college survival skills, academic advising, drug/alcohol counseling, psychological counseling, academic skills center, study technique workshops, career advising, peer counseling, health center, aptitude testing, extended time for tests
- Separate new-student orientation
- Students are not required to work with tutors
- Group and one-on-one tutoring by peer tutors in all academic areas
- Students are assigned an academic adviser. All advisers serve alternative admissions students exclusively
- Placement testing is required in English and math
- A total of 200 full-time faculty at the institution
- Two faculty members assigned to the program, who are trained to work with alternative admissions students
- Alternative admissions students do not take separate classes
- Students are limited to a credit load of 12–14 credits per semester through spring semester of freshman year

REQUIRED COURSES:
- Remedial courses required:
  English Rhetoric (credit-bearing)
  Math (credit-bearing)
  Psychology-Reading/Study Skills (credit-bearing)

- Remedial courses are calculated in GPA

PROFILE OF ALTERNATIVE ADMISSIONS STUDENTS:
- 30 alternative admissions students enrolled
- 40% of the accepted students enrolled
- 100% enter as new students
- 15% of the students transfer to another college after freshman year, 15% transfer after sophomore year
- 30% minority, 50% female
- 60% state residents, no international students
- None 25 years or older
- 12% intercollegiate athletes

- 6% learning disabled
- 65% in top 50% of high school class
- 45% graduate within 4 years
- 55% graduate within 5 years

OTHER FEATURES/ACCOMMODATIONS:
- On-campus housing is available and is guaranteed for alternative admissions students
- On-campus housing is reserved for and required of alternative admissions students

- A meal plan is available. It is required of alternative admissions students
- Financial aid is available

DEADLINES:
- Rolling admission
- April 15 for financial aid

The program is best suited for a student with high grades and rank, but low test scores.

GEOGRAPHICAL INDEX TO COLLEGES

HAWAII (HI)

University of Hawaii at Hilo, 168

IDAHO (ID)

Idaho State University, 73

ILLINOIS (IL)

Aurora University, 11
Elmhurst College, 53
Kendall College, 82
School of the Art Institute of Chicago, 136
Southern Illinois University at Carbondale, 140
Western Illinois University, 198

INDIANA (IN)

Ball State University, 13
Calumet College of Saint Joseph, 21
Huntington College, 72
Indiana Institute of Technology, 75
Indiana State University, 76
Indiana University–Purdue University at Indianapolis,
   77
Indiana University Southeast, 78
Oakland City College, 116

IOWA (IA)

University of Dubuque, 164
University of Northern Iowa, 178
Westmar College, 202

KANSAS (KS)

Bethany College, 17
Kansas Newman College, 81

KENTUCKY (KY)

Morehead State University, 104
Union College, 157
Western Kentucky University, 199

LOUISIANA (LA)

Louisiana College, 88

MAINE (ME)

Husson College, 73
Unity College, 158
University of Maine, 170
University of Maine at Farmington, 170
University of Maine at Fort Kent, 171
University of Maine at Machias, 172
University of Maine at Presque Isle, 172
University of New England, 177
University of Southern Maine, 185

MARYLAND (MD)

Columbia Union College, 35
Morgan State University, 105

MASSACHUSETTS (MA)

Anna Maria College, 7
Atlantic Union College, 9
Boston University, 21
Eastern Nazarene College, 49
Elms College, 54
Emerson College, 55
Emmanuel College, 56
Northeastern University, 112
University of Massachusetts at Boston, 173

MICHIGAN (MI)

Andrews University, 5
Aquinas College, 8
Central Michigan University, 26
Eastern Michigan University, 48
Grand Valley State University, 65
Michigan State University, 99
Siena Heights College, 138
Spring Arbor College, 144
University of Detroit, 163
University of Michigan, 174
Western Michigan University, 199, 200

MINNESOTA (MN)

Bemidji State University, 16
Bethel College, 18
College of St. Scholastica, 34
Concordia College, 36
St. Cloud State University, 130
Saint Mary's College of Minnesota, 133
Southwest State University, 142

MISSISSIPPI (MS)

Alcorn State University, 4
Delta State University, 43
Tougaloo College, 155
University of Southern Mississippi, 186

MISSOURI (MO)

Avila College, 12
Lindenwood College, 85
Northwest Missouri State University, 114
Rockhurst College, 128
William Woods College, 204

NEBRASKA (NE)

Nebraska Wesleyan University, 107
University of Nebraska-Lincoln, 175

Geographical Index to Colleges

NEVADA (NV)

Sierra Nevada College, 138
University of Nevada at Las Vegas, 176

NEW HAMPSHIRE (NH)

Magdalen College, 89
New England College, 109
New Hampshire College, 110

NEW JERSEY (NJ)

College of Saint Elizabeth, 32
Fairleigh Dickinson University, Florham–Madison
    Campus, 57
Ramapo College of New Jersey, 124
Rider College, 125
Saint Peter's College, 134
Upsala College, 192

NEW YORK (NY)

Adelphi University, 1
Colgate University, 30
College of New Rochelle, 31
College of Saint Rose, 34
Dominican College of Blauvelt, 43
D'Youville College, 44
Hofstra University, 70
Houghton College, 77
Iona College, 79
Long Island University/Brooklyn Campus, 86
Long Island University/C. W. Post Campus, 86
Long Island University/Southampton Campus, 87
Manhattan College, 91
Mercy College, 97
Molloy College, 103
Nazareth College of Rochester, 106
New York University, 111
Pace University, 119
Pace University, Pleasantville/Briarcliff Campus, 120
Roberts Wesleyan College, 127
Rochester Institute of Technology, 127
Russell Sage College, 129
State University of New York at Albany, 146
State University of New York at Stony Brook, 147
State University of New York College at Brockport,
    148
State University of New York College at Buffalo, 149
State University of New York College at Geneseo,
    150

NORTH CAROLINA (NC)

Belmont Abbey College, 15
North Carolina School of the Arts, 112
University of North Carolina at Wilmington, 177

OHIO (OH)

Antioch College, 8
Cedarville College, 24
Defiance College, 41
Malone College, 90
Marietta College, 94
Notre Dame College of Ohio, 115
University of Findlay, 165
Xavier University, 205

OKLAHOMA (OK)

Bartlesville Wesleyan College, 14
Cameron University, 22
Central State University, 27
East Central University, 45
Oklahoma City University, 117
Southern Nazarene University, 141

OREGON (OR)

Eastern Oregon State College, 50
George Fox College, 61
University of Oregon, 179
Western Oregon State College, 201

PENNSYLVANIA (PA)

Albright College, 3
Alvernia College, 4
Delaware Valley College, 42
East Stroudsburg University of Pennsylvania,
    46
Elizabethtown College, 52
Gannon University, 59
Geneva College, 60
Gwynedd-Mercy College, 67, 68
Immaculata College, 74
Indiana University of Pennsylvania, 76
La Roche College, 84
Mansfield University, 92
Mercyhurst College, 98
Neumann College, 108
Pennsylvania State University, 121
Pennsylvania State University at Erie, The Behrend
    College, 121
Robert Morris College, 126
Saint Vincent College, 134
Seton Hill College, 137
Thiel College, 155
University of Pittsburgh, 180
Waynesburg College, 194
West Chester University, 196

RHODE ISLAND (RI)

Rhode Island College, 125

ALPHABETICAL INDEX TO COLLEGES

Alphabetical Index to Colleges

Robert Morris College, PA, 126
Roberts Wesleyan College, NY, 127
Rochester Institute of Technology, NY, 127
Rockhurst College, MO, 128
Russell Sage College, NY, 129

Sacred Heart University, CT, 130
St. Cloud State University, MN, 130
Saint Joseph College, CT, 131
Saint Leo College, FL, 132
Saint Mary's College of Minnesota, MN, 133
Saint Peter's College, NJ, 134
Saint Vincent College, PA, 134
Sam Houston State University, TX, 135
School of the Art Institute of Chicago, IL, 136
Seton Hill College, PA, 137
Siena Heights College, MI, 138
Sierra Nevada College, NV, 138
Sioux Falls College, SD, 139
Southern Illinois University at Carbondale, IL, 140
Southern Nazarene University, OK, 141
Southern Vermont College, VT, 142
Southwest State University, MN, 142
Southwest Texas State University, TX, 143
Spring Arbor College, MI, 144
Spring Hill College, AL, 145
State University of New York at Albany, NY, 146
State University of New York at Stony Brook, NY, 147
State University of New York College at Brockport, NY, 148
State University of New York College at Buffalo, NY, 149
State University of New York College at Genesco, NY, 150

Tampa College, FL, 151
Tennessee Technological University, TN, 152
Texas A&I University, TX, 152
Texas A&M University, TX, 153
Texas Wesleyan University, TX, 154
Thiel College, PA, 155
Tougaloo College, MS, 155
Trinity College, DC, 156

Union College, KY, 157
Unity College, ME, 158
University of Alabama, AL, 158
University of Alaska Fairbanks, AK, 159
University of Arkansas at Little Rock, AR, 160
University of Bridgeport, CT, 161
University of California at Santa Barbara, CA, 162
University of Colorado at Denver, CO, 163

University of Detroit, MI, 163
University of Dubuque, IA, 164
University of Findlay, OH, 165
University of Hartford, CT, 166, 167
University of Hawaii at Hilo, HI, 168
University of La Verne, CA, 169
University of Maine, ME, 170
University of Maine at Farmington, ME, 170
University of Maine at Fort Kent, ME, 171
University of Maine at Machias, ME, 172
University of Maine at Presque Isle, ME, 172
University of Massachusetts at Boston, MA, 173
University of Michigan, MI, 174
University of Nebraska–Lincoln, NE, 175
University of Nevada at Las Vegas, NV, 176
University of New England, ME, 177
University of North Carolina at Wilmington, NC, 177
University of Northern Iowa, IA, 178
University of Oregon, OR, 179
University of Pittsburgh, PA, 180
University of Redlands, CA, 180
University of South Alabama, AL, 181
University of South Carolina, SC, 182
University of South Carolina at Aiken, SC, 183
University of South Carolina–Coastal Carolina College, SC, 184
University of Southern Maine, ME, 185
University of Southern Mississippi, MS, 186
University of Texas at Austin, TX, 186
University of Washington, WA, 187
University of Wisconsin at Green Bay, WI, 188
University of Wisconsin at Milwaukee, WI, 189
University of Wisconsin/Parkside, WI, 190
University of Wyoming, WY, 191
Upsala College, NJ, 192

Valdosta State College, GA, 192
Virginia Commonwealth University, VA, 193

Waynesburg College, PA, 194
Webber College, FL, 195
West Chester University, PA, 196
West Texas State University, TX, 197
Western Illinois University, IL, 198
Western Kentucky University, KY, 199
Western Michigan University, MI, 199, 200
Western Oregon State College, OR, 201
Westmar College, IA, 202
Whitworth College, WA, 203
William Woods College, MO, 204

Xavier University, OH, 205

ABOUT THE AUTHOR

STACY NEEDLE has extensive training and experience as a college placement adviser. In the course of her work in matching a great variety of students to appropriate colleges, she visits fifty to sixty campuses every year. Ms. Needle has a master's degree in student personnel services, is a member of the National Association of College Admissions Counselors, and lectures extensively. She lives in New Jersey.